The Official CompTIA® Project +® Study Guide (Exam PK0-004)

The Official CompTIA® Project+® Study Guide (Exam PK0-004)

Course Edition: 1.0

Acknowledgements

PROJECT TEAM

Laurie A. Perry, Project+, Author

John Wilson, Project+, PMP, Author

Brian Sullivan, Media Designer

Peter Bauer, Content Editor

Thomas Reilly, Vice President Learning

Katie Hoenicke, Director of Product Management

James Chesterfield, Manager, Learning Content and Design

Becky Mann, Senior Manager, Product Development

James Pengelly, Courseware Manager

Rob Winchester, Senior Manager, Technical Operations

Notices

DISCLAIMER

TRADEMARK NOTICES

COPYRIGHT NOTICE

The Official CompTIA® Project+® Study Guide (Exam PK0-004)

About This Guide

If you are using this guide, you probably have some professional exposure to the duties of a project manager, or you may be embarking on a career in professional project management. As a project manager, the ability to demonstrate best practices in project management—both on the job and through professional certification—is becoming the standard to compete in today's fast-paced and highly technical workplace. In this guide, you will apply the generally recognized practices of project management to successfully manage projects.

Project managers are always under severe pressure to complete projects on time and within budget. However, most projects fail to meet these demands and as a result, many projects are terminated early. Successful project management requires knowledge and experience. This guide is designed to provide you with the skills needed to be a successful project manager in today's rapidly changing world. Additionally, this guide can be a significant part of your preparation for the CompTIA® Project+® certification exam. The skills and knowledge you gain in this guide will help you avoid making costly mistakes and increase your competitive edge in the project management profession.

Guide Description

Target Student

This guide is designed for individuals in various job roles who have a basic knowledge of project management, and who participate in small to medium scale projects.

This guide is also designed for students who are seeking the CompTIA® Project+® certification and who want to prepare for the CompTIA® Project+® PK0-004 Certification Exam. A typical student taking the CompTIA® Project+® PK0-004 Certification Exam should have a minimum of 12 months of project management experience. Experience with specific project management software is helpful, but not mandatory.

Guide Prerequisites

To ensure your success, you should be familiar with basic project management concepts. Basic computing skills and some experience using Microsoft Office are desirable but not required.

Guide Objectives

In this guide, you will apply recognized practices of project management and understand a project's life cycle, roles, and skills necessary to effectively initiate, plan, execute, monitor, control and close a project.

You will:

- Identify the fundamentals of project management.
- Initiate a project.

- Create project plans, stakeholder strategies, and scope statement.
- Develop a Work Breakdown Structure and activity lists.
- Develop project schedule and identify the critical path.
- Plan project costs.
- Create project staffing and quality management plans.
- Create an effective communication plan.
- Create a risk management plan, perform risk analysis, and develop a risk response plan.
- Plan project procurements.
- Develop change management and transition plans.
- Assemble and launch the project team to execute the plan.
- Execute the project procurement plan.
- Monitor and control project performance.
- Monitor and control project constraints.
- Monitor and control project risks.
- Monitor and control procurements.
- Perform project closure activities.

How to Use This Book

As You Learn

This book is divided into lessons and topics, covering a subject or a set of related subjects. In most cases, lessons are arranged in order of increasing proficiency.

The results-oriented topics include relevant and supporting information you need to master the content. Each topic has various types of information designed to enable you to solidify your understanding of the informational material presented in the guide. Information is also provided for reference and reflection to facilitate understanding and practice.

At the back of the book, you will find a glossary of the definitions of the terms and concepts used throughout the guide. You will also find an index to assist in locating information within the instructional components of the book.

As a Reference

The organization and layout of this book make it an easy-to-use resource for future reference. Taking advantage of the glossary, index, and table of contents, you can use this book as a first source of definitions, background information, and summaries.

Guide Icons

Watch throughout the material for the following visual cues.

Icon	Description
	A **Note** provides additional information, guidance, or hints about a topic or task.
	A **Caution** note makes you aware of places where you need to be particularly careful with your actions, settings, or decisions so that you can be sure to get the desired results of an activity or task.

1 | Defining Project Management Fundamentals

Lesson Time: 2 hours, 45 minutes

Lesson Introduction

Successfully managing your projects requires effective planning up-front and adherence to the industry's best practices through every step of the process. By identifying the processes involved in a project life cycle, you will be better prepared to initiate a project in your organization and position it for success. In this lesson, you will identify the effective practices of project management and related project management processes so that you will be ready to move forward strategically and with confidence.

Lesson Objectives

In this lesson, you will:

- Identify basic concepts and terminology of professional project management.

- Identify and describe the phases and components of the project life cycle.

- Identify and describe the organizational influences on project management.

- Define the Agile methodology.

TOPIC A

Identify Project Management Basics

You want to plan and implement projects that will positively impact your organization. A thorough knowledge of projects and project management is required to efficiently manage your projects. In this topic, you will identify basic concepts and terminology of project management.

Business organizations around the world are using project management as a competitive advantage to achieve corporate strategic objectives. By identifying the main elements involved in project management practices, you can enhance the chances of success over a wide range of projects across application areas and industries.

Projects

A *project* is a temporary work endeavor that creates a unique product, service, or result. It has a clearly defined start and finish. The end of a project is reached when its objectives are met, the need for the project no longer exists, or it is determined that the objectives cannot be met. Projects require resources to perform project activities and lend themselves to a teamwork structure because they draw from a range of disciplines to complete the work. Also, projects vary widely in terms of budget, team size, duration, expected outcomes, and industries. A project is considered to be successful when the specified objectives are met within the specified duration and budget and with the required quality.

Example: The Intranet Website Creation Project

Consider a project authorized by a firm to create an intranet website that will display its employees' information. The outcome of the project is the website, and the duration will depend on the complexity and size of the work involved. The project will come to an end when the website is posted on the server and is ready for use by appropriate users.

Subprojects

A *subproject* is an independently manageable component of an existing project. A project can have multiple subprojects and they in turn can have even smaller subprojects. Usually, a subproject is given on contract either to an external enterprise or to another functional unit in the organization.

Example: Subprojects in a Car Project

The project team working on the interior design of a solar-powered car decided to subcontract the designing of seats and the air-conditioning system to two individual external vendors as subprojects.

Project Management

Project management is the planned effort for executing and monitoring a project in order to accomplish its defined goals and objectives. Managing projects involves scheduling; identifying requirements; establishing objectives; balancing quality, scope, time, and cost; and addressing the concerns and expectations of stakeholders.

Project management is different from the management of routine, ongoing work initiatives called operations. Projects generally involve temporary initiatives, unique circumstances, and cross-functional teams. Projects may involve new or specially formed teams taking on new tasks and attempting unfamiliar skills, processes, or work efforts. Operations, on the other hand, deal with the ongoing day-to-day production of goods and services. Operations management includes such disciplines as human resources, purchasing, sales, and maintenance.

Responsibilities of a Project Manager

In any given project, some of the common responsibilities of project managers include communicating cross-functionally, managing the efforts of the team members who do not report directly to them, and delivering work on time, within the allotted budget and specifications for quality.

 Note: The project manager's roles and responsibilities will be discussed in detail throughout this course.

Linear Presentation

Although project management is an iterative, cyclical process in real life, it is necessarily presented in a linear manner throughout this course.

Programs

A *program* is a group of related projects that have a common objective. It offers great control over constituent projects and delivers benefits that the organization can use to meet its goals. A program is managed by a program manager, and individual projects are managed by project managers who work for the program manager. However, all projects need not always be a part of programs. Projects that do not have a common objective, but still are managed in a group, are generally known as multiple projects.

Example: A Computer Service Expansion Program

A computer servicing firm launched a new program that aims at expanding its business. This expansion program consists of many projects such as market research to establish demand, construction of new branch stores, franchise selection, designing the marketing campaign, and consolidation of customer base by establishing loyalty programs.

Portfolios

A *portfolio* is a collection of projects, programs, and operational work to achieve the strategic business objectives of an organization. The projects in a portfolio may or may not be interdependent, but they are grouped to give management a broader view of the organization's projects and their adherence to organizational objectives. For a project to be part of a portfolio, its attributes such as cost, resource requirements, timelines, strategic goals, and benefits should be in line with other projects in the portfolio. Portfolios are generally managed by a senior manager or senior management teams.

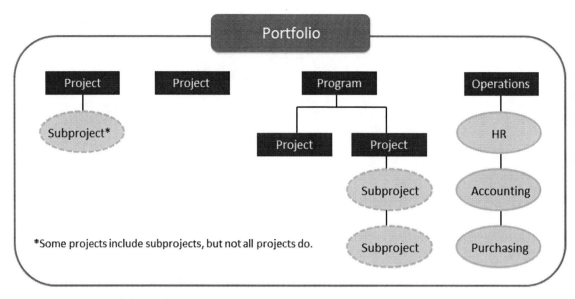

Figure 1-1: A portfolio and its contents.

Example: A Company Portfolio

An alternate energy producing company designed a breakthrough technology capitalizing on solar energy. The company's strategy is to exploit the technical know-how in all possible areas to generate revenue and become a trendsetter. It initiated a portfolio that contains various programs and independent projects to identify the potential use of this technology in power generation, transportation, and domestic and industrial markets. The portfolio also included other operational work such as administration- and logistics-related activities. It is essential for the company to ensure that the operational work continuously supports the projects and programs.

Programs vs. Portfolios

Program management includes related and interdependent projects, whereas a portfolio may include several otherwise unrelated projects if they all support major goals or a significant product line.

Operations

Operations are ongoing, repetitive tasks that produce the same outcome every time they are performed. The purpose of operations is to carry out day-to-day organizational functions, generate income to sustain the business, and increase the value of organizational assets. Operational processes are aligned with the business requirements of an organization. Therefore, when organizations update or adopt new objectives based on organizational needs, customer requirements, or market demand, these processes are continuously revised to accommodate the changes.

The following table highlights the differences between projects and operations.

Projects	Operations
One-time effort	Ongoing effort
Unique product or service	Repetitive product or service

Example: Operations in a Computer Manufacturing Company

In order to meet its increasing customer demands, a computer manufacturing company decided to open a new manufacturing facility. Construction of the facility would constitute a project, and when it opens, everything from that point forward would be an operation. The company plans to reach a break-even point in three years by achieving the desired volume of output from its new facility. The operations to be carried out in the new facility include daily production, routine maintenance, wages and salary credits to employees, grievance handling, logistics, and supply of finished products to the market.

The PMO

The *Project Management Office (PMO)* is a centralized, permanent, ongoing administrative unit or department that serves to improve project management performance within an organization. The people in the PMO provide support for project management concepts, tools, training, and mentoring to project managers; they may or may not actually do hands-on project management themselves. The PMO will try to maintain standards across projects, provide governance, and improve efficiency. It has the authority to make key decisions in the projects. In some organizations, the project managers are provided, or assigned, by the PMO.

PMOs function differently in different organizations, depending on the business needs. Unlike programs, the projects supported by the PMO may not be related to each other. The structure and function of the PMO depends upon the respective organizational requirements. In some organizations, the PMO may be referred to as the "project office," "program office," "central project office," "project management center of excellence," or "program management office."

Some of the primary functions of the PMO include:

- Maintaining project historical information.
- Managing shared resources across projects managed by the PMO.
- Monitoring project timelines, budget, and quality at an enterprise level.
- Identifying and implementing new project management methodologies.
- Creating effective project policies, documentation, and templates.
- Helping project managers develop estimates and schedules.
- Conducting routine quality assurance reviews.
- Managing communication across projects under the PMO.

The PMO may publish their policies, templates, and other documentation on an intranet site, or in a Wiki library. The Wiki can be structured to provide links to specific procedures that should be followed to comply with the directives of the PMO.

Example: A PMO at a Broadband Services Company

A broadband services company identified a business need to introduce a faster, more convenient, and cost-effective service to its customers. The project managers at each broadband exchange came out with new processes and economies of scale to improve the performance of the system. In this case, the PMO introduced standardized processes for calculating, leveling, loading, and developing project budgets and helped the project managers with updating the project schedules. The PMO also planned for developing project data references and organized a best practices sharing session every month.

Project Stakeholders

A *project stakeholder* is a person who has a vested business interest in the outcome of a project or who is actively involved in its work. Stakeholders take on various roles and responsibilities; their participation in the project will have an impact on its outcome and its chances of success.

Stakeholders may have competing interests, needs, priorities, and opinions. They may have conflicting visions for the project's successful outcome. Project managers must identify internal and external stakeholders as early as possible, learn what their needs are, and secure their participation in defining the project's parameters and success criteria. While it may be difficult to negotiate to a consensus early in the project, it is far less painful and costly than getting to the end of the project only to learn that someone's needs were not met or were misunderstood.

Example: Project Stakeholders Involved in Constructing a Power Plant

An alternative energy producing company initiated a new project to harness geothermal energy by building a power plant to utilize the energy for electricity generation. Stakeholders for this project included the staff, management, and owners of the company; local and statewide elected officials; the licensing agencies; and engineers, architects, and construction workers employed by the project.

Project Stakeholder Types

The following table describes the common types of project stakeholders and their responsibilities.

Project Stakeholder	Description
Customers/end-users	*Customers* are individuals or organizations who will receive the product or service generated by the project. Customers can provide some of the resources of an external project. Some of their responsibilities include: • Defining the needs for the project output. • Delivering the project output. • Paying for the project output. Additionally, the customer might also be the *end-user* who will be affected by the product or service generated by the project.
Sponsor/champion	*Sponsors* may be individuals or groups that provide finances, management support, and overall control of the project. The sponsor may be internal or external to the organization. The sponsor: • Has the financial resources for the project. • Signs and publishes the project charter. • Approves initial project baselines, and changes to baselines. • Has the ultimate responsibility for the project's success. • Signs off on all planning documents, including requirements, business case and scope, and change requests. • Authorizes the team to use resources. • Champions and supports the project manager and team. • Reviews progress and quality. • Cuts through red tape, helps deal with roadblocks, and expedites activities. • Helps the project manager "market" the project to stakeholders who may not see the benefit of it.
Portfolio managers/ Portfolio review board	*Portfolio managers* or executives in the portfolio review board are a part of the project selection committees and belong to the high-level project governance side of the organization. Their review considerations may include: • Gauging the Return on Investment (ROI) of the project. • Identifying the value of the project. • Analyzing the risks involved in taking up the project. • Identifying the factors that may influence the project.
Program managers	*Program managers*, in coordination with the project managers, manage related projects in a program to obtain maximum benefits. They also provide guidance and support to every individual project.

Project Stakeholder	Description
Project Management Office (PMO)	A PMO is an administrative unit that supervises and coordinates the management of all projects in an organization. It focuses on providing: • Administrative support services, which include processes, methodologies, policies, standards, and templates. • Any key performance indicators and parameters that will allow projects to measure their success. • Training and mentoring support to project managers and project team members. • Support and guidance in managing projects and usage of tools. • Support for resource allocation. • Assistance in better communication among project managers, sponsors, and other stakeholders.
Project managers	*Project managers* are individuals responsible for managing all aspects of the project. The project manager: • Works with stakeholders to define the project. • Plans, schedules, and budgets project activities with team input. • Works with the team to carry out project plans. • Monitors performance and takes corrective action. • Identifies, monitors, and mitigates risks. • Keeps the sponsor and the stakeholders informed. • Requests and documents scope changes. • Provides timely reports on project metrics. • Acts as a liaison between the project team and other stakeholders.
Project management team	The *project management team* are those members of the project team who perform management activities, such as: • Acting as the procurement manager for projects that involve multiple contracts and vendors. • Being responsible for inputting data into the Project Management Information System (PMIS) and confirming the accuracy of that data. • Assuming the role of Project Manager in his or her absence.
Project coordinator	The *project coordinator* role exists when the organizational structure does not warrant or support a full-scale project manager. The project coordinator has limited decision-making responsibilities. This role requires cross-functional coordination and duties can include: • Administrative support and documentation assistance. • Time and resource scheduling. • Quality control checking.

Project Stakeholder	Description
Scheduler	The *scheduler* creates and maintains the project timeline. The scheduler is proficient at using project management software such as Microsoft® Project and other applications. Other duties might include: • Communicate timeline and schedule changes. • Monitor schedule status and solicit task status from resources. • Report schedule performance.
Project team	The *project team* comprises the project manager, the project management team, and other individual team members. The individual team members perform project work and may not be involved in the management side of the project. The project team contains people from different groups who possess knowledge on specific subjects or have unique skill sets to carry out project work. The project team's duties include: • Use expertise to contribute to completing project tasks. • Contribute deliverables on schedule. • Provide estimates of task duration. • Provide estimates of costs and dependencies.
Vendors and business partners	*Vendors* are external parties who enter into a contractual agreement with the organization and provide components or services needed for the project. Seller, contractor, and supplier are also used when referring to vendors. In the same way, *business partners* are external to the company and provide specialized support to tasks such as installation, customization, training, or support.
Functional managers	*Functional managers* are individuals who provide resources (people) to the project manager, who in turn assigns them to project activities. Examples of functional managers are engineering managers, IT managers, and other department heads. They sometimes act as subject matter experts or may provide services needed for the project.
Operations managers	*Operations managers* manage the core business areas such as the design, manufacturing, provisioning, testing, research and development, or maintenance side of the organization. Some of their functions include: • Directly managing the production and maintenance of the final products and services that the organization provides. • Handing off technical project documentation and other records to the operations management group upon project completion.

Positive and Negative Stakeholders

Positive stakeholders usually benefit from the successful outcome of a project, whereas negative stakeholders see negative outcomes of a successful project. A good example of positive stakeholders is business leaders from a community who benefit from an industrial expansion project because it involves economic growth for the community. In this scenario, the negative stakeholders will be the environmental groups who are more concerned about the environment and will consider the project as harmful to the environment.

Furthermore, the positive stakeholders can go to the extent of getting the needed permits to proceed with the project because they are more interested in the project's success. But, the negative stakeholders can block the progress of the project by demanding more environmental reviews.

The Project Manager Role

Project managers are responsible for meeting project objectives and their job role is different from that of a functional or operations manager. Based on the organizational structure, a project manager may report to a portfolio or program manager. The project manager works in tandem with his or her manager to meet the project objectives and ensure that the project plan is in alignment with the overall program plan.

A project manager should have the following characteristics:

- **Knowledge:** Having good knowledge of project management.
- **Performance:** Performing well in projects by applying project management practices.
- **Personal effectiveness:** Including the project manager's attitude, personality, and leadership skills.

TOPIC B

Describe the Project Life Cycle

Before you can begin planning and managing your project, you need to define the project's needs, determine which processes are appropriate, and ascertain the degree of rigor needed to meet the project objectives. To do this, you will identify the project management processes that are generally recognized as good practices in most projects across industry groups. In this topic, you will describe the project life cycle.

Effective project managers combine their skills and knowledge with appropriate processes to meet project objectives and deliver results in line with corporate strategies. By identifying the main elements of effective project management processes, you can enhance the chances of success over a wide range of projects across application areas and industries.

The Project Life Cycle

In order to improve management control, projects are broken down into manageable, sequential phases of work activities. *Project phases*, taken together, are referred to as the *project life cycle*. Project life cycles may have four or five phases, which can vary because the life cycle is customized to meet the needs of specific projects. A project life cycle is marked by the beginning and the end of the project. During the initial phase, the project's general scope and timing are determined. During the intermediate phases, detailed planning occurs along with the actual work activities. In the final phase, project-closing activities occur.

 Note: CompTIA uses the term "project phases" to mean what the Project Management Institute's PMBOK® Guide calls "process groups." The PMBOK Guide specifically defines a phase as a group of activities that result in one or more deliverables, and a process group as a group of project management processes. For example, the Initiating Process Group, the Planning Process Group, and so on. This course will use the terms *process group* and *phase* interchangeably.

Project Life Cycle Characteristics

Though projects differ in nature, size, and complexity, they display certain common characteristics. At the beginning of the project, the cost and staffing levels are quite low. They reach the peak once the work is carried out and drop rapidly upon project completion. Influences, uncertainties, and risks involved with stakeholders are high at the project start and diminish over the life of the project.

Likewise, the ability to influence the characteristic of the final product, without impacting the project cost, is high during the initial stages of a project and low toward project completion.

Project Management Processes

A *process* is a sequence of activities designed to bring about a specific result in response to a business need. *Project management processes* are all the activities that underlie the effective practice of project management; they are grouped into initiating/pre-project setup, planning, executing, monitoring/controlling, and closing a project. Project management processes may produce project deliverables, such as schedules and performance reports, or product deliverables, such as software interface specifications or a building's foundation.

Project management processes are recognized within the profession as good practices; applying them appropriately improves the chances of success on nearly any project.

Project Life Cycle Phases (Process Groups)

The processes in a project life cycle are organized into five phases (process groups).

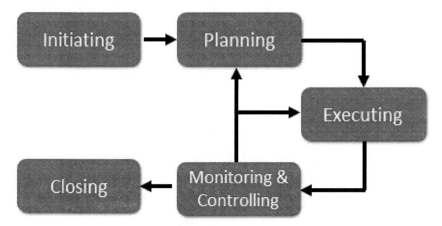

Figure 1–2: The process groups in a project life cycle.

Phase (Process Group)	Involves
Initiating	Defining the need for a new project or the new phase of an existing project, validating the project, preparing a project charter, and obtaining approval for the project charter to move forward.
Planning	Creating the project management plan. This plan addresses scope, time, cost, quality, risk, communications, procurement, human resources, and stakeholders. During planning, project objectives are refined and a strategy is developed to accomplish the work in the project or phase.
Executing	Carrying out the work mentioned in the project management plan in order to meet project specifications.
Monitoring and Controlling	Regular monitoring of project performance and tracking progress made in the project or phase. They also include changes that are to be made to the plan when required and corrective actions needed to get back on track.
Closing	Finalizing the project activities, handing off the project or phase output, gaining formal acceptance, tying up administrative and contractual loose ends, and finally closing the project or phase.

Tailoring

Not every process in the project life cycle takes place in every project. Determining which processes are appropriate for a given project is referred to as *tailoring*. The project manager and the project team are responsible for tailoring the applicable processes to meet the needs of a specific project or phase.

Project Life Cycle Outputs

Specific outputs are generated at the end of each process group.

Process Group	Outputs	
Initiating	• Project purpose • Goals and objectives • Project charter • Business case	• Assignment of a project manager, management sponsor, functional manager, and user representative • Constraints and assumptions • High-level scope definition • High-level risks
Planning	• Project management plans • Scope management plan • Scope statement • Work Breakdown Structure (WBS) • Activity list • Project network diagram • Activity duration estimates • Project schedule • Schedule management plan • Resource requirements	• Cost estimates • Cost management plan • Cost baseline • Quality assurance plan • Communications plan • Resource management plan • Roles and responsibilities • Assignment of resources • Risk management plan • Procurement management plan • Statement of Work (SOW)
Executing	• Intermediate or final work results/deliverables • Change requests • Project records	• Quality improvements • Proposals and contracts
Monitoring and Controlling	• Performance reports • Change requests • Project plan updates • Corrective actions	• Risks/Issues log • Change control reports • Budget changes
Closing	• Formal acceptance and closure • Project archives • Contract file • Lessons learned	• Customer sign-off • Sponsor sign-off • Transition/training

 Note: The Work Breakdown Structure is a logical grouping of project deliverables arranged in a hierarchical structure that defines the total scope of work required to complete the project. This output is discussed in more detail in future lessons.

Project Prototyping

Project prototyping is the process of creating a mock-up of a product or system. A prototype is usually built for demonstration purposes. In the software development life cycle, a working model on a smaller or partial scale of the system is built, tested, and reworked until an acceptable model is achieved. This in turn facilitates the development of the complete system or product. Project prototyping works best in scenarios where complete project requirements are not available in advance.

Prototyping Models

The following table describes four different prototyping models.

Model	Enables You To
Proof-of-principle	Check some aspects of the product design without considering the visual appearance, the materials to be used, or the manufacturing process.
Form study	Check the primary size and appearance of a product without simulating its exact function or design.
Visual	Check the design and imitate the appearance, color, and surface textures of the product but will not contain the functions of the final product.
Functional	Check the appearance, materials, and functionality of the expected design.

Project Stages

A *project stage* is a group of related project activities that results in the completion of a major deliverable. Each stage in a project is marked by the completion of one or more deliverables, the review and approval of which may occur before the project can go on to the next stage. Documents and information that are created in one stage are used as an input for the next stage. A project stage can, but does not need to, contain all phases, or process groups.

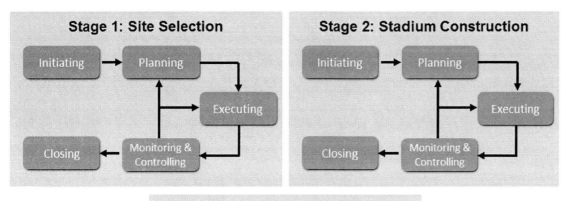

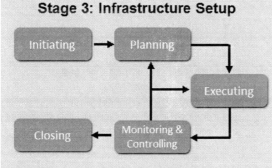

Figure 1-3: The three-stage project of constructing a stadium.

Project Governance

Project governance is a comprehensive methodology to control a project and ensure its success. It is carried out throughout the life cycle of a project and provides guidance in the form of project phase reviews, to monitor and control the project. Every phase in the project is formally initiated to decide on the deliverables expected out of that phase. A management review is performed at the start of every phase to decide whether to begin the activities of a particular phase. This assumes significance in cases where the activities of the prior phase are not yet complete.

Governance Activities in a Project

At the beginning of each phase, it is a good practice to verify and validate the former assumptions made to the project, analyze risks, and explain in detail the processes required to achieve a phase's deliverables. After the key deliverables of a particular phase are produced, a phase-end review is necessary to ensure completeness and acceptance. Even though this method signifies the start of the subsequent phase, a phase can be closed or the project can be terminated when huge risks are involved for the project or when the objectives are no longer required.

Phase-Gate Reviews

A *phase-gate review*, also known as a governance-gate review, is a check point review of project deliverables and performance that occurs at the end of each phase of a project where a management review or sign-off may be required. Each review is used to check if each phase has fulfilled the exit criteria and is eligible to move to the next phase. The advantage of this approach is that the project is controlled by incremental decisions based on information, rather than one big decision based on speculation and conjecture. The disadvantage of this approach is that it may create the impression that the project team keeps approaching management for assurance, approval, and support and provides management with an opportunity for mentoring and guiding the project.

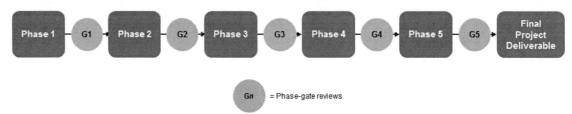

Figure 1-4: An illustration of phase-gate reviews in the project life cycle.

Software development projects can utilize a special type of phase gate called a *quality gate*. It is located before a phase that is strongly dependent upon the outcome of a previous phase. The Quality Gate process is a formal way of specifying and recording the transition between stages in the project life cycle.

 Note: Like phase-gate reviews, tollgate reviews also check if a project phase in a Six Sigma project has met all the set objectives and is eligible to move to the next phase. When a phase receives tollgate approval, the project can proceed with the next phase.

Phase-to-Phase Relationships in a Project

Multiphased projects generally follow a sequential process that ensures greater control over the project and aids in achieving the desired product, service, or result. There are three types of phase-to-phase relationships: sequential, overlapping, and iterative. Sometimes, multiphased projects will have more than one phase-to-phase relationship occurring during the life cycle of a project. In such cases, certain factors, such as the level of control, effectiveness, and the degree of uncertainty, decide the relationship that can be applied between phases. Based on these factors, all three types of relationships can be applied between different phases of a project.

Phase-to-Phase Relationship Types

Each phase-to-phase relationship has specific characteristics.

Relationship Type	Description
Sequential	• Contains consecutive phases. • Starts only when the previous phase is complete. • Reduces the level of uncertainty, which produces reliable cost and duration estimates but which may eliminate the possibility of reducing the project duration later in the project cycle.
Overlapping	• Contains phases that start prior to the completion of the preceding phase. • Increases the level of risk and can cause rework if the subsequent phase begins before it receives accurate information from the previous phase.
Iterative	• Includes one phase at a time that will be planned and carried out. • Requires planning for the next phase as the work in the current phase progresses. • Is largely helpful in environments that are quite uncertain and undefined. • Reduces the need for long-term planning. • Helps in minimizing project risk and maximizing the business value of the product. • Is an extension or corollary of the overlapping relationship, but in this case the same phase repeats itself multiple times—once in each iteration.

Progressive Elaboration

Progressive elaboration is defined as the process of increasing the level of detail in a project management plan as more information and more accurate estimates become available. At the beginning of a project, very little is known—perhaps only a high-level scope and some objectives. As the project moves forward, requirements are determined; the scope is written; a Work Breakdown Structure is developed; and time and cost estimates are prepared. Thus, the project management plan becomes more detailed as the project progresses. Progressive elaboration applies to work within a phase, as well as work between phases.

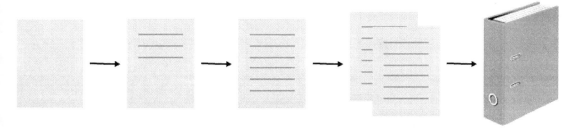

Figure 1-5: Detail is added to plans in progressive elaboration.

Rolling Wave Planning

Rolling wave planning is a technique in which work to be accomplished in the near term is planned in detail, whereas future work is planned with much less detail. As time progresses, the "wave" rolls forward so near-term work is always planned in more detail.

TOPIC C

Identify Organizational Influences on Project Management

As you advance in your development as a project manager, carefully integrating the roles and responsibilities of everyone involved with the projects will effectively ensure that they have a clear understanding of their duties. In this topic, you will examine some organizational structures and project interfaces and document the roles, responsibilities, and reporting relationships of the people working on your project.

As project manager, you want to ensure that everyone working on your project is assigned appropriate duties. In order to ensure this, you need to clearly understand the influences of organizational cultures and styles on the projects you manage and document the roles, responsibilities, and relationships among each individual in the organization.

Organizational Cultures and Styles

Projects are greatly influenced by the various cultures followed by organizations. Some of the factors that form a part of organizational culture are policies, values, management styles, and work environment.

Factor	Description
Policies	Organizational policies and procedures influence the projects the company undertakes. For example, the organizational procedures will determine how to implement new strategies and if the work environs will be formal or informal.
Values	Values, beliefs, and expectations of an organization have a major impact on the organizational culture. For example, the organization's strategic decision-making choices, preferences, and approach will vary, based on its values and beliefs.
Management style	Management style of the organization is another factor that affects the organizational culture. For example, certain factors, such as managers following a coaching style of management or a controlling style of management, the employees being allowed to give feedback, and the implementation of their feedback, are all dependent upon the different styles followed by management.
Work environment	Work ethics followed by the organization also constitute the organizational culture. For example, some organizations may allow employees to work anytime from 7:00 A.M. to 7:00 P.M. and some others may want them to work strictly from 8:00 A.M. to 5:00 P.M. and work late nights if their workload is high.

The Organizational Culture's Influence on Projects

Several aspects of projects are influenced by the organizational culture.

Project Aspect	Description
Project policies and procedures	The project policies and procedures should reflect the organization's cultures, policies, and procedures.

Project Aspect	Description
Project selection	The criteria for the selection of projects are determined by the organizational culture. For example, a competitive, ambitious, and assertive organization will select projects with high risks, whereas a highly rigid and authoritarian organization may not take projects with high risks.
Project management style	A project manager should adapt to the management style of an organization. For example, a project manager cannot follow a permissive management style in an autocratic organization where all decisions are made unilaterally.
Team performance assessments	A project manager should adhere to a company's policies when assessing the performance of a team. For example, an employee should not be promoted to the next level unless he or she meets all the standards set by the organization.

Organizational Process Assets

Organizational process assets are entities that can be used to influence the success of a project. Policies, procedures, guidelines, formal and informal plans, templates, lessons learned documents, and even historical information come under the organizational process assets. They may also include completed schedules, earned value data, and risk data. Any updates to the organizational process assets are handled by the project team members.

Organizational process assets can be classified into two categories.

Category	Description
Processes and procedures	These are the processes and procedures the organization uses for performing project-related tasks. Examples may include: • Policies, product and project life cycles, and quality policies and procedures. • Standard guidelines, proposal evaluation criteria, work instructions, and performance measurement criteria. • Templates such as Work Breakdown Structures, project definition and business case forms, the project schedule, the milestone report, and contract templates. • Tailored guidelines and criteria for organizational processes that will satisfy specific project needs. • Organizational communication requirements and project closure guidelines.

Category	Description
Corporate knowledge base	This is a corporate knowledge repository for storing and retrieving information. This repository can reside in a company intranet site, or you can use a collaboration tool such as Microsoft® SharePoint® or similar software. Examples may include: • Process measurement databases that provide measurement data on processes and products. • Project files such as scope, cost, schedule, and quality baselines; performance measurement baselines; project calendars; and risk registers. • Lessons learned knowledge bases and historical information. • Issue and defect management databases. • Configuration management knowledge bases. • Financial databases.

Enterprise Environmental Factors

Enterprise environmental factors are the internal or external factors that can have a positive or negative influence on the project outcome. These factors can either support or limit the project management options and act as inputs for planning processes. Examples of enterprise environmental factors may include organizational culture, the human resources pool, marketplace conditions, stakeholder risk tolerances, political situations, and project management information systems.

Expert Judgment

Expert judgment is advice provided by individuals having expertise in a specific knowledge area, an application area, an industry, or discipline. It is typically used to make informed decisions on a project. Expert judgment may be obtained from internal or external sources such as stakeholders, professionals, subject matter experts, industry groups, the PMO, consultants, and functional units. Expert judgment can be obtained either through individual consultations, such as one-on-one meetings and interviews, or through a panel format, such as focus groups, workshops, and surveys.

 Note: During the project life cycle, expert judgment may be required only once or continuously, for a very short period or for an extended period.

Example: Expert Judgment in Building a Financial Management Software Application

A project team is assigned to develop a financial management software application for one of their customers. Because the project manager and the team are well versed with the software technical aspect but are not familiar with the financial concepts, the project manager felt that the project team required a financial expert to be present, to help them develop the software. The expert will help analyze the ease of use, coverage of the applications to the current financial laws, and ease of customizing the parameters based on his knowledge of frequently changing parameters in financial systems. The expert will also provide financial data needed to carry out usability and reliability tests on the application while selecting an appropriate application. The expert will also suggest some typical use cases or situations that occur while dealing with and managing a financial system. The project manager, therefore, decided to contract a financial expert from a financial services firm. The expert will provide his or her services throughout the project life cycle.

Organizational Theory

Organizational theory provides information on the organization of work processes and operating practices through organizational structure, power, culture, compensation and benefits, and behavior of people, among other things. Effective use of this information helps in planning human resources efficiently. Project managers must understand that various organizational structures influence or impact the individual response time and performance differently.

Project Interfaces

Project interfaces are the various reporting relationships that occur within a project and on the boundaries of the project.

Interface	Description
Organizational	Reporting relationships among different organizational units. They may be internal or external to the parent organization and include interfaces among the project team, upper management, other functional managers that may need to support the team, and even the organization's customers.
Technical	Reporting relationships among technical disciplines on the project that can occur during a phase or during the transition between phases. They reflect informal and formal relationships with people on the project team and outside the team.
Interpersonal	Formal and informal reporting relationships among individuals working on the project, whether internally or externally.
Logistical	Relationships between project team members who are distributed geographically across different buildings, states, counties, and time zones.

Organizational Structures

An *organizational structure* is the compositional makeup of an organization that describes how various groups and individuals within the organization interrelate. The structure of an organization strongly affects how projects are managed. The type of organizational structure can influence, or limit, the availability of resources and the terms under which those resources are available to the project.

An *organization chart* is a visual representation of a project's organizational structure. Its purpose is to show both the reporting relationships within the project and the project's relationship to the parent organization.

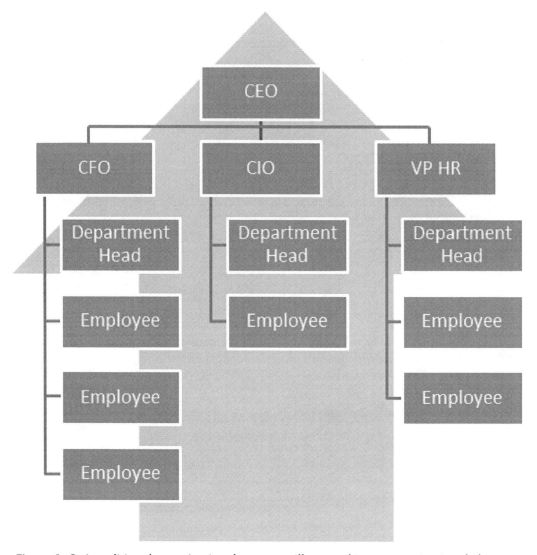

Figure 1-6: A traditional organizational structure illustrated in an organizational chart.

Types of Organizational Structures

The following table describes the four types of organizational structures: functional, projectized, matrix, and composite.

Organizational Structure	Description
Functional	• Each department is responsible for carrying out a specific, similar set of activities.
	• Multiple people perform each type of activity.
	• Reporting is hierarchical, with each individual reporting to a single manager.
	• The project manager's authority is low, relative to the functional manager's authority.

Organizational Structure	Description
Matrix	• A blend of functional and projectized structures in which individuals report upward in the functional hierarchy, but they also report horizontally to one or more project managers. • The matrixed reporting scheme may be permanent or temporary. • May be characterized as weak, balanced, or strong, depending on the relative authority of the project manager to the functional manager. An organization is said to have a strong matrix when the project manager's authority is higher than that of the functional manager.
Projectized	• The project manager and a core project team operate as a completely separate organizational unit within the parent organization. • Core team members are responsible for the work of extended team members in their functional area. • Team members are often co-located. • The project manager reports to a program manager and has a significant amount of authority and independence. • Some projectized organizations may contain their own support systems, such as a separate procurement or personnel department, or share support systems with the parent organization.
Composite	Most modern organizations involve all the above structures at various levels. It is a combination of all the other types of organizations.

Functional Organizational Structure

In a functional organization, team members are loyal to their department and report only to their functional manager. The project manager is part-time on the project and reports to a functional manager; the team members are part-time as well. The project manager role is usually assigned to a staff member who has only limited authority over team members because they report to the functional manager. Overall, a functional organization makes for an inefficient project organization. Examples of a functional organization include organizations that are dominated by *silos*, which are defined as compartmentalized functional units, such as sales, engineering, production, and so on.

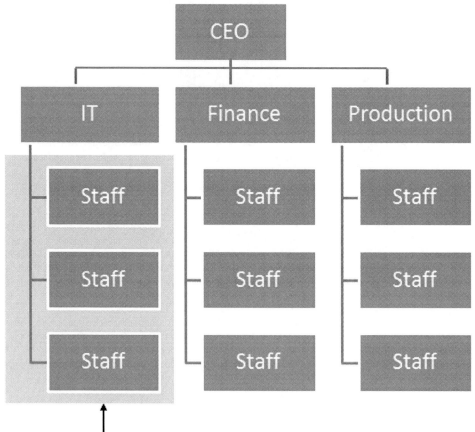

One departmental staff member is assigned the Project Manager role.

Figure 1-7: Functional organizational structure.

Matrix Organizational Structures

In a matrix organization, team members maintain a home in their department and report to both the functional manager and the project manager. The project manager is full-time on the project while team members are part-time. Overall, a matrix organization constitutes a complex and costly but reasonably effective project organization.

The strength of the matrix is influenced by the project manager's authority over the project team and how divided the resources are between the project and their functional department. The following figure illustrates a matrix organizational structure.

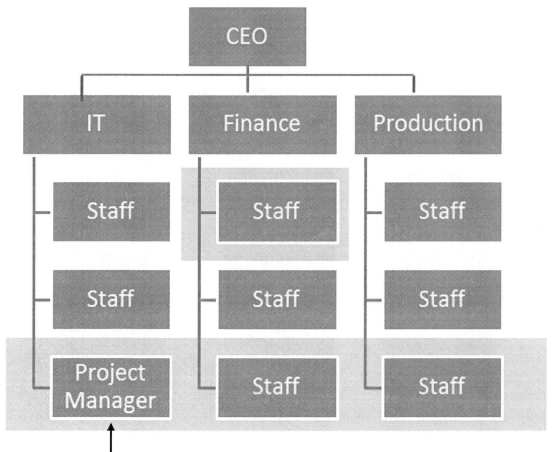

Project Manager and 3 Staff assigned to project.
Resources are shared between functional areas and project.

Figure 1-8: Matrix organizational structure.

 Note: The authority of the project manager is what defines a strong, balanced, or weak matrix. The project manager's authority level is not indicated in the functional organizational structure shown in the figure.

Projectized Organizational Structure

In a projectized organization, team members do not belong to a department so they can be loyal to only the project. This provides flexibility in assigning ad hoc resources to a specific project. Both the project manager and team members are full-time on the project, and the project manager has full authority over team members because they report to only him or her. Overall, a projectized organization makes for an efficient project organization. Examples of a projectized organization include all organizations that exist solely to run projects, such as consulting firms or engineering firms.

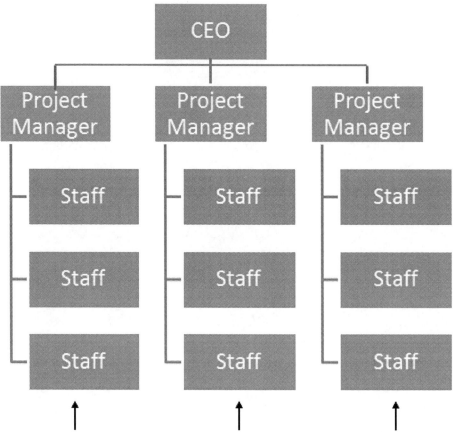

Each project assigned a Project Manager and 3 Staff as team members.

Figure 1-9: Projectized organizational structure.

 Note: A purely projectized organizational structure like the one shown in the figure is only theoretical because it does not allow for functional areas.

Relative Authority in Organizational Structures

Relative authority refers to the project manager's authority relative to the functional manager's authority over the project and the project team. In a purely functional organizational structure, the project manager's authority is low relative to that of the functional manager. Conversely, in the project-based organizational structure, the opposite is true.

The following table illustrates the relationships found in each organizational structure.

Relationship	Functional	Matrix	Projectized
Team members are loyal to	Functional department	Conflicted loyalty	Project
Team members report to	Functional manager	Both functional manager and project manager	Project manager
Project manager's role is	Part-time	Full-time	Full-time
Team members' role is	Part-time	Part-time	Full-time

Relationship	Functional	Matrix	Projectized
Control of project manager over team members is	Low	Medium	High

Example: Relative Authority at a Manufacturing Company

A computer hardware manufacturing company has a functional organizational structure and its management is hierarchical. A project manager coordinating the company's participation in a trade show has engineers, designers, and sales and marketing executives assigned to the project, but does not have functional authority over those resources; they all report to their functional managers in their own departments. The authority of the project manager is low relative to that of the functional managers. Conversely, a web design company has a project-based organizational structure, with independent project teams working on their own projects. A project manager in this organization has much more autonomy and authority.

TOPIC D

Define Agile Methodology

Many of the projects you manage will follow the methodology addressed throughout this course. However, you should be aware of an alternative methodology that is becoming increasingly popular, particularly in the IT profession. Many application developers are using it to deal with the frequent challenges that development and programming projects face. This topic will introduce you to Agile project management.

Basics of Agile Methodology

Agile project management is an iterative and incremental project management approach that focuses on customer value and team empowerment. In Agile project management, the product is developed in iterations by small and integrated teams. Each iteration can span anywhere from two to four weeks, and after each iteration, the working product with increased functionality is shared with the client for feedback. These frequent feedback sessions allow the developers to continuously improve the product and reduce the risk associated with product development. In Agile project management, the teams are involved in the project right from the planning stage and are responsible for estimation. Therefore, there is a shift in the role of the project manager from the taskmaster role taken in traditional projects to that of a facilitator.

To be successful in using any methodology, you need to understand the underlying values and be able to identify with them. These values control the way a theory is implemented. Similarly, you must be aware of the underlying values for successfully implementing Agile. Knowledge about the values of Agile will guide you to change your behavioral practices to implement Agile. Usually, in any project, short-term individual goals act as a hindrance to long-term team goals. Such focus prevents teams from effectively finishing the project. To prevent this, Agile is based on a set of basic values, which include communication, simplicity, feedback, courage, and humility.

Principles of Agile

There are six basic principles of Agile that you should follow to successfully implement the Agile project management approach. The following table defines the principles of Agile.

Principle	Description
Customer Value	Agile project management focuses on providing value to customers in terms of the product, time, and cost. The customer is an integral member of the team. Requirements that are most important to the customer are developed first followed by requirements that are lower on the priority list. Further, customers can change either this priority or the features that are to be developed before each iteration.
Iterative and Incremental Delivery	With this iterative and incremental delivery, you can adapt the features to be developed in subsequent iterations based on customer feedback. This principle reduces monetary risks associated with the project, and reduces effort spent on nonessential features by focusing on high-priority items at any given point.

Principle	Description
Intense Collaboration	Customer requirements are first documented in a simple list that is defined and prioritized by the customer and any change to these requirements is acceptable. Intense collaboration among team members is critical to ensure common understanding of the requirements. You can ensure intense collaboration by facilitating face-to-face communication among team members as they design, develop, test, and document the feature. Additionally, intense collaboration is necessary to bring together the business and development teams of the project.
Small and Integrated Teams	Ideally, an Agile team for each iteration should be small—comprising two to eight members who are talented, competent, and self-disciplined individuals. Keep the overall team size to a minimum number so you can co-locate team members and facilitate smooth, face-to-face communication. In addition, ensure that each Agile team has members with diversified roles to include a variety of perspectives and suggestions and better plan each iteration. It also facilitates the estimation of time for the different features of the product.
Self-Organizing Teams	All customer requirements are subject to change and just enough planning that is essential for each iteration is used. Therefore, teams need to be self-organized so they can make timely decisions, and are empowered to do so. This increases their ability to organize themselves in a way that accomplishes project goals most efficiently. Agile project management can be a success only if all Agile team members commit to the process and discipline themselves to follow it.
Small and Continuous Improvements	Agile project management contains small development cycles that are used to develop the product by feature and receive client feedback on each feature. This allows teams to adapt to change and, in the process, reflect and learn, thus leading to continuous improvements in features in subsequent development cycles. When the product is developed in small development cycles, Agile teams frequently go through the complete development process, which gives the teams the opportunity to make continuous improvements in development procedures, team communications, and customer interactions.

The Scrum Process

Scrum is an Agile methodology that has been developed over the last decade and can be applied to a variety of projects. It focuses on iterative and incremental delivery of products. Scrum owes its popularity to a simple approach, high productivity, and its scope for applicability to multiple areas. When you use Scrum as a development process, you create the product by using customer requirements as the starting point. Then, you assign a priority to each of these requirements based on their priority to the customer. The list is shared with the team, which then breaks each requirement into sub-tasks. The whole team works simultaneously on the sub-tasks that are part of a single client requirement. Each team member picks a sub-task, gives an estimate, and starts working on the assigned sub-task. The requirement is worked on by the team and becomes a set of features of the finished product. Then, the team starts working on the next requirement in the queue. As sections of the product are created, they are shared with the client for review and approval.

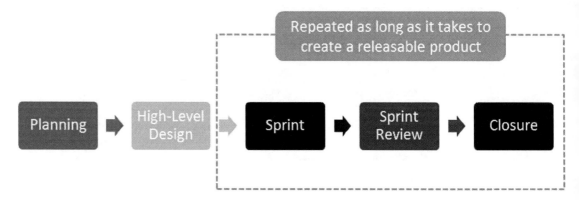

Figure 1-10: The Scrum process.

 Note: The term Scrum is derived from rugby, in which "scrum" refers to "the method of beginning play in which the forwards of each team crouch side by side with locked arms."

User Stories

User stories are customer requirements or features. Each user story emphasizes the functionality of the feature and how it adds to the final product. User stories can vary in size and complexity. Based on a common theme, smaller user stories can be combined into an epic for convenience. These are also called parent and child stories.

Scrum Roles and Responsibilities

When you decide to implement Scrum management, you first start with identifying the various roles in Scrum as they are different from the traditional roles. Scrum requires each of these roles to be actively involved in the development process.

- **Product Owner**—an individual or an organization who is responsible for gathering inputs about a product from the customer and translating the requirements into the product vision for the team and stakeholders.
- **Scrum Master**—an individual who serves, protects, and supports the team like a coach or facilitator and works closely with the Product Owner but does not control the Scrum team. The Scrum Master can be either part-time or full-time.
- **Scrum Team**—dedicated, self-managing, cross-functional, fully empowered individuals who deliver the finished work required by the customer. The size of the team can range from 3 to 15, depending on the project.
- **Stakeholders**—individuals who can affect or be affected by the project either positively or negatively. Most importantly, the customer is included and engaged as a relevant stakeholder.
- **Customers**—an individual, or representative for an organization, who requires the end product.

Role	Responsible for
Product Owner	• Consolidating all client requirements into a prioritized set of deliverables. • Defining the features of the product based on market value. • Managing project ROI and risk. • Adjusting features and their priority on a regular basis. • Participating actively in all planning and review meetings of the project. • Providing answers to questions raised by project teams from time to time. • Determining the release plan for deliverables and communicating it to all stakeholders. • Accepting or rejecting work results.
Scrum Master	• Helping the team by trying to resolve issues or blocks that the team faces. • Improving the productivity of the team and keeping it effective. • Enabling close cooperation among various roles and functions. • Keeping track of training requirements for the team to avoid delay in deliverables. • Protecting the team from outside interference or disruption. • Protecting the interest of the Product Owner and maximizing the ROI. • Organizing and facilitating Scrum-related activities and meetings. • Ensuring that the team follows Scrum standards.
Scrum Team	• Selecting the goal and specifying work results. • Organizing the team and work. • Demonstrating work results to the Product Owner. • Providing the Product Owner with inputs and ideas about the final product. • Working within project guidelines to reach the goal.
Stakeholders	• Helping the product owner define the goal and vision of the project. • Attending planning meetings and helping team members with prioritizing components on a regular basis. • Optionally attending daily team meetings but not participating in the proceedings. • Attending review meetings to assess regular progress.
Customers	• Defining the product requirements. • Being involved in the review phase of each deliverable. • Participating throughout the process.

Stages of the Scrum Process

The Scrum process is based upon a workflow that contains the following steps which are used to manage a Scrum project. Noted within each of the four major steps are detailed substeps.

1. Create a vision for the project.
   a. Talk to the customer.
   b. Talk to the stakeholders.
   c. Interview potential users.
2. Create a Product Backlog.

    a. Itemize the customer requirements.

    b. Verify the order of importance for each of these items from the customer.

    c. Perform market research to decide on the priority of these items.

    d. Use this input to create a prioritized Product Backlog.

3. Set a broad release plan.

    a. Choose a release type.

    b. Identify a release date.

    c. Identify major components in the release.

4. Create a Sprint Backlog.

    a. Organize a Scrum Team.

    b. Identify a senior team member as the Scrum Master.

    c. Invite the Product Owner, Scrum Master, and team members for a planning meeting.

    d. Ask the Product Owner to explain the project vision.

    e. Allow the team to decide on the Sprint goal.

    f. Set the timeline for the Sprint.

    g. Allow the participants to identify tasks from the Product Backlog for the Sprint Backlog.

    h. Split large tasks and combine smaller ones.

    i. Validate the items on the Sprint Backlog with the team.

Product and Sprint Backlogs

There are two different types of backlogs that are used in Scrum. A *Product Backlog* is a prioritized list of customer requirements and it is the first step of Scrum. Here, priority is based on the riskiness and business value of the user story. The Product Owner creates the Product Backlog based on a user story, with input from each stakeholder including the team, customer, end users, and other interested parties. A Product Backlog can hold items of varying size.

A *Sprint Backlog* is a list of user stories selected from the Product Backlog that the Scrum Team chooses and commits to complete in that Sprint cycle. The team decides upon highly cohesive, low coupled chunks of work that form the Sprint Backlog and is used to create a deliverable at the end of the cycle. Once the team decides on the Sprint Backlog, nothing more can be added to the list during the cycle. If the customer requirement changes or the Product Owner identifies any additional stories, they are added to the Product Backlog and not to the Sprint Backlog. This ensures high productivity as the team focuses on the agreed plan even when there are additional customer requirements. However, this approach does not lead to loss of flexibility to accommodate change because change requests are incorporated in subsequent Sprints.

The Sprint Cycle

A *Sprint* (or *Sprint cycle*) represents a complete process from planning to delivery and demo of a part of the product. When the Product Owner defines and prioritizes the Product Backlog, the Sprint cycle begins.

The first step in this cycle is to arrange a Sprint planning meeting to create a detailed plan. The Product Owner reviews the vision, release plan, and Product Backlog with the Scrum Team at the start of the Sprint cycle. A Sprint cycle lasts one to four weeks, during which an agreed upon amount of work is completed to create a deliverable. As a result, analysis, design, development, review, and closure occur in every Sprint. At the end of every Sprint cycle, the team has a working product that is demonstrated to the Product Owner, other team members, the Scrum Master, customers, stakeholders, experts, and executives.

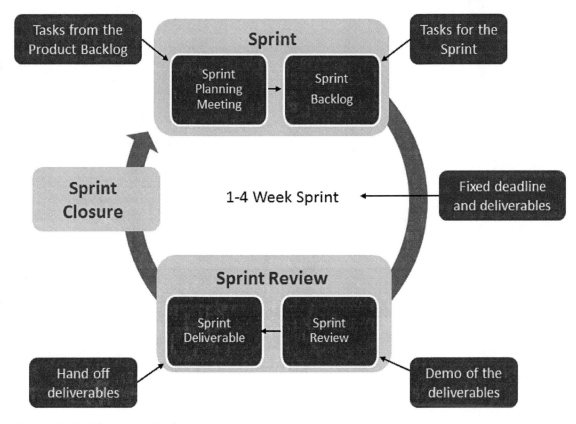

Figure 1-11: The Sprint Cycle.

Iterative Approach

In each Sprint, a chunk of the project is planned, developed, and delivered. User stories within the scope of the Sprint are designed, developed, and tested. At the end of the Sprint, the set of stories that are tested and ready is delivered as a near-releasable product to the customer and the team receives early feedback from the customer. This feedback helps develop subsequent Sprints. A Sprint is completed on a set date whether or not the work is completed. If a team is unable to meet the set target at the end of a Sprint, then the team is expected to acknowledge that it did not achieve set goals. Incomplete tasks are then added to the Product Backlog.

The Agile management principle is based on reasonable intensity and a sustainable pace. Therefore, there is no downtime between Sprints. One Sprint Review leads to the next Sprint planning meeting.

Burndown Charts

A *burndown chart* is a tool that is used to track the progress of the project by plotting the number of days of Sprint against the number of hours of work remaining. Unlike other tracking charts that are used to track how much work has been completed to date, a burndown chart is used to track the pending work until the team's commitment is complete. The burndown chart displays the progress of the team toward the goal.

In an ideal situation, the burndown chart is expected to be a downward sloping graph that will hit zero on the last day. However, this is not always the case because as the project progresses, the team might discover unexpected complexities or issues that may cause work to slow down, which further leads to increased number of hours of work remaining. If the burndown chart is not a downward sloping graph, then it signals the team to do things differently or increase the pace of their work. It also creates a feedback loop and enables the teams to improve the estimation by committing to only the amount of work that they can accomplish in a Sprint. Usually, the teams over or under commit in the first few Sprints. However, this improves after some time and the commitments are aligned with the work accomplished. You can create a burndown chart using a paper and pen or a whiteboard rather than creating the chart electronically.

 Note: When you use a burndown chart to track a Sprint, the burndown chart is referred to as Sprint burndown chart. However, when you use the burndown chart to track a release, it is known as a release burndown chart. In a release burndown chart, you plot the iteration number against the X-axis and the number of story points against the Y-axis.

Task	Task Owner	Day 1	Day 2	Day 3	Day 4	Day 5
		Hours of Work Remaining				
Automate server connection and authenticate to the provider system	Chris	6	4	3	6	1
Read provider's data directory	Sandra	3	6	2	5	3
Parse the current temperature out of the data	Tracy	5	3	1	4	4
Push the temperature data to the client	John	5	2	3	3	2
Parse snow/rain data from the provider's data	Sandra	3	4	1	2	2
Push the snow/rain data to the client	Susan	2	1	4	3	2
Resdesign client screen a bit	Tom	2	2	2	2	4
Refactor the server code	Tom	4	4	4	3	4
Total		**30**	**26**	**20**	**28**	**22**

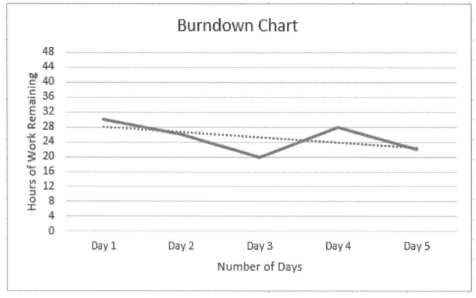

Figure 1-12: Burndown chart and the supporting data.

Daily Standup Meetings

The *daily standup meeting* is a meeting in which the complete team gets together for a quick status update. These meetings are short, 15-minute meetings that are conducted by standing in a circle. The standup meetings should be ideally conducted at the start of working hours, and the presence of all team members involved in the Sprint is mandatory. In these meetings, each team member who is a part of the Scrum is expected to summarize the tasks that were completed on the previous day, the tasks that are to be completed on the present day, and any roadblocks that the member might be facing.

The daily standup meetings enable team members to self organize and lead to a professional and appreciative environment. To ensure effective daily standup meetings:

- Time the meetings and keep the duration of the meetings to a maximum of 15 minutes.
- Ensure that the standup is a huddle rather than a meeting.
- Make sure all attendees stand up during the daily standup meeting.
- Signal the end after the meeting ends.
- Establish high-energy levels by discussing solutions for complicated problems offline.

The Closure Process

The Closure phase of the Sprint cycle consists of three stages: Sprint retrospective, Starting next Sprint, and Release planning.

Closure Phase	Activity
Sprint retrospective	The Product Owner, Scrum Master, and the Scrum Team attend the Sprint retrospective meeting to analyze from a process perspective what is working well and what is not and to agree upon changes to implement. This meeting may even have an outside facilitator if it adds value to the discussions. This is a critical part of the Scrum process where the team is empowered to change the process if it is not working. This is in line with the Scrum philosophy of making the process work for the team, not the other way around.
Starting next Sprint	The next Sprint starts soon after the previous Sprint finishes. After the Sprint review and retrospective meetings, the Product Owner consolidates the input from the meetings and the additional priorities that came in during the Sprint and incorporates them in the Product Backlog. The team then goes back into Sprint planning and decides the backlog for the next Sprint.
Release planning	It is possible while closing a Sprint that the customer may want to close the release and start using the product, so that the value from the completed features is delivered sooner. It should be part of the Closure process of a Sprint to determine if the entire product or some of the features can be released to the customer before proceeding with new development. The Product Owner could either decide on a set release date or a set of products to be released. A special "Release Sprint" may be planned to integrate all the modules and do a final testing before the launch.

Agile Comparison to Other Methodologies

In the world of project management, you might encounter other methodologies, such as PMI's PMBOK and PRINCE2. Each methodology has its own principles and processes that make it unique to its adopters and practitioners. When comparing Agile to other project management methodologies, there are some notable differences. The comparisons listed are general in nature, and do not provide detail of specific methodologies.

- Agile is considered to be more informal while others can be seen as more formal.
- An iterative approach (Agile) enables quicker bursts of output rather than the result of a longer, sequential approach where all planning is completed before execution begins (Waterfall).
- Agile is cyclical and not linear, whereas others tend to be linear.
- The outputs are incremental deliverables that are constantly being improved rather than a single final product.
- Self-empowered teams collaborate with customers to achieve the best possible output while other methodologies focus on process and tools.
- Responding to lessons learned ensures continued improvement while others can be hindered by sticking to the plan.

Each methodology follows its own specialized doctrine and history of how it came to be commonly known. For Agile, this began with the *Agile Manifesto for Software Development*. For more information about Agile, see **agilemethodology.org** or one of the many websites related to Agile project management.

Although the information provided here is a brief comparison of Agile and other project management methodologies, there is more information than what can be summarized in this course. You will definitely want to do some research on your own. Here are two links to help you get started.

- Project Management Institute (PMI) and the *PMBOK* Guide (**www.pmi.org**)
- PRINCE2 (**www.axelos.com/best-practice-solutions/prince2**)

ACTIVITY 1-1
Defining Project Management Fundamentals Review

Scenario
Answer the following review questions.

---

1. What types of project management experiences have you had?

2. How does the ability to tailor each of the project management process groups to each project or phase improve your chances of project success?

Summary

In this lesson, you discovered that a solid foundation is the essential building block to successfully manage projects. You identified the project management phases, or process groups, that are recognized as good practices in any given project across industries. Now, you are better prepared to initiate a project in your organization.

2 | Initiating the Project

Lesson Time: 1 hour, 45 minutes

Lesson Introduction

Project management is an integrated endeavor composed of five interlinked phases (process groups) and their component processes. Initiating is the first of five process groups that you will perform on virtually every project you manage. Starting a project is like starting a new job; the more you know about the company, your team members, and what is expected of you, the more likely you are to hit the ground running and make a good impression. Ensuring that your project starts out right will save you time and resources. It will also eliminate the need to backtrack once your project is officially underway. In this lesson, you will initiate a project, a critical first step in laying the foundation for your project's success.

Lesson Objectives

In this lesson, you will:

- Identify the project selection process.

- Prepare a project statement of work.

- Create a project charter.

- Identify project stakeholders.

TOPIC A

Identify the Project Selection Process

Projects should solve a business problem or seek to achieve a business opportunity. So, it is important to clearly identify and define the problem or opportunity your project seeks to address. Once you understand the project, it is imperative for you to ensure that the project's requirements align with the stated operational or strategic goals. Additionally, you need to identify the ways in which decision makers make critical choices among competing projects. In this topic, you will identify some of the most significant components of project selection.

In increasingly competitive business environments, there will always be projects competing for funding, resources, and priority. As a professional project manager, you will not be responsible for selecting projects that your organization will pursue, but you need to understand the methodologies behind making sound choices about what projects to pursue, prioritize, fund, and when. Applying appropriate project management methodology to this area will increase your chances for success.

Strategic and Operational Relevance

Strategic relevance of a project determines whether the project should be done—in other words, does it align with the company's strategic goals. Strategic relevance serves as a checkpoint and requires that the project objectives and the strategic priorities are clearly defined and communicated by senior leadership. It is important to remember that strategic objectives are inherently dynamic and can be influenced by unpredictable market events.

Note: A project can meet the business requirements of solving a particular business problem in a particular department, but may not be deemed strategically relevant by senior management. Senior management determines the prioritization of resource allocation for the organization. If your project is not strategically relevant, you will lose sponsor support.

Establishing *operational relevance* is a responsibility that requires the project objectives and operational priorities be clearly defined and communicated by tactical management and decides if the project should be taken up. It is important to remember that operational priorities will be heavily influenced by both established and emerging strategic priorities

Relative Authority

The relationship between the project manager and functional managers is going to be heavily influenced by organizational context. In strong matrix organizations, the balance of power rests with the project manager, whereas in a weak matrix organization, the balance of power rests with the functional manager. In many ways, both project and functional managers share tactical responsibilities with varying degrees of authority. This reality can cloud the process of establishing the operational relevance of any project. While strategic relevance is often easy to determine and because the source of organizational direction is more clearly defined, the determination of operational relevance requires that the accountability and authority for operational priorities be clearly established and communicated.

Reconciliation of Strategic, Tactical, and Operational Goals

It is important to attune the project's business, functional, and technical goals with the organization's strategic, tactical, and operational goals. Primarily, the organization's strategic goals are set by the executive management. These goals need to be reconciled to the project's business requirements. Then, the functional requirements must be reconciled to both the project's business goals and the organization's tactical goals, which are set by project and functional managers.

Similarly, the project's technical requirements must be reconciled to both the organization's operational goals and the functional and business requirements.

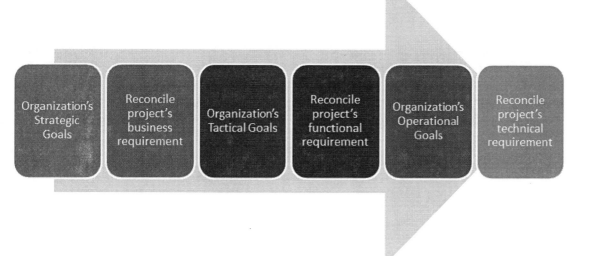

Figure 2-1: The process of reconciling a project to the organization's strategic, tactical, and operational goals.

Project Requirements

A *project requirement* is a statement that defines the functionality that a project is designed to accommodate and how the functionality will be achieved and satisfied by the solution. Project requirements can be classified as business, functional, or technical.

- *Business requirements* define *why* the project is being conducted, and every project must satisfy a business need or it should not be pursued. Projects typically address pressing organizational needs or market stimuli that drive decision makers to sponsor projects and prioritize competing projects.
- *Functional requirements* refer to *what* the project will accomplish. These requirements detail the desired functionality, capacity, or capability expected from the project.
- *Technical requirements* detail *how* the project will meet the business and functional requirements, including technical needs that are crucial for a project.

Business Requirements

- Provide online access to low-cost airfares for a given city pair.
- Provide online access to all available flights provided by low-cost carriers.
- Realize cost savings to customers of at least 20% and hence increase market share by 10% after one year.

Functional Requirements

- Real-time electronic access to carriers—ABC, WYZ, and DEF routing and fare information.
- Response time to low-cost carrier information must be less than 20 seconds.

Technical Requirements

- Interface to carrier information must be compliant to current Leaps & Bounds Travel's desktop and network standards.
- Leaps & Bounds Travel's interface must comply with external suppliers' security guidelines.

Figure 2-2: A list of project requirements for a travel reservation company to increase its market share.

Project Selection Criteria

Project selection is the act of choosing a project from among competing proposals. *Project selection criteria* are the standards and measurements an organization uses to select and prioritize projects. The organization's strategic goals provide a source for at least one dimension of selection criteria. Any project selected should be clearly linked to one or more strategic goals. Other selection criteria may be qualitative or quantitative. Qualitative criteria deal with the project's suitability with the organization's capabilities, while quantitative criteria may specify financial targets that the project must meet.

Example: Project Selection Criteria at a Financial Services Organization

A financial services organization considering a project proposal to integrate their customer and financial databases may develop the following project selection criteria:

- Links to the organization's strategic goal of obtaining a technological advantage over the competition.
- Qualitative criteria—feasible to produce using only internal resources.
- Quantitative criteria—meet or exceed the defined internal goal of increasing new sales revenue by 10 percent.

Project Selection Methods

Project selection methods are systematic approaches that decision makers use to analyze the value of a proposed project. These evaluations may be formal and detailed or informal "guesstimates," depending on the organization and its needs. Ideally, project selection methods should take into account the organization's strategic objectives and historical information about past successes and failures.

Example: Selecting Projects

A financial services firm that has the opportunity to implement two new projects, but has resources for only one, may perform an analysis of the projected cost, projected duration, and projected financial benefits to prioritize the one that will give greater financial return within a specific period of time.

Project Selection Decision Models

Project selection can be difficult because each project may present a complex array of seemingly incomparable selection criteria. Economic and technological considerations often influence project selections. In many application environments where ecological, health, and ethical impacts are increasingly important, often the only way to choose from many different project alternatives is by relying on unsubstantiated professional judgment or past experience. To improve the efficiency and effectiveness of the assessment, many organizations use formal decision models to select the appropriate project to initiate.

A *project selection decision model* provides a framework for comparing competing project proposals by helping decision makers compare the benefits of one project with another.

Decision Model Type	Description
Benefit measurement models	Analyze the predicted value of the completed projects in different ways. They may present the value in terms of forecasted revenue, ROI, predicted consumer demand in the marketplace, or the *Internal Rate of Return (IRR).*
Mathematical models	Use different types of mathematical formulas and algorithms to determine the optimal course of action. Variables such as business constraints, the highest possible profit that could be made on a project, and the laws and safety regulations that govern business operations may be considered.

Capital Budgeting

Capital budgeting helps senior executives make decisions about when and whether to make significant investments in capital expenditures such as new equipment, machinery, and facilities. Capital budgeting is often used if a project is large or if it is likely to involve the purchase of fixed assets. In these cases, the decision makers may use formal methods such as *payback period, Discounted Cash Flow (DCF),* and *Net Present Value (NPV).*

Scoring and Rating Systems

A scoring and rating system is used to find the best available solution or outcome.

Rating System	Description
Decision tree	In a decision tree model, selection criteria are arranged along the branches of a tree flowchart. The project is evaluated against criterion #1 on branch #1. If the project meets the criterion, it travels down to branch #2, where it is evaluated against criterion #2, and so on. If the project fails to meet any one criterion, it is removed from consideration.

Rating System	Description
Criteria profiling	This is similar to the decision tree model in that the project is evaluated using one criterion at a time. However, in this model the project continues to be considered even if it fails to meet some of the criteria. At the end of consideration, the project is scored on the number of criteria met. The score is then compared to other projects also under consideration. The standard format of criteria profiling is considered an unweighted factor model because the same score is assigned to each criterion in the profile.
Weighted factor	This type of model is similar to criteria profiling, but different criteria may be weighted and factored into the scoring. For example, a project may get one point for meeting a low-priority criterion and three points for meeting a high-priority criterion.
Q-sorting	In a Q-sorting model, groups of people rate the relative priority of a number of projects. The process begins by determining rating criteria. Each group member is given a deck of cards with a different project listed on each card. Each group member sorts the deck into high, medium, and low priority, based on the predetermined criteria. The high-priority projects are further sorted to identify very high priority projects. The group compares their high priority project selections. Any projects they decide to pursue will be chosen from among the consensus of high-priority projects.
Delphi technique	This technique allows experts to be located remotely and remain anonymous, yet still participate in group decision making. People participating in a Delphi process are given criteria, asked to rate a project on a zero-to-ten scale, and provide reasons for their ratings. The resulting statistics are fed back to the participants along with a summary of the group's reasoning. Participants can then revise their ratings based on the group findings. The process repeats until some predetermined stop criterion (number of rounds, achievement of consensus, etc.) is reached.

Feasibility Analysis

Feasibility analysis is an evaluation method for proposed projects to determine if they are feasible to the organization in terms of financial, technical, and business aspects. It gives management the technical and operational data needed to make a decision about project selection. In many cases, the feasibility analysis is based on expert judgment about current technological developments, in-house technical capabilities, and historical data relating to previous project phases.

If the feasibility analysis is a formal study, it should include:

- The description of the problem that the project is expected to solve.
- The summary of relevant historical data about previous project phases.
- The summary and evaluation of available technologies that could be used to solve the problem, including the potential output quality of each.
- The evaluation based on current assessment of the organization's technical capability and readiness to use each technology.
- The estimate of costs and time to implement each alternative.
- The statement of assumptions or constraints used to derive the previous evaluations and estimates.
- Recommendation as to the best alternative to pursue, based on projected cost, time, and quality.
- The statement of project goals and major development milestones.

Example: Feasibility Analysis Performed by a Utility Company

A Canadian utility company produced a feasibility analysis for a proposed project involving the use of wind turbines to generate renewable electricity and offset losses incurred from rising oil prices. The data to be analyzed included:

- Historical data such as wind data collected over a year, a wind energy assessment, and a wind speed frequency distribution.
- Technical data, including the analysis of the anticipated power quality and stability.
- Financial and economic data, including detailed information about projected costs, capital expenditures, and operational and management costs.
- A summary of impacts on the environment, sound, wildlife, public safety, and land use.
- A conclusion that summarized the analysts' findings and a recommendation regarding the wind turbine project's feasibility.

Cultural Feasibility

Cultural feasibility is an organizational characteristic that measures the extent an organization's shared values support the project's goals. The proposed solution must be accepted and implemented for the organization to derive any real benefits. In order to determine the feasibility of a project, the cultural issues that may prevent the absorption of the proposed change must be detected. This can be achieved by looking at the relationship among people, processes, and platforms involved in the implementation of the solution.

In order to thoroughly examine cultural feasibility, you should consider these questions:

- What key business processes are involved in the proposed change?
- What is the essence or nature of those business processes?
- Who within the organization supports those key business processes?
- What is the technical proficiency of the staff and can they handle the proposed change?
- What is the technical proficiency of the intended audience or customers and can they handle the proposed change?
- Does the intended audience believe that the proposed project solution can help or benefit them?

Example: Initiatives to Improve an Organization's Sales Performance

The sales group for a toy manufacturer was consistently failing to meet their sales goals. In order to help them out, senior management purchased each salesperson a wireless PDA to help them manage their relationships and contacts. Six months after the PDAs were rolled out, the sales numbers had not improved. When senior management inquired as to how the PDAs were helping the sales force, they discovered that the PDAs were not being used. As it turned out, the PDAs were incompatible with the database that the sales force was accustomed to using. A vast majority of them did not know how to use the new tool and were not interested in learning. Even those who did learn were forced to enter all their contact information on two separate systems, which took time that could have been spent with customers. Most salespeople just left the PDAs in the trunks of their cars. In this case, a project that was designed to increase sales was a failure.

Let us revisit the same toy manufacturer. Again, the sales force was failing to meet its goal. This time, however, senior management took into account the anti-technology culture of their sales force. Instead of supplying the salespeople with PDAs, management provided higher-end sales kits, such as including marketing slicks and promotional materials, that could be used to help them get in the doors of major toy distributors. This time, the sales number improved, because the salespeople were given tools they were more inclined to use.

Technical Feasibility

Technical feasibility is a study to analyze the technical considerations of a proposed project. The technical feasibility of a project cannot be determined until the impact to existing systems is fully quantified. A *Subject Matter Expert (SME)* should be brought in to assist in the quantification of the systems' impact when you encounter the following situations:

- The proposed project has never been attempted before.
- The proposed project will interact with any key business process or mission-critical systems.
- The project team for the proposed project does not contain personnel sufficiently knowledgeable or certified in key aspects of the technology in question.
- The systems' impact cannot be accurately re-created and tested in a simulation environment.

Example: Local Deli's Technical Feasibility

Let's look at the example of a local deli that specializes in providing takeout services for a nearby set of large office buildings. The owners of the deli had one of their employees, Jim, who is a student at the local university, build a Microsoft® Access® database for the purpose of tracking information surrounding their growing takeout business. Several successful marketing campaigns developed an awareness of the deli's services, and the takeout business was now responsible for over 60 percent of revenue and 75 percent of profit. Predictably, the information in the database grew dramatically, and within 18 months, the business had outgrown the original database. The owners want to upgrade the database, but are unsure if they should bring in outside help or let Jim handle the situation. Let's compare this situation to our definition:

- Neither the deli owners nor Jim have ever done anything like this before.
- The proposed IT project will interact with a vital revenue stream that contributed 75 percent of the total profit.
- The project team does not contain anyone certified as an expert with the platform.
- The deli owners do not have the technical or financial resources required to construct a testbed environment that will allow for a test of any upgrade.

The deli owners decide to bring in an outside firm to help them with this situation because they met the conditions described as requiring an SME. Within the first 15 minutes of the discussion, the owners are told that all the information in their database can be transferred to a more capable database platform, but they lacked the expertise to upgrade Access to SQL or Oracle®. A database designer is brought in and within a month the deli owners are up and running with a powerful new solution that Jim is being trained to administer.

First-Time/First-Use Penalty

Many IT projects suffer from what is called a *first-time/first-use* penalty, which means that a particular type of project has never been done before and nobody within the organization has any experience with the operation of this new capability. One of the more serious first-time/first-use penalties is the proper quantification of the impact that the change will make to existing systems. Because nobody within the organization has experience with the situation at hand, SMEs will be needed to provide a detailed look at the system's expected impact. It is exceedingly difficult to determine the technical achievability of any IT project until the effect on existing systems is fully quantified.

Cost-Benefit Analysis

Cost-benefit analysis presents a project's estimated costs alongside its predicted benefits to help decision makers make informed decisions about project selection. Cost-benefit analysis may be formal or informal. Although the analysis contains quantitative information, it is merely forecast expectations rather than hard data. It is important to recognize and document any assumptions used to derive cost and benefit forecasts.

The costs include current operating costs and expected project costs related to the function under analysis. The benefits include quantifiable benefits, such as increased sales or reduced costs expected as a result of the project, and intangible benefits such as enhanced image or brand awareness that can only be described subjectively.

Example: Cost–Benefit Analysis for Developing an E-commerce Capability

Senior management of a large retail firm is considering a proposal for the development and addition of an e-commerce capability on their existing website to increase revenue. Before committing, management asks each department director to evaluate the feasibility and provide rough cost estimates. The directors then agree that the project is indeed feasible given their current capabilities and should cost around $25K.

The VP of Sales and Marketing estimates that the e-commerce site will generate a five percent increase in sales in the next five years. Given the company's current sales of $1 million, the estimated improvement will result in an additional $50K in sales over the next five years. With $25K in upfront costs, the net benefit is estimated to be $25K. The cost-benefit analysis results in a rough estimation of the company's net gain.

Workflow Analysis

Workflow analysis is a technique that formally documents the manner in which work gets done and displays that work in a flowchart. This type of analysis can be helpful in breaking down large or complex jobs into discrete tasks and decisions, but it requires that you already know how to do the work. Sometimes, you may encounter situations where you have limited experience with the problem at hand. In these cases, you need help to precisely determine the functional requirements. Once the discrete steps involved in getting a piece of work completed are identified, technology can be applied to improve efficiency.

Example: Automating Processes in a Bank

Every day people go to the bank to make deposits. The image shows what a workflow analysis for this particular task may look like. Millions of people automate this process with direct deposit, which is a form of Electronic Funds Transfer (EFT). The automation of this business process means that those bright and sunny Saturday mornings no longer need to be spent at the bank. In the same way, automating business processes can free up time spent on rote activity so that more important issues can be addressed.

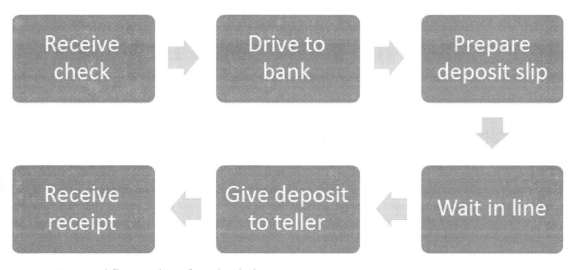

Figure 2-3: Workflow analysis for a bank deposit.

Business Process Automation

Increased efficiency is usually accomplished by automating redundant tasks within the workflow that require complex calculations. The most common task automated in our everyday working environment is information retrieval.

Use Cases, Prototypes, and Scenarios

Use cases, prototypes, and scenarios are tools that are used to create or refine functional requirements by providing a perspective or point of interaction that did not previously exist. This newly created point of interaction allows for more detailed input to the design process.

Tool	Description
Use case analysis	A method for designing systems by breaking down requirements into user functions. Each use case is an event or sequence of actions performed by the user.
Prototype	A simulated version of a new system; essential for clarifying information elements.
Scenarios	A method for developing potential or likely eventualities for different situations.

Example: Use Case Analysis and Prototype for a Lawn Mowing Project

Imagine for a moment that you have been told to mow a lawn and that although you have a vague understanding of the process, you have never done this before. A Business Analyst, John, shows up and questions you about how you would like to cut the grass. He performs a use case analysis by breaking down the larger task of cutting grass into a sequence of actions, such as start the mower, push over grass, stop the mower, and empty the bag.

A day later an engineer shows up in your driveway with a prototype lawn mower on a trailer. The engineer patiently spends about an hour explaining the proper operation of the mower and answering any questions that you have. Without really knowing what to expect, you start the mower and begin to cut the grass. Hours later, you complete the task and the Business Analyst returns to ask how the mowing went. You inform him that the mower was too loud, it stalled in thick grass, and was very difficult to push. The interaction with the prototype lawn mower succeeded in providing concrete feedback that otherwise would not have been possible. Based on the feedback given, the analyst decides to perform further testing using other scenarios such as mowing in very thick grass, wet grass, and on uneven terrain.

TOPIC B

Prepare a Project SOW

One of the first documents you will prepare for your project is a Project Statement of Work. It is generally a narrative description of the work that the project is going to perform, and it is the starting point from which many other project documents will be written. In this topic, you will focus on creating an effective Project Statement of Work.

SOW

A *Statement of Work (SOW)* is a document that describes the products or services that the project will supply, defines the business need that it is designed to meet, and specifies the work that will be done during the project.

A SOW can be internal or external.

- An internal SOW is supplied by the project's sponsor in response to an organizational need. It is generally referred to as the Project SOW.
- An external SOW is usually supplied to a potential client during the procurement process. An external (or procurement) SOW could be included with a request for a proposal or as part of a contract. The Procurement SOW is discussed in detail in the *Planning Project Procurements* lesson.

Project SOW

The Project SOW describes the products, services, or results that the project will deliver. It either contains or references the following:

- **Business need**. There are several business-related reasons that an organization might undertake a project. These include:
  - Market demand
  - Technological advance
  - Legal requirement
  - Government regulation
  - Environmental consideration
- **High-level scope definition**. This includes the characteristics of the product, service, or result. It is generally brief, because it is too early in the project to have much detail available. This information also includes any high-level project risks that are known at this time.
- **Strategic plan**. This contains the organization's strategic vision, goals, and objectives, and possibly a high-level mission statement. Every project should be aligned with the organization's strategic plan.

Guidelines for Preparing a Project SOW

A Project SOW will provide direction and definition to a project. Because this document will be used as a reference when creating other project-related documents, it's important to provide the appropriate definition and description of the project in the SOW. Use the following guidelines when preparing your Project SOW:

- Provide the description and the high-level scope of the project. This might include its benefit to the organization and the business need that is driving the project.
- Identify the major deliverables and any anticipated milestone events.
- Identify any known resource requirements, such as human resource needs, hardware, software, funding, and so on.

- Identify any high-level project risks or concerns that might affect the project.
- Define the criteria that will indicate when the project is complete.
- Use the mandated Project SOW format, if your organization has one. If not, you can modify a Project SOW from a previous, similar project.

TOPIC C

Create a Project Charter

Determining the appropriate project management processes to apply to your project is an important step in initiating the project. However, before you can apply organizational resources to project activities, you need to obtain formal authorization for the project. In this topic, you will create a project charter.

To accomplish project objectives, you need the organization's support. Without it, you may be unable to convince anyone that your project is valuable to the organization or obtain the resources you need. An effective project charter ensures that you gain your organization's support for the project and the authority to apply resources to project activities.

Business Case

A *business case* is a document that justifies the investments made for a project and describes how a particular investment is in accordance with the organization's policy. It outlines the technical, investment, and regulatory factors that influence the project. The business case provides a framework to link an investment proposal to the achievement of an organizational objective. While project managers are not always the people who write the business case, it's important that they understand it.

Example: A Business Case for a Geothermal Energy Project

GCCG is considering a geothermal energy project as an element of its strategy to diversify its business portfolio. Senior management at GCCG has scheduled a meeting to review project selections by the PMO. The project sponsor, Barbara Tolliver, will present a business case that outlines the technical, investment, and regulatory factors influencing the project. She prepared a business case that includes:

- Details of the proposed investments with the timeline.
- Expected returns from the project with the proposed timeline.
- Expected ROIs.
- Reference to the payback period in the context of organizational strategies and project objectives.

Business Case Components

A business case can include a number of components, as described in the following table.

Component	Description
Business need	Substantiates the business reason for conducting the project.
Project contribution	Determines the project's contribution toward the organization's objectives.
Stakeholders	Lists the project stakeholders, their expectations, and contributions toward the project.
Constraints	Compiles the limitations of the project.
Strategic risks	Lists the risks that the project may face and the possible risk management measures.
Benefits evaluation	Analyzes and outlines the key benefits to be obtained.

Component	Description
Project roles	Lists the members of the project team and their respective job roles in the project.
Benefits realization plan	Provides an outline of the benefits of the proposed project.
Contingency plan	Outlines the alternate solutions for unplanned events.

Project Charter

A *project charter* is a document that formally launches and authorizes a new project, or authorizes an existing project to continue with its next phase. A project receives authorization when the initiator signs the project charter. To be successful, the project must link to the ongoing work of the organization and it must match its goals and capabilities with business requirements. The project charter may be developed by an initiator, such as a sponsor, or it may be delegated to the project manager. If the project charter is created by the sponsor, it is advisable that the project manager also be involved in the development process.

> **Note:** Project charters can be publicized by using a company intranet. However, all project stakeholders will not be given the rights to view the published charters.

Project Charter

I.   Project Name
GCCG E-banking Portal

II.   Authorities
 A.   Initiating Authority
Vicky Morris, Director

 B.   Project Manager
<Student Name> is authorized as project manager for this project and will be the primary point of contact. *<Student Name>* is responsible for meeting all key milestones within the time, cost, and performance constraints of this project. Furthermore, *<Student Name>* has the authority to apply organizational resources to accomplish the goals of this project.

III.   Business Need the Project Addresses
The GCCG E-banking Portal will create awareness among consumers on the services provided by the bank. The portal should enable easier access, effectively support the relationship banking experience of the consumer, enhance product acceptance, and thereby improve market share in each of the bank's product lines.

IV.   Project Description
 A.   Product/Service Characteristics
  • Integration of banking services

Figure 2-4: The project charter for the GCCG e-Banking Portal project.

Project Charter Components

Like many project management documents, the format and level of detail contained in the charter is determined by the PMO or senior organization management. Some charters are relatively brief, whereas others can contain some or all of the components as described in the following table.

Component	Description
Project purpose	A clear description of the reason for undertaking the project.
Problem statement	A description of the problem or opportunity that the project must address.
Project authorization	A list of individuals who are authorized to control and manage the project with the respective authority statement.
Scope definition	A description of the scope of work that the project must include. It can also specify what the project will and will not include.
Project objectives	A description of the business benefit that an organization achieves by performing the project.
Project description	A high-level list of what needs to be accomplished in order to achieve the project objectives. This section should also specify when it is deemed that the specified objectives must be met.
Project deliverables	A list of deliverables that must be produced at the end of each phase of the project.
Project milestones and cost estimates	A list of project milestones and the cost estimates.
General project approach	A short description of the project approach, which includes project deliverables, process stages, quality objectives, and project organization.
Constraints and assumptions	A description of the constraints and assumptions that are made when initiating the project, and their impact on scope, time, cost, and quality.
Risks	A list of high-level risks involved in undertaking the project.
Project stakeholders	A list of key project stakeholders.
Related documents	A list of references to the documents that are used to make assumptions.
Project organizational structure	A list of key roles and responsibilities, including signatories.
Issuing authority	Name of the sponsor and signature or formal acknowledgement of the charter contents.

Example: Creating a Project Charter for an Internal Process Improvement Project

The vice president of a software development company, Catherine Long, is authorized to initiate an internal process improvement project. She asked her program manager to help her draft the project charter. Catherine, along with her program manager, develops a project charter to formally authorize the project. The Process Improvement project is named in the memo and the memo's date serves as the authorization date. The memo establishes the authority of her colleague, John, as the project manager and provides John's contact information. Because Catherine is the project sponsor, she also includes her contact information.

The business need to improve the internal processes and procedures to improve time to market, while striking the appropriate balance between quality and speed, is clearly stated. The memo provides a brief description of the service and product of the project, which is to analyze the current processes and procedures and make recommendations.

The known constraints of completing the project with minimal impact on current project schedules within three months are included in the memo. Catherine's signature is on the memo, which is being distributed to all the department directors, vice presidents, and project managers who may be affected by or involved in this project. It also establishes the priority of the project and asks these groups to lend their support.

Guidelines for Creating a Project Charter

An effective project charter clearly communicates the project's importance to the organization and formally authorizes the project. To create an effective project charter, follow these guidelines:

- Gather the prerequisites required to create a project charter.
  - From the project SOW, gather the products or services to be delivered by the project.
  - Use a business case to understand the market demand, organizational and social requirements, and customer requests.
  - Mention the contract information if the project is commissioned for an external customer.
  - Keep in mind that many factors, such as company culture, government or industry standards, stakeholder risk tolerances, market conditions, human resources, and information systems, have an impact on the project charter development process.
- Use a corporate template, if one exists in your company.
- Involve an expert who can provide relevant information to develop a project charter.
- Include the project and authority identification information, such as the title of the project and the date of authorization, the project manager's contact information, and the contact information of the initiating authority (usually the customer or sponsor).
- Include a clear, concise description of the business need, opportunity, or threat that the project is intended to address:
  - Does the project charter clearly identify all the pertinent information about the project?
  - What are the circumstances that generated the need for the project?
  - What is the market demand for the product or service?
  - Consider any legal requirements associated with the project.
  - Has all extraneous information been clearly excluded from the project charter?
- Include summary descriptions of the product or services of the project—the required outcome of the project and the critical characteristics of the product or service.
- Include a description of the project's relationship to the business need it is intended to address—the importance of doing the project now, and how the project addresses the business need, opportunity, or threat for which it is intended.
- Consider any known constraints and assumptions:
  - Are there any known time, cost, scope, quality, or resource issues or factors that will limit the way you and your project team can approach the project?
  - Are there any factors or issues that you and your project team will presume to be true, real, or certain in order to begin planning your project?
  - Is there a risk of any project delays?
  - Are there any budget constraints?
  - Are there going to be problems with resource availability?
  - Will the project require internal or external resources?
- Ensure that the person signing the document has the appropriate signing authority.
- Distribute the signed charter to the appropriate project stakeholders, such as the project team members, customer and any relevant vendors, relevant functional managers, and the Finance and Accounting departments.

TOPIC D

Identify Project Stakeholders

You have a project charter providing the formal authorization to apply organizational resources to project activities. Before you can begin the planning process, it is vital to identify the groups or individuals who will have a role to play either directly or indirectly in the project. In this topic, you will identify the stakeholders of your project.

Stakeholders are an integral part of any project and extensively support the success of the project. It is imperative that you document relevant information regarding stakeholders' interests and expectations because they strongly influence a project's product or service.

Stakeholder Analysis

Stakeholder analysis is the formal process of gathering and analyzing quantitative and qualitative information to identify all the stakeholders of a project. It also involves building coalitions at the onset of a project by identifying stakeholder needs, objectives, goals, issues, and impact.

Stakeholder analysis is performed through a series of steps:

1. Identify all potential stakeholders of the project.
2. Classify stakeholders based on their potential impact or support on the project.
3. Plan for likely stakeholder reaction or response and plan how to enhance stakeholders' support and mitigate potential negative impact on the project.

Ideally, project managers will question the stakeholders about their interest in the project, their desired outcome, their goals, and any lessons learned from prior projects. This increases the effectiveness of the stakeholder analysis process. As the project progresses, the analysis will be validated against the current state of project work and stakeholders' changing needs.

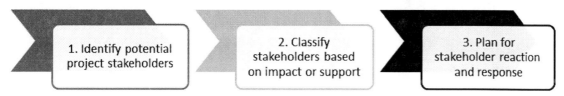

Figure 2–5: The process of analyzing project stakeholders.

Stakeholder Register

A *stakeholder register* is a document that identifies stakeholders of a project. Typical stakeholder register entries may include the stakeholder's name, organizational position, location, role in the project, contact information, requirements, expectations, influence on the project, specific interest in the project or a phase, and whether the stakeholder is internal, external, for, against, or neutral to the project.

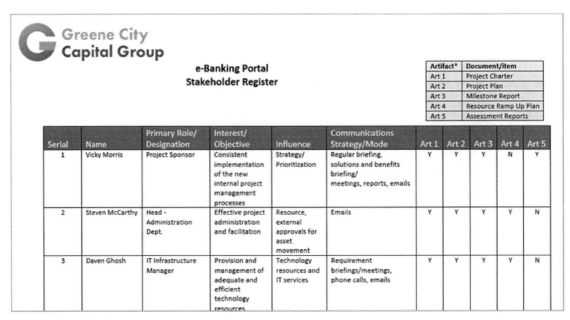

Figure 2-6: A portion of the stakeholder register for the e-Banking Portal project.

Stakeholder Management Strategies

A *stakeholder management strategy* is created to ensure maximum support and minimize the negative impacts of stakeholders throughout the project life cycle. The stakeholder management strategy is created by the project manager when identifying stakeholders, and might not be shared with the project team. The strategy information is ideally represented in a stakeholder analysis matrix.

Components of a Stakeholder Management Strategy

A typical stakeholder management strategy could include:

- Stakeholder identification—a list of the identified stakeholders along with their identification-related information.
- The stakeholder map—a chart showing the interest of different stakeholders and levels of participation required from each identified stakeholder.
- The stakeholder analysis influence and importance matrix—a matrix that describes the stakeholders based on their influence and importance to the project.
- The stakeholder list—a list of various stakeholder groups involved in the project and their management.
- Stakeholder communication—a description of how the project will engage various stakeholders, the communication routes, and the frequency of communication for each stakeholder or group of stakeholders.
- Communication efficiency—specifies how the efficiency of the communication process will be measured.

The Stakeholder Analysis Matrix

The *stakeholder analysis matrix* is a document that lists the project stakeholders and describes their interests and the ways in which they influence the project. The stakeholder analysis matrix is a shared document, and therefore it is imperative that the project manager exercises proper judgment and due caution with regards to the kind of information and detail that needs to be included in it.

Stakeholder	Project Role	Interests	Impact Assessment (1==Low, 5=High)	Potential Strategy
Bob	Project manager	Schedule is critical	5	Weekly status meetings
Sally	Web designer	User-friendly website	3	Encourage creativity
Larry	Trainer	Easy-to-follow training materials	3	Needs tech. writer and graphics support

Figure 2-7: An example of a stakeholder analysis matrix.

Example: Identifying the Computer Networks Upgrade Project Stakeholders

Andrew is the project manager for the Computer Networks Upgrade project in a training development company. He collects project information that includes the project charter, the organization structure, the organization's policy documents, the lessons learned and the stakeholder register of previous projects, and other relevant documents related to the current networking and computer resources deployed within the company. He studies the information gathered to identify the stakeholders from senior management.

Andrew interviews the key stakeholders, such as the department heads for Marketing, Finance, Human Resources, Content Development, Media Development, Quality Control, and Operations, and expands the list of identified stakeholders based on these interviews. The additional stakeholders are the department heads for IT services, customer support, purchase, administration, and accounts. Further, Andrew classifies the stakeholders based on their potential impact or support to the project. He documents the details of the stakeholders in the stakeholder register and based on his assessment of each stakeholder, he defines the stakeholder management strategy in a stakeholder analysis matrix.

Guidelines for Identifying Project Stakeholders

It is important to identify stakeholders early in the project; analyze relevant information regarding their interests, expectations, importance, and influence; and devise a strategy to ensure their involvement to maximize positive influences and mitigate potential negative impacts. To identify project stakeholders, follow these guidelines:

- Perform a review of project and related information to ascertain the list of internal and external parties who may be impacted by the project. The documents or information are a valuable source for stakeholder identification. These may include:
  - The project charter
  - Procurement documents
  - The organization or company structure
  - The organization or company culture
  - Government or industry standards
  - Stakeholder register templates
  - Lessons learned from previous projects
  - Stakeholder registers from previous projects
- Gather the relevant documents that help you identify the stakeholder requirements.
  - Use the project charter to identify the external parties who are impacted by the project, such as the project sponsor and customers, and the team members participating in the project.
  - Use the procurement documents to identify if the project involves procurement or is based on an established contract.
  - Use existing documents, such as stakeholder registers and lessons learned from previous projects, to determine the stakeholder needs.
- Identify groups or individuals with specialized training or knowledge who can help in the comprehensive identification and listing of the stakeholders.

- Interview the identified stakeholders to gain knowledge of their roles, departments, interests, knowledge levels, expectations, and influence levels within the organization.
- Analyze your lists to identify the key stakeholders of the project. These include anyone in a decision-making or management role who is impacted by the project outcome, such as the sponsor, the project manager, and the primary customer.
- Determine and classify the potential impact or support that each stakeholder could generate during the project life cycle and define an approach strategy. You need to prioritize the key stakeholders to plan for efficient communication and management of their expectations.
- Assess how stakeholders will react or respond in various situations, especially bad news, during the project life cycle. You need to plan how to influence the stakeholders to enhance their support of the project and also to mitigate any potential negative impacts arising from them.
- Document stakeholder information to include identification, assessment, and stakeholder classification in the stakeholder register.
- Devise a stakeholder management strategy to increase support and minimize negative impacts of stakeholders to the project.

ACTIVITY 2–1
Initiating the Project Review

Scenario

Answer the following review questions.

1. How is the project initiation phase (process group) important while managing a project in your organization?

2. How do you think creating the Project SOWs in your organization helps you manage your projects?

Summary

In this lesson, you explored the significant elements of initiating a project, which is one of the five interlinked process groups and a critical part of every project you will ever manage. By effectively initiating your project and laying a solid foundation for the work that will follow, you will significantly increase your chances for project success.

3 | Planning the Project

Lesson Time: 1 hour, 45 minutes

Lesson Introduction

With your project defined at a high level and authorized by the sponsor, you are ready to begin planning your project. Project planning is the second of the five project management process groups that you will perform on most projects you manage.

As a project manager, it is up to you to define how the project will be carried out. You will also be responsible for identifying the stakeholders' needs so that you can ensure their satisfaction. With the project objectives and scope clearly defined and documented, you can lead your project toward the agreed-upon measures of success. In this lesson, you will plan project strategy.

Lesson Objectives

In this lesson, you will:

- Identify the elements of the project management plan and subsidiary plans.

- Determine stakeholder needs.

- Create a scope statement.

TOPIC A

Identify Project Management Plan Components

Your project has been authorized and the charter identifies you as the project manager. While you are eager to get started, it's advisable that you begin by planning how the team will manage the project to its successful completion. In this topic, you will identify the elements of a project management plan and the additional plans that support the project.

Developing a realistic, usable, dynamic project management plan helps the project team stay focused on the objectives and purpose of your project. Continually updating your project management plan when new information is available will help you circumvent problems before they develop and ensure that project work occurs according to the plan.

Project Management Plan

A *project management plan* is a document that details how a project will be executed to achieve its objectives. A well-defined plan consists of certain components, including:

- A description of the project management processes that will be used and the level of implementation for each.
- A description of the tools and techniques that will be used to complete those processes.
- Plans for monitoring and controlling changes to the project.
- Details on configuration management (documented procedures for authorizing and controlling changes to a product, service, or result).
- A description of the techniques that will be used to create and control the project's performance baselines (scope, time, and cost).
- Techniques for communication with stakeholders.
- A definition of the project life cycle.
- A plan for identifying, documenting, and addressing open issues.

Example: A Project Management Plan for a Supermarket Chain

A national supermarket chain sought to reduce the average amount of time its customers spend waiting in the checkout lines. The project management plan listed the necessary management processes and the tools needed to complete those processes.

The plan also included the tasks to be completed, such as hiring more clerks and expanding checkout areas, methods for controlling changes to the project, details on configuration management, performance measure baselines, stakeholder communication plans, such as weekly regional manager meetings, a project life cycle, such as implementation, evaluation, and analysis, and the procedure for addressing open issues.

The plan also contained a cost management plan and a quality assurance management plan.

Subsidiary Plans

Project management plans might be detailed or a simple summary, and might include any number of subsidiary management plans that are described in the following table.

Subsidiary Plan	Description
Scope management plan	Provides guidance on how project scope will be defined, documented, verified, managed, and controlled.

Subsidiary Plan	Description
Requirements management plan	Documents how requirements will be analyzed, documented, and managed throughout the project.
Schedule management plan	Describes the scheduling methodology, the scheduling tools to be used, and the format and established criteria for developing and controlling the project schedule.
Cost management plan	Describes the format and establishes the criteria for planning, structuring, estimating, budgeting, and controlling project costs.
Quality management plan	Describes how the performing organization's quality policy will be implemented by the project management team throughout the project.
Process improvement plan	Details the steps for analyzing work processes to identify activities that enhance their value.
Human resource plan	Provides guidance on how human resources required for a project should be defined, staffed, managed, controlled, and eventually released.
Communications management plan	Provides details that document the approach to communicate efficiently and effectively with the stakeholders.
Risk management plan	Describes how risk management is structured and performed on the project.
Procurement management plan	Describes how the procurement processes will be managed from developing procurement documents through contract closure.

 Note: Subsidiary plans may be formal or informal, detailed or broadly framed, and are created based on the requirements of the project.

Scope Management Plan

A scope management plan is a planning document that describes how a project team will define, verify, manage, and control the project scope. The plan can be either formal or informal, depending on the needs of the project.

Example: A Scope Management Plan for the Geothermal Energy Program

The project manager of the geothermal energy program, Rachel Tagon, worked with the core project team to construct the scope management plan. The plan contains a description of how frequently and extensively the scope is expected to change, how the project team will identify, discuss, and classify changes to the scope, and who will approve the changes.

Requirements Management Plan

A requirements management plan is a document that describes how project requirements will be analyzed, documented, and managed throughout the project life cycle. Phase-to-phase relationships between various phases of the project strongly influence how requirements are managed. Components of the requirements management plan require project managers to choose the most effective relationships to aid the success of the project and document this approach in the plan.

Components of the requirements management plan include:

- Methods to plan, track, and report requirement activities.
- Configuration management related activities.

- Processes for requirements prioritization.
- Formats and guidelines on developing a traceability matrix for requirements.

Example: A Requirements Management Plan for GCCG's Warehouse Management Software Project

The project manager for GCCG's Warehouse Management Software project, Mark Anderson, prepares the requirements documentation for the project. Mark documents the requirements collected during the Warehouse Management Essential Requirements workshop and through subsequent interviews conducted with each stakeholder. He creates the requirements management plan with information on how these requirements will be analyzed, documented, and managed throughout the project life cycle.

Schedule Management Plan

A schedule management plan, one of the subsidiary plans in the overall project plan, is an approach to develop, maintain, and manage the project schedule.

A typical schedule management plan describes:

- The purpose of the plan.
- Approved schedule development tools and techniques such as a particular project management software application.
- The number, types, and purposes of the project schedules to be developed and maintained.
- How changes to the schedule baseline will be managed.
- Who is responsible for developing and maintaining the project schedules.
- How and when schedule performance will be reported.

Example: A Schedule Management Plan for a Warehouse Management Software Project

The schedule management plan clearly describes the project team's approach to developing the schedule and for making changes to the schedule baseline. The plan names the person responsible for maintaining the project schedules and contains a policy for schedule performance reporting.

Cost Management Plan

A cost management plan is a document that outlines the guidelines for planning, estimating, budgeting, and controlling project costs. It describes how risk budgets, contingencies, and management reserves will be communicated and accessed. It also provides the planning and structure necessary to control project costs and keep them within the budget limits. The plan can be formal or informal, detailed or brief, depending on the needs of the project.

Example: A Cost Management Plan for a Construction Project

You are the project manager of a construction project, and you want to develop the cost estimate and budget for your project. You believe that setting up a base document enlisting the guidelines for cost management will help the project. You tailor the existing guidelines and define the cost management plan incorporating the estimate, methods, and procedures required for calculating direct and indirect costs involved in the project. You also mention the process for calculating contingency costs.

Quality Management Plan

A quality management plan is a document that describes a team's approach to implementing the quality policy. It explains how quality control and quality assurance will be performed. It may be formal or informal, depending on the project's requirements.

Example: Ensuring Quality in an Outsourced Task

A manufacturer of high-end clothing may seek to reduce costs by outsourcing some of its labor. The quality management plan will articulate exactly how quality control and assurance will be performed, to ensure that the new source of labor can meet the company's high standards. The plan will also identify who will be responsible for quality control; how, when, and to what degree they will conduct inspections for quality; and how the team will respond to any quality issues that arise.

Process Improvement Plan

A process improvement plan is a document that describes the steps to analyze and determine areas of improvements in creating the project deliverables. The areas of process improvements include process boundaries, process configuration, process metrics, and targets for improved performance.

Example: A Process Improvement Plan at a Software Development Company

Sharon Parker is a project manager at a software development company. When managing one of the high-priority projects, Sharon realized that the product testing process was taking longer than required. She decided to review the existing process followed by her project. The process of testing software involves a senior developer review at the end of each phase, unit testing, systems testing, user acceptance testing, SME review, and customer review.

Sharon discussed the issue with the process managers and other senior managers. She created a process improvement plan to reduce the time taken to test the product. The plan included information on the long- and short-term goals, the purpose of the goals, actions to be taken, priority levels, time estimates, and who will perform which activity while improving the process.

Long and Short Term Goals	Purpose of the Goal	Actions	Priority Level	Time Estimate	Responsibility
Reduce product review cycle for high-priority tasks with critical activities.	Reduce time taken to review product quality.				
Set priorities for high-priority tasks.		Check progress and take corrective action during development.	1		
		Review project commitments with senior managers, engineers, and the customer to obtain agreement.	2		

Figure 3–1: A portion of a process improvement plan.

Human Resource Plan

A human resource plan is a document that provides guidance on how the human resources required for a project should be defined, staffed, managed, controlled, and eventually released after the project is completed. It includes the components necessary for developing cost estimates such as the project staffing attributes, personnel rates, and related rewards and recognitions. The plan illustrates the project's organizational structure and includes the staffing management plan that describes the project management team's approach to managing the increase and decrease of project staff across the project life cycle.

Example: The Sales Force Automation Project

Ria is the project manager of a large scale Sales Force Automation project. She will have to deal with a vast pool of human resources with varying skill sets and costs. She has to ensure optimum utilization of resources; that is, the right amount of human resources with the right skill sets are used at the right time. Based on the project schedule, she creates a human resource plan that describes the human resource requirements for the project. The plan defines:

- The required qualifications of the work force.
- The employment contract, whether it is permanent or fixed employment, independent contractor, or volunteer.

- Availability status, whether resources are available, developed, or hired.
- Duration, whether it is full-time or part-time or has limited duration.
- Cost of each resource—the estimated cost to obtain the human resources needed, including gross payment, development cost, and hiring cost.
- When the resources will be released from the project.
- Resource training needs, if any.

Communications Management Plan

A communications management plan is a document that describes the project team's approach to communicating information about the project. It documents what information must be communicated to whom, by whom, when, and in what manner. It also documents how information is collected, archived, and accessed.

Example: A Communications Management Plan to Arrange for a Company's Annual Meeting

A project manager in charge of presenting a company's annual meeting with shareholders will have many stakeholders from different departments and at different levels of company management. The communications management plan may include regularly scheduled status meetings with the employees assigned to the project, with meeting minutes to be distributed to upper management. It may also stipulate an email distribution list with all stakeholders and resources included on all relevant project communication.

Risk Management Plan

A risk management plan is a document that describes the team's approach to identifying risks. It identifies:

- The methodology, approaches, and tools that will be used.
- The roles and responsibilities of those involved.
- The budgeting and scheduling for risk management activities.
- The risk categories.

 Note: The risk management plan does not address responses to risk. These are addressed in the risk response plan.

Example: A Risk Management Plan for a New Project

Entrepreneurs seeking funding from venture capitalists for a new business will present a risk management plan to their potential investors. For a proposed amusement park, the risk management plan will describe business risks, such as operational risks of potential losses due to employee theft, and insurable risks, such as liabilities for injuries sustained on the park's rides.

Procurement Management Plan

A procurement management plan is a document that outlines the guidelines for obtaining or purchasing work from outside sources. It specifies the types of contracts that will be used, describes the process for obtaining and evaluating bids or proposals, mandates the standardized procurement documents that must be used, and explains how multiple providers will be managed. The plan also states how procurement activities will be coordinated with other project management activities, such as scheduling and performance reporting. Depending on the needs of the project, the procurement management plan may be formal or informal, brief or detailed.

Example: Procurement Management for an Advertising Agency

A small advertising agency will procure contracts from external sources for some of the work considered necessary but beyond its core capabilities, such as specialized printing and professional photography services. The procurement management plan will outline the company's processes for soliciting and evaluating bids or proposals from competing service providers and will specify how management will schedule contract work, schedule payments to providers for the work done, and evaluate the quality.

TOPIC B

Determine Stakeholder Needs

You identified the elements and are integrating the various subsidiary plans into the project management plan. In the process of finalizing your project management plan, you need to be aware of the project stakeholder requirements and document them so as to avoid missing critical information. In this topic, you will determine stakeholder needs.

As a project manager, you have to analyze the needs of the project stakeholders. A clear and authentic documentation of those needs will be critical to the project's success. If the stakeholders are not in agreement about project expectations, timelines, and cost, they will not be satisfied with the outcome of the project. By determining the needs of the stakeholders, you can obtain a consensus and prevent misunderstandings on the requirements of varied stakeholders of the project.

Project Objectives

Project objectives are the criteria used to measure whether a project is successful or not. Projects can have one or more objectives, and sub-objectives can be added to the project to further clarify project goals. However, each project must include at least one objective and the objectives must be:

- Specific in terms of the scope.
- Quantifiable in terms of time, cost, and quality.
- Realistic and attainable.
- Consistent with organizational plans, policies, and procedures.

Example: Project Objectives for the Arithmetic on a Stick Project

The following objective was developed for a project devoted to the development of an educational product, "Arithmetic on a Stick."

"Develop a hand-held interactive math game for three- to six-year-olds that includes four levels of instruction, practice, and remediation in early math skills, based on national math standards, produced by June 1, 2017, for less than $2.5 million."

Note how the objective has the characteristics of a quantifiable objective:

- The objective specifies the scope: handheld interactive math game for three- to six-year-olds that includes four levels of instruction, practice, and remediation in early math skills.
- It is quantifiable in terms of time: by June 1, 2017.
- It is quantifiable in terms of cost: less than $2.5 million.
- A quality measurement is specified: based on national math standards.

Customer Requirements

As the name suggests, a *customer requirement* is the documented list of customers' needs and expectations that must be met in order to meet the project objectives. Some of the requirements criteria include conformance to specific standards, quality, functional interface, data, security and control, content, technical, training and performance support, and deployment. The requirements need to be elicited, analyzed, and recorded in sufficient detail from the customers to enable measurement during project execution. The collected requirements form the basis for planning the cost, schedule, and quality for the project.

Requirements are further categorized into project requirements and product requirements, depending on the needs of the project. Project requirements could typically include the business, project management, and delivery requirements of the project. Product requirements could typically include the technical, security, and performance requirements of the product.

Example: Analyzing Customer Requirements

Senior management of a large firm decided to undertake the development of an e-commerce capability on their existing website. When interviewing the customer, the project manager received a lot of requirements that were project specific. The project manager recorded the customer requirements in sufficient detail and ranked the requirements based on priority. Because there was an increased demand for the product, the customer wanted the product to be delivered ahead of schedule. The project manager included this requirement to the existing list of customer requirements.

Stakeholder Requirements Collection Methods

There are various methods to collect project or product requirements from stakeholders, such as:

- Interviewing
- Focus groups
- Facilitated workshops
- Group creativity techniques
- Group decision-making techniques
- Questionnaires and surveys
- Observations
- Prototypes

Interview Techniques

Interviewing is a technique that uses one-to-one interaction to know more about project requirements from individual stakeholders. This is used to identify the stakeholder's individual requirements, goals, or expectations relating to the project. This method gives opportunity to build questions and receive detailed answers while developing a good rapport with the stakeholders. It aids in identifying and defining the features and functions of the desired project deliverables.

Focus Groups

Focus groups are trained moderator-guided interactive discussions that include stakeholders and SMEs (Subject Matter Experts). They are a form of qualitative research that is used to elicit stakeholders' and SMEs' expectations and attitudes toward the proposed product, service, or result of the project.

Example: The Focus Group

Consider a company that is developing an online documentation system. For one of the projects, a focus group of system administrators was formed to discuss their thoughts and preferences on issues, such as distributing and replicating huge documentation files across multiple servers and whether or not they needed faster access to local copies of the documentation on specific client machines. Although they had the option of having usability studies to check if the administrators were able to operate the system, the project manager felt that having a focus group was more efficient to discuss the issues in a single session.

Facilitated Workshops

Facilitated workshops are group sessions that bring together key multidisciplinary or cross-functional stakeholders to define project or product requirements. Facilitated workshops are an important technique to quickly define cross-functional requirements of the various stakeholders of the project. They help build trust, foster relationships, reconcile differences, and improve communication among the stakeholders, thereby leading to enhanced stakeholder consensus.

Because multiple perspectives are available, the issues or questions related to the requirements are resolved quickly.

Example: Conducting Facilitated Workshops for GCCG's Warehouse Management Software Project

The project sponsor, Vicky Morris, approved the project charter for GCCG's Warehouse Management Software project. The project charter lists stakeholders from various departments, such as the Process Development and Implementation department, and the key project managers and administration personnel, especially those arranging the training logistics. It also includes key PMO staff and the Chief of the Business Transformation team. To build stakeholder consensus, the project manager of GCCG's Warehouse Management Software project, Mark Anderson, decides to conduct a facilitated workshop rather than holding one-on-one interviews with the key stakeholders. He invites the key project stakeholders for a "Warehouse Management Essential Requirements" workshop.

Mark coordinates discussions with key stakeholders during the workshop to define the requirements of this project. Discussions in the workshop highlight the differences among various stakeholder requirements. Mark is not only able to reconcile the stakeholder differences, but also to obtain a consensus on all the project requirements.

Group Creativity Techniques

Group creativity techniques are group activities established within organizations to identify project or product requirements for a project.

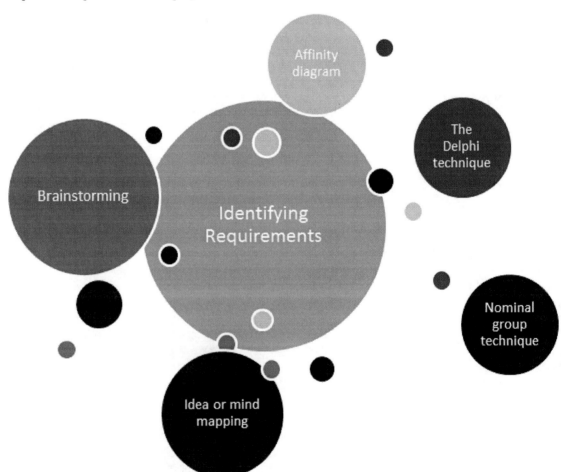

Figure 3-2: Group creativity techniques.

Group Creativity Technique	Description
Brainstorming	This technique is used to generate and create multiple ideas related to the project and product requirements.
Nominal group technique	This technique uses a voting process to rank the most useful ideas obtained through brainstorming. Ranking allows for further brainstorming or for prioritization.
The Delphi technique	This is a group technique that extracts and summarizes anonymous group input to choose among various alternatives.
Idea (or mind) mapping	This technique consolidates ideas created through brainstorming in a map that reflects the commonality, differences in understanding, and generation of new ideas.
Affinity diagram	This technique enables the sorting of a large number of ideas collected during brainstorming into distinct categories for review and analysis.

Group Decision-Making Techniques

Group decision-making techniques are assessment processes that evaluate multiple alternatives to arrive at an outcome. These techniques are used to generate, classify, and prioritize project or product requirements. The outcome is the resolution of future action for the project.

Various methods are adopted to reach a group decision.

Method	Description
Unanimity	Everyone in the group agrees on a single course of action.
Majority	Requires support from more than 50% of the members of the group to indicate the selected decision.
Plurality	The largest batch in the group decides for the group even if a majority is not achieved.
Dictatorship	One individual makes the decision for an entire group.

Other Requirement Collection Techniques

Various other techniques to collect project or product requirements are also available.

Technique	Description
Questionnaires and surveys	Written sets of questions designed to quickly accumulate information from a broad audience. Used when statistical analysis is appropriate for collecting stakeholder requirements.
Observations	A direct way of viewing individuals in their work environment or while using the product to identify the project or product requirements. Also referred to as *job shadowing*.
Prototypes	A method of obtaining feedback on requirements by providing a working model of the expected product.

Requirements Documentation

Requirements documentation describes how individual requirements meet the business need of the project. The requirements that are documented in the requirements documentation must be unambiguous, traceable, complete, consistent, and acceptable to key stakeholders of the project.

Greene City Capital Group

Requirements Document

Project: GCCG e-Banking Portal

Version

Document Release	Date	Author	Description
1.0	<Today's Date>	<Student Name>	Original version

1. Introduction

1.1 Purpose/Scope

This document describes the requirements and other relevant information of the GCCG project.

1.2 Assumptions, Dependencies, and Constraints

Assumption:

- Since this is a new foray of integrating banking services into a consumer e-banking portal, the company will expect the technology and technical skills required for this integration to be made available for project execution.

Dependencies:

- Availability of hardware and software before needed according to the schedule.
- Availability of a business consultant.
- Feasibility of integrating the different banking-related services depending on the technologies and platforms the services are built on.

Constraints:

- The project completion must be on or before August 20th.
- The project must be completed within the $1 million budget.

Figure 3–3: A requirements document for the GCCG e-Banking Portal project.

The RTM

The *Requirements Traceability Matrix (RTM)* is a tabular document that links the project or product requirements to their origin and traces them throughout the project life cycle. It links each requirement to the business and project objectives, Work Breakdown Structure, product design and development, and test scenarios. It ensures that approved requirements in the requirements documentation are met at the end of the project. The RTM also provides a structure for managing changes to the project or product scope.

Project: GCCG Warehouse Management Software

Req No	Requirements Specification	S/W Module	Test Specification	Test Case	Verification	Forward Traceability
R5	Adherence to W3C and related standards	N/A	N/A	N/A	Verified	U8
R6	Distributed access and control	Several service modules	System integration testing	5.7.8	Partially verified	U17
R7	User custom and interface	Custom modules	System integration testing	5.10.3	To be verified	U84

Figure 3–4: An RTM for the GCCG Warehouse Management Software project.

 Note: Forward traceability in the figure implies that it is possible to trace a requirement to elements in the outputs of later phases in the project life cycle.

Example: Identifying the GCCG Warehouse Management Software Project Requirements

The project manager for GCCG's Warehouse Management Software project, Mark, is defining and documenting the requirements for the project. From the project charter authorized by Vicky Morris, he lists the high-level project requirements and product descriptions. He interviews the key stakeholders of the project who provide him with the detailed project and product requirements. He also analyzes the stakeholder register to determine the other stakeholders of the project and enhances his list of project requirements by conducting a facilitated workshop to determine the remaining needs and expectations of the stakeholders.

Mark gets the project team to develop a prototype for the Warehouse Management software, distributes it to key stakeholders for their review, and obtains their feedback on the functional requirements of the project.

Using the requirements obtained from the stakeholders, Mark creates the requirements documentation for the project. He also creates the requirements management plan, which includes the RTM that documents how the requirements will be analyzed, documented, and managed throughout the project life cycle.

Guidelines for Determining Stakeholder Needs

Care should be taken in defining and documenting the needs and expectations of various project stakeholders in order to meet the project objectives. The success of a project depends on the effective capture and management of the various project and product requirements. To effectively define and manage project and product requirements, follow these guidelines:

- Study the project charter to identify the high-level project requirements and product descriptions.
- Examine the stakeholder register to identify stakeholders who can provide information on detailed project and product requirements.
- Use various methods to collect project or product requirements. These methods include interviews, focus groups, facilitated workshops, group creativity techniques, group decision-making techniques, questionnaires, surveys, and observations.
- If possible, provide a working model or prototype of the expected product to obtain feedback on requirements.
- Create the requirements documentation to describe how individual requirements meet the business need for the project. Ensure that the requirements are measurable, testable, traceable, complete, consistent, and acceptable to key stakeholders.
- Review and validate the requirements management plan along with the key stakeholders and make sure that it:
  - Describes methods to plan, track, and report requirement activities.

- Describes configuration management related activities.
- Includes process for requirements prioritization.
- Includes project or product related metrics.
- Provides a traceability matrix for requirements.

TOPIC C

Create a Scope Statement

You have the first of many subsidiary plans incorporated into your project management plan. Now, you can focus on defining the project scope, a critical element essential to achieving project success. A clear and concise scope statement will help you define the success that will guide your project. Without a strong scope statement, you could end up spending valuable time and resources on work that isn't even supposed to be part of your project. In this topic, you will create a scope statement.

The Project Scope Statement

The *scope statement* defines the project and what it does and does not need to accomplish. It is created at an early stage in the project to reflect the stakeholders' common understanding of major activities to be performed in the project and provide a basis for future project decisions about what should and should not be included in the project.

Depending upon the size and scope of the project, a project scope statement should typically include:

*   Project objectives, deliverables, exclusions, and requirements.
*   Project constraints and assumptions.
*   Product acceptance criteria.

It may also include initial project organization, defined risks, schedule milestones, initial WBS, and approval requirements.

Greene City Capital Group

Project Scope Statement

Project Name: GCCG e-Banking Portal
Department: *<Department Name>*
Project Manager: *<Student Name>*
Date: *<Today's Date>*

Prepared By

Document Owner(s)	Project/Organization Role
<Student Name>	Project Manager

Version History

Version	Date	Author	Change Description
1.0	*<Today's Date>*	*<Student Name>*	Created document

Project Description

The e-Banking Portal project will provide the following features as components in the project:
- Single-sign-on and authenticated access to the consumer e-banking portal.
- Integration of banking services.
- Response time during transactions to be in the bandwidth of zero to four seconds.

Project Justification

GCCG e-Banking Portal will integrate all banking-related services through a single-sign on feature to customers of the bank. This portal will ensure that these applications and hardware networks will seamlessly integrate and provide services through a single window to the customer.

Figure 3-5: The project scope statement for the e-Banking Portal project.

 Note: In the scope statement, requirements and objectives are defined with specific measurable success criteria.

Project Scope Statement Components

The following table describes some of the components found in the scope statement.

Component	Description
Project objectives	These are the measurable success criteria for the project. Project objectives are called critical success factors in some organizations.
Product description	The characteristics of the product, service, or result of the project undertaken.
Project requirements	The conditions or capabilities that the deliverables of the project must meet to satisfy a standard, contract, specification, or government or industry regulation.
Project deliverables	Any tangible, measurable result or outcome required to complete a project or portion of a project. The scope statement should include a list of the summary-level subproducts that, taken together, constitute completion of the project.
Project boundaries	The parameters of what is and what is not included within a project.

Component	Description
Product acceptance criteria	The process and criteria for accepting finished products or services resulting from a project.
Project constraints	Factors that limit the way that the project can be approached. These limitations may concern time, cost, scope, quality, resources, and others. For example, you may be given a project deadline or overall budget that your project must work within.
Project assumptions	Statements that must be taken to be true in order for the planning to begin. For example, if your project requires that you incorporate energy costs into your budget, you may want to make the assumption that the price of oil on the project start date will remain the same as it is today in order to create project cost estimates.

 Note: Key Performance Indicators (KPIs) are metrics that are used to evaluate factors crucial to the success of a project or organization. KPIs differ from organization to organization.

Constraints

Constraints are limitations that concern scope, time, cost, and ultimately quality. These factors are interrelated and exist in a state of equilibrium. As the project progresses, if one of these factors is altered, the other two factors should be balanced to accommodate the change without compromising on the quality of the product or service.

For example, if the project schedule is shortened due to a change in stakeholder requirements, the cost and/or the scope will be affected. The cost can increase because more resources are needed to meet the shortened schedule, or the scope can decrease so all of the work can be finished per the revised schedule. In either of these situations, the quality (what the stakeholders expect from the project) will change.

This re-prioritization of constraints can occur at any time during the project, and in large or complex projects it can occur several times. It can be due to requests from any stakeholder, either on the project team or the sponsor, or from someone not on the team (i.e., a customer, someone in management, or a functional manager). It can even result from a project manager on another project, when both projects are competing for the same resources.

Figure 3-6: The constraints triangle.

Product Analysis

Product analysis is an evaluation of the project's end product and what it will take to create the product. It translates project objectives into tangible deliverables and requirements.

Product Analysis Techniques

The following table describes some available product analysis techniques.

Technique	Description
Functional analysis	Analyzing all the things that a product does, including primary and related functions, to identify unnecessary functions that may drive up cost on a product.
Value engineering and value analysis	Identifying and developing the cost versus benefits ratio for each function of a product. It is a method for controlling costs while maintaining performance and quality standards, and is very common in military and construction contracts.
Quality function deployment	Identifying what the customer's needs are and translating those needs into technical requirements. It is appropriate for each stage of the product development cycle.
Systems engineering	Analyzing products holistically and integrating factors such as users, usage environment, and related hardware or software, with which the product must function.

Alternative Identification Techniques

Alternative identification techniques are methods for generating as many alternative solutions and plans as possible during project planning.

Technique	Description
Lateral thinking	A creative approach to problem solving in which the team attempts to think about a problem in new ways and generate a fresh solution.
Brainstorming	A general creativity technique for generating possible alternatives. Brainstorming methods can be structured or unstructured in approach. The goal is to generate as many ideas as possible from as many team members as possible.
Delphi technique	A group technique that extracts and summarizes anonymous expert group input to choose among various alternatives. Often used to arrive at an estimate or forecast.

Guidelines for Creating a Scope Statement

A well-defined scope statement provides a basis for project stakeholders to make future decisions about the project's scope. It also serves as a baseline for monitoring the scope during execution. To create an effective detailed scope statement, follow these guidelines:

* Refine the project objectives, deliverables, and product scope description from the requirements documentation.
* Reexamine the project requirements from the requirements documentation. Do they need to be re-prioritized with respect to the results of the stakeholder analysis?

- Review the project boundaries in the project charter. If the stakeholder analysis revealed expectations that are out of alignment with the project objectives, it may be necessary to add these expectations to the list of excluded items.
- Update the preliminary project constraints, risks, and assumptions from the requirements documentation. As the project scope comes more into focus, the constraints, risks, and assumptions need to be reconsidered.
- Create schedule milestones so that the client and project team have dates for setting goals and measuring progress.
- Include a revised overall cost estimate and define any cost limitations that were listed in the business case, project charter, or requirements document.
- Identify and document known risks as noted in the project charter.
- Map out the internal organization with regard to personnel, including management, project teams, and stakeholders as noted in the stakeholder register. Be sure to include the management requirements, which will define how the project scope and changes therein are managed.
- Document product specifications and approval requirements that were provided in the requirements documentation.
- Finalize the procedure for accepting completed products.

ACTIVITY 3–1
Planning the Project Review

Scenario
Answer the following review questions.

---

1. Which factors are important to your organization while defining the project scope?

2. In your experience, what are the most critical inputs for developing a project scope statement?

Summary

In this lesson, you learned that an effective project management plan will ultimately define the execution, monitoring, controlling, and closing of your project. You examined the various components of a successful project management plan. You created the requirements document, which records your stakeholder requirements. Using these components, you developed a scope statement that met the requirements. With this knowledge and skills, you are better prepared to not only create a strong project plan, but also manage it successfully.

4 Preparing to Develop the Project Schedule

Lesson Time: 3 hours

Lesson Introduction

Now that you have prepared your project scope, you are ready to begin developing the project schedule, which will drive and guide all the work in your projects. In this lesson, you will advance your skills by examining the tools used in schedule development.

Lesson Objectives

In this lesson, you will:

- Develop a WBS.

- Create an activity list.

- Identify the relationships between activities.

- Identify resources.

- Estimate time.

TOPIC A

Develop a WBS

You developed a scope statement that clearly states the objectives and lists your project's major deliverables. Now, you can break down the major deliverables into smaller, more manageable pieces. In this topic, you will develop a Work Breakdown Structure (WBS).

It's always easier to successfully complete a project by breaking it down into smaller, more manageable chunks. Creating an effective Work Breakdown Structure (WBS) helps improve the accuracy of your time, cost, and resource estimates by providing a baseline for performance measurement and project control.

The WBS

A *Work Breakdown Structure (WBS)* is a logical grouping of project deliverables arranged in a hierarchical structure. A WBS defines the total scope of work required to complete the project. The deliverables and their component sub-deliverables are represented on the WBS in levels of descending order.

The smallest, most granular deliverable that is represented on the WBS is called a *work package*. A work package must describe a deliverable that can be adequately scheduled, budgeted, and assigned to an individual person or group.

In a WBS, major components of work can be grouped by:

- Major project deliverables.
- Life cycle phases.
- Organizational or functional responsibility.
- Geographical location.

> **Note:** Deliverables listed at each level on the WBS equal the sum of all the items on the level directly beneath them.

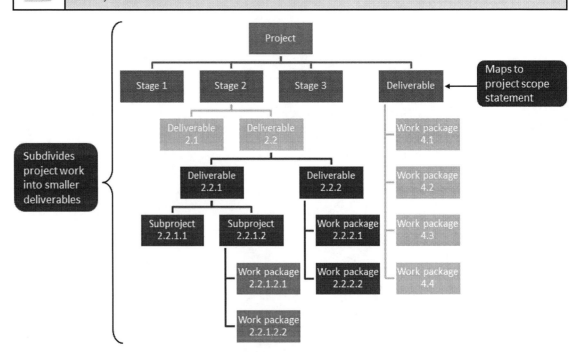

Figure 4–1: A WBS displaying a logical grouping of project deliverables.

Thorough Work Breakdown Structures feature several input elements, such as organizational process elements, the project scope statement, the project scope management plan, and approved change requests.

Example: A WBS in Movie Making

Movie making is a great example of a process that commonly employs Work Breakdown Structures. A film director is responsible for the coordination of several different departments, such as the set designers, photographers, and editors.

Creating a robust WBS allows the director to easily manage the numerous crews working on the film. It will organize every component of the film into separate work packages, each with its own deliverables, deadlines, and budget.

The WBS Dictionary

The *WBS dictionary* is an auxiliary document containing details about each element in the WBS. It may contain information, such as description of work, code of accounts identification, milestones, contract information, cost, quality requirements, resource requirements, time estimates, or resource information, for measuring performance and completeness.

Site Improvements: Roads and Amenities (3.3.1.3.2)	
Both aggregate-surfaced and asphalt-paved roads are provided. All roads and paved areas around the building are to be constructed over 2 feet of classified fill. All parking areas and asphalt paved roads consist of a 2-inch asphaltic concrete surface over a 4-inch aggregate base over an 8-inch aggregate subbase.	
A. Roadways	Excavate peat soil above the final design elevation. Provide aggregate roads, including all panel surfaces, bases and shoulders, curbs, signs, and sidewalks.
B. Parking Lots	Excavate and remove peat soil above the final design elevation. Provide parking at various locations as indicated in the facility sections. Parking stall dimensions are 10 feet wide by 20 feet in length. Provide heater plugs at all parking locations and curbs where needed, to protect walks and heater plug stands.
C. Site Development	NA
D. Walks, Steps, and Terraces	NA
E. Landscaping	Landscaping in terms of trees, shrubs, and specimen plants is not included in this contract. Only selected areas around the Readiness and Control facility will be seeded.
F. Special Construction	NA

Figure 4–2: An example of a WBS dictionary for a construction project.

Decomposition

Decomposition is a technique for creating the WBS by subdividing project work to the work package level. An analysis of the scope statement will help identify the project work. The level of decomposition varies for different projects. Decomposition of project work is stopped when the components of the work packages are sufficient to complete the work and can be assigned to an individual person or group, cost estimated, scheduled, and monitored.

Code of Accounts

A *code of accounts* is any system that is used for numbering the elements in a WBS. A code of accounts system allows project managers to easily track individual WBS components. This system is helpful in the areas of performance, reporting, and costing.

Example: Code of Accounts Specified by a School District

A school district requires its schools to comply with a uniform code of accounts so that it can easily record, track, and document specific types of revenues and expenditures in every school. The code of accounts could be shown as Function/Category/Program. If functions include administrative salaries (30), teacher salaries (31), and consultants' fees (32); categories include para-professional expenditures (100) and professional expenditures (101); programs include regular instructional (411), special education (417), and languages (419), then the fee paid to a consultant leading a teacher training workshop in special education services will be coded 32/101/417.

The Scope Baseline

Scope baseline describes the need, justification, requirements, and boundaries for the project. It is a component of the project management plan. Components of the scope baseline include the detailed project scope statement, the WBS, and the WBS dictionary.

Guidelines for Developing a WBS

You can use the following guidelines to create a Work Breakdown Structure:

- Gather the reference materials and other inputs you will need. Some of the materials needed include: the scope statement, the requirements documentation, a WBS template (if available), constraints and assumptions, relevant historical information, and other planning inputs that may impact scope definition.
- Determine how the project work will be organized. Regardless of the organization, these elements represent the level directly below the project name on your WBS. The WBS can be created using various methods.
  - Subdividing the project into phases as the first level of decomposition and then subdividing the phases into product deliverables as the second level of decomposition.
  - The project can be subdivided into major deliverables, which can be the first level of decomposition.
- Identify the major deliverables or subprojects for the project. The major deliverables should be listed in the scope statement or contract, but your team may think of more deliverables that are necessary to achieve the project's objectives. If you are organizing your project work by major deliverables, this will represent the level directly below the project name. If you are organizing your work by some other method, the major deliverables will probably be two levels below the project name.
- Analyze each element to determine whether it is sufficiently decomposed. Can each deliverable be adequately scheduled, budgeted, and assigned to an individual person or group? If yes, you have reached the work package level; decomposition for this element is complete. If no, further decomposition is required for this element.
- Break down each WBS element into sub-deliverables until you reach the work package level. For each element, ask yourself, "In order to create this deliverable, what sub-deliverables will we have to produce?"
- Validate your WBS using a bottom-up approach. Starting at the work package level, ensure the following:
  - The lower level components are necessary and sufficient for the completion of each decomposed item.
  - Each element is described as a deliverable (preferably as a noun), and is distinguishable from all other deliverables.
  - Each element can be adequately budgeted, scheduled, and assigned to an individual person or group.
- Remember that, although it is not necessary to have the same number of levels for each deliverable, a disproportionate number of levels may indicate that the deliverable is inappropriately decomposed. Analyze the element to determine whether one of the higher level

components should be broken into two sub-deliverables or whether two or more sub-deliverables should be combined. Make any necessary modifications before assigning a unique numeric code to each element.

- Use your organization's or project's code of accounts to assign a unique numeric cost code for each element, indicating its branch and level on the WBS for cost performance tracking and reporting.

TOPIC B

Create an Activity List

The next step in developing a project schedule is to accurately define project activities so that you can be sure that the activities are tied to the project scope and you can mitigate scope creep. In this topic, you will gather the WBS and other relevant information to create an activity list.

The activity list is a fundamental building block for an effective project schedule and budget. Defining the activities helps ensure that all project activities remain within the project scope, so you can avoid missing critical activities. If you define exactly what needs to be done, you can avoid performing unnecessary work.

Duration

Duration is the amount of time that a particular task or work package will take to complete. The metrics used to express duration are units of time such as days, weeks, months, or years.

- *Fixed duration* is a term that is used to describe a task or work package that requires a set amount of time to complete. The application of additional resources will not change the time required.
- *Elapsed time* is the actual calendar time required for an activity from start to finish. An activity that requires two weeks to complete will take four calendar weeks of elapsed time if there is a two-week plant shutdown in the middle.

Figure 4–3: An example of duration.

Effort

Effort is the measure of labor that must be applied to the completion of a particular task or work package. The metrics used to express effort are the number of resources multiplied by the duration of the work; generally "person-hours," "person-days," and "person-months."

- *Effort-driven* is a term that is used to describe a task where the effort (or work) remains fixed regardless of the number of resources used to complete the work. In other words, the task can be completed faster through the application of additional energy or labor resources.

Figure 4-4: An example of effort.

Work Packages

A work package refers to the planned work or the deliverables that are contained in the lowest level component of the WBS. The work package can also be described as manageable work effort, or a level at which the cost and schedule for the work can be easily estimated. Work packages can be broken down or subdivided into smaller, manageable, and executable components called *activities*.

 Note: Because activity definition is a step in project scheduling, activities are also referred to as schedule activities.

Note that every single component of work is not tracked on the master project schedule. However, work package owners—those responsible for the completion of the work packages—may develop a schedule containing the itemized components of work necessary to complete the activities in the work package.

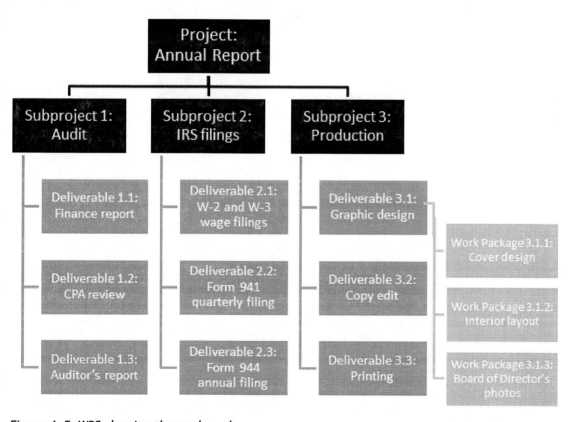

Figure 4-5: WBS showing the work packages.

The 8/80 Rule

The *8/80 rule* refers to a general guideline regarding work packages; they require more than 8 and fewer than 80 hours of effort to be completed. The 8/80 rule helps project managers create the work package list by identifying which work components should be considered work packages. Any work component that can be completed in fewer than 8 hours does not rise to the level of a work package; it can be combined with other work. Also, any work component requiring more than 80 hours of work is too large to be categorized that way; it should be broken into smaller components.

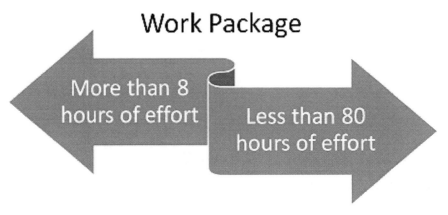

Figure 4-6: The hours of effort that define a work package.

 Note: While the 8/80 rule may be a useful guideline in small projects, it will be impractical to apply it to large projects, which will necessitate tracking millions of work packages.

Activities

An activity is an element of project work packages that requires action to produce a *deliverable*. Activities lay the foundation for estimating, scheduling, executing, and monitoring and controlling the project work. The characteristics of an activity are:

- It has expected duration.
- It consumes budget and human resources.

In each of the following examples, actions are required to produce deliverables. Each has an expected duration and will consume budget and human resources:

- Revising a user manual.
- Making a sales presentation.
- Reserving a conference room.

 Note: The term activity refers to the components of work performed during the course of a project. The term task is used sparingly, only in reference to brands of project-management software.

Activity Lists

An *activity list* is a definitive list of activities that must be completed to produce the desired project deliverables. It includes an activity identifier and a description of the scope of work for each activity so that each team member understands the work required for completion. The activities in an activity list are listed in a sequential order and are used to estimate project duration and create the project schedule.

For example, the work packages for conducting a training session will include:

1. Determine training budget

2. Schedule training date
3. Set training requirements
4. Identify trainers
5. Confirm attendees
6. Reserve conference room
7. Set up audio-visual materials
8. Acquire training software
9. Train attendees
10. Collect feedback

Continuing with the training session example, you can break down an individual activity into smaller components. For example, the work package of reserving the conference room could be broken down into the following activities:

1. Determine size requirement
2. Determine date needed
3. Identify possible room alternatives
4. Select room
5. Call to reserve room
6. File confirmation when received

Example: Creating an Activity List for a Web Design Project

A project team for a web design company used the WBS and activity list from a previous, similar project to create an activity list for their project. The team used historical records of the previous project to help identify activities that may be required to complete each deliverable. Depending on the activities they select, the length of time may be lengthened or shortened.

Additionally, an outside multimedia expert was consulted about activity identification. Finally, to make sure that the activities supported the project objectives, the team reviewed the scope statement.

The project team gathered inputs and resource materials to create the activity and milestone lists and activity attributes for the work package.

Activity Attributes

Activity attributes contain additional information about all activities in an activity list. Similar to the WBS dictionary but for activities, the activity attributes describe the activities by listing the different components associated with the activities, which include responsible team members and the level of effort required. Activity attributes are used to develop project schedules and select, order, and sort planned activities.

Milestones

A *milestone* is a control point event in a project with zero duration that triggers a reporting requirement or requires sponsor or customer approval before proceeding with the project. Milestones serve as markers and are defined by the project manager, customer, or both.

Example: Milestones for a Construction Project

A construction firm that is building a new house will include several milestones at the beginning and end of the project and at each phase of the contract that involves deliverables. The major milestones will include: completing the site preparation, foundation, basement, crawl space, floor, roof frames, porch, windows and doors, plumbing, electrical and insulation work, drywalling, and furnishing.

Milestone Lists

A *milestone list* is a document that contains the project milestones and indicates if achieving the milestones is mandatory or optional for the project to move to the next phase. Milestone lists are used as indicators of a project's progress and the goals that must be reached. They may also list the scheduled dates for each milestone. Milestone lists are usually accompanied by milestone charts.

Activity	Required	Duration (in Days)	Resources
Site preparation completion	Yes	0	Site preparation crew
Foundation completion	Yes	0	Mason
Basement completion	Yes	0	Mason
Crawl space completion	Yes	0	Mason
Flooring completion	No	0	Framing crew
Roof framing completion	No	0	Framing crew
Porch completion	No	0	Framing crew
Windows and doors completion	No	0	Framing crew
Plumbing completion	Yes	0	Plumbing crew
Electrical and insulation completion	Yes	0	Electricians
Dry walling completion	Yes	0	Dry wall installers
Furnishing completion	Yes	0	Carpenters

Figure 4-7: A list of project milestones for a construction project.

Entry/Exit Criteria

Entry/exit criteria are conditions or circumstances that are required to enter into or exit from a particular milestone. An entry criterion corresponds to a condition that has to exist for the work to begin. An exit criterion corresponds to what must be accomplished for the milestone to be considered complete. The exit criterion for the completion of one or more milestones is the entry criterion for the next subproject work.

The figure illustrates that the exit criterion for Subproject #1 is the entry criterion for Subproject #3, and the exit criteria for Subprojects #2 and #3 are the entry criteria for Subproject #4.

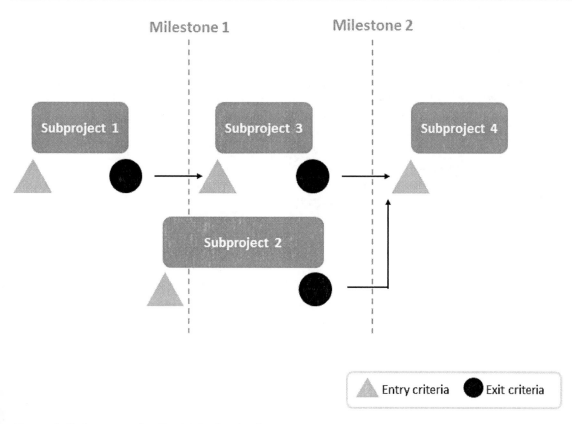

Figure 4-8: An example of entry/exit criteria.

How to Create an Activity List

Accurately defining project activities ensures that all project activities are tied to the project scope, which will mitigate the potentially damaging effects of scope creep.

Create an Activity List

To define activities and create an activity list, follow these guidelines:

1. First, gather the inputs and resource materials you will need. These may include:
   - The WBS
   - An activity list template
   - The scope statement
   - The scope baseline
   - Relevant historical information
   - Constraints and assumptions
2. Analyze and decompose each work package of the WBS into activities that will be required to produce the deliverable.
   - Conduct brainstorming sessions with the project team to ensure that no required activities are overlooked.
   - Consult the scope statement to ensure that activities will enable you to meet the project objectives.
   - Ensure that you conduct progressive elaboration for work packages that cannot be defined at the project start; i.e., create detailed activities for short-term WBS work packages.
3. Consult records of similar projects to identify possible activities.
4. Consult SMEs about unfamiliar material.
5. Evaluate all constraints and assumptions for their possible impact on activity definition.

6. Once you decomposed each work package into activities, evaluate your activity list:
   - Ensure that the descriptions accurately reflect the actions to be performed.
   - Verify that the activity descriptions are as specific as possible. For example, if the desired outcome is a revised user manual, describe the activity as "revise user manual," rather than "produce new user manual."
   - Confirm that the activities listed for each work package are necessary and sufficient for satisfactory completion of the deliverable.
   - Verify that the list is organized as an extension of the WBS.
7. Create activity attributes for each activity in the activity list by determining responsible team members and the level of effort required.
8. Define the milestones in the project and create a milestone list.

TOPIC C

Identify the Relationships Between Activities

You created an activity list for your project. Now, you can sequence the project activities and establish a relationship among them. In this topic, you will delve into the process of sequencing activities and creating a project schedule network diagram. You will also examine the sequencing process and scheduling tools.

You are the project manager for the launching of a new product line. If you do not understand the sequence in which the project work must occur, you cannot develop an effective schedule. You will end up with rework and additional costs. Creating a project schedule network diagram for your project will help you uncover the relationship between tasks, avoiding unnecessary work and expense.

Activity Dependencies

An *activity dependency* is a logical relationship that exists between two project activities. The relationship indicates whether the start of an activity is contingent upon an event or input from outside the activity. Activity dependencies shape the sequence among project activities.

Example: Activity Dependencies for Designing Room Layouts

An architect, Brian, designed a residence and has a vision for room layouts. However, he will not be able to assess the functionality of the design until the builders frame in the structure with walls, windows, and a roof. Once the structure is in place, he will be able to reassess the plans to determine if modifications are necessary.

Activity Dependency Types

Three common types of activity dependencies are available.

Dependency	Description
Mandatory	A *mandatory dependency* is inherent to the work itself. It is usually affected by physical constraints. Activities must be performed in a specific sequence for the work to be successful. Mandatory dependency is also known as "hard logic." **Example:** Books can't be bound before they are printed.
Discretionary	A *discretionary dependency* is defined by the project and the project management team at their discretion. It is defined based on the best practices followed in a specific application area or on specific requirements. If there is no mandatory or external dependency between two activities, the team has some flexibility in activity sequencing. It is also known as "soft logic," "preferential logic," and "preferred logic." **Example:** The sponsor would like to see the book's cover design as soon as possible, so the team may decide to have the cover artwork done before the inside illustrations.
External	An *external dependency* is contingent on inputs from outside the project activities. Can be either mandatory or discretionary. **Example:** The books can't be printed until the shipment of paper arrives.

Dependency	Description
Internal	An *internal dependency* is contingent on inputs from within the organization. Like external dependencies, internal dependencies can be either mandatory or discretionary.

Precedence Relationships

A *precedence relationship* is the logical relationship between two activities that describes the sequence in which the activities should be carried out. Each activity has a Start and Finish. The precedence relationship considers appropriate logic while connecting these points. Precedence relationships are always assigned to activities based on the dependencies of each activity.

- The *predecessor activity* drives the relationship. In most relationships, the predecessor activity comes first.
- The *successor activity* is driven by the relationship.

Dependency determination is the identification of the dependencies of one activity over the other. It involves establishing the precedence relationships among activities and creating logical sequences.

Precedence Relationships Types

Precedence relationships may vary in the way they start and finish.

Precedence Relationship Type	Description and Example
Finish-to-Start (FS)	The precedence relationship between two activities where the predecessor activity must finish before the successor activity can start. It can be expressed as, "Activity A must finish before Activity B can begin." The total time for these two activities is the sum of A and B.
	Example: The foundation for a house must be finished (Activity A) before the framing can start (Activity B).
Finish-to-Finish (FF)	The precedence relationship between two activities where the predecessor activity must finish before the successor activity can finish. It can be expressed as, "Activity A must finish before Activity B can finish." The total time to complete both activities is based on when B begins.
	Example: The construction must be finished (Activity A) before the building inspection can be finished (Activity B).
Start-to-Start (SS)	The precedence relationship between two activities where the predecessor activity must start before the successor activity can start. It can be expressed as, "Activity A must start before Activity B can start." The total time to complete both activities is based on the latest finish time of A or B.
	Example: The building design must start (Activity A) before the electrical layout design can start (Activity B).

Precedence Relationship Type	Description and Example
Start-to-Finish (SF)	The precedence relationship between two activities where the predecessor activity must start before the successor activity can finish. It can be expressed as, "Activity A must start before Activity B can finish." In this relationship, the successor activity begins before the predecessor activity. The total time to complete both activities is the sum of A and B. **Example:** The electrical inspections must start (Activity A) before you can finish the drywalling (Activity B).

Lag

A *lag* is a delay in the start of a successor activity. Some relationships require a lag before a subsequent activity can begin. Lags are determined by an external or mandatory dependency and may affect activities with any of the four precedence relationships.

There are several reasons why lags occur. Examples of two possible lags are:

- The permit application takes six weeks to process.
- The adhesive must dry until tacky before the laminate can be installed.

In the first example, the activity that follows the submission of the permit application is delayed by six weeks due to an external dependency of the application processing time. In the second example, the installation of the laminate activity is delayed by the amount of time the adhesive takes to dry. This is a lag due to a mandatory dependency because the delay is inherent to the work itself.

Effects of a Lag in an FS Relationship

When a lag is introduced in an FS relationship, the overall elapsed time required for the chain of activities increases. The start and finish dates of the successor activity are delayed when there is a lag.

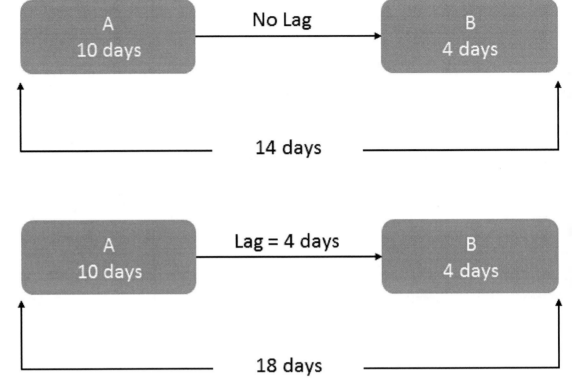

Figure 4-9: An FS relationship with a lag.

Lead

A *lead* is a change in a logical relationship that allows the successor activity to start before the predecessor activity ends in an FS relationship. A lead is implemented when you need to accelerate a successor activity in order to shorten the overall project schedule.

Leads will vary in length, depending on the acceleration required by the amended schedule. Sometimes, a lead introduces a risk of rework because the successor activity starts before the completion of the predecessor activity, and the complete, comprehensive inputs may not be available. Leads are sometimes referred to as "negative lags" because in project management software, leads are displayed as negative numbers.

For example, the programmer for a website may decide to start programming the home page four days before the interface design is approved. Starting the programming may shorten the overall project schedule by four days. However, if the design is not approved, there may be significant rework for the programmer, resulting in the loss of some or all of the four-day gain.

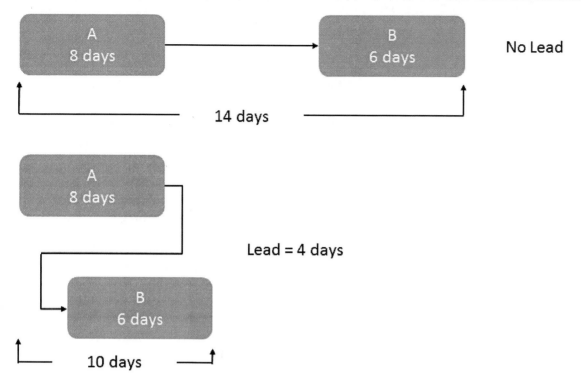

Figure 4-10: An FS relationship with a lead.

Project Schedule Network Diagram

A *project schedule network diagram* is a graphical representation of the sequence of project activities and the dependencies among them. Project schedule network diagrams read from left to right or top to bottom and are typically accompanied by summary information. The diagram can either include the entire project or just specific parts of it. Parts of a schedule network diagram may be referred to as a subnetwork or a fragmented network.

 Note: Summary information describes the basic approach that is used to sequence project activities.

Project schedule network diagrams may differ in that they may be:

* Detailed or high level.
* Generated manually or with software.
* Constructed using a variety of methods.

The PDM

The *Precedence Diagramming Method (PDM)* is a project schedule network diagramming method that uses rectangular boxes or nodes to represent activities and arrows to represent precedence relationships between activities. These types of diagrams:

* Always read from left to right.
* Show duration only in the nodes.
* Are created manually or with software.
* Report a group of related activities as an aggregate activity.
* Can use all precedence relationship types.

The following figure shows a project schedule network diagram that was constructed using the PDM.

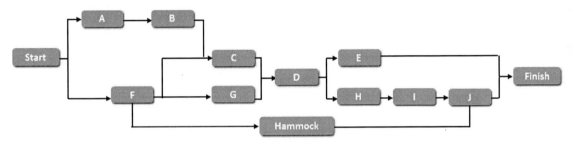

Figure 4-11: A network diagram using PDM.

Summary Activities

A *summary activity* is a group of related activities that, for reporting purposes, is shown as a single aggregate activity in a bar chart or graph. It may also be called a *hammock activity*. Summary activities have their own internal sequence of activities.

Figure 4-12: A summary or hammock activity in a network diagram.

Conditional Diagramming Methods

Activity sequences that must be revisited or repeated are called *loops*, whereas activities that will be implemented only under specific conditions are called *conditional branches*. A *conditional diagramming method* is any network diagramming method that allows for non-sequential activities such as loops or conditional branches. Typically, activities in these types of diagrams are represented by rectangles, decision points are represented by diamonds, and directional flow is indicated by arrows.

Conditional diagramming methods vary based on the method used. The most common conditional diagramming method is the *Graphical Evaluation Review Technique (GERT)* model.

> **Note:** When creating a network diagram, you may want to create a "Start" node that connects by arrows to all the nodes for activities with no dependencies.

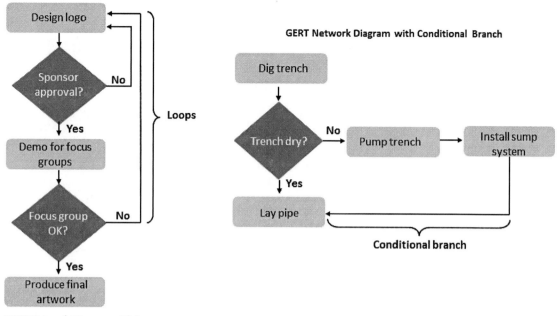

GERT Network Diagram with Loops

Figure 4-13: GERT network diagrams with loops and a conditional branch.

How to Create a Project Schedule Network Diagram

You can create a project schedule network diagram using the PDM, the most commonly used type, with all the activities having the appropriate precedence relationships.

Create a Project Schedule Network Diagram

Use the following procedure to create a Finish-to-Start (FS) PDM:

1. Determine the dependencies among project activities.
   - Use the activity list to identify all the activities that must be sequenced to create a project schedule.
   - Use the activity attributes to determine the sequence of events or their defined predecessor and successor relationships.
   - Use the milestone list to identify the logical starting point for sequencing of activities.
   - Review the project scope statement that contains the product description, which could affect sequencing.
   - If there are any existing documents related to project scheduling, use them when creating the project schedule.
2. Determine the leads and lags between activities.
3. Identify predecessor and successor activities.
4. Identify the precedence relationships between activities.
5. Create nodes for all activities with no predecessor activities or dependencies.
6. Create nodes for all activities that are successor activities to the nodes already created.
7. Draw arrows from the predecessor activities to the successor activities.
8. Continue drawing the network diagram, working from left to right until all activities are included on the diagram and their precedence relationships are indicated by arrows. Include any known lags or leads.
9. Verify the accuracy of your diagram. Check to ensure that:
   a. All activities on the activity list are included in the diagram.
   b. All precedence relationships are correctly indicated by arrows going from the predecessor activities to the successor activities.

c. Any known lags or leads are indicated on the diagram.

TOPIC D

Identify Resources

You identified the logical dependencies and precedence relationships between the project activities and created a project schedule network diagram for your project. Now, you can determine the types and quantities of resources needed to accomplish project work. In this topic, you will estimate activity resources.

It is very common for projects to involve numerous people, including vendors or strategic partners, and require different types of materials. Without a clear understanding of who is doing what, efforts may be duplicated or may lead to costly mistakes or misunderstandings. Firmly establishing who is involved, what role they play, who has authority for what, and what materials will be needed will make the project run smoothly and aid in the success of the project.

Project Resources

Project resources refer to any useful materials or people needed to complete the project work. Project resources will vary greatly in size, cost, and function. Resources can be labor, materials, facilities, equipment, consultants, services, supplies, or utilities. Project resources are almost always limited in quantity and, therefore, require thoughtful allocation.

Resources can be divided into three major categories: work, materials, and cost. Within each of these categories, you can have different types of resources. The following table defines different types of resources.

Resource Type	Description
Shared resources	Resources that are used for multiple projects and must be managed as such.
Dedicated resources	Resources that have been committed for your project's use.
Benched resources	Skilled resources that are retained during downtime but are not performing "billable" tasks. The benefit is that they can be put into service immediately when the need arises.
Low-quality resources	Resources that do not possess specialized skills or qualities.

Example: Resources Required to Organize a Seminar

A project for an HR department could be to present an annual employee health and wellness seminar. Resources will include the conference room, which will be used for the seminar; the tangible information materials, such as brochures and pamphlets that will be given to employees; the visiting consultants, who will be hired to make presentations and answer employees' questions; and the vendors, who will participate in the seminar and offer their services.

Resource Availability Constraints

In most organizations, the number and availability of suitable resources is limited and the project manager must find and assign the most appropriate resources for each project activity. Several situations can arise that make this task difficult.

- When the best resource is not available within the organization, the shortage can be handled by either hiring someone with the needed skills, using a temporary employee provided by a staffing agency, subcontracting the work to another company, or teaming with another company to share a portion of the scope. In each of these cases, the project cost can be affected, and the project manager will need to address it with a change request.

- When the best resource is assigned to an activity, it is tempting to give that person more work than they can handle in their scheduled work hours. This overallocation can be handled by either delaying some of the work until the resource can do it within their schedule, assigning some of the work to another resource, or changing the scope. A fourth alternative is to permit the overallocation and compensate the resource with overtime pay. As with the shortage situation, cost will likely be impacted with these solutions.

- Resources in many organizations will be assigned to multiple projects, and the managers of these projects will compete for a resource's time. This competition will create an imbalance, resulting in shortages and overallocations as discussed.

Resource Calendar

A *resource calendar* is a calendar that lists the time during which project resources can participate in the project tasks. It helps prevent resource scheduling conflicts because it includes details such as vacation time and other project commitments. Composite resource calendars will list additional information such as the available list of resources and the skills and capabilities of human resources.

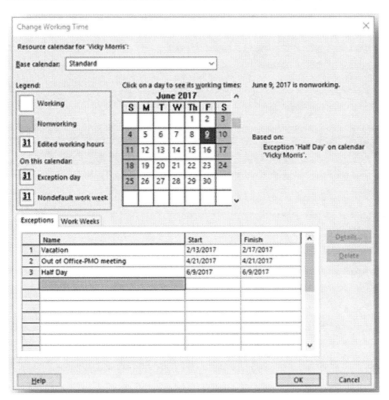

Figure 4-14: A resource calendar in Microsoft Project.

Alternatives Analysis

Every project's activities can be accomplished using different methods. *Alternatives analysis* is the process of examining the different methods of accomplishing activities and determining a preferred method. The analysis may involve selecting among different skills, tools, and equipment and determining whether the project work can be accomplished by the project team or must be procured from outside the organization.

Published Estimating Data

Published estimating data is information found in commercial publications about production rates, resource cost, and labor requirements. For example, if a publication states that an experienced concrete finisher can smooth x square yards of concrete per hour, extrapolation can be used to determine how many finishers will be needed to smooth 5x square yards of concrete.

Project Management Software

Project management software is a software application that generates and organizes resource information, such as cost estimates, Work Breakdown Structures, and project schedules. It also helps optimize resource utilizations. Project management software provides ways of tracking planned dates versus actual dates and forecasting effects of changes to the project schedule and possible project results.

Project management software can be used as a desktop application or a web-based app that's available from any location on multiple devices. Applications can range from a single-user application to a multi-user app that enables collaborative use. Some examples of project management software include:

- Microsoft® Project 2016—part of the Microsoft® Office suite of applications.
- Oracle® Primavera—project management software for enterprises.
- LiquidPlanner®—an online project management application for collaborative IT projects.
- Smartsheet®—an online project management application.
- Atlassian® JIRA Agile™—a software development application used by Agile teams.

 Note: There are many software solutions available to create and manage project schedules. An excellent resource that summarizes almost 90 software applications can be found at *www.projectmanagementsoftware.com*.

Activity Resource Requirements

The availability of resources will influence the accomplishment of project activities. *Activity resource requirements* are the descriptions of resources, such as people, equipment, and location, and the quantities of resources necessary to complete project activities. Resource requirements will be progressively elaborated when developing the human resource plan.

The Resource Breakdown Structure

The *resource breakdown structure* is a hierarchy of identified resources, organized by category and type. Category includes labor and equipment and type includes resource skills and grade levels. The resource breakdown structure helps organize and report project schedule information along with the resource utilization data.

Example: Determining Resources for the Website Design Project

Robert is trying to determine the resources required for the initial design work package of a website project. The art director provided him with a list of resources he will need. Because there are no in-house graphic designers available, Robert authorizes him to hire a contractor.

The computer, workstation, and black-and-white printer are overhead items that are already available to the art department. However, there is no color printer on site and the software program will need to be purchased. The company's policies require that this equipment be rented rather than purchased. As an alternative, Robert directed the art department to utilize a commercial printing facility for presentation items that require color.

Guidelines for Identifying Resources

Accurate estimations of the resources required to complete project deliverables are vital in developing a realistic project schedule and budget. You can follow these guidelines to determine the resource requirements for your project:

- Determine the resources necessary to complete each activity in the work packages.
- Determine the quantity of resources necessary to complete each activity.
- Refer to the resource calendars to identify the availability of each resource.
- Generate possible alternatives for unavailable resources and areas where:
  - Resources are known to be constrained.
  - The work is new to your organization so new resources will need to be brought in.
  - Many different resourcing options are known to exist.
  - There have been disagreements about resource requirements in the past.
  - Certain activities have high risk.
- Analyze the scope statement to ensure that you identified all the resources required to perform the project work.
- Consider organizational policies that could affect resource acquisition and usage.
  - Can you use contract labor to take advantage of lower hourly rates for certain types of work?
  - Is renting equipment preferred over purchasing?
  - Must suppliers be selected only from a list of those approved and qualified?
  - Are there any resource usages that require authorization from upper management?
- Identify and use resources that provide expertise, such as project team knowledge, internal organizations, industry colleagues, technical or professional associations, SMEs, and other project managers of projects with aspects similar to your project.
- Analyze the resources currently available, such as in-house staff as well as materials, facilities, and equipment.
- If necessary, use project management software to plan, organize, and manage project schedules and resources.

 Note: Most project managers use a spreadsheet program to capture the resource requirements for their projects. This allows flexibility in formatting the information and lets you output the columns you want for a particular purpose.

TOPIC E

Estimate Time

You identified the activity resources that will be needed for each scheduled activity in a work package. Now, it is time for you to determine how long each activity will take. In this topic, you will estimate activity duration.

Inaccurate time estimates will affect the schedule and may frustrate the team involved in meeting the schedule. By minimizing potential adjustments to the schedule, you and other stakeholders will not have to work overtime and you can preserve your reputation as a project manager.

Reserve Analysis

Reserve analysis is the process of identifying and adding extra time that will serve as contingency or management reserves to the duration estimates.

- *Contingency reserves* serve as buffers in recognition of scheduled risks or setbacks. These reserves are usually determined by the project manager.
- *Management reserves* are buffers added to the project for unforeseen changes to project scope and cost. These reserves are usually determined by the sponsor.

As the project progresses, reserve analysis is used to determine if the remaining or planned buffer is adequate for project completion. Reserve analysis runs the risk of inflating a cost estimate.

Example: Reserve Analysis at a Cell Phone Manufacturing Company

A cell phone manufacturing company contracted a vendor to integrate a new telecommunication technology with their current system. The project manager, Bob, has been assigned to manage this new project. He creates a schedule to complete the project within one month. Bob anticipates that if the technical integration aspects are unavailable, the project will need to be extended for one more month. Therefore, he specifies this in the project management plan and retains a contingency reserve of one month. Senior managers, upon reviewing the project management plan, advised Bob to add two more weeks as management reserves to the project in order to accommodate the risks that may occur due to unknown-unknowns.

The Analogous Estimating Technique

Analogous estimating or *top-down estimating* is an estimating technique in which managers use their experience, historical information from similar projects, and expert judgment to determine the total project cost or time estimate. The resulting total is then apportioned across the major categories of project work. Estimates are generated for the top levels of the WBS and then apportioned downward through the levels of the WBS.

Analogous cost estimating is used when:

- You have a limited amount of detailed information about the project.
- You have a similar project to use for comparison.
- Those preparing the estimates have the requisite expertise.

Example: Estimating Duration to Prepare a Report

Laurie has been asked to provide an estimate to prepare a report. It is early in the project, and she does not have many details about what will go into the report. However, she has written many reports for similar projects, and remembers that most of them took her about four weeks to prepare. This new project is slightly more complex than her other ones, so she adds a week and estimates that she can complete it in five weeks.

The Parametric Estimating Technique

Parametric estimating is a technique that is used to predict duration or cost by using historical data in a mathematical model. The most common parametric model uses simple multiplication, as shown in the following example. The accuracy of a parametric estimate will only be as good as the accuracy of the data used in it.

Example: Parametric Estimating for a Web Design Project

A project manager for a web design firm, William, may use parametric estimating to produce cost and time estimates for new accounts. He will base his estimates on past experience and expert judgment. If several other similar sites, each of which included five pages and basic functionality, took approximately 15 hours to develop, then he could fairly estimate that a site with 10 pages will require 30 hours of development time.

The Three-Point Estimating Technique

Three-point estimating is a method of activity duration estimating in which three types of estimates are incorporated into a singular duration estimate scenario: optimistic, most likely, and pessimistic. Optimistic estimate is the best-case estimate of the time required to complete the specified work. Most likely estimate is the time required to complete the work under normal conditions. Pessimistic estimate is the worst-case estimate or the time required to complete the work if any unanticipated delays occur. These estimates are generally based on historical information and help in increasing the level of accuracy in estimating project duration. Three-point estimating is based on Program Evaluation Review Technique (PERT) analysis.

The most commonly used formula for three-point estimating is:

```
[Optimistic time + 4(most likely time) + pessimistic time] / 6
```

Example: Three-Point Estimating for a Marketing Campaign Project

You are the project manager for the creation of an innovative marketing campaign project across the country. Several similar projects conducted previously required three months to complete (most likely estimate); one was completed in one month (optimistic estimate); and one took eleven months to complete (pessimistic estimate). Therefore, you estimate that the time for the current project will be four months, based on the formula:

```
[1 + 4 * 3 + 11] / 6
```

The Bottom-Up Estimating Technique

Bottom-up estimating is a method of estimating the duration or cost of each work package in the WBS. The estimates are then rolled up or aggregated for progressively higher levels within the WBS. The project manager reviews the estimate figures to compile the total project duration or cost. Bottom-up estimating is the most accurate method but it is also challenging, costly, and time consuming.

Use bottom-up estimating in the project life cycle when:

- More detail is available about the work packages.
- You need more accurate estimates.
- You have the time to invest in making the estimates.

You should also use bottom-up estimating for work packages with the highest level of uncertainty associated with cost. Make sure that you weigh the additional accuracy provided by bottom-up estimating against the additional cost of making the estimates.

Guidelines for Estimating Time

Accurate activity time estimates form the basis of an accurate project schedule because they include a careful review of effort required, the duration of tasks, the delivery date or deadline, and customer priorities. You can use the following guidelines to ensure that your estimates are as accurate and realistic as possible:

- Gather all the prerequisites, such as activity lists, activity attributes, resource calendars, activity resource requirements document, and project products, required to estimate the duration of each activity in the project.
- Involve the work package owners or others who are familiar with the work of the activity.
- Consult historical information.
  - Are there any detailed records from previous, similar projects that you could use to derive your estimates?
  - Are there any relevant commercial duration estimating databases?
  - Do any project team members have experience with similar activities?
- Determine which technique you want to use to estimate the activity duration. The techniques include:
  - Analogous estimating
  - Bottom-up estimating
  - Parametric estimating
  - Three-point estimating
  - Reserve analysis
- Determine how you want to quantify the work that needs to be done: in terms of the estimated hours of labor that will be needed, the number of units to be produced, and the number of customers to be served.
- Consider resource requirements and capabilities. For example, who will be assigned to the activity and how will the skills of the assigned staff affect the duration estimates?
- Determine the appropriate estimation method to use.
  - If it is early in the planning phase or if there is good historical data, consider using analogous estimating.
  - If there is inadequate historical data, consult SMEs.
  - Use quantitatively based duration to estimate activities when quantities of work units can be multiplied by the productivity rate.
  - If you are using the three-point estimating technique, ask the estimators for the optimistic, most likely, and pessimistic estimates.
- Modify the constraints and assumptions from the other planning processes.
- Verify the accuracy of your estimates.
  - What is the probability associated with this estimate?
  - What was this estimate based upon?
  - Are there any risks associated with this estimate?
- Consider the need for reserve time. As more information becomes available about the activity or work package, the reserve time can be modified.
- Include the list of assumptions made in the creation of the estimates.
- Include a range of variance for each estimate.
- Update all project documents that require changes.

ACTIVITY 4-1
Preparing to Develop the Project Schedule Review

Scenario

Answer the following review questions.

---

1. How do you think creating an activity list for projects will help ensure that your project activities are tied to the project scope?

2. Reflect on the advantages of creating a project schedule network diagram. How do you think this will help you organize your project more effectively?

Summary

In this lesson, you identified the major elements of project schedules, which include activity lists, project network schedule diagrams, estimates of activity duration, and techniques for making estimates. You will now be able to develop effective project schedules and manage schedules in response to organizational constraints on time and resources so that you can complete your projects on time and on budget.

5 Developing the Project Schedule

Lesson Time: 2 hours, 45 minutes

Lesson Introduction

The project schedule is an essential component of any project management effort. As you strive to advance your skills as a professional project manager, you need to have a good command of all project schedule-related elements. Developing effective project schedules and skills to manage the schedules in response to organizational constraints on time and resources will help you complete your projects on time and on budget. In this lesson, you will develop the project schedule.

Lesson Objectives

In this lesson, you will:

- Develop a project schedule.

- Identify the critical path.

- Optimize the project schedule.

- Create a schedule baseline.

TOPIC A

Develop a Project Schedule

You identified the necessity of effective activity duration estimating in successful schedule planning. Now, you will put that to use by moving on to the next stage of schedule development. In this topic, you will develop a project schedule.

The project schedule is one of the most important tools for keeping upper management and project stakeholders informed about the project's status and for tracking performance. Given its importance and high visibility, you want to make sure that the schedule you create is realistic. If you don't take the time to establish realistic start and finish dates, it is unlikely that your project will finish on time and within the quality and cost targets.

Project Schedules

A *project schedule* is the project team's plan for starting and finishing activities on specific dates and in a certain sequence. The schedule also specifies planned dates for meeting project milestones.

The purpose of the project schedule is to coordinate activities to form a master plan in order to complete the project objectives on time. It is also used to track schedule performance and keep upper management and project stakeholders informed about the project's status.

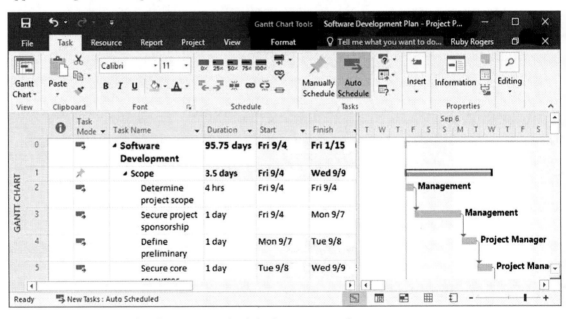

Figure 5-1: An example of a project schedule from Microsoft Project.

The Critical Path

The *critical path* is the network path that has the longest duration. Activities on the critical path cannot be delayed or the whole project will be delayed unless subsequent activities are shortened.

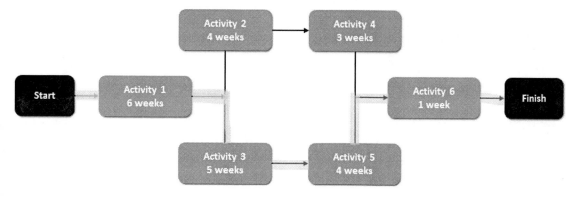

$$1[6w] + 2[4w] + 4[3w] + 6[1w] = 14 \text{ weeks}$$

$$1[6w] + 3[5w] + 5[4w] + 6[1w] = 16 \text{ weeks } \textbf{Critical Path}$$

Figure 5-2: A network diagram showing the critical path of activities.

Float

Float is the amount of time an activity can be delayed from its Early Start (ES) without delaying the project finish date or the consecutive activities. Float occurs only in activities that are not on the critical path. Float is also called *slack*. There are two types of float: total and free.

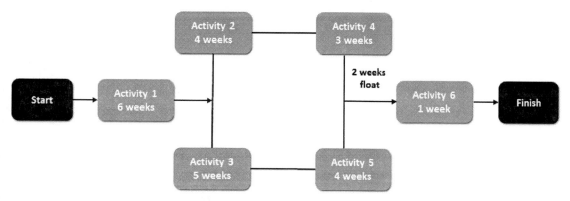

Figure 5-3: A schedule network diagram showing float.

Standard Schedule Diagramming Notations

When representing float, it might be helpful to use the standard schedule diagramming notations. Project network diagrams use the standard diagramming nomenclature as described in the following table.

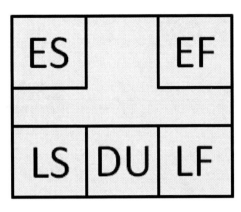

Figure 5-4: Standard schedule diagramming notations for an activity.

Notation	Description
ES	**Early Start** is the earliest time an activity can start. Usually, the ES of the first activity in a network diagram is zero. The ES of all other activities is the latest Early Finish (EF) of any predecessor activities (assuming that any successor activity starts as soon as all its predecessor activities are finished).
EF	**Early Finish** is the earliest time an activity can finish. The EF for the first activity is the same as its duration. For all other activities, EF is the latest EF of all the predecessor activities of an activity plus its duration.
LF	**Late Finish** is the latest time an activity can finish. The LF for the last activity is the same as its EF time. The LF for any predecessor activity is the earliest LS of any of its successor activities.
LS	**Late Start** is the latest time an activity can start. The LS for the last activity is its EF minus its duration. The LS for any predecessor activity is its LF minus its duration.
DU	**Duration** is the number of work periods required for the completion of an activity.

Total Float

Total float is a type of float where the total amount of time an activity requires can be delayed without delaying the project finish date. Total float for an activity can be calculated by subtracting its EF from its LF or its ES from its LS. The total float for every activity on the critical path is zero.

 Note: When you see the term float by itself, it generally refers to total float.

In the following Critical Path Method (CPM) diagram, Activity C has an ES of 25 days. However, should it begin on its LS date, the value is 36. Therefore, the amount of time the start date can be delayed without affecting the finish date is 11 days. The Total Float (TF) value is 11 (36 - 25 = 11).

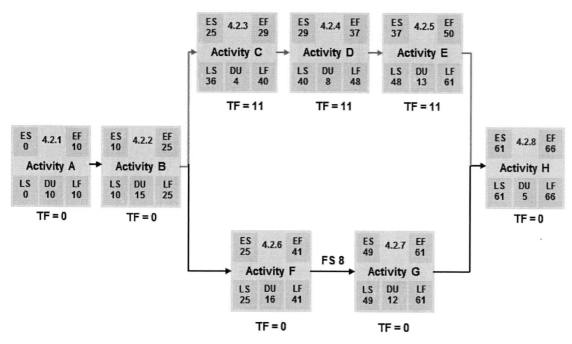

Figure 5–5: A CPM network diagram with total float.

Free Float

Free float is the amount of time an activity can be delayed without delaying the ES of any activity that immediately follows it. It allows flexibility of the start or finish time within that activity only. If there is a string of activities with float, free float will be available only for the activity at the end of the string. Free float for an activity is calculated by subtracting the EF of the activity from the ES of its successor activity.

In the CPM diagram, the free float for Activity E can be calculated by subtracting its EF from the ES of the successor activity, which in this case is Activity H. The free float value is Activity H's ES (61) - Activity E's EF (50), or 61 - 50. The free float is 11.

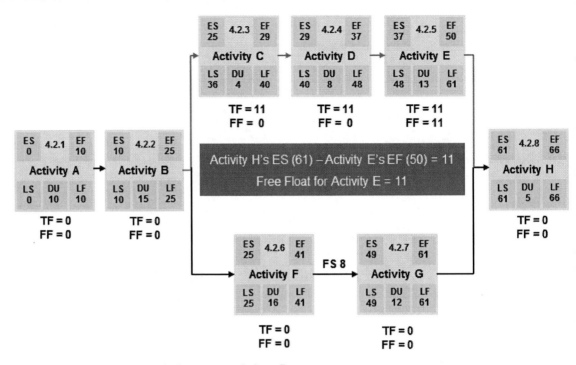

Figure 5-6: A CPM network diagram with free float.

Schedule Network Analysis

Schedule network analysis is a technique that is used to calculate the theoretical early and late start and finish dates for all project activities. In other words, it helps create a project schedule. This method also generates float or slack.

Schedule network analysis may be achieved using one of the four methods:

- Critical Path Method (CPM)
- Critical chain method
- What-if scenario
- Resource leveling

Example: Developing a Schedule for a Marketing Campaign Project

You are trying to craft a schedule for the creation of a new marketing campaign, which will involve finding a new advertising agency, creating the advertisements, and producing marketing materials. Because the project contains so many different work packages, you decide that schedule network analysis is necessary. Using a project management software application, you are able to define the network path from "request for proposals" to "launch campaign." From there, you can estimate the points in the schedule where there is slack and adjust the activities accordingly.

The CPM

The *Critical Path Method (CPM)* is a schedule network analysis method that estimates the minimum project duration and determines the amount of scheduling flexibility that exists in a project. It uses all four precedence relationships and calculates one early and late start and finish date for each activity using a single-duration estimate. The longest path through the network—the critical path—is identified. Then float is calculated to identify activities where there is some scheduling flexibility. CPM is the mathematical analysis technique used in most types of project management software.

Activity	Start	Finish	Early Start	Early Finish	Late Start	Late Finish	Critical
⊟ **Tradeshow, Planning, Execution, and Wrap-Up**	**Apr 2**	**May 1**	**Apr 2**	**May 1**	**Apr 2**	**May 1**	**Yes**
⊟ **Perform Preliminary Research**	**Apr 2**	**May 1**	**Apr 2**	**May 1**	**Apr 2**	**May 1**	**Yes**
Research potential tradeshows	Apr 2	Apr 6	Apr 2	Apr 6	Apr 2	Apr 6	Yes
Review inputs from lines of business (LOB)	Apr 9	Apr 13	Apr 9	Apr 13	Apr 9	Apr 13	Yes
Review individual tradeshow information	Apr 16	Apr 18	Apr 16	Apr 18	Apr 16	Apr 18	Yes
Tradeshow exposure for your organization	Apr 19	Apr 19	Apr 19	Apr 19	Apr 19	Apr 19	Yes
Tradeshow value for your organization	Apr 20	Apr 20	Apr 20	Apr 20	Apr 20	Apr 20	Yes
Review tradeshow fees	Apr 23	Apr 23	Apr 23	Apr 23	Apr 23	Apr 23	Yes
Establish preliminary tradeshow budget	Apr 24	Apr 27	Apr 24	Apr 27	Apr 24	Apr 27	Yes
Evaluate relevance for your organization	Apr 30	Apr 30	Apr 30	Apr 30	Apr 30	Apr 30	Yes
Evaluate alignment to Corporate Strategy Goals	May 1	May 1	May 1	May 1	May 1	May 1	Yes
Evaluate competitive advantages	Apr 9	Apr 9	Apr 9	Apr 9	Apr 23	Apr 24	No
Determine company tradeshow objectives	Apr 10	Apr 10	Apr 10	Apr 10	Apr 24	Apr 25	No
Review company attendee list (past and current)	Apr 11	Apr 11	Apr 11	Apr 11	Apr 25	Apr 26	No
Review competitor participation	Apr 12	Apr 12	Apr 12	Apr 12	Apr 26	Apr 27	No
Review audience demographics	Apr 13	Apr 13	Apr 13	Apr 13	Apr 27	Apr 30	No
Review organization marketing plan	Apr 16	Apr 16	Apr 16	Apr 16	Apr 30	May 1	No
Preliminary Research Complete	May 1	May 1	May 1	May 1	May 1	May 1	Yes

Figure 5-7: The Critical Path Method involves calculating one early and late start and finish date for each activity.

The Critical Chain Method

The *critical chain method* is a schedule network analysis method that allows you to consider resource limitations and adjust the schedule as appropriate to work within those limitations. The critical chain is established by analyzing the critical path alongside the resources that are actually available. The critical chain method is also used to plan and manage reserves or buffers and helps mitigate possible cost and schedule risks.

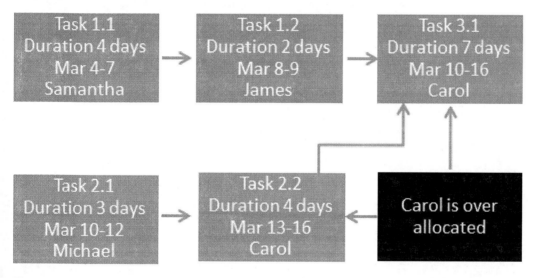

Figure 5-8: A critical chain project schedule allows you to consider resource limitations and adjust the schedule.

What-If Scenario Analysis

The *what-if scenario analysis* method allows you to consider different situations that may occur and influence the schedule; it assesses the feasibility of the schedule under various adverse conditions. It allows you to compute different schedules based on potential delays or unplanned events that are a normal part of business life, such as key employees resigning during a project. The outcomes are also used to mitigate the impact of unexpected situations when preparing risk response plans. This method helps in selecting the optimum plan.

Example: What-If Scenario Analysis for a Planned Move of a Corporate Headquarters

The project manager, David, used the what-if scenario analysis method to compute different schedules for a planned move of the corporate headquarters to a new facility. He based his computations on several scenarios, such as: What if the contractor for the new building brings the goods in late? What if key decision makers are allocated elsewhere during the planning process? What if there is a union strike affecting the construction workers?

Resource Leveling

Resource leveling is used to analyze the schedule model. It allows you to readjust the work as appropriate so that people are not overly allocated. It is also used to address scheduling activities when critical resources are only available at certain times. Resource leveling is normally done after the critical path has been initially identified. The critical path frequently changes as a result of resource leveling.

Resource leveling tools are found in many types of project management software. You need to consider automated leveling and resource smoothing when using resource leveling tools.

- **Automated Leveling**: Most project management software packages have resource leveling capabilities. However, make sure that you analyze the results before accepting them. Automated leveling often pushes out the project's completion date. Resources may be reallocated to work at times that are inappropriate due to other constraints.
- **Resource Smoothing**: A resource leveling technique that involves rescheduling activities in a project to ensure that appropriate resources are allocated to each activity. Resource smoothing does not create a delay in the project completion date. It only allows for delays in the activities within their float.

 Note: The most common scheduling conflicts are under-allocation of resources to a critical task and over-allocation of a critical resource.

Example: Resource Leveling at a Construction Company

Daniel, a project manager who worked for a construction company, always managed several projects simultaneously. His project resources included construction workers who were paid varying hourly wages. By using the resource leveling method via a tool in his project management software, Daniel could make sure that the most expensive hourly workers, including electricians and stone masons, were appropriately and consistently allocated.

Schedule Formats

The project schedule can be presented in different formats, depending on the circumstances. Three commonly used schedule formats are:

- Gantt chart
- Milestone chart
- Project schedule network diagram with dates

Gantt Chart

Created by Henry Gantt, the *Gantt chart* is the visual representation of a project schedule in bar chart form. Tasks in the Gantt chart are listed down the left side and dates are listed across the top or bottom with bars to indicate start and finish dates. Time is represented with horizontal bars that correspond to the activities. Gantt charts may also show the dependencies of the project activities, as well as the percentage of the activity completed to date and the actual progress in relation to planned progress.

These charts are often used when presenting the project status to upper management. A detailed view of the chart is used when reviewing the project status with the project team.

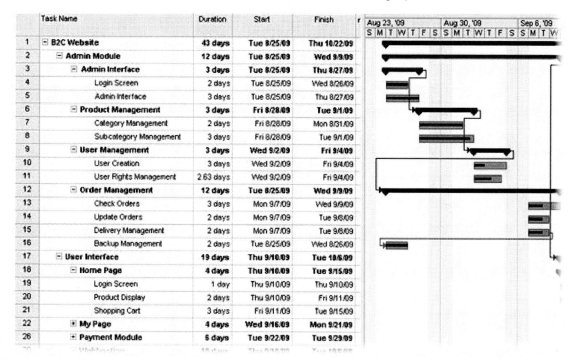

Figure 5-9: An example of a Gantt chart.

Milestone Chart

A milestone chart provides a summary level view of a project's schedule in terms of its milestones. Milestones are typically listed from the left to right of the chart, and icons or symbols are used to show scheduled milestone events. Time intervals—divided into hours, days, weeks, or months—are usually presented horizontally across the top or bottom of the chart, as illustrated in the figure. Milestone charts can be effective in demonstrating the project's overall schedule to project team members, stakeholders, and upper management.

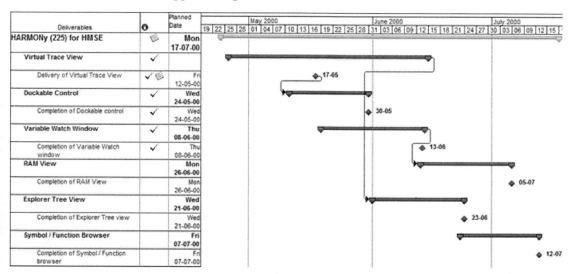

Figure 5-10: A milestone chart.

Project Schedule Network Diagram with Dates

Adding dates to the project schedule network diagram helps when assigning start and finish dates to activities on the project schedule network diagram. These types of charts can be useful when you need to communicate the project status in terms of activity precedence relationships.

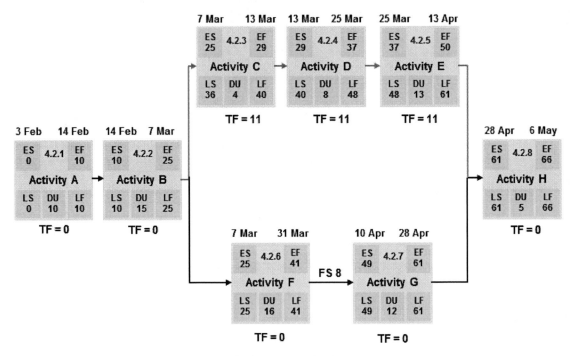

Figure 5-11: A project schedule network diagram with dates.

How to Develop a Project Schedule

As the project manager, the project schedule enables you to coordinate activities and ultimately complete the project objectives on time.

Develop a Draft Project Schedule

Use the following procedures to develop a draft project schedule:

1. Perform a mathematical analysis to determine the time periods within which activities could be scheduled once resource limits and other known constraints are applied.
2. Evaluate the possible impact of any constraints and assumptions on schedule development.
3. Consider the availability of your resources.
   - Will you have the staff you need to perform the work when it is scheduled to be done?
   - Will you have access to materials, facilities, and equipment you need to perform the work when it is scheduled to be done?
4. Consult project calendars and assign dates to activities.
   - Are there any holidays during which your project team will not conduct work activities?
   - Will your project team conduct work activities on weekends?
   - When will your key project team members be taking vacations?
   - Are there any unmovable milestone dates that must be met?
5. Assess the feasibility of the schedule under adverse conditions by conducting what-if scenario analysis.
6. Consider external resource date constraints, if applicable.
   - Are there any regional or national holidays not previously accounted for?
   - Do you need to make considerations for travel time for meetings?

7. Select project management software that best meets the needs and budget of your project. If your organization does not require the use of a particular software program, ask yourself the following questions to make the selection:

    • How complex is the project?
    • Do I need to manage more than one project at a time?
    • How easy will the software be to learn and to use?
    • How well will the software adapt to projects that vary greatly?
    • What type and depth of analyses do I need to perform?
    • What is the reputation of the software company?
    • What do other project managers in the field use and what do they recommend?

8. Review rough drafts of the schedule with the project team, sponsor, and customer. You may also need to review the rough drafts with functional managers to ensure that there are no conflicts with functional resources.

9. Choose the format in which you will publish the schedule.

    • If your audience only requires a summary-level view of the project's progress in terms of milestones, consider using a milestone chart.
    • If you are reviewing the schedule with your project team, consider publishing a detailed bar chart or a network diagram with dates.
    • If you are preparing a presentation for key project stakeholders or upper management, consider printing the schedule in several different formats to show various views of the project's progress versus planned progress.

10. Distribute the preliminary schedule to all program office personnel, functional team members, functional management, and customers or sponsors to obtain approval.

11. Following approval, baseline the schedule and distribute it to the team.

TOPIC B

Identify the Critical Path

Now that you drafted a project schedule, you are ready to establish the start and finish times for each of the activities in your project and determine the duration of the entire project. That means you will need to know the critical path through your project activities. In this topic, you will identify the critical path.

Sometimes, the resources you are counting on may not be available when they are scheduled to be. How do you know when your project cannot be successfully completed? The answer is that you must identify the critical path when developing the project schedule. Identifying the critical path allows you to determine which activities have scheduling flexibility before you complete your project schedule.

Critical Activities

Critical activities are the activities that are on the critical path. Generally, for all activities along the critical path, ES = LS and EF = LF. There can be no flexibility in the start time or the finish time for these activities. Activities that are not on the critical path usually have some flexibility in their start and finish times. Activities on the critical path have a total float of zero.

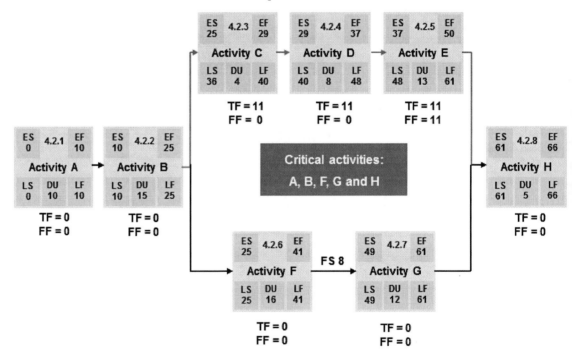

Figure 5-12: Critical activities lie on the critical path (Activities A, B, F, G, and H).

Note the following characteristics in the CPM graphic:

- The ES for the first activity (A) equals zero.
- The EF for the first activity is its ES plus its duration (0 + 10 = 10).
- The ES for all successor activities is the latest EF of any of its predecessor activities plus any lags or minus any leads between the two activities.

   For example, the ES for Activity D is the same as the EF for Activity C (29) and the ES for Activity G is the EF for Activity F (41) plus an 8 FS lag, which is indicated as FS 8 (41 + 8 = 49).

> **Note:** Although the ES of the first activity can be zero, it can also have the value one. But when the ES of the first activity is one, then the EF should be calculated as ES + DU - 1. The ES of the successor activity will then be the EF of the predecessor activity plus one. For example, if the ES of the first activity is one, then its EF will be 1 + 10 - 1 = 10 and the ES of the second activity will be 11.

- The EF for all subsequent activities is its ES plus its duration. For example, the EF of Activity B (25) is its ES (10) plus its duration (15).
- The LF for the last activity is the same as its EF time (66).
- The LS for the last activity (61) is its EF (66) minus its duration (5).
- The LF for any predecessor activity is the same as the earliest LS of any of its successors plus or minus any leads or lags between the two activities.

   For example, the LF of Activity E is the same as the LS of Activity H (61), and the LF for Activity F (41) is the LS for Activity G (49) minus the 8 day FS lag (49 – 8 = 41).

- The LS for any predecessor activity is its LF minus its duration. For example, the LS for Activity E (48) is its LF (61) minus its duration (13).
- Only the three activities that are not on the critical path (C, D, and E) have total float (TF = 11).
- Only the last activity in that string (Activity E) has free float (FF = 11).
- The critical path is indicated by bold lines with arrows and includes activities A, B, F, G, and H. It is the path with the longest duration and zero float.

How to Identify the Critical Path

Use the following procedures to identify the critical path.

Identify the Critical Path

To identify the critical path for a project with FS precedence relationships:

1. Conduct a forward pass to determine the ES and EF for each activity.

   a. Use zero (0) for the first activity's ES.
   b. Enter the first activity's duration as its EF.
   c. Calculate the ES for each successor activity using the latest EF from any of its predecessor activities plus or minus any lags or leads.
   d. Calculate the EF for each successor activity by adding its duration to its ES.
   e. Move through all the activities until you have an ES and EF for each one.

2. Perform a backward pass to determine the LS and LF for each activity.

   a. Enter the last activity's EF as its LF time.
   b. Subtract the last activity's duration from its EF to determine its LS.
   c. Calculate the LF for each predecessor activity using the earliest LS from any of its successor activities plus any leads or minus any lags.
   d. Calculate the LS for each predecessor activity by subtracting its duration from its LF.
   e. Move backward through all the activities until you have the LF and LS for each one.

3. Calculate float.

   a. For each activity, subtract its EF from its LF to determine total float.
   b. For each string of activities with float, calculate free float for the last activity in the string by subtracting its EF from its successor activity ES.

4. Identify the critical path as the path with the longest duration and zero float.

TOPIC C

Optimize the Project Schedule

Now that you drafted your project schedule and identified the critical path, you are ready to begin the hands-on management of the schedule, which involves successfully negotiating organizational constraints on time and resources. To do so, you must identify the tools that project managers use to respond to resource fluctuations, setbacks, and delays while responding to the perennial business need of delivering the project on time. In this topic, you will optimize the project schedule.

Setbacks, delays, constraints on time and resources, and competing priorities are all part of everyday life in business, and they will affect every project you work on. You want to be able to work effectively in the face of these challenges by optimizing your project schedule, which means using project management tools to work around these problems, so that you can support the needs of the business.

Schedule Compression

Schedule compression is the shortening of the project schedule without affecting the project scope. Setbacks or revised deadlines can cause production problems, in which there is little time to do a lot of work. When these issues occur, product quality is often sacrificed. Schedule compression alleviates the pressure of completing too many activities in a short time without negatively affecting the project scope. Compression may be achieved in one of two ways: fast-tracking and crashing.

Fast–Tracking

Fast-tracking is the process of compressing the project duration by performing some activities concurrently that were originally scheduled sequentially. Typically, fast-tracking involves identifying FS relationships that could be done in parallel, either as FF, SF, or SS relationships, or by simply adding some leads to FS activities.

Some fast-tracking may entail looking very creatively at the network diagram to see if some discretionary dependencies could be done completely independently. Usually no added costs are incurred from fast-tracking; however, it can result in increased risk and rework.

Example: Fast–Tracking Activities to Produce a New Product

Sponsors are pressuring Carol to bring a new product to market quickly. Carol decides to fast-track some activities by placing a lead relationship between the development of the new product and the writing of the associated user manual. The total duration of the two activities is shortened, because writing the manual can start before the product development is complete. Consequently, the project duration is shortened.

Crashing

Crashing is a schedule compression method that analyzes cost and schedule trade-offs to determine how to obtain the greatest schedule compression for the least incremental cost. Crashing typically involves allocating more resources to activities on the critical path in an effort to shorten their duration, thereby increasing project costs.

To crash a schedule, analyze:

- Duration estimate under normal (for example, not compressed) conditions.
- Cost associated with the normal condition.
- Duration estimate under the crash condition.
- Cost associated with the crash condition.

The formula for calculating crash costs per week is:

```
(Crash Cost - Normal Cost) / (Normal Time - Crash Time)
```

Example: Crashing the Company Website Project

As project manager for the company website project, you are asked to compress the schedule for the design deliverable. There are eleven activities, five of which are on the critical path. Using the formula (Crash Cost - Normal Cost) / Normal Time - Crash Time), you calculate the crash costs per week for each of the five activities to determine which activities will provide the greatest duration reduction for the least incremental cost. Your calculations are:

	Normal Time (wk)	Crash Time (wk)	Time Saved	Normal Cost ($)	Crash Cost ($)	Cost Increase	Crash Cost/Wk ($)
A	10	8	2	15,000	23,000	8,000	4,000
B	12	11	1	10,000	14,500	4,500	4,500
C	8	6	2	5,000	8,000	3,000	1,500
D	6	3	3	6,000	7,500	1,500	500
E	9	6	3	12,000	18,000	6,000	2,000
Total	45	34	11	48,000	71,000	23,000	-

While you have not yet analyzed the effect of crashing the activities, you can determine from your calculations that:

- Activities D and C are the best candidates for crashing.
  - Activity D has a net gain of three weeks at a cost of just $500 per week.
  - Activity C reduces the schedule by two weeks at a cost of only $1,500 per week.
- Activity E is another possible candidate with a three-week reduction at a cost of $2,000 per week.
- Activity B, which has a crash cost of $4,500 per week and a reduction of only one week, is the worst candidate for crashing.
- The order in which the activities should be crashed is D, C, E, A, and B.
- The total number of weeks by which the project could be shortened if all of the activities on the critical path are crashed is 11 (45 - 34).
- The total additional cost if all activities on the critical path are crashed is $23,000 ($71,000 - $48,000).

Crash Cost Plotting Methods

Crash cost plotting methods are techniques for analyzing the crash costs by creating a graph or a visual representation that clearly illustrates those costs. With the X-axis showing the duration and the Y-axis showing the cost, the activities are plotted on the grid from right to left, starting with the activity with the lowest crash cost per week. Activities with flatter slopes are the activities with relatively larger time savings for the associated cost. These are the best candidates for crashing. Crashing may result in increased risk and rework; the project team needs to identify the point where it becomes impractical to crash the schedule any further.

Example: Presenting a Project's Crash Costs

In this example, the project manager plotted the crash costs against total project costs and total project duration in weeks. Notice that the crash cost plotting illustrates the activities that have greater savings of time and associated costs.

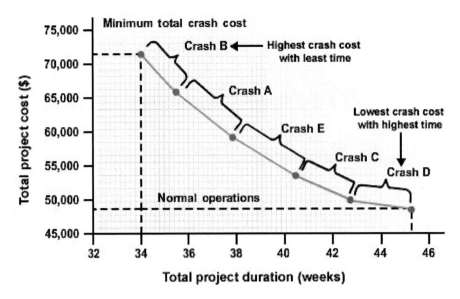

Figure 5-13: Plotting crash costs on a graph.

Delaying

Project resources may not always be available whenever required. *Delaying* is a project scheduling process where activities are postponed to accommodate the availability of resources. Delays may be caused by internal or external resources. The first resource on an activity that allows the activity to be delayed is the delaying resource.

Guidelines for Optimizing the Project Schedule

You can use the following guidelines to optimize and compress the project schedule:

- Consider your resource leveling options.
  - Can you pull needed resources from activities with float and apply them to critical activities?
  - Can you authorize overtime or comp time to meet your project requirements?
  - Is shift work possible?
  - Can an activity be contracted out to free up resources during a critical period?
- Consider fast-tracking the project.
  - Can any activities on the critical path be done concurrently that were originally scheduled sequentially?
  - Are there any discretionary dependencies that could be done completely independently?
  - Are there any increased costs associated with fast-tracking activities?
  - What are the associated risks?
- Analyze activities on the critical path to determine if crashing the schedule will produce a viable option.
  - Are there any activities on the critical path that can be shortened if more resources are added?
  - What are the costs associated with crashing those activities?
  - Which activities will provide the biggest duration decrease while incurring the least amount of incremental cost?
  - What are the resource allocation implications of crashing the activity? Will some key resources be overextended? Will all resources be available when needed?
  - Are there any quality implications associated with crashing the activities?
- Identify if any resources are overly allocated. Prioritize the project tasks the resources are responsible for and delay those tasks that can be performed later, to avoid over allocation.

- Analyze each activity on the critical path to determine whether reducing the scope is a viable option for reducing duration.
- Recalculate the critical path after compressing the schedule.
- Review any schedule changes with key stakeholders.
- Revise the schedule and distribute to the team.

TOPIC D

Create a Schedule Baseline

Now that you optimized the schedule, you need to create a schedule baseline in order to get management approval for your project schedule. In this topic, you will establish a schedule baseline.

As a project manager, it is your responsibility to get management approval for your project schedule so that you can begin your project on the right footing, setting the stage for proper monitoring and measuring of schedule performance throughout the life cycle of the project. The schedule baseline is the key mechanism for gaining that approval, and so your ability to generate the appropriate baseline will be critical to project success.

Schedule Baselines

A *schedule baseline* is the management-approved version of the project schedule; it is drawn from the schedule network analysis and includes baseline start and finish dates. It provides the basis for measuring and reporting schedule performance. It is a formal part of the project management plan.

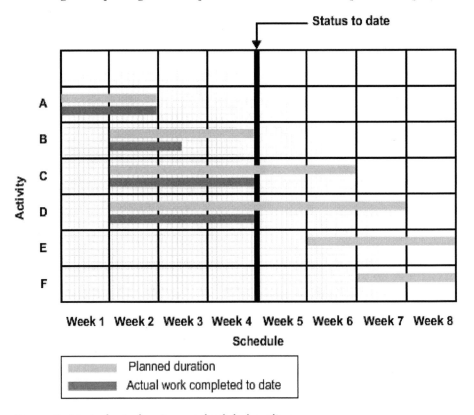

Figure 5-14: A chart showing a schedule baseline.

Example: Establishing the Schedule Baseline when Launching a New Line of Products

A cosmetics company is launching a new line of products. The project manager needs to establish a schedule baseline and secure approval from both company management and the group of stakeholders, which includes the company's sales and marketing teams. The project manager will begin by distributing the preliminary product rollout schedule along with resource calendars, cost estimates, and any related constraints. He will distribute the schedule to the appropriate parties for formal approval.

Before the team members give their approval, they will submit changes to the schedule; the project manager will be responsible for incorporating those changes. Making these changes will impact the cost baselines, and the project manager will need to follow the organization's formal change process and secure approval from management before continuing. Finally, the project manager will save the original schedule baseline and preserve the historical data related to this product launch.

Guidelines for Establishing a Schedule Baseline

Obtaining approval from the stakeholders for your project will be vital as you move through the project life cycle and monitor the schedule performance. By establishing a schedule baseline, you will further enhance the project's integrity by securing approval from the project management team and stakeholders. To establish the schedule baseline, follow these guidelines:

- Gather your preliminary project schedule, which includes the project's start and finish dates. Make sure that all of its components are accurate and up-to-date, including the resources, duration, calendars, predecessor dates, task dependencies, cost estimates, and constraints. Confirm that resources have not been overly allocated.
- Distribute the proposed schedule baseline to the appropriate stakeholders and project management team for approval. This approval is a formal requirement, and as such, it should be received in writing from the project sponsor.
- Incorporate any changes to the schedule baseline as required by the management team.
- Changes to your schedule baseline may require additional resources or more time; these changes will affect the project cost and will require you to update your cost baseline as well.
- Revisions made to the schedule baseline after it has been approved will need to be made through a formal change process approved by management.
- Save the original schedule baseline. During the life cycle of the project, changes will be made as the schedule baseline is updated and revised; you will need to preserve the historical data included in your original schedule baseline.

ACTIVITY 5–1
Developing the Project Schedule Review

Scenario

Answer the following review questions.

---

1. In your experience, which schedule format do you find to be the most beneficial and why?

2. When developing a project schedule, which element or component of the schedule do you find to be the most crucial?

Summary

In this lesson, you developed a project schedule by taking all of the constraints into consideration. You identified the critical path so you know which activities have scheduling flexibility when you are completing your project schedule.

6 | Planning Project Costs

Lesson Time: 1 hour, 30 minutes

Lesson Introduction

Good project management requires the ability to create accurate estimates regarding the costs of project completion. It also requires you to have a budgeting process that helps you monitor progress against expectations and work with the sponsor to make adjustments to the schedule or the scope as changes arise.

The ability to deliver projects on time and on budget is a key element of good project management. You want to be able to create accurate estimates regarding the work that must be done and the costs that will be incurred and monitor progress against expectations. By identifying methods for creating accurate cost estimates and budgets that will guide your projects, you can effectively meet expectations and deliver the desired results. In this lesson, you will plan project costs.

Lesson Objectives

In this lesson, you will:

- Estimate project costs.
- Estimate the cost baseline.
- Reconcile funding and costs.

TOPIC A

Estimate Project Costs

You developed the project schedules and determined the activities and resource requirements for your project. But how much will those activities cost? Estimating project costs will provide the answer. In this topic, you will estimate project costs.

High cost estimates may discourage sponsors from pursuing projects that have potential for success, while estimates that are too low can waste precious resources on a project that ultimately proves unfeasible. As a project manager, it is your responsibility to estimate project costs as accurately and realistically as possible. Mastering the techniques for estimating project costs will help you effectively control project costs.

Common Cost Estimate Types

The following table describes some of the common cost estimate types and their associated degrees of accuracy. The accuracy levels noted here are approximations rather than hard percentages.

Estimate Type	Description and Accuracy Rating
Rough Order of Magnitude (ROM) estimate	Developed without any detailed base data and often based on high-level historical data, expert judgment, or a costing model. ROM is generally made early in the project. **Accuracy:** -25 percent to +75 percent
Range of estimate	Often used as an alternative to ROM where the accuracy of the estimate is not well known. So, rather than $10M $\pm$30 percent, the estimate can be stated as $7M to $13M. **Accuracy:** $\pm$35 percent
Approximate estimate	Based on more information than ROM estimates, but still lacks the detail required for high accuracy. Approximate estimate may be possible if the project is similar to previous ones with reliable historical data for costing or where a proven costing model is applicable. **Accuracy:** $\pm$15 percent
Budgetary estimate	Often used for appropriation purposes. **Accuracy:** -10 percent to +25 percent
Definitive (or **control** or **detailed**) **estimate**	Based on detailed information about project work. Definitive estimate is developed by estimating the cost for each work package in the WBS. **Accuracy:** -5 percent to +10 percent
Phased (or **rolling wave** or **moving window**) **estimate**	Allows the use of ROM or approximate estimates for later parts of work, while work that must be done earlier in the project life cycle is estimated at the definitive level. **Accuracy:** $\pm$5 percent to $\pm$15 percent in the window closest to present time; $\pm$35 percent farther in the future

Project Management Estimating Software

Project management estimating software is any software application that assists in cost estimating while managing projects. This helps simplify the usage of cost estimating techniques and facilitates effective cost estimate alternatives.

 Note: Some examples of project management estimating software include Microsoft® Excel®, Microsoft® Project, and Oracle® Primavera.

Vendor Bid Analysis

Vendor bid analysis is a cost estimation technique based on the bids obtained from vendors. The proposed costing from vendors is considered while developing estimates for the project. Generally, a part of the project is outsourced to a vendor, so the costing for that outsourced part of the project can be sought from the vendors through their proposals, bids, or quotations. The costing can be indicative figures with less accuracy or very accurate detailed figures.

Example: The Solar Car Model Program

Consider the company that has taken on the design and launch of the new solar car model program. This can be further divided into several small projects for creating major components such as the engine, chassis, drive system, solar panels, exterior, and interior. These projects have a bigger objective and are interrelated to each other. The company decides to outsource the project that deals with the making of solar panels and allots $100,000 for that project. The project manager sends an invitation to vendors to obtain the best bids for the project. The costing suggested by the vendors helped the project manager to refine the cost estimates. Later, the company decided to select a bid that includes all the project deliverables and supports the final total project cost.

Activity Cost Estimates

Activity cost estimates provide estimates of costs necessary to finish project work. This includes costs on direct labor, materials, equipment, facilities, services, information technology, contingency reserves, and indirect costs. Cost estimates for each activity are added together to create an overall cost estimate for the work package.

Example: Estimate Project Costs for a Website Project

You are estimating the costs of the company website project with a budget of $100,000. Although you have rough estimates from some of the work package owners, it is early in the project life cycle. Therefore, you decide to use analogous estimation. After researching outsourcing costs and consulting several financial references, you apportion the money across major deliverables. After reviewing the individual estimates to make sure that they are assigned to the proper accounts, you submit your cost estimate and a list of assumptions.

Basis of Estimates

The basis of estimates involves supporting and additional information needed to justify cost estimates. Details can include the project scope, justification for the estimate, assumptions, constraints, confidence level on the estimate, and expected range of estimates.

Advantages and Disadvantages of Estimating Techniques

There are several benefits and drawbacks in using the analogous, bottom-up, and parametric estimating techniques.

Technique	Advantages	Disadvantages
Analogous estimating	Ensures that no work is inadvertently omitted from work estimates.	Can be sometimes difficult for less experienced managers to apportion cost estimates.
Bottom-up estimating	Accurate and gives lower level managers more responsibility.	Might be time consuming and can be used only after the WBS has been well-defined.
Parametric estimating	Not time consuming.	Might be inaccurate, depending on the integrity of the historical information used.

Guidelines for Estimating Project Costs

Accurately estimating project costs will avoid overruns and unforeseen expenditures. Making good cost estimates will help create a strong cost baseline, which will ultimately be used for measuring project cost performance. To develop accurate cost estimates, you can follow these guidelines:

1. Involve the work package owners.

    - When possible, the cost figures that go into the cost estimates for individual work packages should be provided by those who will actually provide the resources. As always, it is the people who will do the work, provide the service, or supply the material that can best estimate what the associated costs will be. It is the project manager's responsibility to compile these cost figures into realistic estimates.
    - For some projects, though, the project manager will be solely responsible for generating the cost estimates. This may be the case for:
        - Small projects in which the project manager is familiar with the activities required.
        - Projects with well-defined resource requirements.
        - Projects that are similar to past projects for which the costs are well documented.
    - Even in such cases, the project manager may want to do a quick reality check with the resource supplier to make sure that incorrect assumptions have not been made.

2. Gather any relevant input information, such as estimating publications and resource rates, that may help you prepare the estimates.

3. Determine which estimating technique to use.

    - Use analogous estimating when you have a limited amount of detailed information about the project, you have a similar project to use for comparison, and the work package owners preparing the estimates have the requisite expertise.
    - Use parametric estimating to estimate work packages when you have reliable parametric models and the work conforms closely to those models.
    - Use bottom-up estimating later in the project life cycle, when more detail is available about the work packages, you need more accurate estimates, and you have the time to invest in making the estimates. Also use bottom-up estimating for work packages with the highest level of uncertainty or risk associated with cost. Make sure that you weigh the additional accuracy provided by bottom-up estimating against the additional cost of making the estimates.
    - Use a combination of estimating techniques when you have a combination of circumstances for different deliverables on the WBS.

4. Look for alternative costing options. Some options you may explore can include:

    - Using stock components versus custom-made.
    - Stretching the duration of an activity to eliminate overtime charges.
    - Leasing versus purchasing of capital equipment.
    - Outsourcing as opposed to handling the work in-house.

5. Determine the units of measure that will be used.

- Estimates should all be in the same unit of measure (usually monetary).
- Units must be clearly defined and easily interpreted.

6. Consider possible risks that may impact cost.
7. Ensure that all cost estimates are assigned to the appropriate account, according to the chart of accounts, the accounting tool that maps to the accounting ledger.
8. Make sure that your cost estimates include the following key elements:

- Estimated costs for all resources that will be charged to the project. Use the WBS and resource requirements document to develop the estimates.
- The level of estimate (degree of certainty).
- A list of assumptions made when developing the estimates.
- How long the estimate will be valid.

TOPIC B

Estimate the Cost Baseline

After estimating project costs, you need to consolidate the costs into a project budget and prepare the project cost baseline. In this topic, you will estimate the cost baseline.

Costs are one of the major constraints of any project, and your ability to manage the project's costs will directly correlate to its success or defeat. You need to be able to employ sound methodology when estimating costs and carefully monitor expenditures throughout the project life cycle. In addition, you need to be able to track project costs associated with each work package in the WBS at the points in the project life cycle when those costs will be incurred. By establishing a cost baseline, you can track those project costs, set up the cash flow for the project, and measure cost performance.

Cost Baselines

A *cost baseline* is a time-phased budget that will monitor and measure cost performance throughout the project life cycle. It is developed by adding the estimated costs of project components by period. The cost baseline typically includes a budget contingency to accommodate the risk of incurring unidentifiable, but normally occurring costs, within the defined scope. Cost baselines will vary from project to project, depending on each project's unique budget and schedule.

 Note: Once the baseline is established, the cost becomes a commitment from the project manager's perspective. The project manager should try to closely match the project's committed funds to the baseline, from a timing perspective.

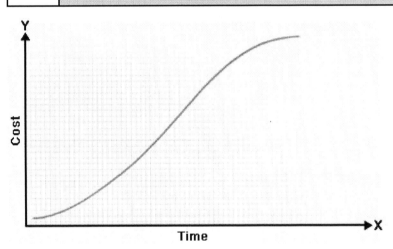

Figure 6-1: A generic cost baseline shown as an S-curve.

Example: Cost Performance Baseline

Many project management software packages can create an S-curve of the cost baseline for you; a generic example of a cost baseline displayed as an S-curve is shown here. Cost is plotted on the Y-axis and time on the X-axis. Developed by totaling the estimated project costs by period, this cost performance baseline shows how the cumulative planned project costs are distributed across the project's duration.

Cost Aggregation

Cost aggregation is a technique that is used to calculate the cost of a whole component by finding the aggregate cost of the constituent parts of the whole component. Activity costs are combined into work package costs, which are then aggregated up the WBS until a single project cost is produced. Cost estimation uses the cost aggregation method. You can aggregate the cost of all project components to determine the total cost of the project.

Contingency Allowances

Contingency allowances are additional funds that are sometimes built into cost estimates to allow for unanticipated events. Planning contingency allowances for a project ensures that the project manager is able to manage unforeseen costs and expenditures.

There are two types on contingency allowances. Contingency reserve is added at the activity level of the project by the project manager, to account for risks that might affect an activity; for example, an additional $1,000 for renting a piece of equipment for one more week than scheduled. Management reserve is added at the project level by the sponsor, to account for unknown-unknowns; for example, 5% would be added to the project for things that cannot be identified or envisioned.

When adding a contingency reserve to your budget:

- Avoid contingency on contingency. Based on the WBS input, make sure that the work packages do not already have a contingency amount tacked onto the basic estimate.
- As the project manager, you must release contingency funds only through a closely controlled and well-documented process, which is included in the cost management plan. A contingency reserve is not to be used as a slush fund without controls.

Example: Contingency Allowances for the Jazz Festival

Every year, the city of Montreal hosts the world's largest jazz festival with thousands of performances and more than two million attendees. Contingency reserves for this event might include funds to cover risks, such as a headlining act cancelling. Such a cancellation will force the festival to issue ticket refunds while incurring overhead costs, including theater rental and advertising. Contingency reserves will not be used for general operating support; for example, if ticket sales failed to meet expectations. A management reserve of 5% of the project budget might be added by the sponsor.

Cost Assignment Methods

Consider the way costs are assigned when establishing the baseline; this is important because the cost should be earned or tracked in the same way it is assigned.

Cost Assignment Method	Description
50/50 percent rule	50 percent credit is given when the activity begins and the remaining 50 percent credit is given when the work is completed. For example, if an activity is budgeted to cost $3,000, the activity will receive $1,500 when the work begins and the other $1,500 when the work is complete. This same method can vary in the percentage values. You can also use a 25/75 or 75/25 rule, for instance. Some of the variants to the 50/50 percent rule include 20/80 and the 0/100 rule.
Percentage complete rule	Completion percentages are estimated and assessed at specified reporting intervals. This is perhaps the most commonly used rule, and also generally considered to be the most accurate.

Cost Assignment Method	Description
Weighted milestones	The total work package value is divided up and assigned to milestone intervals within the work package. Each milestone carries a budgeted value. The value is earned when the milestone is achieved. This method works well for long work packages with multiple activities.

Note: There are certain activities that are not measurable; for example, research-based activities. It becomes difficult to account for earned values for such activities. So, to avoid the inability to measure an activity, use the 50/50 rule. The moment activity starts, 50% work completion credit is given to the activity. However, no further credit is given until the activity is complete.

Project Funding Requirements

Project funds are determined from the cost baseline and funding occurs in increments. These incremental amounts are not continuous but are done periodically, sometimes quarterly or annually, based on the project's funding requirements. The total amount of funds includes the cost baseline plus the management reserve. Project funding requirements help define the amount of funds required and when they are required. They also help optimize the funds' inflow to the project.

Historical Relationships

Historical relationships involve relationships that are used in parametric or analogous estimates to develop simple or complex mathematical models for calculating project costs. The cost and accuracy of the parametric and analogous estimates will vary widely. They can be relied upon when the historical information used is accurate, parameters used are quantifiable, and when the models are scalable.

Guidelines for Estimating the Cost Baseline

You can estimate a cost baseline to assist in the monitoring and measuring of cost performance throughout the project life cycle. You can use the following guidelines to estimate the cost baseline:

- Gather the inputs you will need to establish the baseline, such as the WBS, the project schedule, the cost estimates, and the risk management plan.
- Use the project schedule to determine when activities will be taking place.
- Using one of the methods for assigning costs, allocate funds for each activity or work package for the time period in which it will be taking place.
- Consider adding a contingency reserve to accommodate the risk of incurring extra expenses.
- Avoid adding contingency reserves for activities with low risk values.
- Total the costs for each time period.
- Plot the costs for each period on a chart to create an S-curve of the baseline.
- Publish and distribute the cost baseline to the appropriate project stakeholders.

TOPIC C

Reconcile Funding and Costs

Once costs are estimated, you need to verify that there is no discrepancy between the funding committed and the costs of the work to be done. You want to be able to reconcile the funding with the actual costs to make sure that your project stays on track. In this topic, you will identify methods of reconciling funding with costs.

Funding Limit Reconciliation

Funding limit reconciliation is a method of adjusting, spending, scheduling, and allocating resources in order to bring expenditures into alignment with budgetary constraints. Most budgets are created on the premise of steady incoming and outgoing flows. Large, sporadic expenditures are usually incompatible with organizational operations. Therefore, funding limits are often in place to regulate the outgoing capital flow and to protect against overspending.

Budgets must be reconciled with such limits. This will affect the scheduling of project work and possibly reshuffle WBS work packages entirely. The schedule, in turn, can affect the distribution or acquisition of resources.

Example: Set Funding Limits for Projects

Customers set funding limits for large projects based on internal considerations such as when their fiscal years begin and end and how healthy their cash flows are. A customer who wants to spread the costs of a project over two quarters may authorize $250,000 to be spent during Quarter 1 and $350,000 during Quarter 2. In response, the project manager will have to align the resources, schedules, and activities so that the project work does not exceed the limits on funding.

Guidelines for Reconciling Funding and Costs

Frequently, it is only at this point in a project, after you established a cost baseline, that funding deficiencies become apparent. It is your responsibility as a project manager to reconcile the costs with the funding that has been approved by the sponsor. To reconcile funding and costs, follow these guidelines:

- Gather the materials you will need, including:
  - The project budget and the schedule.
  - The project scope statement, which may contain information regarding funding constraints.
  - The cost estimation and activity cost estimates, so that you can monitor expenditures against estimates.
  - The WBS, so that you can monitor deliverables.
  - Contracts, so that you can monitor the commitments and requirements that must be met.
- Map the project budget, the scope statement, and the schedule to the funding available.
  - Make sure that the promised work and the promised funding are in alignment.
  - Review the project scope statement, making sure that the budget accounts for the funding constraints.
  - If there is already a clear disconnect between the work that has been promised and the funding that has been allocated, you must alert the sponsor now.
  - Identify alternatives. If funding deficiencies are apparent, look for suggestions of alternatives that the sponsor could agree to, which are typically a reduction in the scope, an increase in the budget, an extension of the schedule, or some combination of those.
- Involve the project sponsor.

- Reconciliation requires good communication. Now is the time to discuss funding limitations, expectations, changes to the project scope, and options for resource allocation and schedule revisions.
- Work with the sponsor on an ongoing basis from this point forward to adjust the project's scope, schedule, and cost to be in line with the funding that the sponsor is willing to formally commit.
- Make sure that the sponsor is apprised of changes in resource allocation that may affect deliverables.
- Partner formally with the company's financial decision makers.
  - Discuss the initial project overall cost validation and mapping of financial transactions for cash flow reasons.
  - Discuss the on-going monitoring of the project's financial performance to enhance the financial integrity of the project.
- Reconcile funding with costs on an iterative basis throughout the project. Many problems can be avoided through careful monitoring and adjusting resources in response to the changes that will arise.
- Actual costs may exceed the estimated costs during different time frames. Keep the sponsor (and the external customer, if there is one) apprised of any additional costs that are incurred.
- Monitor spending.
  - As work begins on the project, you will need to monitor expenditures both in terms of cash and in terms of effort, or hours of labor.
  - Monitor and document unexpected expenses as they arise, such as rework that may be required. Unexpected expenses will affect the budget and schedule and must be discussed with the sponsor.
- Monitor the schedule. As work begins on the project, it will be your responsibility to monitor the activities as they are completed or partially completed so that you can identify and adjust for delays before they derail the project.
- Monitor the risks that have been identified for your project. Alert the sponsor if those risks become reality, so that appropriate changes can be made to the scope or the schedule. Make sure that any risks that arise during reconciliation are reflected in an updated risk register.

ACTIVITY 6-1
Planning Project Costs Review

Scenario
Answer the following review questions.

1. How do you think the ability to effectively estimate costs will improve your performance on the job?

2. How do you think incorporating good funding reconciliation practices will help in completing a project within the allocated budget?

Summary

In this lesson, you identified methods of creating accurate cost estimates and the budgets that will guide all the work done on your projects so that you can effectively meet expectations and deliver the desired results. Delivering projects on time and on budget is the cornerstone of good project management.

7 | Planning Human Resources and Quality Management

Lesson Time: 1 hour, 45 minutes

Lesson Introduction

As you continue progressive elaboration of your project work, how you handle competing demands for time, resources, and quality can have a significant impact on the success of your project. One of the ways by which you can minimize potential resource conflicts, and misunderstood quality standards, is to enlist the support of project stakeholders, both internal and external, to help create effective quality and human resource plans. In this lesson, you will plan human resources and quality.

Lesson Objectives

In this lesson, you will:

- Create a human resource plan.

- Create a quality management plan.

TOPIC A

Create a Human Resource Plan

You developed the project schedule and schedule baselines. Now, you want to make sure that you acquire the right resources for your project, everyone working on the project knows what their roles and duties are, and those responsibilities are clearly articulated and documented. In this topic, you will create a human resource plan.

While managing a project, handling competing demands of human resources can have a significant impact on the success of the project. You can efficiently organize human resources in a project by acquiring appropriate resources, identifying and documenting the roles and responsibilities of each resource in the project, and coordinating and managing the team to execute the work according to the project plan.

Project Interfaces

Project interfaces are the various reporting relationships that occur internally or externally to a project. There are five types of project interfaces.

Interface	Description
Organizational	These are reporting relationships among different organizational units. They may be internal or external to the parent organization and include interfaces among the project team, upper management, other functional managers who support the team, and even the organization's customers.
Technical	These are reporting relationships among technical disciplines on the project that occur during a phase or during the transition between phases. They reflect informal and formal relationships with people on the project team and outside of the team.
Interpersonal	These are formal and informal reporting relationships among individuals working on the project, whether internally or externally.
Logistical	These are relationships between project team members who are distributed across different buildings, countries, and time zones.
Political	These are relationships inside an organization. Different people have different interests in the organization and its projects. Depending upon interpersonal dynamics and individual aspirations, people will try to satisfy their disclosed or undisclosed interest.

The RAM

The *Responsibility Assignment Matrix (RAM)* chart links key project stakeholders to specific project deliverables or activities by assigning responsibilities to each stakeholder for each element of work.

Some of the questions the RAM attempts to answer include:

- Who is accountable for the completion of a specific deliverable or activity?
- Who has sign-off authority on the deliverable or activity?
- Who must be notified of the completion?
- Who makes the acceptance or rejection decision?

Note: In a large or complex project, a matrix may be used to show the responsibilities for major deliverables only. A lower level matrix may be developed to show work package roles and responsibilities within each deliverable. Work package owners may develop a RAM that assigns responsibilities to each activity in the work package.

	Project Manager	Engineering Manager	Quality Assurance Manager	Purchasing Manager	Manufacturing Manager
Create Blueprints	S	A	P		p
Manufacture Circuit Board	S	A	P		P
Test Circuit Board	S	P	A		P
Order Components	S	P	P	A	P
Assemble	S		P		A

S = Sign-off   A = Accountable   P = Participant

Figure 7–1: A RAM links key project stakeholders to project deliverables.

In the RAM, the deliverables or activities are listed vertically with the key project stakeholder positions, titles, or names listed horizontally. Responsibility for each deliverable or activity is assigned to one of the stakeholders.

The RACI Chart

A *RACI chart* is a type of RAM that helps depict the level of responsibility for each project team member. RACI stands for Responsible, Accountable, Consulted, and Informed. The RACI matrix helps identify who is responsible for making decisions and how the people responsible are supported. RACI is generally used to provide clarity on the roles and responsibilities assigned to each project team member. The RACI chart is also called a RASI chart, where "S" stands for "Support."

	Project Manager	Engineering Manager	Quality Assurance Management	Purchasing Manager	Manufacturing Manager
Create Blueprints	A	R	C	I	C
Manufacture Circuit Board	I	C	C	I	A
Test Circuit Board	I	R	A	I	R
Order Components	C	C	I	A	I
Assemble	I	R	C	I	A

R = Responsible   A = Accountable   C = Consulted   I = Informed

Figure 7–2: A RACI chart.

Ownership

Ownership refers to a condition where everyone in the project claims to understand the assigned roles and responsibilities. A sense of ownership in employees can be achieved by clearly defining their roles and responsibilities and making them accountable for the tasks they are expected to do.

Example: The Corporate Intranet Project

You are the project manager for a corporate intranet project, and during the execution phase, the Software Tester, Daniel, fell ill and has taken a week off. To keep the project going without any hassles, you decide to bring in another Software Tester to replace Daniel. In the meantime, Gavin, from the Integration and Testing department, volunteers to take up Daniel's work. The roles and responsibilities defined by the management for the Integration and Testing personnel also involves software testing besides other responsibilities. You appreciate Gavin for his sense of responsibility and ownership of taking up the job of a Software Tester.

Networking

Networking is a technique that is used during human resource planning. It helps build an excellent rapport with the functional managers and other stakeholders, internal and external, to know their readiness, willingness, and bandwidth to provide resources. It also helps in understanding the interpersonal relationships among stakeholders. Efficient networking involves understanding the political and interpersonal factors in an organization that influence staffing management. Use of human resource network activities, such as proactive correspondence, informal conversations, luncheon meetings, and trade conferences, will help you obtain the best resources for the project team. Networking also enhances the professional project management practices of a project manager at different phases of a project.

Example: Reserving Resources Through Networking

You are the project manager for the business process project, and you report to the Director of the Project Management Office, Susan Long. This is an internal project intended to revolutionize work through business process re-engineering across all departments of the organization. You and Susan worked out the charter and are now focusing on the resources required to provide a high-level budget. You identified the functional areas from where you will need resources. You and Susan started interacting with the functional department heads. It is your rapport, which was built over a period of time, that helped you and Susan get connected with them. You asked them to earmark some resources, which you may require, and they agreed to do so.

Staffing Management Plans

A *staffing management plan* is part of the HR plan that forecasts what types of staff will work on a project, when they will be needed, how they will be recruited, and when they will be released from the project. Depending upon the project requirements, the staffing management plan may be formal or informal, exhaustive or brief. The plan is a subsidiary plan to the human resource plan and is an important input during the human resource planning process.

Example: Staffing Management Plans for Writing a Book

To coincide with a company's 100th anniversary, the CEO decided to document the company's growth and evolution. The staffing management plan for this project will stipulate external resources with expertise in writing, designing, printing, and publishing, but it will also include internal resources with specialized knowledge about the company history. The staffing management plan will identify who will be needed to help with the book, when they will be needed, what they will be expected to contribute, and how long they will be expected to participate.

Staffing Management Plan Components

Several components of the staffing management plan evolve as you develop the project plan.

Component	Description
Staff acquisition	When planning resources, consider whether you will use team members from within the organization or from external sources, the costs associated with the level of expertise required for the project, physical location of resources, and the amount of assistance that can be provided by other departments for the project management team.
Resource calendars	The staffing management plan details the time frame required for a project and for each project team member. Optimizing the use of resources on a project will help finish the project on time and within budget. Resource calendars identify the working days and times that each resource is available; they also include vacations and other periods when the resources cannot work on the project. Use of human resource charting tools, such as resource histograms, can help illustrate the number of hours that a person, department, or entire project team will need for each week or month over the course of the project.
Staff release plan	Developing a plan for releasing resources helps control project costs by using team members' expertise or skills as and when they are needed. Planning for staff release also allows a smooth transition to other projects and the mitigation of human resource risks that may occur during the final phases of the project.
Training needs	A training plan can be developed for team members who need to improve their competency levels or who may need to obtain certifications that will benefit the project.
Recognition and rewards	Creating incentives for meeting milestones or other project deliverables can have a positive effect on morale. An effective recognition plan rewards team members for meeting goals that are under their control.
Compliance	If the contract requires compliance with government regulation or other standards, this should be stipulated in the staffing management plan.
Safety	Projects where specific safety precautions must be taken, such as on construction sites or nuclear power plants, can have documented policies and procedures for the protection of team members. These procedures should also be documented in the risk register.

Example: The Human Resource Plan for a Construction Firm

The project manager, Charles, is working on a project team at a construction firm and starts creating a human resource plan. He decided to document the roles and reporting relationships of the project team members. Charles reviewed the staffing requirements of the project, which state that a senior foreman must oversee the primary labor force and should report directly to the assistant project manager.

Also, he reviewed the project constraints and identified that the plumbing subcontractor requires at least five full-time laborers for the duration of the project. The subcontractor must report to the union branch chief.

Charles identified all the key stakeholders on the project and created an organization chart. Using this information, he then created a RAM. He included all these details in the human resource plan and distributed it among the team members and stakeholders.

Guidelines for Creating a Human Resource Plan

A well-drafted human resource plan will help you analyze the skills of the existing workforce and forecast your resource needs to optimize the available resources and obtain the best results while executing the project. To create an effective human resource plan, follow these guidelines:

- Review the staffing requirements that were previously identified during resource planning, and the external relationship requirements with clients, consultants, and vendors.

  - Identify the required resources.
  - Determine the level of expertise required for resources.
  - Estimate the cost of resources.
  - Consider methods like networking for the acquisition of human resources. They can be sourced from within the organization, outside the organization, or both.
  - Obtain assistance from the human resource department of your organization for staff acquisition.

- Identify any constraints that may limit your organizational planning options.
- Address the organizational structure of the performing organization and how this affects the structure of the project team.
- Document the roles, responsibilities, and reporting relationships of the project personnel.

  - If necessary, incorporate required roles and reporting relationships from any contractual agreements with unions or other employee groups.
  - Consider the competencies of expected staff members and how they affect the project's reporting relationships or roles and responsibility assignments.
  - Ensure that all key project stakeholders with reporting relationships are indicated in a hierarchical format on the chart.
  - Assign roles and responsibilities to stakeholders who are directly involved with the project work rather than to senior managers or customers who have limited or indirect involvement.

- Create an organization chart to document the reporting relationships among your project team. Use any available template to create this chart.
- Analyze the formal and informal project interfaces that exist among the organizational units, technical disciplines, and individuals for their possible impact on your organizational planning.
- Create a Responsibility Assignment Matrix (RAM) to document the roles and responsibilities for key project stakeholders.

  - Create the RAM as early as possible in the project and update it responsively to reflect changes in personnel or project focus.
  - Account for each element of the project's scope in the RAM and provide a key to describe responsibility codes.

- As part of the human resource plan, create the staffing management plan that includes the following components: staff acquisition, resource calendars, staff release plan, training needs, recognition and rewards, compliance, and safety.
- Distribute the human resource plan to all project team members and other key project stakeholders.

TOPIC B

Create a Quality Management Plan

You now need to set standards and define parameters to assess project quality. Poor quality management is a major cause of project failure, and as a project manager it is your responsibility to ensure that your major deliverables are completed with an acceptable level of quality. In this topic, you will create a quality management plan.

What good is a project that is completed on time and within budget if the quality is inconsistent or even substandard? Clearly defining quality standards for project stakeholders ensures a common understanding of how project quality will be measured and achieved.

Quality

Quality is the "totality of features and characteristics of a product or service that bear on its ability to satisfy stated or implied needs." It is the degree to which the characteristics of a project fulfill its requirements. Remember that quality is inside the project management triangle; quality represents what the stakeholders expect from the project. The stated and implied quality needs are inputs for devising project requirements. In business, quality should be feasible, modifiable, and measurable. Quality is the key focus of project management.

 Note: This definition is provided by the International Organization for Standardization, ISO Standard 8402: Terms and Definitions.

The Quality Process

Quality management includes three stages: quality planning, quality assurance, and quality control.

Figure 7–3: The three stages in a quality process.

Stage	Description
Quality planning	Identifying the standards which apply to the project and deciding how to meet these standards, with a focus on establishing sponsor or customer requirements, designing products and services to meet those requirements, establishing quality goals, defining processes, and establishing controls to use in monitoring the processes.
Quality assurance	Evaluating overall project quality regularly and systematically during the execution process so that all stakeholders have confidence that the project will meet the identified quality standards and legal and regulatory standards. Quality assurance is prevention oriented.
Quality control	Evaluating specific quality results against quality standards and identifying ways to improve quality and eliminate causes of unsatisfactory quality. Quality assurance is conducted during the monitoring and controlling processes of the project.

Variables Affecting Quality

Throughout the life cycle of a project, there are a number of variables that could arise, affecting the quality of the deliverable. Some of those variables include:

- Cost associated with a particular problem.
- Time loss associated with a particular problem.
- Degree of hazard associated with a particular problem, such as health or safety.
- Pressure to get a product to market.
- Poor design.
- Unclear directions.
- Issues with vendors.
- Burned out team members.

TQM

Total Quality Management (TQM) is an approach to improve business results through an emphasis on customer satisfaction, employee development, and processes rather than on functions. TQM should be viewed as a long-term, ongoing process rather than a one-time event. The following table describes various TQM implementations by different quality theorists.

Theorist	Approach
W. Edwards Deming	The Deming cycle focuses on continuous process improvement in which quality must be continuously improved in order to meet customer needs.
Joseph M. Juran	The Juran trilogy breaks quality management into quality planning, control, and improvement. Quality improvement leads to breakthrough improvement, meaning improvement that raises the quality bar to an unprecedented level.
Philip Crosby	This method focuses on four absolutes: • Quality is conformance to requirements rather than a measure of how good a product or service is. • Quality is achieved by prevention rather than inspection. • Everyone in the company must work to a standard of zero defects. • Quality can be measured by determining the cost of quality.

Theorist	Approach
Genichi Taguchi	The Taguchi method emphasizes that quality should be designed into the product so that factors that cause variation can be identified and controlled.
William (Bill) Smith, Jr.	Six Sigma emphasizes responding to customer needs and improving processes by systematically removing defects. Originally developed by a Motorola, Inc. engineer named Bill Smith, Six Sigma is now closely associated with General Electric, Inc. and other major industrial companies such as Eastman Kodak.

 Note: As part of your quest to further your project management skills, you should consider investigating some of the major motivational and leadership theories that are a key part of serious project management efforts today. Many organizations are increasingly using project-based continuous improvement approaches; the work of W. Edwards Deming provided the foundation for this effort. Deming's 14 Points for Management, included in his book *The New Economics for Industry, Government, Education*, provides a systematic and pragmatic approach to transforming a western style of management in industry, education, or government to one of optimization. For further reading, see *Out of the Crisis* by W. Edwards Deming.

Standards and Regulations

Standards are voluntary guidelines or characteristics that have been approved by a recognized body of experts such as the International Organization for Standardization (ISO). In some cases, the standards body will provide certification that suppliers conform to the requirements of their standards. Often, the conformance to standards is a customer requirement.

Regulations are compliance-mandatory characteristics for specific products, services, or processes. Standards often start out as accepted or *de facto* best practices describing a preferred approach and may later become *de jure* regulations, such as using the Critical Path Method in scheduling major construction projects.

 Note: There are also de facto standards that aren't approved by a standards body. For example, TCP/IP is the de facto standard protocol for all modern computer networks. It is the approved standard for the Internet, but everyone uses it on private networks as well.

Example: Standards and Regulations in Toy Manufacturing

In the U.S., consumer-safety legislation governs the manufacturing of products, including toys. In 2007, a recall of millions of toys produced with lead-based paint compelled lawmakers to introduce stricter federal regulations with criminal penalties for noncompliance. But major U.S. toy retailers, in response to public demand, went further; they forced their suppliers to meet even tougher standards regarding lead in surface paint.

The ISO 9000 Series

The *ISO 9000 series* is a quality system standard that is applicable to any product, service, or process in the world. It was developed by the ISO, which is a consortium of approximately 100 of the world's industrial nations. There are limits to the certification, which does not guarantee that an organization will produce quality products or services; it simply confirms that appropriate systems are in place. Subsections of the standard address particular industries or products.

Project managers must be aware of the local, state, and federal laws that may directly or indirectly affect the project. Managers should ensure that the laws used at the workplace comply with both the federal and state guidelines.

Note: For more information about the ISO 9000 series, visit the ISO website at **www.iso.org**.

Cost of Quality

Cost of quality refers to the total cost of effort needed to achieve an acceptable level of quality in the project's product or service. These costs include all the work necessary to ensure conformance and all the work performed as a result of non-conformance to requirements.

The four types of cost associated with quality are prevention costs, appraisal costs, internal failure costs, and external failure costs. Prevention and appraisal costs are called *conformance costs*—amounts spent to avoid failures. Internal and external failure costs are called *non-conformance costs*—amounts spent to rectify errors.

Type of Cost	Description	Example
Prevention costs	Upfront costs of programs or processes needed to meet customer requirements or design in quality.	• Design plans • Quality plans • Employee and customer training • Process evaluations and improvements • Vendor surveys • Other related preventive activities
Appraisal costs	Costs associated with evaluating whether the programs or processes meet requirements.	• Inspections • Testing • Design reviews • Destructive testing loss
Internal failure costs	Costs associated with making the product or service acceptable to the customer after it fails internal testing and before it is delivered to the customer.	• Scrap or rejects • Design flaws • Rework or repair • Defect evaluation
External failure costs	Costs due to rejection of the product or service by the customer.	• Product returns • Liabilities • Evaluation of customer complaints • Maintenance costs • Corrective action • Loss of contract

Checklists

A *checklist* is a job aid that prompts employees to perform activities according to a consistent quality standard. Items on checklists are phrased as either imperatives, such as "Make sure that this file is saved correctly," or questions, such as "Does this image match the description in the database?" Checklists can be simple or complex and may range in detail, depending on the experience and skill level of the employees and the complexity of the situation.

Example: An Image Quality Checklist

A sample checklist for printing images is shown. Note that the checklist prompts the graphic artist to create images according to a consistent quality standard. The items on the list are phrased as interrogatives. If the artist cannot answer all the questions in the affirmative, the image should not be handed off.

Obtain a printout of the image specifications from the graphics database. Use this checklist to ensure that the images are ready to be handed off to the programmer.

#	Item	Yes	No
1	Does the image match the description in the database?	☐	☐
2	Does the style meet the specifications set for the course or lesson?	☐	☐
3	Does the quality of the image meet the standards set for the course?	☐	☐
4	Is the image size correct?	☐	☐
5	Is the image named correctly?	☐	☐
6	Is the border on the image correct?	☐	☐
7	Is the image placed in the correct palette?	☐	☐
8	Is the opacity correct (transparent or opaque)?	☐	☐
9	Is the bit-depth correct?	☐	☐
10	Is the resolution correct?	☐	☐
11	Does it have the correct extension?	☐	☐
12	Have all stray pixels been cleaned up?	☐	☐

Figure 7–4: A sample checklist.

Flowcharts

A *flowchart* is a diagram that shows the relationships of various elements in a system or process. Flowcharting techniques can assist the team's efforts in identifying potential quality problems and the possible effects of those problems. The two most widely used flowcharting techniques are:

- Process (or system) flowcharts
- Cause-and-effect diagrams

Process Flowcharts

A *process flowchart*, a process diagram, or *system flowchart* shows the sequence of events and the flow of inputs and outputs between elements in a process or system. There is a definite beginning and end along with decision points clearly called out with the actions to be taken, based on the result of each decision.

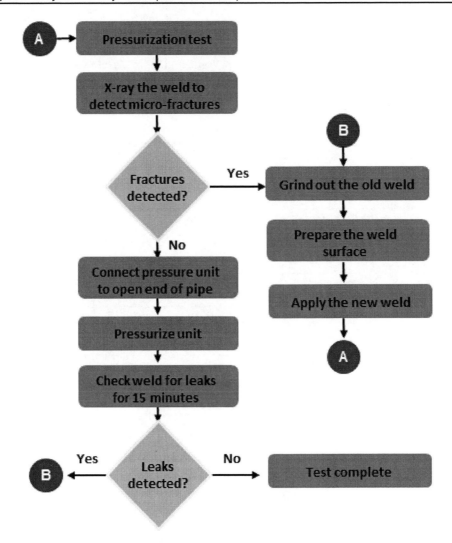

Figure 7–5: A sample process flowchart.

Cause–and–Effect Diagrams

- A *cause-and-effect diagram* is a type of flowchart organized by category. The cause-and-effect diagram provides a structured method to identify and analyze potential causes of problems in a process or system. This method organizes potential causes of problems into defined categories. Using these defined categories promotes the identification of potential causes.
- Some common categories include, but are not limited to:
    - Material
    - Method
    - Environment
    - Personnel
    - Measurement
    - Energy

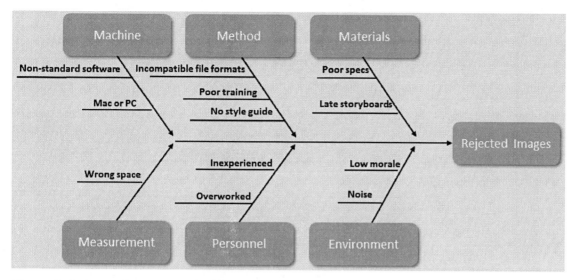

Figure 7-6: A sample cause-and-effect diagram.

 Note: The cause-and-effect diagram is also called the Ishikawa diagram (named after its creator, Kaoru Ishikawa of Japan) or the fishbone diagram (named for its shape).

Control Charts

Control charts are graphs that are used to analyze and communicate the variability of a process or project activity over time. Control charts help show the potential capability of the process and also suggest the range of variability in the process. This range of variability can assist a project manager in determining if the variance is caused by common or assignable sources. If the process variability fluctuates around the *average*, or statistical mean, the process shows very little variability and is said to be stable.

The components of a control chart include the process mean, the *Upper Control Limit (UCL)*, and the *Lower Control Limit (LCL)*. The process mean is determined by taking samples from the actual process and calculating the statistical mean. As additional samples are taken and tested, they are evaluated in terms of standard deviations from the process mean. For most repetitive processes, the UCL will be three standard deviations above the mean, while the LCL will be three standard deviations below the mean.

Control charts have measurements that indicate instability because they each have measurements that exceed the range between the UCL and LCL. Analysis of the first chart shown is that there are more than seven consecutive points above the mean. In the second chart, more than seven consecutive points are below the mean. This seven-point variance is called the *seven-run rule*. Run rules are used to indicate situations that are out-of-statistical control. When seven or more consecutive points lie on one side of the mean, it indicates that there should be a shift in the mean.

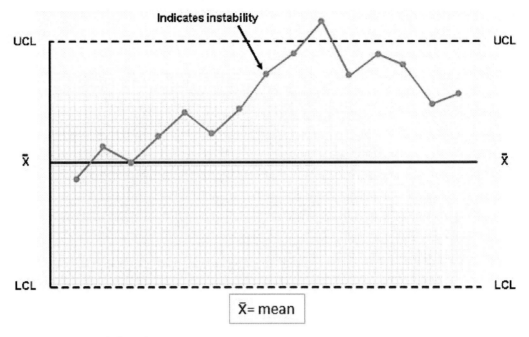

Figure 7-7: Variability above UCL.

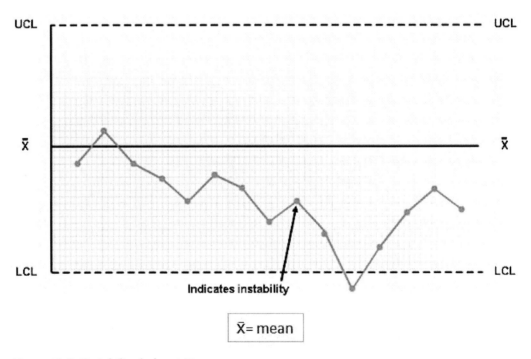

Figure 7-8: Variability below LCL.

Benchmarking

Benchmarking addresses the evaluation of a group's business or project practices in comparison to those of other groups. It is used to identify the best practices in order to meet or exceed them. Benchmarking can be conducted between identical processes in a variety of ways: in similar or dissimilar industries and with internal or external organizational areas.

Benchmarking is commonly used to determine:

*   The products or services to offer and the features that should be included.
*   The processes used by other groups to achieve customer satisfaction.

- The metrics or goals used to measure the processes or products that achieve customer satisfaction.

Example: Benchmarking the Espresso-Based Beverages

Twenty percent of Americans drink espresso-based beverages every day, and the multi-billion dollar premium coffee market is expected to grow significantly in the next several years. Several leading fast-food retailers benchmarked the performance of Seattle-based Starbucks Corp., the world's largest chain of coffee houses. McDonald's, Dunkin' Donuts, and Tim Horton's expanded their menus of premium coffees to compete in this arena and offer similar, high-quality coffee products.

DOE

Design of Experiments (DOE) is a technique that is used to systematically identify varying levels of independent variables. DOE can determine:

- Which variable has the greatest effect.
- What the relationship is between each variable and the customer-focused quality specifications.
- What the best value is for each variable, to ensure optimal quality or value.

When done properly, DOE can result in significant improvements to products and processes, including shorter development cycles, more robust products, and cost reductions.

Example: DOE for Producing a New Style of Jars

A cannery was about to bring forth a new style of jar into production. As development of the packaging moved forward, questions arose regarding the ability of the in-line capper to deliver the precise amount of torque when rotating the lid onto the new jar. Early testing demonstrated that lid torque less than three inch pounds will result in a leaky package. Torque greater than eight inch pounds will mar the finish on the screw-on lid.

Given the task of determining the optimum torque requirement for the new packaging, the project team used a DOE software program to generate statistical information about how torque was affected by other interconnected factors. Two of the factors tested were spindle speed and conveyor speed. The results indicated that these speeds had the greatest effect on lid torque.

Armed with this information, it was a simple exercise in determining adjustments to these settings that will result in consistent optimum torque. The experiment employed by the project team was successful because it was able to identify the variable that had the greatest effect and its relationship to the quality specification of lid torque.

Quality Metrics

Quality metrics is an actual value that describes the measurements for the quality control process. It determines which elements of the project are going to be measured, how they will be measured, and how they are factored into the project. Some examples of quality metrics include timely performance, budget control, defect density, reliability, rate of failure, and test coverage.

Example: Quality Metrics for a Cellphone Company

One of the leading cellphone manufacturers defined their quality policy for software development. They mentioned a few measurement areas in their quality policy, which included:

- Delivered defects per size
- Total effectiveness throughout the process
- Schedule adherence
- Accuracy of estimates
- Number of open customer problems
- Time that problems remain open
- Cost of non-conformance

- Software reliability

Process Improvement Planning

Process improvement planning is the process of analyzing and identifying areas of improvement in project processes and enumerating an action plan based on the project goals and identified issues. The process involves:

- Describing operational theories and project roles and responsibilities.
- Identifying long- and short-term goals.
- Describing process improvement objectives and activities.
- Identifying risks and resource requirements.
- Determining process improvement activities.
- Creating a process improvement plan.
- Receiving approval from stakeholders and senior managers.
- Executing the process improvement plan.

Example: The Quality Management Plan

A project team is given the task of creating a quality management plan. The team discovers that the company has an adequate quality policy. However, it does not address potential problems. The team assigns roles and responsibilities to the individuals responsible for project quality and includes a project quality assurance coordinator.

The team reviews the baseline performance requirements and customer-requested quality requirements. They ascertain that a cost-effective quality trade-off will be to repeat the design process and peer plan reviews. Finally, the organization's quality manual is referenced in regard to approved approaches to each relevant quality assurance and control item, including specifications, change control, checking criteria, and control logs.

Guidelines for Creating a Quality Management Plan

Creating a quality management plan will ensure that the organizational structure, responsibilities, procedures, processes, and resources are in place to implement quality management. To create an appropriate quality management plan, follow these guidelines:

- Collect the documents required to create a quality management plan.

  - The project management plan
  - The scope baseline that includes the scope statement, the WBS, and the WBS dictionary
  - The stakeholder register
  - The cost performance baseline
  - The schedule baseline
  - The risk register
  - Any regulations, rules, standards, guidelines, and operating conditions that may affect the application area
  - Quality policies, procedures, guidelines, and historical information
- Review the organization's quality policy and determine how your project team will implement the policy.

  - How will your team identify potential quality problems and their impact on the quality of the project's product, service, systems, or processes? Will you use particular flowcharting methods, benchmarking, design of experiments, or other techniques?
  - Are there any standards and regulations that are applicable to your project?
  - Are there any activities or components that require the development of operational definitions to provide a common understanding of the project's quality standards? If so, who is responsible for developing them?

- Does your organization have any standard checklists that can be modified, or used as is, to prompt employees to perform certain activities according to a specific quality standard? If not, should checklists be developed? Who is responsible for developing them? What are the conditions under which they should be developed?
- Review the product description to identify customer or stakeholder quality requirements.
- Identify the variables affecting the quality of the deliverable.
- Determine the cost of quality trade-offs.
  - How will your team define quality to avoid expensive rework?
  - Are the proposed processes and systems worth the cost of implementing them?
- Review the quality management plan and make sure that it:
  - Describes the project management team's approach to implementing its quality policy (quality assurance, quality control, and quality improvement approaches).
  - Describes the resources required to implement quality management.
  - Includes quality management roles and responsibilities for the project.
  - Is as detailed and formal as required, based on the quality needs of the project.
  - Includes how customer satisfaction will be measured and managed.

ACTIVITY 7-1

Planning Human Resources and Quality Management Review

Scenario

Answer the following review questions.

1. Which components will you include while creating a staffing management plan in your organization?

2. What is the purpose of a quality management plan in your organization?

Summary

In this lesson, you identified project team interactions, and quality standards and metrics for measuring quality performance. These steps help in creating a necessary framework to effectively plan for project staffing and quality management.

8 | Communicating During the Project

Lesson Time: 1 hour, 30 minutes

Lesson Introduction

One of the most important skills in project management is the ability to communicate efficiently and effectively with all of the project stakeholders during the project. As a project manager, up to 90% of your time might be spent communicating about the project. Therefore, it's critical that you have a strategy for effective communication. In this lesson, you will examine communication techniques and develop a communications plan.

Lesson Objectives

In this lesson, you will:

- Identify communication methods and factors that influence communication.

- Create a communications management plan.

TOPIC A

Identify Communication Methods

It's important to identify the different communication methods that are available and to know when one method might be more appropriate than another. Additionally, communication technologies are continuously changing so it's important to stay informed about what is available. As the project manager, you will also need to be aware of the many factors that can influence the team's communication among themselves and with other stakeholders.

Communication Methods

Communication methods are techniques that are used to share and manage information among stakeholders in a project. They help the team communicate project performance and progress. These ensure that the concerned people in the issue resolution process are aware of the impending severity of the issue, which enables them to take immediate action. Communication methods are specified in the communications management plan.

Communication methods can be broadly classified into three types:

- **Interactive communication:** Involves communication between multiple people performing multi-directional information exchange.
- **Push communication:** Involves sending information to a receiver. It ensures that the information has been distributed but does not guarantee that it has reached the receiver.
- **Pull communication:** Involves receivers accessing information whenever required.

Communication Types

The communication medium and type that you choose will depend on who is communicating, what type of message is being communicated, and how much feedback (verbal or non-verbal) the speaker wants or needs. Common examples of communication types include, but are not limited to, the following.

Type	Benefits	Constraints
Face-to-face meetings	• Provides the opportunity for instant feedback—auditory and visual. • Can immediately clarify if there are questions or confusion. • Can be scheduled or impromptu.	• Requires parties to be in the same physical location. • Requires a meeting date and time.
Video and voice conferencing (virtual meetings)	• Eliminates the need to be in the same physical location. • Can provide beneficial audio and visual feedback. • Can be scheduled or impromptu.	• Potential for message to get lost in translation. • Crossing time zones can be problematic. • Requires special equipment and connection.

Type	Benefits	Constraints
Email	• Enables parties to communicate when it's convenient and works with their schedules. • Can provide an official paper trail. • Enables receiver to have a record of communication.	• Not always the most timely. • Security/hacking might be an issue for confidential messages.
Fax	• Convenient and easy to send. • Software enables you to send a fax from your computer.	• Equipment and connection required. • Outdated form of communication that not all offices have set up.
IM—Instant Messaging	• Immediate real-time communication. • Can be setup and configured by an organization (i.e., Skype for Business).	• Message content can be limited. • Informal nature might be seen as "unofficial."
Text messaging	• Immediate communication. • Available and accessible to anyone with a mobile device.	• Requires a mobile device and app. • Limited to short bursts of communication.
Printed media and documents	• Provide official documentation and legal archives. • Gives a sense of legitimacy to the message.	• Costly to produce. • Is a permanent record of the communication, which can be a disadvantage in some situations.
Social media	• Low-overhead method of broadcasting a message. • Specialized method to communicate with a specific demographic.	• Communication can tend to be one-way. • Limited amount of feedback.
Company website	• Enables consistent, dynamic communication to broad base of recipients. • Reduces the geographic location factor.	• Requires personnel to manage and update. • Two-way communication is not real-time and feedback can be limited.

Communication Model

Communication models determine how information must flow from the sender to the receiver. The major components of the communication model include the sender, the receiver, and the message. The communication model must be considered when planning for project communications. During the communication process, it is the responsibility of the sender to send information that is clear and complete so that the receiver receives the information correctly and understands it properly. The receiver is responsible for confirming that the information from the sender has been received, verifying the completeness of the message, and ensuring it has been understood properly. The project can be negatively impacted if the communication between the sender and receiver fails.

Communication Technology Considerations

Communication technology is any type of technology that is used for communicating information, including websites, email, instant messaging, phones, and video conferencing. Some technologies are instantaneous, while others take time; some are interactive, while others are one-way only. Some provide a historical record of what was communicated, while others are transient.

Questions to ask when determining communications technology for each type of communication are:

- How quickly must the information reach the audience?
- Is there likely to be feedback from the communication? How will it be collected and integrated?
- Must there be a record of the communication? What type of record is required?
- What technologies are available for transmitting the given communication? Are they appropriate to the type and value of the communication?
- What technology will the audience need to receive the communication? Is it likely that the receiving technology is in place? If not, how expensive is it?
- Are there technical difficulties or learning curve issues with communicating via the technology?
- Are there access issues, such as security-protected sites, which could limit the number of audience members who could receive the communication?
- What types of archival technology will be used to store the communication? Where will the communication be stored? Are there compatibility or access issues that must be addressed?
- Is the particular mode of technology (transmittal, storage, or reception) likely to become outdated before the project is completed?
- What is the relative cost of each technology, taking into account the number of communication channels and number of members who must receive the communication?
- Consider any relevant global communication issues that may affect your project; how will they influence your choice of the most appropriate technology?

Communication Method Considerations

There are many factors that can influence the project team's communication methods and their effectiveness. Although it's tempting to try to control the factors, as the project manager, the key is having an awareness of the factors and knowing which communication will work best in each situation.

Factor	Description
Language barriers	When stakeholders span across countries, language can be one of the biggest barriers to effective communication. You must strive to find a common language or provide translators and interpreters who can ensure that the message is sent and received clearly. When language is a potential barrier, you might choose to use written or printed material that can be translated rather than spoken words that can be misinterpreted or misunderstood.
Geographical factors	When team members are scattered across time zones or global hemispheres, the time zone difference can affect the timely delivery of messages. It's important to consider the message's destination when choosing how and when you will communicate. Voice and video conferencing can help to bridge the geographical gap, but be careful to avoid meeting when someone should be sleeping.
Technological	Having the appropriate technological resources will be important for everyone on the project team to be able to send and receive clear messages. Something as simple as making sure everyone has functioning speakers with little or no static can help to make your video calls go more smoothly.
Cultural	When different cultures are involved, it's important that the communication method be inclusive and take any cultural beliefs into consideration.

Factor	Description
Inter-organizational	The method of communication between two or more organizations might be dictated in an official organization procedures manual, but most likely, it will depend on the parties involved, what needs to be communicated, how frequently the communication needs to happen, and so on.
Intraorganizational	Within an organization, the communication methods and channels are probably well-defined; however, having an understanding of the most effective methods will be invaluable in conveying the message.
Personal preferences	Some team members might have a preference for email while others appreciate a phone call. Knowing the individual preferences can help you choose the best communication method.
Rapport/relationship building	When the goal of communication is to build rapport or relationships, a personal touch is often more effective. A phone call or a personal email can be more persuasive than a mass email.
Message content	Some messages won't be easy to deliver because they contain news that the receiver does not want to hear. In that case, you need to be ready for the variety of reactions to how the message is received. While it might be tempting to avoid conveying bad, or undesirable, news in person, that might be the best method to get your message across. Using a personal touch might provide the support that the receiver needs to actually hear the message.
Criticality	For project messages that are of the highest importance and critical to the success of the project, you will want to ensure that your communication method is appropriate.
Stakeholder requirements	Documentation for official tracking and monitoring purposes might be the driving force for the chosen communication method.

TOPIC B

Create a Communications Management Plan

Now that you are aware of the different communication methods and technologies available, you need to create a strategy or plan for the best way to communicate with your project team and other stakeholders. In this topic, you will create a communications management plan to ensure effective communication.

Communications Management Plan

An effective communications management plan ensures that the right people receive the right information in the most appropriate format at the right time. Efficient communication means that the right amount of information and level of detail is given at the right time. You don't want your resources expending unnecessary energy reporting on details that are not required at that time. Nor do you want to spend hours generating unnecessarily long reports. Mastering the techniques to develop an effective communications management plan will ensure that you deliver significant information to stakeholders when they need it.

As a project manager, your communication plan needs to identify the audience (who), the types of information they should receive (what), the frequency (when), and the communication method and technology (how) that will be used. The plan can be in a table or spreadsheet format as shown in the following example.

Stakeholder	Message	Method/Format	Frequency	Responsible
Sponsor	Status report	Written document providing quick reference on project issues.	Weekly or Monthly	Project Manager
Customer	Project plan	Formal plan document	At beginning of the project	Project Manager
End-user	Results of the project	Training via class or one-on-one	At the end of the project	Assigned trainer
Team	Collecting project data	Web-based database	As needed	Team members
Team	Project issues	Team meetings	As needed	Project coordinator
Team	Progress reports	Informal written documents	Weekly	Project Manager

Example: Creating a Communications Management Plan for a New Project

You are working on a project for a multinational company. Communication for this project has been particularly difficult, with members missing vast amounts of information being generated or acting on misinformation. These errors cost thousands of dollars in lost work hours. You discovered that the problem is due to the geographic dispersal of team members and the irregular schedules of several stakeholders.

Based on these considerations, you determined that the communications management plan will use a web-based template that allows deployed staff to submit their information to a uniform database. To facilitate information collection and dissemination, you determine that an online form will categorize the data while the online program organizes the data and automatically prepares reports in email format that are delivered on a schedule, based on the needs of all stakeholders. You integrate all the information in the communications management plan and provide copies to all project stakeholders.

Stakeholder Communication Requirements Analysis

Communication requirements are the project stakeholders' documented communication needs. They include relevant information that contributes to the success of a project and analysis of cost, time, and logistics. Not all stakeholders will require the same amount, level, or timeliness of communication. The variances must be factored into the communication requirements.

Communication requirements analysis is an investigation that leads to a clear articulation of the stakeholders' communication needs and helps the project manager make effective choices regarding the technologies to be recommended in the communications management plan. It should also address special communication needs, such as time zones, communication preferences, functional or hierarchical barriers, language barriers, technological barriers, and cultural differences, when working with remote teams or team members.

This analysis should take the form of a grid, questionnaire, or survey that documents the communication and technology requirements for each stakeholder. It will also enable the project manager to obtain buy-in from stakeholders and shape their perceptions by providing the right information at the right time.

A project manager conducting communication requirements analysis may survey stakeholders regarding their communication needs by asking some basic questions, such as:

- How often will you like to receive status reports?
- How will you prefer to receive information: by phone, by email, or in face-to-face meetings?
- What level of detail are you expecting?

Issues of appropriateness, level of detail, timeliness, and cost should be considered in addition to the preferences and technology capabilities of stakeholders.

Communication Channels Calculation

Project managers need to identify the number of communication channels, or paths, which will indicate the complexity of the project's communication. The number of channels, or the number of ways that a team can communicate, is identified with the formula:

```
(n(n - 1)) / 2
where n = number of stakeholders
For example: 12 stakeholders: (12 x 11) / 2 = 66 communication channels
```

The relevance of this relationship becomes apparent when we recognize that the number of channels also represents the number of ways that we can miscommunicate—66 potential ways for a group of 12 stakeholders.

Communication Triggers, Target Audience, and Rationale

The following table describes the types of events that can trigger the need for communication from the project manager, identifies the target audience, and provides a rationale.

Trigger	Target Audience	Rationale
Audits	Project team	Timeframe of audit
Project planning	Project sponsor, client	Impact on project planning documents
Project change	Project team	Impact on schedule, cost, or risk

Trigger	Target Audience	Rationale
Risk register updates	Project sponsor, project team	Impact on schedule or cost
Milestones	Project sponsor, client	Milestone reporting requirement
Schedule changes	Project sponsor, functional managers, client	Impact on schedule, cost, or risk
Task initiation/completion	Project team	Impact on upcoming tasks
Stakeholder changes	Project team, affected stakeholders	Impact on schedule, cost, or risk
Gate reviews	Project team	Reporting requirement
Business continuity response	Project team, project sponsor	Impact on project
Incident response	Project team	Impact on schedule, cost, or risk
Resource changes	Functional managers, project team	Impact on schedule, cost, or risk

Situational Communication Responses

Certain situations require specific responses on the part of the project manager, as described here.

- **Personality conflicts between team members.** Meet with the two team members separately and try to understand their individual issues and concerns. Then meet with them together to discuss and resolve the differences.
- **The project is significantly behind schedule.** Discuss the issue with the sponsor.
- **Minor organizational changes have occurred.** Discuss the issue with the project team during the team's regular meeting.
- **An important milestone has been successfully completed.** Notify the sponsor and senior management of the achievement.
- **A team member leaves the organization.** Discuss the team member's exit and its effect on the project during the team's regular meeting.
- **A team member passed away unexpectedly.** Immediately hold an emergency meeting with the project team to discuss its effect on the project.
- **The main vendor is unresponsive.** First meet with the vendor and review the contract requirements and deliverables. Immediately following that, the sponsor should be notified. In order to protect your legal standing, document your objections to the vendor in writing.
- **Significant budget cuts have occurred.** Call an emergency meeting of your project team and announce the change and how it's going to affect the scope, project, and resources needed for the project. If required, also meet with the vendor and negotiate new contract terms.

Guidelines for Creating a Communications Management Plan

Effective communications management plans ensure that all project team members are aware of the type and format of information shared with project stakeholders for the success of the project. To create an effective communications management plan, follow these guidelines:

- Gather and distribute contact information for all involved parties.
- Determine the communication needs of project stakeholders.
  - Work from an organization chart to avoid omitting a key stakeholder.
  - Ask for your project sponsor's input.
  - Ask open-ended questions.

- As a rule of thumb, project team members require more detail on a more frequent basis. Senior management typically requires summary information on a less frequent basis.
- Analyze the value to the project of providing information.
- Evaluate any constraints and assumptions to determine their possible impact on communications planning.
- Determine the appropriate communication technologies to use for communicating project information.
    - Determine the immediacy of the need for information.
    - Analyze the availability of technology systems.
    - Evaluate the expected project staff to identify their knowledge of and access to proposed technology.
    - Conduct research to determine the likelihood that there will be changes to the proposed technology before the project is over.
- Make sure that your communications management plan includes all key elements:
    - A description of the type of information required for each project stakeholder.
    - A collection and filing structure that describes the methods the project team will use to collect and file project information.
    - A distribution structure describing to whom and by whom project information, such as status reports, data schedules, and meeting minutes, should be provided.
    - The methods that will be used to distribute the various types of information.
    - Schedules for the production of each type of communication.
    - Methods for accessing information between scheduled communications.
    - A method for updating and refining the communications management plan throughout the project life cycle.
    - Identify the functional or hierarchical barriers, language barriers, technology barriers, and any cultural differences in the project and document them in the communications management plan.
- Integrate the communications management plan into the overall project plan.
- Distribute the plan to project stakeholders.

ACTIVITY 8-1
Communicating During the Project Review

Scenario

Answer the following review questions.

1. In your experience, which communication methods did you find to be the most effective? Which methods were the least effective?

2. Share a situation when you were required to communicate a difficult message about the project to its sponsor or a top-level executive. What approach and communication method did you take?

Summary

In this lesson, you identified the importance of developing a communications management plan to ensure that everyone on the project team understands the strategy for communicating the project's progress. As the project manager, you must facilitate and demonstrate efficient and effective communication throughout the life of the project.

9 | Planning for Risk

Lesson Time: 3 hours

Lesson Introduction

You have created several important components of a sound project management plan, including plans for managing the schedule, cost, quality, and communication. Unexpected events can upset your work plan or bring your project to a screeching halt. Experienced project managers take steps to plan how to manage potential risks to projects. Risk analysis and planning allow you to be proactive, identifying and circumventing potential issues, rather than scrambling to respond to problems. Your risk management plan will help identify and neutralize risks before they can affect the project. In this lesson, you will develop a risk management plan so that you can identify and respond to the risks to your project.

Lesson Objectives

In this lesson, you will:

- Create a risk management plan.

- Identify project risks and triggers.

- Perform qualitative risk analysis.

- Perform quantitative risk analysis.

- Develop a risk response plan.

TOPIC A

Create a Risk Management Plan

All projects carry risks. As a project manager, it is your responsibility to conduct effective risk management planning to proactively respond to any potential issues. In this topic, you will plan and execute risk management activities and examine a risk management plan.

Project management carries with it inherent risk that things can go differently than you had hoped or planned. Deciding how to approach and plan for project risks early in the planning phase can help you maximize opportunities in positive risks and minimize the consequences of adverse risks that may occur during the life of your project.

Risk

A *risk* is an uncertain event that may have either a positive or negative effect on the project. Its primary components are a measure of probability that a risk will occur and the impact of the risk on a project. Some common ways to classify risk are effect-based classification, source-based classification, and level of uncertainty.

Example: Weather Risks

Due to its relative unpredictability, the weather is a risk common to business. An organization planning an outdoor festival will likely choose a location and day with the highest probability for agreeable weather. In this scenario, the threat of rain is a risk that could seriously affect attendance and revenue. Because the weather is known to be a possible risk but its impact is yet unknown, this risk will be classified as known-unknown.

Negative Risks

Negative risks are risks that have a negative impact on the project. These can also be referred to as *threats*. Project managers strive to prevent these risks from occurring or reduce their impact.

Example: Negative Risk in a Project

Because a competitor introduced a new and improved product, the demand for the existing product may decrease; therefore, the revenue will be impacted.

Positive Risks

Positive risks are risks that when taken, produce a positive project outcome. These can also be referred to as *opportunities*.

Example: Positive Risk in a Project

An example of positive risk is the increase in market demand and revenue for a product due to effective marketing strategies and need for the product.

Effect-Based Risk Classification

Effect-based risk classification is a method of analyzing the way that risks to a project could impact its success. A risk can have an effect on time, cost, quality, and scope. All these effects are interrelated; therefore, any changes to one element will affect all the others.

A project manager may choose to use effect-based risk classification for a complex project in which many of the risk factors are interrelated, such as a large-scale corporate endeavor or initiative in which many departments, teams, and external resources are participating. Any one department's failure to produce will impact on the rest of the project.

Source-Based Risk Classification

Source-based risk classification is a method of analyzing risk in terms of its origins. Sources may be internal or external to the project, and technical, nontechnical, industry-specific, or generic.

For a project requiring internal and external resources, such as an advertising campaign, a project manager may classify the risks in terms of where they originate. One source of risk could be the potential rise in the price of advertising time on network television, which could affect cost and scope. Another source of risk could be the failure of an external advertising agency to meet its deadlines, which would affect the schedule and scope.

Business Risk vs. Insurable Risk

Project risks are of two types: business and insurable. A *business risk* is one that is inherent in a business endeavor, such as when a company assumes that it will spend money and make money, and that any project undertaken carries with it the potential for success or failure, profit or loss. *Insurable risk* is a risk that has only the potential for loss and no potential for profit or gain. An insurable risk is one for which insurance may be purchased to reduce or offset the possible loss.

Example: Risks in a Retail Store

For a retail store owner, the outlay of money to purchase inventory without a guarantee that it will sell is a business risk. A loss of inventory due to a fire is an insurable risk.

Business Risk Types

Project managers should be aware of some of the common types of business risks.

Business Risk	Description
Competitive	Risks such as the risk of increased competition in the marketplace and a rival company developing a superior product.
Legislative	Risks such as the risk of new laws or changes in regulations governing your products, goods, or services, that require your company to spend more to maintain compliance.
Monetary	Risks such as the risk of increased prices for raw materials, increased taxes, increased operating costs, and losses due to nonpayment by customers.
Operational	Risks such as the risk of fraud, theft, employee injury, workplace accidents, and damage to equipment.

Insurable Risk Types

Several types of insurable risks are available.

Insurable Risk	Description
Direct property	Risk of property damage due to weather, fire, and so on.
Indirect property	Risk of additional expenditures needed to recover from property loss.
Liability	Risk of needing to make good after causing damage to another.

Insurable Risk	Description
Personnel-related	Liability risk for damage to employees.

Probability Scales

A *probability scale* is a graph showing the assignment of value to the likelihood of a risk occurring. Probability scales are designed using a variety of values, such as linear, nonlinear, or an ordinal scale using relative probability values ranging from not very unlikely to almost certain. A risk's probability score can range in value from 0.0 (no probability) to 1.0 (certainty). While this is a common way to assign probability, any other set of values can be used instead—for example one to five, or one to ten.

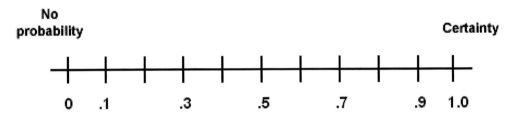

Figure 9–1: A probability scale with values showing the likelihood of a risk occurring.

Basics of Probability

When you perform probabilistic analysis, you will need to apply some of the basic principles of probability.

Principle of Probability	Description
Sum of probabilities	The sum of the probabilities of all possible events must be equal to 1 (100%).
Probability of single event	The probability of any single event must be greater than or equal to 0 and less than or equal to 1.
Mean	The sum of the events divided by the number of occurrences.
Median	The number that separates the higher half of a probability distribution from the lower half. It is not the same as the average, although the two terms are often confused.
Standard deviation	This is the measure of the spread of the data, or the statistical dispersion of the values in your data set.

Probability Distribution

Probability distribution is the scattering of values assigned to likelihood in a sample population. It can be visually depicted in the form of a *Probability Density Function (PDF)*. In a PDF, the vertical axis refers to the probability of a particular value that is depicted on the horizontal axis. The zero on the horizontal axis represents the mean, and the plus and minus numbers represent standard deviations from the mean.

Probability can be assigned subjectively or objectively. *Subjective probability* is based on people's opinions, which may be shaped by information, experience, and attitude. Even if they are given the same set of facts, they may make very different determinations of the probability of an event. *Objective probability* is deduced mathematically.

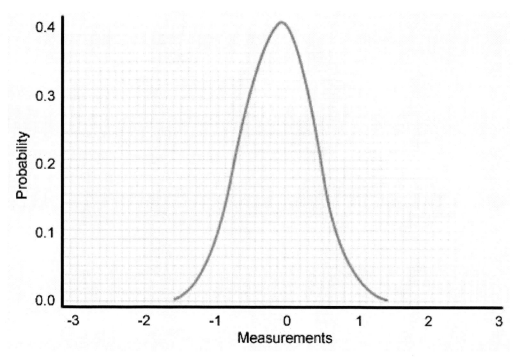

Figure 9–2: A probability density function graph displaying the probability of a measurement with a specific value.

The Normal Distribution PDF

A *normal distribution PDF* results when there is a symmetrical range or variation in the probabilities of each outcome. Visually, the data is distributed symmetrically in the shape of a bell with a single peak, resulting in the common term bell curve. The peak represents the mean; the symmetry indicates that there are an equal number of occurrences above and below the mean.

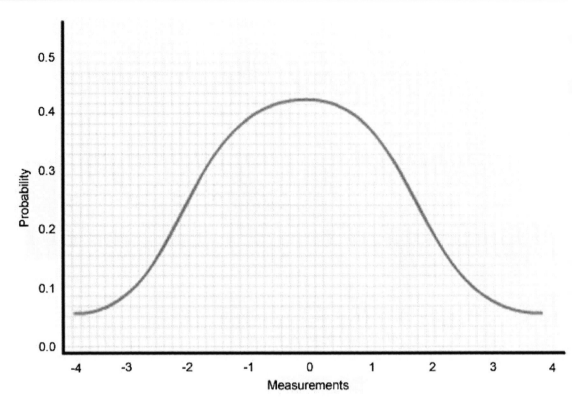

Figure 9–3: A normal distribution PDF graph.

The Triangular Distribution PDF

A *triangular distribution PDF* results when there is an asymmetrical distribution of probabilities. Visually, the data is skewed to one side, indicating that an activity or element presents relatively little risk to project objectives. If either the probability of occurrence is low or the impact is low, then this necessarily indicates that there is little risk.

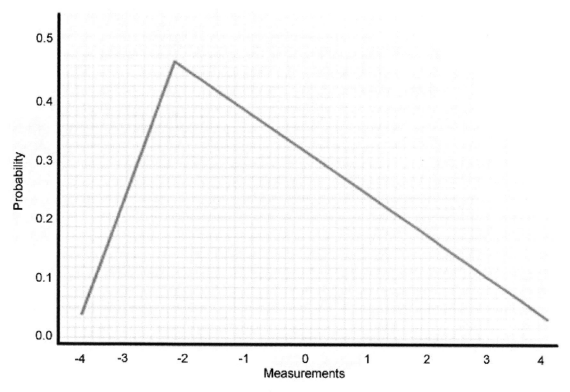

Figure 9–4: A triangular distribution PDF graph displaying asymmetrical distribution of probabilities.

Impact Scale

An *impact scale* is a rating system of values that reflect the magnitude of the impact of a risk event on project objectives. The impact scale can be ordinal, using values of very low, low, moderate, high, and very high. Numbers are assigned to these values. To improve the integrity and quality of the data and make the processes consistent and repeatable, organizations typically develop definitions for each value to help the risk management team assign each risk's impact score consistently. As with the probability scale, any set of numbers can be used to correspond to the range of impacts.

Figure 9–5: Impact scale.

The following table shows an example of an organization's impact scale.

Impact Rating	Impact Level	Definition
1	Very low	If this risk occurs, the impact on the project's objectives would be minor and not noticeable outside the project.
3	Low	If this risk occurs, the impact on the project's objectives would be minor but noticeable to the customer or sponsor.

Impact Rating	Impact Level	Definition
5	Moderate	If this risk occurs, the impact to the project's objectives would be significant and would create customer or sponsor dissatisfaction with the project.
7	High	If this risk occurs, the impact on the project would be significant and would create major customer or sponsor dissatisfaction. The project would be in jeopardy.
9	Very high	If this risk occurs, the impact would be catastrophic. The project would be cancelled.

Levels of Uncertainty

Levels of uncertainty describe the risks of a project based on how much is known about the source and effect of the risk, which are often described as knowns, known-unknowns, and unknown-unknowns.

Level of Uncertainty	Description and Example
Known	Items that you know could affect you, and for which you can roughly predict the nature and extent of the effect.
	Example: A 50% staff turnover in the fast food industry.
Known-unknown	Items that you know could affect you, although you are not able to predict how or how much they will affect you.
	Example: Competition in the marketplace.
Unknown-unknown	Items that are beyond your ability to foresee, predict, or prepare for.
	Example: Hurricane Katrina in the U.S. in 2005.

The Project Risk Management Process

The project risk management process is a high-level process that includes the following outputs: risk management planning, risk identification, qualitative risk analysis, quantitative risk analysis, and risk response planning.

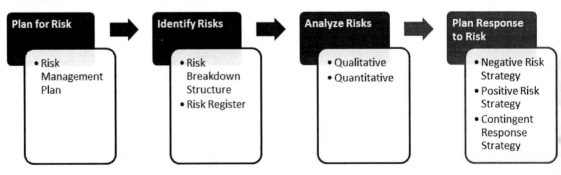

Figure 9–6: The project risk management process outputs.

Risk Management Plan

A risk management plan is a document that describes the team's approach to manage risks. It determines the methodology, approaches, and tools that will be used; documents the roles and responsibilities of those involved; identifies the budgeting and the scheduling for risk management activities; and lists the risk categories.

 Note: The risk management plan does not address responses to risks. Those are addressed in the risk response plan.

Example: A Risk Management Plan for a New Project

Entrepreneurs seeking funding from venture capitalists for a new business will present a risk management plan to their potential investors. For a proposed amusement park, the risk management plan will describe business risks, such as operational risks of potential losses due to employee theft, and insurable risks such as liabilities for injuries sustained on the park rides.

Risk Management Plan Components

A good risk management plan will include several components.

Component	Description
Methodology	Defines the tools, approaches, and data sources that may be used to perform risk management on the project.
Roles and responsibilities	Defines the lead, support, and risk management team membership for each type of action in the risk management plan. Participants might include project team members and a risk officer.
Definitions of risk probability and impact	Scales of risk probabilities and impact are defined for use in qualitative risk analysis using terms such as "very unlikely" to "almost certain" with respective values in numbers for these terms. For instance, "very unlikely" may have 0.05 as a probability value.
Probability and impact matrix	Predefined matrix with risk priority areas earmarked, which has product of impact value on the X-axis and probability value on the Y-axis.
Revised stakeholder tolerances	Stakeholder tolerances may need to be updated as a result of planning for risk management.
Budgeting	A budget for project risk management should be established and included in the risk management plan.
Timing	Defines how often the risk management activities will be performed throughout the project life cycle.
Risk categories	Documentation, such as a Risk Breakdown Structure (RBS) or categories from previous projects, will help identify and organize risks.
Reporting formats	Defines how outputs of this process will be documented, analyzed, and communicated.
Tracking	Documents how risk activities will be recorded and audited.

RBS

A *Risk Breakdown Structure (RBS)* is a hierarchical arrangement of identified risks that helps project managers to organize potential sources of risk to the project. Functioning much like a WBS, an RBS arranges categories into a hierarchy. This approach allows the project team to define risk at detailed levels.

Level 0	Level 1	Level 2	Level 3
Project Risk	Management	Corporate	• History/experience/culture • Organizational stability • Financial
		Customer & stakeholder	• History/experience/culture • Contractual • Requirements definition & stability
	External	Natural environment	• Physical environment • Facilities/site • Local services
		Cultural	• Political • Legalize/regulatory • Interest groups
		Economic	• Labor market • Labor conditions • Financial market
		Requirements	• Scope uncertainty • Conditions of use • Complexity
	Technology	Performance	• Technology maturity • Technology limits
		Application	• Organizational experience • Personnel skill sets & experience • Physical resources

Figure 9–7: An RBS displaying the different levels of project risks.

Risk Analysis

Risk analysis is the evaluation of the probability and impact of the occurrence of a risk in a project. Risk analysis is typically conducted through either qualitative or quantitative techniques. The level of risk to the project is the product of the probability of the risk occurring and the predicted impact that the risk will have on the project's success.

Example: Risk Analysis for a New Venture

A manufacturing company would conduct various kinds of risk analyses before launching a new line of products. It would evaluate the probability and impact of the risks, such as the costs of research and design; the potential for future sales and revenue from a new product line; fluctuating consumer demand; competition from rivals; and pending consumer-safety legislation associated with this new venture that may govern the manufacturing of the new products.

Risk Tolerance

Risk tolerance refers to the level of risk acceptable to a project manager or key stakeholder when the investment is compared to the potential payoff.

Stakeholders may perceive risk differently. Some stakeholders may be interested in only conservative, low-risk projects that are similar in nature and scope to many past successes. Other stakeholders may seek out high-risk ventures in uncharted territory; they may be willing to risk a great amount of capital on a speculative project with the potential for large returns.

Risk Tolerance Levels

There is a range of risk tolerance levels starting with the risk-averter to the extreme risk-seeker. Most people find themselves comfortable somewhere in between the averter and the seeker.

Risk Tolerance Classification	Description
Risk-averter	Not likely to take a risk that is considered a high risk.
Risk-neutral	Tolerance to risk is proportional to the amount of money at stake.
Risk-seeker	Accepts an uncertain outcome and may be willing to take a high risk regardless of the consequences.

Guidelines for Creating a Risk Management Plan

Creating an effective risk management plan provides the project team with a secure approach to identifying, analyzing, responding to, monitoring, and controlling project risk. To create an effective risk management plan, follow these guidelines:

- Collect the cost, schedule, and communications management plans to know how budget, schedule, and contingencies and management reserves will be communicated and accessed.
- Determine how you will organize your project's risk management team.
  - Consider assigning a risk officer to coordinate all risk management activities. While not all organizations have risk officers, it may be a helpful option to consider.
  - Define the roles and responsibilities for each person on the risk management team.
  - The sponsor may be able to assist in some risk management activities, such as developing response strategies for all risks classified as high risks.
- Conduct risk planning meetings to develop the risk management plan.
- Establish a budget for risk management.
- Consult your organization's risk management policy and make sure that your risk planning complies with the policy. If your organization has a risk management plan template, use it and make modifications to meet the specific needs of your project.
- Describe the approaches, tools, and data sources that may be used to perform risk management activities for this project.
  - How will the risks be identified? Will you conduct brainstorming sessions? Will you use the Delphi technique? Will you use SMEs?
  - How will the identified risks be scored and analyzed so that effective response strategies can be developed? Is there organizational policy mandating a specific scoring and prioritization method?
- Determine and describe the schedule for performing risk management activities.
- Determine and describe how your team will document risk response efforts.
  - What tools will your team use to store risk information and track responses?
  - How will the risk response efforts be communicated to the project stakeholders?
- Determine and describe how the lessons learned from your risk management activities will be documented for the benefit of future projects.
- If an organization, sponsor, or customer has specific guidelines or requirements regarding risk thresholds, this information should be included in your risk management plan.

TOPIC B

Identify Project Risks and Triggers

In the previous topic, you created a risk management plan. Using the approach outlined in the plan, you can begin the process of identifying potential risks that may affect your project. In this topic, you will delve into the risk identification component process and identify project risks and triggers.

Identifying risks and triggers helps you determine the most effective action to take for each risk. Mastering the tools and techniques to identify project risks and triggers ensures that you are prepared to take the appropriate action.

Triggers

Triggers are the early warning signs or indications that a risk to your project is about to occur. They could be external factors that influence your project, such as proposed changes in relevant legislation. They could also be internal factors that influence your project, such as proposed changes in staffing, governance, or funding within your organization. Triggers must be examined during regularly scheduled risk review sessions held during the life of the project.

Example: Trigger Indicators

For a project involving the production of an independent documentary for television, news of an impending television writers' strike will be a trigger. If the writing on the documentary is not yet complete, the trigger could indicate a negative risk that critical external resources will not be available during the strike. If the writing on the documentary is complete, the trigger could indicate a positive risk that the networks' demand for the product could increase in the absence of other new programming.

Example: Identify Project Risks and Triggers

A car manufacturer conducted an internal study and concluded that passengers had difficulty buckling the company's standard seat belt. A team was commissioned to redesign the belt buckle. The project manager directed the risk management team to review the project documentation and results of the study. The risk management team brainstormed a list of potential risks and their triggers for the new buckles. Two risks identified were that the buckles would fail to provide proper slack during regular use and that the buckles may accidentally release during a collision.

The project team examined old test results for similar buckle designs and commercial safety studies concerning seat belts. After reviewing the information, these risks were categorized as technical. The project manager called for tests that would specifically check the probability of these risks occurring. Because public safety was at risk, the team agreed that even one failed test would trigger an immediate risk response plan. The team noted all their results in the initial project risk register for later analysis.

Information-Gathering Techniques

Information-gathering techniques are methods that are used to collect data that will assist the project team in identifying risks and risk triggers to the project.

Technique	Description
Brainstorming	Used to identify overall project risks or may focus on the risks within a particular project segment or work package.

Technique	Description
Delphi technique	Used to generate a consensus among project risk experts who anonymously submit their risk list to a facilitator. Because it relies on achieving consensus, the Delphi technique may be difficult to implement in many organizations.
Root cause analysis	Used to identify problems, discover the root cause, and develop corrective actions.
Interviewing	Used to get information from people with wide experience across many projects, such as stakeholders, team members, project managers from previous projects, and functional management peers, to quantify the probability and impact of risk on project objectives. The output is a statistical interpretation of the data from which a range of probability can be expressed against a level of confidence that the risk will or will not occur, such as optimistic or low and pessimistic or high.
	There are two interviewing methods used for generating risk probabilities: Direct and Diagrammatic.
	• **Direct**: Approaching an expert to assign subjective probabilities to a given range of values, providing a lowest possible value, most likely value, and highest possible value.
	• **Diagrammatic**: Using diagrams to seek advice from an expert to assign subjective probabilities to a given range of values, providing a lowest possible value, most likely value, and highest possible value.

Documentation Reviews

Documentation reviews are the structured reviews of project plans and related documents that are conducted to improve the quality of the documents. They also help in determining if there are any discrepancies between the documents and the stated project requirements, which may be indicators of project risks. The documents of previous projects that are used in the current project may also be reviewed along with other documents.

Example: Documentation Reviews in a Global Service Providing Company

A global service providing company, situated in several locations across the world, decides to incorporate an ERP system within the organization and customize business processes to suit the organization's requirements. Because the company conducted a similar project earlier, the PMO decides to use the project documents created for the previous project. While reviewing the documents, the PMO identified that the activity list was not updated with some changes made during the later phases of the project. The PMO rectified this in the current project.

Checklist Analysis

Checklist analysis is the process of systematically evaluating the pre-created checklists and developing a checklist based on relevant historical information. It serves as a standardized way to identify risks and is applicable to any process or system, including equipment and human issues. This analysis is generally performed by experts and the quality of evaluation is primarily based on the knowledge and experience of people creating the checklists. It is recommended to review the checklist during project closure and incorporate the lesson learned for future use on projects.

The steps involved in checklist analysis include:

1. Determine the process or system of interest.
2. Define the areas of interest.
3. Classify the process or system.

4. Create relevant checklists.
5. Subdivide the elements of the activity or system if necessary.
6. Respond to the questions related to the checklists.
7. Use the results for making validations, recommendations, or improvements.

Assumptions Analysis

Assumptions are statements that must be taken to be true in order to begin project planning. *Assumptions analysis* is the process of validating the assumptions made during project planning. It involves documenting the assumptions and then determining the risks that may be caused due to inaccuracy, instability, or incompleteness of the project assumptions. Assumptions analysis can be carried out at any phase of the project life cycle.

Diagramming Techniques

Different diagramming techniques are used to identify project risks.

Diagramming Technique	Used To
Cause-and-effect diagrams	Identify the causes of project risks.
Flowcharts	Identify process elements that have risk associated with them.

SWOT Analysis

SWOT analysis is the process of examining the project from the perspective of strengths, weaknesses, opportunities, and threats. SWOT analysis identifies the objective of the project and the external and internal factors that may positively or negatively impact the project. The analysis can be used for making decisions and developing strategies or plans that help an organization achieve its business objectives.

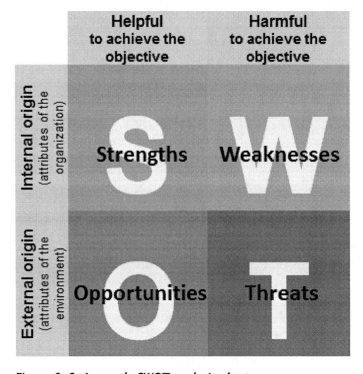

Figure 9–8: A sample SWOT analysis chart.

Risk Registers

The *risk register* is a living document that identifies and categorizes risks, potential risk responses, and their triggers, or warning signs. If risk categories are changed, the risk register must be updated. Any possible risk responses included in the risk register are forwarded for use in planning risk responses. The risk register will be updated with the results of other risk management processes and provided to project team members involved in project risk management.

 Note: The risk register will ultimately contain the outcomes of other risk management processes, including the results of the qualitative risk analysis, quantitative risk analysis, and risk response planning. In its initial stage, the risk register does not necessarily contain information regarding planned responses to risks. However, the sample risk register shown in the following figure is a completed one.

Risk Register

	Description	Trigger	Risk Category	Impact	Probability	Risk Score	Strategy	Status
1	PM out with lengthy illness	Chronic illness	Resource Availability	5	1	5	Mitigation	Open
2	Transportation strike	Newspaper article	Union Issues	4	2	8	Mitigation	Open
3	Client late approving scope	Snowstorm closes office	Inadequate Time	1	1	1	Acceptance	Closed
4	Company merger cancels project	Memo from CEO	Change of Project Priority	5	2	10	Acceptance	Open
	Total 4 Risks					24.00		1 of 4 closed.
				Score for Open Risks		23.00		
				Closed Risks (%)		4.17%		

Figure 9–9: An example of a completed risk register.

Risk Categories

Risk categories divide project risks into areas reflecting common sources of the risk.

Risk Category	Examples
Technical, quality, or performance risks	• Technical changes. • Changes to industry standards during the project. • Reliance on unproven or complex technology. • Unrealistic performance goals.
Project management risks	• Inadequate time and resource allocation. • Ineffective project plan development. • Poor cost estimates.
Organizational risks	• Resource conflicts with other projects. • Inadequate project funding. • Inconsistent management support.
External risks	• Union issues. • Change of management in customer's organization. • Regional security issues.

Guidelines for Identifying Project Risks and Triggers

It is important to identify and document the characteristics of risks that affect the project so that the project team can determine the most effective action to take for each risk. The project risks and triggers identified will determine the type of risk analysis to be performed. To identify project risks and triggers, follow these guidelines:

- Perform a structured review of documents and processes with key project stakeholders to ensure an understanding of the risks involved. These documents are a valuable source for risk identification and they may include:
  - The project charter.
  - The WBS.
  - The product description.
  - The schedule and cost estimates.
  - The resource plan.
  - The procurement plan.
  - The list of constraints and assumptions.
- Use a consistent method to identify risks and their possible triggers. Techniques may include:
  - Information-gathering techniques such as brainstorming, interviewing, the Delphi technique, and SWOT analysis.
  - Risk identification checklists (make every effort to itemize all types of possible risks to the project on the checklist).
  - Assumptions analysis.
  - Diagramming techniques such as cause-and-effect diagrams and system flow charts. You can also use *influence diagrams*, which provide a graphical representation of a problem showing causal influences, time ordering of events, and other relationships among variables and outcomes.
- Apply the selected method systematically. Before the project begins, identify risks in every project segment and work package. At the start of each project segment, reexamine the risks for that segment. Update your list of risks at the close of each project segment.
- Think outside the box. Apply your method consistently, but be on the lookout for special circumstances that may arise in any project segment. Those checklists and templates are in place to help get the risk identification process going, but they are far from complete. As the project progresses, circumstances change. Be on the lookout for changed assumptions, new risks, or additional impacts from previously identified risks.
- Consult relevant historical information, such as risk response plans and final reports from previous similar projects, that may include lessons learned describing problems and their resolutions. Another source of historical information for risk identification is published information, such as commercial databases, academic studies, and benchmarking results.
- Collect the historical information and other project-related documents and perform a checklist and assumptions analysis. Conduct a SWOT analysis to identify the risks involved in achieving the project objectives.
- Once risks have been identified, group them into categories that reflect common sources of risk for your industry or application area.
- Examine each identified risk to determine what triggers will indicate that a risk has occurred or is about to occur.
- Use the results of your analysis to initiate the risk register.
  - Consider implementing any risk-register software that may be in common usage at your company. You can also create a risk register without specialized software by using a spreadsheet or table.
  - Include the project's name, sponsor, key stakeholders, and objectives.
  - Identify the risks inherent in your project with a description of each.

TOPIC C

Perform Qualitative Risk Analysis

You identified the risks that may affect your project and documented their characteristics. Now, you must assess the impact and likelihood of these identified risks. In this topic, you will perform qualitative risk analysis, where you will rank and prioritize project risks according to their potential effect on project objectives.

Identifying risks is only one part of an effective strategy to minimize work activity disruptions that could cause your project to go over budget or exceed its promised deadline. It is important to rank their importance so that precious time isn't wasted addressing risks with low priority. Qualitative risk analysis lays the foundation for effectively quantifying high-priority risks in your project.

Qualitative Risk Analysis

Qualitative risk analysis is the process of determining the probability of occurrence and the impact of identified risks by using logical reasoning when numeric data is not readily available. This is then used to determine the risk exposure of the project by multiplying the probability and impact. The qualitative risk analysis process ultimately provides the list of prioritized risks for further actions.

Example: Performing Qualitative Risk Analysis for a Music Concert

An event management company is planning to organize a jazz concert in a coastal city. An initial marketing survey undertaken by the company indicates that the response for the concert will be good, because the general population of that city likes jazz music. Also, historical data shows that the response toward similar musical concerts held in this city has been very encouraging.

However, a recent weather bureau announcement indicated that there is a slight possibility that the low-pressure area that developed beside the coastal city can cause heavy rains on the day of the concert. The organizing committee officials decide to have a discussion about the weather risk with all the stakeholders involved, to evaluate the impact of risk on the project objectives on the basis of a scale of low, medium, and high.

The members discuss the issue, list different areas of concern, and rate them. The members find that in the worst case scenario, the low-pressure area over the coast may develop into a tropical storm, accompanied by very heavy rains and wind. But the chances of that are remote, because the weather bulletin does not project a tropical storm and indicates that there is only a slight possibility of heavy rains.

Secondly, some of the members were concerned that heavy rains may force people to stay indoors and reduce the incremental revenue from ticket sales at the box office on the day of the event, as well as from sales of souvenirs and concessions at the event. But on the contrary, others felt that because the concert is to be held inside an auditorium, the chance of rain having a big impact on the audience turnout is remote. Also, even a seat occupancy rate of 50% would ensure that the expenditure involved with this event can be reclaimed.

Based on the deliberations, the organizing committee finally concludes that the risk exposure is low or at the worst moderate in nature. The event managing company documents the information in the risk register.

Risk Matrix Criteria

To create a numerical risk matrix, you must identify the probability and impact of each risk on a project. The following table is an example of a one-to-five scale that can be used for probability and impact.

Risk Level	Criteria
5—Very high	Will break the project. For example, if the technology doesn't meet basic quality requirements, the system will seriously disrupt a mission-critical business function.
4—High	Significant additional resources in time and cost will be required to complete the project. Sponsor may need to handle the risk.
3—Medium	The project will be delayed, but can still be completed with moderate additional resources. The project manager can handle this risk with the support of the sponsor.
2—Low	The project can be completed with minor additional resources in time or cost. The project manager can handle this risk.
1—Very low	Minor inconvenience. For example, an important internal skill resource becomes unavailable, but external equivalent skill resources are readily available at equivalent cost. The project manager can handle this risk.

Risk Data Quality Assessment

Risk data quality assessment is a technique that involves the evaluation of the reliability of the available data concerning a risk. It includes examining the data obtained about a particular risk for the amount of data available, the quality of data available, the extent to which the source of the information understands the risk, and the legitimacy and dependability of the data.

Example: Risk Assessment for a Restaurant Chain

As project manager for a restaurant chain, Barry is responsible for the new site development. The company is interested in expanding to a location in the northern section of the city, and Barry conducted a risk assessment to determine whether or not it would be financially sound to purchase property in a large shopping plaza there. The risk assessment includes the average cost per square foot of real estate within that neighborhood; this figure indicates that real estate is selling at a very reasonable price. Upon detailed examination of the risk data, however, Barry discovers that the information used to calculate the average cost per square foot is five years old. Barry's quality assessment indicates that the data is too out-of-date to be useful in the risk analysis, and purchasing property based on this information would be a poor idea.

Risk Probability and Impact Assessment

Risk probability and impact assessment is a risk assessment technique that is used to evaluate the likelihood of occurrence and potential impact of the identified project risks. The *risk probability* and *risk impact* factors are often ranked either as very high, high, moderate, low, and very low or else as numbers from one through ten. Then, probability and impact of a risk are multiplied to identify the risk score, which is used to set the priority for each identified risk. The methods used to assess risk probability and impact include meetings, interviews, expert judgment, and drawing from historical information.

Ref. #	Risks	Probability	Impact	Risk score
1	Changing market conditions	2	4	8
2	Changing organizational policies and procedures	3	4	12
3	Communciation failure	4	4	16

5 - Very high	4 - High	3 - Medium	2 - Low	1 - Very low

Figure 9-10: A chart used to assess a project's risk probability and impact.

Probability and Impact Risk Rating Matrix

The *probability and impact risk rating matrix* is a graph showing the assignment of risk rating to risks or conditions. The matrix combines the probability and impact scales to prioritize and identify risks that are likely to require further analysis. Risk rating is calculated by multiplying the risk's impact score by its probability score. It may indicate risk thresholds by applying shading, color, or line variations. The probability and impact risk rating matrix will guide the response plans.

The sample probability and impact risk rating matrix shown here is a simplified example; the shadings of color indicate the levels of probability and impact. A real probability and impact risk rating matrix will be used to assess very complicated risks with many factors and data points.

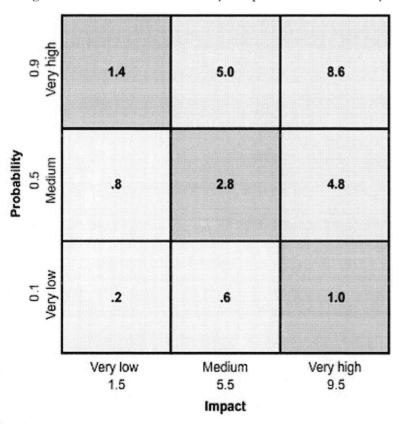

Figure 9-11: A simplified probability and impact risk rating matrix.

Example: Qualitative Risk Analysis for a Fast Food Company

A fast food company wanted to reduce its long lines and increase its hourly sales. The company discovered that by reducing the cooking time of hamburgers by 30 seconds, they could average 10 more customers served per hour. The shift managers decided to perform qualitative risk analysis to identify potential problems with this plan. Most of the risks they identified centered around food safety and were based on existing health and safety standards for the cooking of meat products. These regulations forced the restaurant chain's risk threshold to be very low.

A probability and impact matrix was created and each identified risk was scored on the matrix. Highest in the ranking was the cook's inability to guarantee consistency of internal food temperature based on a formula of cooking times.

Risk Urgency Assessment

Urgent risks are risks that require immediate attention. *Risk urgency assessment* is the task of evaluating project risks and prioritizing them based on their urgency. The assessment may also include specific information on timing for responding to each risk.

Example: Assessing Risk Urgency in a Construction Project

David is managing a small construction project. During project execution, he identifies that the building's scaffolding support is inadequate, which may lead to a fatal accident on site. This risk will require immediate attention while other risks, such as unavailability of resources and weather threats, though equally important, will be less urgent.

Risk Register Analysis

There are several ways that the data in a risk register can be analyzed, as shown here.

Analysis	Description
Relative ranking or priority list of project risks	The overall risk ranking for a project can be determined by adding the individual risk factor scores and dividing by the number of risks.
Risks grouped by categories	Placing risks in categories may reveal areas of risk concentration. It may also highlight common causes of risk, allowing you to improve risk anticipation and response.
Causes of risk or project areas requiring particular attention	Identifying specific frequently occurring causes in risk occurrence enables better risk response planning.
Lists of risks requiring response in the near term	Some risks may require action in the near term. These can be grouped separately from the risks that will be addressed at a later date.
List of risks for additional analysis and response	Risks that may require additional analysis and management typically include risks classified as high or moderate. For example, a schedule risk that threatens to delay the project end date beyond acceptable limits will require quantitative analysis.
Watchlist of low-priority risks	Risks that are not urgent and do not require near-term action can be documented on a watchlist for monitoring.
Trends in qualitative risk analysis results	As qualitative risk analysis is repeated, a trend may result that can make risk response or further analysis more urgent or less urgent.

The Ongoing Risk Assessment Process

The *ongoing risk assessment process* is an iterative process of identifying, analyzing, and documenting the risks facing your project; it is conducted throughout the project life cycle. This is primarily an organizational issue that requires the project manager, or the PMO, to have project managers outside the project shadow the project manager and provide oversight and fresh perspective during risk management reviews.

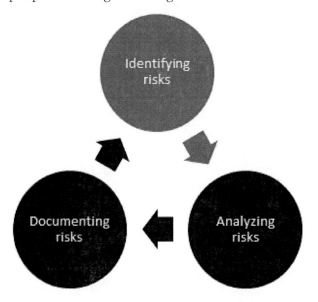

Figure 9-12: The ongoing risk assessment process.

Guidelines for Performing Qualitative Risk Analysis

Performing qualitative risk analysis provides a method by which you can rank and prioritize risks. Effective qualitative risk analysis can assist an organization with the decision-making process when selecting which project to do and what resources are assigned. To perform qualitative risk analysis, follow these guidelines:

- Use the risk register to examine the list of identified risks.
  - Are all the risks identified?
  - Are all the risks completely documented?
- Analyze the data available for each risk, and assign a data precision ranking score, if you find that helpful.
  - Does the source of the data fully understand the risk?
  - Is the source reliable and trustworthy?
  - Is the amount of data sufficient to adequately analyze the risk?
  - What is the accuracy and quality of the data?
  - Are there risks that require further monitoring? Should they be placed in the risk register for scrutiny?
- Determine the organization's risk threshold for this project.
- Analyze the assumptions identified during risk identification as potential risks against the validity of the assumption and the impact on the project if false. Use the help of an expert if necessary.
- Analyze the probability and impact of each identified risk using well-defined probability and impact scales.
- Determine the risk factor scores using a probability and impact risk matrix.
- Prioritize the risks according to the risk management plan. Identify risks that require further analysis.
- Determine the overall risk for the project and compare it with the organization risk threshold.

- Document all changes to the risk register.

TOPIC D

Perform Quantitative Risk Analysis

You performed a qualitative risk analysis for your project. Now you can determine the extent of the risk exposure to your entire project. In this topic, you will perform quantitative risk analysis.

Taking advantage of opportunities can often mean turning a negative outcome into a positive one. By performing a quantitative risk analysis, you can take steps to maximize the positive consequences of the opportunities facing your project.

Quantitative Risk Analysis

Quantitative risk analysis is a technique that is used to assess the risk exposure events to overall project objectives and determine the confidence levels of achieving the project objectives. Quantifying risk can help you identify time and cost contingencies of a project. It further refines and enhances the prioritization and scoring of risks produced during qualitative analysis.

In most everyday project management scenarios, conducting qualitative risk analysis is adequate to meet the project manager's purposes; only in sophisticated, mature project management environments is there much additional value added by conducting quantitative risk analysis.

Example: Quantitative Risk Analysis for the Supply–Chain Management Software Project

The project team on the Supply-Chain Management Software project identifies process data for a statistical analysis using a Monte Carlo simulation to determine the confidence level that the project will be completed on time and within the budget. The team identifies critical project parameters, which affect the project schedule. The team further determines project success rate and makes decisions about viable project alternatives taking into account the risks within the project.

Quantitative Risk Analysis Update Components

Several quantitative risk analysis update components are available.

Component	Description
Probabilistic analysis of the project	Once risks are qualitatively and quantitatively analyzed, the project team should be able to forecast the possible completion dates and costs and provide a level of confidence for each.
Probability of achieving the cost and time objectives	Using quantitative risk analysis, the project team can estimate the likelihood of achieving the project objectives under the current plan and with the current knowledge of the project risks.
Prioritized list of quantified risks	Identified risks are prioritized according to the threat they pose or the opportunity they present to the project. This prioritized list includes a measure of the impact of each identified risk.
Trends in quantitative risk analysis results	Repeating the quantitative risk analysis allows the project's risk management team to analyze the trends and make adjustments as necessary. Information on project schedule, cost, quality, and performance gained when performing quantitative risk analysis will help the team to prepare a quantitative risk analysis report.

Project Risk Ranking

Project risk ranking is the overall risk ranking for producing the final deliverable of the product or service of the project. It allows for comparisons among other projects, assisting in project initiation, budget and resource allocation, and other decisions.

In the following example, the project risk management team created a probability and impact matrix that illustrates the relative position of threats as identified in the qualitative risk analysis. The team now calculates the percent exposure of the top four risks.

Qualitative risk analysis already suggested the descending order of risks. The following table displays the total exposure of all the risks for the project as 3.22 and the exposure of the top four risks as 2.37. Considering the top four risks, the team determines the exposure to these risks as 73.6%.

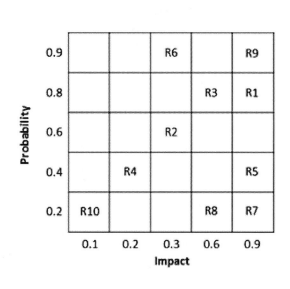

R9	0.9	0.9	0.81
R1	0.8	0.9	0.72
R3	0.8	0.6	0.48
R5	0.4	0.9	0.36
R6	0.9	0.3	0.27
R7	0.2	0.9	0.18
R2	0.6	0.3	0.18
R8	0.2	0.6	0.12
R4	0.4	0.2	0.08
R10	0.2	0.1	0.02
Total exposure			3.22
Exposure of top 4 risks			2.37
% Exposure of top 4 risks			2.37 / 3.22 x 100
			73.6%

Figure 9-13: A probability and impact matrix and risk exposure table for the risk ranking example.

Quantitative Analysis Methods

Quantitative analysis methods allow project managers to consistently determine the probability and impact of each risk.

Method	Description
Sensitivity analysis	Places a value on the effect of changing a single variable within a project by analyzing that effect on the project plan.
Decision tree analysis	Factors both probability and impact for each variable, indicating the decision providing the greatest expected value when all uncertain implications and subsequent decisions are quantified.
Simulation	Uses models that calculate potential impact of events on the project, based on random input values.
Expected Monetary Value (EMV) analysis	Assesses the average outcome of various unknown scenarios.

Note: EMV and decision tree analysis are commonly used together to arrive at a final decision.

Sensitivity Analysis

Sensitivity analysis is a method of assessing the relative effect of changing a variable in the project to gain an insight into possible outcomes of one or more potential courses of action.

Sensitivity analysis is probably the simplest method of analyzing the impact of a potential risk and its results are easy for project stakeholders to understand. However, it does not lend itself well to assessing combinations of risks and how they may affect a project. Furthermore, the sensitivity diagram does not provide an indication of anticipated probability of occurrence of the risk event.

Often, sensitivity analysis is performed independently on a number of variables. When displayed on a single graph or sensitivity diagram, the results allow you to compare which variables have the highest likely impact on project performance. Typically, it is only performed for variables that are likely to have a major impact on project performance in terms of cost, time, or economic return.

Decision Tree Analysis

Decision tree analysis is an assessment of the data obtained using the decision tree method to evaluate various possible outcomes. Decision trees allow decision makers to evaluate both the probability and impact for each branch of every decision under consideration, making it a useful tool for risk analysis. Solving the decision tree indicates the decision that will provide the greatest expected value when all the uncertain implications, costs, rewards, and subsequent decisions are quantified.

Simulation

Simulation is a technique that uses computer models and estimates of risk to translate uncertainties at a detailed level into their potential impact on project objectives. For schedule development, simulation involves calculating multiple project duration with varying sets of assumptions regarding project activities.

Example: Using Simulation for Planning a Multimedia Campaign

You are planning a multimedia campaign for a client. Your team is divided as to which printing contractor to use. Printer A has handled similar projects for you in the past. However, they are poorly staffed and turnaround time can be slow. Printer B is a large company with modern equipment and fast turnaround time. However, their remote location will add at least a day for each shipment of the product.

Your team simulates the two project activities duration using each of the printers. Your simulation takes into account factors such as previous turnaround times for similar projects, realistic shipping times, and maximum production capabilities. Based on your simulation results, you decide to stick with Printer A.

Monte Carlo Analysis

Monte Carlo analysis is a simulation technique used by project managers to make predictions about the statistical distribution of activity durations or cost estimates for a project. It is a form of simulation, where the project model is run many times with input values (durations or costs) chosen at random for each iteration from the duration or cost probability distributions. This analysis does not produce a single result, but calculates a range of possible results.

In more general business terms, Monte Carlo refers to not one single analysis method but to a wide class of techniques, mostly making use of sophisticated computers and inputs of random numbers, probabilities, and algorithms. It has a wide range of applications in many fields, including finance and engineering; because it works effectively with large inputs of numbers, it is well suited for complex project management problems in which more than a few inputs such as costs, activity, and duration are unknown.

Example: Monte Carlo Analysis for a Project

Stakeholders asked George Allen, a project manager, to estimate how long it will take to complete a project involving three tasks and an inexperienced team. The first task is scheduled to take 30 days, the second task is scheduled to take 60 days, and the third task is scheduled to take 90 days. But with inexperienced resources, the tasks' durations could take more time. Using a software application, George will run a Monte Carlo simulation analysis using repeated (potentially thousands of) random duration values for each task. The result of these calculations will be a statistical distribution of durations for the project. From this distribution, George estimates that this project has a 40% probability of being completed within 170 days, a 60% probability of being completed within 180 days, and an 80% probability of being completed within 200 days.

EMV Analysis

Expected Monetary Value (EMV) analysis is a method of calculating the average outcome when the future is uncertain. Opportunities will have positive values and threats will have negative values.

EMV is found by multiplying the monetary value of a possible outcome by the probability it will occur. This is done for all possible outcomes and their figures are added together. The sum is the EMV for that scenario.

This technique is used in decision tree analysis; EMV must be calculated in order for the analysis to find the best outcome. The best outcome is the lowest combination of cost and EMV.

Guidelines for Performing Quantitative Risk Analysis

Performing quantitative risk analysis enables the project team to prioritize risks according to the threat they pose or the opportunity they present to the project. The prioritized list can be used to develop an effective response plan for each risk. To effectively perform quantitative risk analysis, follow these guidelines:

- Review the risk, cost, and schedule management plans to identify project risks.
- Begin with your original estimate of time or cost. Break out the various components of the estimate into manageable chunks. Determine the variable that you wish to investigate and identify its likely range of variation.
- Calculate and assess the impact of changing the range of results on the overall project estimate for each value in the range.
- Consult historical information, such as similar completed projects, studies of similar projects by risk specialists, and risk databases for information, that may be useful for quantitative risk analysis on your project.
- Use the appropriate interviewing technique and obtain probability distributions from stakeholders and subject matter experts.
  - If expertise resides with more than one person and the problem does not lend itself to precise analytical techniques but can benefit from subjective judgments on a collective basis, consider using the Delphi technique.
  - Consider using the direct method when time or resource constraints do not allow for more complex, resource-intensive methods and questions can be phrased clearly and concisely.
  - If your expert has a solid understanding of probability concepts and is familiar with PDFs, consider using the diagrammatic method.
- Depict the distributions in a PDF.

- Perform a sensitivity analysis to determine which risks have the most potential impact on the project by examining the extent to which the uncertainty of each element affects the objective being examined if all other uncertain elements are held at their baseline values. Use the decision tree analysis technique to examine the implications of choosing alternatives by incorporating the probabilities of risks and the costs or rewards of each logical path of events and future decisions.
- Conduct a project simulation using a model to translate uncertainties at a detailed level into their potential impact on project objectives at the total project level. Prioritize the quantified risks according to the threat they pose or the opportunity they present to the project objectives. Include a measure of each risk's impact. Document all changes to the risk register.
- Update the risk register, project management plan, and other project documents.

TOPIC E

Develop a Risk Response Plan

You performed a qualitative or quantitative risk analysis for your project. Now, you need to decide how you are going to address these project risks. In this topic, you will perform risk response planning, the final risk planning component process, by developing a risk response plan.

Whether you realize it or not, each planned response stems from an identified risk. Developing a risk response plan provides insurance for your project because you are taking steps to ensure that each possible scenario has an action plan.

Negative Risk Strategies

Negative risk strategies specify how to deal with risk scenarios that have a possible negative impact on the project.

Strategy	Description
Risk avoidance	Involves changing the project plan to prevent a potentially detrimental risk condition or event from happening. One way to eliminate a risk is to reduce or change the scope of the project in an attempt to avoid high-risk activities. The scope change could involve the project requirements or specifications, or it can mean changing the approach to meeting the requirements or specifications.
Risk transference	Involves shifting the impact of a risk event and ownership of the risk response to a third party. This strategy is used in connection with financial risk exposure and most often involves payment of a risk premium to the party assuming the risk.
Risk mitigation	Attempts to reduce the probability or impact of a potential risk event to an acceptable level. Mitigation may involve implementing a new course of action in an effort to reduce the problem or changing the current conditions so that the probability of the risk occurring is reduced. Sometimes, when reducing the probability is not possible, the focus must be on reducing the consequences of the risk event.
Risk acceptance	Involves accepting that a risk exists. The acceptance may be passive or active. Active acceptance indicates that a plan is ready for execution if the risk occurs. Passive acceptance indicates that no action is planned if the risk occurs and whatever action is suitable will be executed on an extempore basis.

Positive Risk Strategies

Positive risk strategies address how to deal with risk scenarios that have a possible positive impact on the project.

Strategy	Description
Risk exploitation	Often used when a project team wants to make sure that a positive risk is fully realized. This is often done by hiring the best experts in a field or ensuring that the most technologically advanced resources are available to the project team.

Strategy	Description
Risk sharing	Entails partnering with another party in an effort to give your team the best chance of seizing the opportunity. Joint ventures are a common example of risk sharing.
Risk enhancement	Attempts to increase the probability that an opportunity will occur. This is done by focusing on the trigger conditions of the opportunity and trying to optimize their chances for occurrence.
Risk acceptance	Involves accepting the risk and actively responding to it as it comes, but not through pursuit.

Contingent Response Strategies

A *contingent response strategy* is a risk response strategy developed in advance, before things go wrong; it is meant to be used if and when identified risks become reality. An effective contingent response strategy allows a project manager to react quickly and appropriately to the risk event, mitigating its negative impact or increasing its potential benefits. A contingent response strategy may include a *fallback plan*, which is implemented if the initial response strategy is ineffective in responding to the risk event. A contingent response strategy is also called a *contingency plan*.

Example: Contingent Response Strategy for an Outdoor Event

A rain date is a classic example of a contingent response strategy. For an outdoor event, such as a company picnic, that could be spoiled by inclement weather, the project manager can announce in advance the contingent response strategy: in case of rain, the picnic will be postponed by one week.

Contingency Reserves

A contingency reserve is a predetermined amount of additional time, money, or resources set aside in advance to be used to further the project's objectives in the event that unknown risks or accepted known risks become reality. Contingency reserves cover risk events that are not accounted for in the project's schedule and cost baselines. The amount of reserve is determined by the potential impact of the risk, but should include enough to implement a contingency plan and a buffer for dealing with unidentified risks.

Example: Contingency Reserve for a Trade Show

A project manager in charge of company participation at a trade show may solicit help in the form of employees willing to participate. His contingency reserve will take the form of human resources; he could solicit more volunteers than he expects he will need. In the event that some employees are not able to participate at the last minute, he will have a reserve of other employees to call upon.

Risk-Related Contract Decisions

Risk-related contract decisions are risk response approaches agreed upon by both parties when procuring materials from a third party. These decisions are made when:

- Planning risk responses for the project.
- Sharing or transferring part or all of the risk (opportunity or threat, respectively).
- Enhancing or mitigating part or all of the opportunity or threat, respectively, faced by an organization.

Some of the risk-related contract decisions include agreements for insurance, bonding, services, Letter of Credit (LoC), bank guarantee, and other items as appropriate for the project.

Example: Risk Response Plan for a New Product

You and your team have been asked to create a new line of exercise equipment. Your project team reviews all documentation for risks. From these documents, the team identifies three risks that need risk response planning. Because the first risk deals with loss of time due to possible worker injuries, the team decides to employ risk transference, paying a premium for insurance.

The second risk involves a scenario in which the new products could be first to market. To address this opportunity, the team settles on risk exploitation by hiring more staff to ensure the positive outcome. After a lengthy review, the team is unable to determine a course of action for the final risk, which is the possibility that a key patent may not be approved in time for production. For this risk, the team develops a contingency plan and the team then documents all changes in the risk register, risk management plan, and project plan.

Guidelines for Developing a Risk Response Plan

An effective risk response plan describes the response strategies for each identified risk. The selected response strategies should take advantage of opportunities and reduce the probability and impact of threats to project objectives. You can follow these guidelines to develop an effective risk response plan:

- Examine each identified risk to determine its causes and how it may affect the project objectives. Brainstorm possible strategies for each risk to identify which project stakeholders can be assigned responsibility of a risk. Involve those people in your risk response planning.
- Choose the response strategy that is most likely to be effective for each identified risk. Ensure that the chosen risk response strategies are:
  - Enough to bring the risk to a value below the organization's threshold.
  - Appropriate to the severity of the risk.
  - Cost effective.
  - Timely enough to be successful.
  - Realistic within the context of the project.
  - Agreed to by all parties involved.
  - Owned by a responsible person.
- If you are unable to bring a risk's rating below the organization's risk threshold, ask your sponsor for help. Develop specific actions for implementing the chosen strategy.
- Identify backup strategies for risks with high risk factor scores.
- Determine the amount of contingency reserves necessary to deal with accepted risks. Consider how much the contingency plan will cost and how much time the contingency plan will add to the schedule.
- Determine how much of a contingency reserve you should set aside for unknown risks (ones that have not been identified).
- Consult the risk management plan for the description of the content and format of the risk response plan. Include the following elements in your risk response plan:
  - A description of the identified risks along with the area of the project affected (i.e., the WBS element).
  - Risk owners and assigned responsibilities.
  - Qualitative and quantitative risk analysis results.
  - Response strategies selected and the specific actions for implementing the strategies.
  - The level of residual risk expected to remain after the response strategies are implemented.
  - The budget and schedule for responses.
  - Contingency plans and fallback plans for all accepted risks with high risk values.
- Incorporate the risk response plan into the overall project plan so that the strategies can be implemented and monitored. As the project progresses through the life cycle, examine trends in the qualitative and quantitative analyses results that may guide your response strategies.

ACTIVITY 9–1
Planning for Risk Review

Scenario

Answer the following review questions.

1. How could your organization benefit from comprehensive risk planning?

2. Which tools and techniques will you use to effectively perform qualitative risk analysis for future projects you manage?

Summary

In this lesson, you analyzed risks and planned risk responses. You created a risk management plan that describes how project risk management activities are structured and performed throughout the project. By taking a proactive approach during risk planning, you arm yourself with the necessary information required to manage potential risks to your projects and ensure the best possible environment for success.

10 | Planning Project Procurements

Lesson Time: 1 hour, 45 minutes

Lesson Introduction

You planned for project risk and are almost ready to transition your project to the executing process group. But before you can do that, you need to identify ways of securing external resources when necessary.

Competitive pressure and increased time-to-market force many companies to look outside their organizations to fill resource gaps and gain a competitive advantage. By clearly defining your expectations and requirements, you enhance the chances of finding qualified, responsive suppliers who can help you achieve a successful outcome for your project. In this lesson, you will plan project procurements and create a procurement management plan.

Lesson Objectives

In this lesson, you will:

- Collect the input needed to create a procurement management plan.

- Prepare a project procurement management plan.

- Prepare procurement documents.

TOPIC A

Collect Project Procurement Inputs

Before you transition your project to the executing process group, you need to plan for the project procurements based on the resource requirements that you identified. In this topic, you will plan project procurements.

Before you commence with the execution of a project, the project purchasing requirements and decisions are to be identified and documented. This requires the identification of resources that need to be procured from outside the project organization and an approach to identify potential sellers for the project. A good procurement plan ensures that risks and changes to the project schedule are minimal.

Procurement Management

Procurement management is the management of processes involved in acquiring the necessary products and services from outside the project team. Procurements are managed by constructing and implementing a procurement management plan, which specifies the procurements that will be used, determines the process for obtaining and evaluating bids, mandates standardized procurement documents that must be used, and describes how multiple providers will be managed.

Procurement management includes the management of project contracts and change control processes developed to administer project procurements. When managing contracts, a project manager ensures compliance with the terms and conditions stipulated in the contract and documents any change in the terms that are made to the contract during execution.

 Note: Not all organizations have a procurement department; however, there might be someone responsible for procurements. As the project manager, it's important for you to know how procurements are managed in your organization.

Outsourcing

Outsourcing refers to moving beyond the organization to secure services and expertise from an outside source on a contract or short-term basis; it is done for core work that has traditionally been done within the organization. Outsourcing is used frequently because it allows businesses to focus more on their core competencies. On the other hand, many businesses are emphasizing that work should be kept in-house whenever possible, in an effort to maintain stricter quality controls and security measures. As a project manager, you will need to work within the expectations and constraints that result from either situation.

Example: Outsourcing by a Clothing Manufacturer

A U.S. clothing manufacturer that has been producing its own buttons for decades may find that it is more cost-effective to move this part of its operations to an outside source. By outsourcing the button production to a vendor in a different locale, the company may realize significant cost savings while focusing on its core operations.

Make-or-Buy Analysis

Make-or-buy analysis is a technique that is used to analyze various parameters, such as cost of making versus buying, capacity (based on size) of making, legal eligibility of making, and technical feasibility of making, and determine whether it will be better to produce a product or service in-house or procure it from an outside seller. Make-or-buy decisions can significantly impact project time, cost, and quality. In the case of a buy decision, you must also consider if the product needs to be purchased, leased, or rented.

Example: Make-or-Buy Analysis for Developing Training Materials

A multimedia company was required to deliver several days of training to a client on the operation of its flagship product. The company's project team had to decide whether to increase staff in order to develop the training materials in-house or to outsource the work to a seller. The company's budget constraints and relative inexperience made it cost-effective to contract with an experienced outside firm.

Factors in Make-or-Buy Decisions

When making a make-or-buy decision, it is important to consider several factors.

Factor	Description
Impact	Consider the impact on cost, time, or quality. For instance, if current personnel must be retrained for services requiring a new skill set, it may be less expensive to outsource those services.
Ongoing need	If the organization will continue to need a specific skill set—even for future, unrelated projects—it may be a worthwhile investment to train current personnel to perform that service.
Learning curve	While it may make financial sense to develop an in-house solution, there may not be enough time to train personnel and implement the necessary policies and equipment to produce that solution.
Cost-effectiveness	If the required resources are readily available internally, organizations will usually use them. However, if the project involves technology, skills, materials, or resources that are beyond the organization's capabilities, it may be cost-effective to hire outside help.

The Lease, Rent, or Buy Decision

The *lease, rent, or buy decision* refers to business analysis that determines the most cost-effective way to procure the necessary equipment for a project if purchasing is not an option. Such a decision is primarily based on financial analysis.

Example: Lease, Rent, or Buy Decisions for Acquiring a High-Speed Copier

A project requires a high-speed copier with collating capabilities. If it is a small, one-time project and the equipment is very expensive and prone to breaking, it may be cost-effective to lease the equipment and take advantage of a service agreement. But if the project is ongoing over a period of months and service needs are not anticipated, it may be more cost-effective to rent a copier for the duration of the project. For a long-term project requiring extensive copying resources, it may be more cost-effective to purchase the equipment.

Market Research

In addition to the formal procurement documents, project managers should use whatever tools are available to them to discover, learn about, and research potential vendors. Some of the available tools that might offer useful information include:

- Vendor websites
- Vendor knowledge bases
- Industry analyst reports

- Consumer buying guides
- Internal experts

Example: Enterprise Solutions from Deltek

Headquartered in Virginia, Deltek (**www.deltek.com**) is a market research firm that provides market research, buyer guides, and solutions to assist organizations in outsourcing. One buyer guide offers suggestions on selection criteria, which include reputation and past performance, industry knowledge, strategic partnership, and the ability to meet needs. Input's research shows that most contracts include provisions to safeguard against unsatisfactory partnering, but most companies hesitate to exercise the provisions. Buyers should look for a supplier with a proven record of excellence and reputation for quality.

Teaming Agreements

A *teaming agreement* is a legal contractual agreement between two or more parties to form a joint venture or any other arrangement as defined by the parties to meet the requirements of a business opportunity. The parties can be internal or external to the organization executing the project. When a teaming agreement is created for a project, it significantly impacts the planning processes for the project and predefines issues such as the scope of work and competition requirements.

Example: GCCG's Agreement with Develetech Industries

GCCG and Develetech Industries have been associated partners for the last four years. The agreement insists that GCCG will have to procure the hardware from Develetech Industries for any implementation-related and turn-key projects executed by GCCG in the North American region. However, this arrangement is not obligatory when the implementation is done in any other area.

Specifications

Specifications are descriptions of the work to be done or the service or product to be provided; they define the requirements that must be met in exacting detail. These descriptions can be in the form of words, pictures, or diagrams. Specifications may relate to a product's design, performance, or functionality.

Guidelines for Collecting Procurement Inputs

Effectively planning project procurements helps document the project purchasing decisions, specify the approach to be used in project procurements, identify potential sellers for the project, and add this information to the procurement management plan. To generate an effective procurement management plan, follow these guidelines:

- Identify the project needs that can be fulfilled by acquiring products, services, or results. Determine:
  - What is to be acquired.
  - How to acquire.
  - How much to acquire.
  - When to acquire.
- Study the various input documents required for planning procurements to determine information related to the procurement requirements. The documents include:
  - The project scope baseline.
  - The requirements documentation.
  - Existing teaming agreements.
  - Project risk registers.
  - Risk-related contract decisions.

- Activity resource requirements.
- The project schedule.
- Activity cost estimates.
- The cost performance baseline.
- Appropriate enterprise environmental factors.
- Existing organizational process assets.
- Consult technical experts to define specifications for the project needs clearly, concisely, and completely.
- Perform a make-or-buy analysis to determine whether particular work can be accomplished by the project team or must be procured from outside the organization. If procuring from the outside, will it be something that you need to lease, rent, or buy?
- Determine the contract types to be used for specific procurement needs of the project.
- Document the procurement information that was collected to use it in the development of the procurement management plan.

TOPIC B

Prepare a Procurement Management Plan

You have collected the necessary project input documents and are now ready to create the plan for managing the project procurement. In this topic, you will prepare a procurement management plan.

Procurement Management Plan

After gathering all of the project procurement inputs, the next step is to assemble the information into a procurement management plan, which outlines the following:

- Whether or not to procure
- What to procure
- How to procure
- How much to procure
- When to procure

You must understand the need to procure products or services and the input required for procurement planning. You must clearly define the scope of the project, the products, market conditions, and constraints and assumptions before undertaking procurement planning.

Example: Creating a Procurement Management Plan for a Warehouse Management Software Project

The project manager of GCCG's Warehouse Management Software project, Mark Anderson, is creating the procurement management plan for the project. Mark discusses with stakeholders the various project requirements that include the warehouse management software, related computer hardware, networking, database, and project staffing. He studies the project scope baseline to determine the scope of the warehouse management software implementation within GCCG. He goes through the requirements documentation for each of the project requirements.

Mark involves Brian Wells, the IT Consultant of GCCG, to draw up the technical specifications of the project requirements. Further, discussions with Brian indicate that the warehouse management software and other requirements of this project have to be procured from outside the organization because the current infrastructure at GCCG does not support the requirements of this project.

Based on the procurement information collected, Mark prepares the procurement management plan for GCCG's Warehouse Management Software project.

Source Selection Criteria

Source selection criteria are the standards used to rate or score proposals, quotes, or bids and form a part of the procurement solicitation documents. Criteria can be objective or subjective.

- **Objective criteria** can be readily demonstrated, specific, and measured.
- **Subjective criteria** are open to different interpretations.

The following table provides examples of objective and subjective criteria.

Objective Criteria	Subjective Criteria
Ph.D. chemist with at least five years of experience in chromatographic research.	Experienced laboratory chemist with strong analytical skills.
80,000–90,000 square-foot storage area within three miles of the Dallas-Fort Worth Airport.	Ample square-foot storage area near Dallas-Fort Worth Airport.

Source selection criteria can be set in different ways.

Source Selection Criteria	Description
Understanding of need	Does the seller's proposal effectively address the procurement SOW while demonstrating a clear understanding of the needs?
Overall or life-cycle cost	Does the selected seller produce the lowest total cost of ownership, which includes the purchase cost and operating cost?
Technical capability	Does the seller have or is the seller expected to acquire the technical skills and knowledge needed for the project?
Management approach	Does the seller have or can the seller reasonably develop the management processes and procedures to ensure a successful project?
Technical approach	Do the seller's proposed technical methodologies, techniques, solutions, and services meet the project requirements?
Warranty	Does the seller provide a warranty for the final product and for what duration?
Financial capacity	Does the seller have or is the seller expected to obtain the necessary financial production capacity and interest resources?
Production capacity and interest	Does the seller have the capacity and interest to meet the project requirements?
Business size and type	Does the seller's company meet a specific category of business defined by the buyer, or established by a governmental agency, and included as a condition in the contract? Categories could include small, women-owned, or disadvantaged small businesses.
Past performance of sellers	Does the company have past experience with selected sellers?
References	Does the seller provide references from previous customers verifying the seller's work experience and compliance with contractual requirements?
Intellectual property rights	Are intellectual property rights established by the seller in work processes or services to be used for the project?
Proprietary rights	Are proprietary rights ensured by the seller in the work processes or services to be used for the project?

Guidelines for Preparing a Procurement Management Plan

To generate an effective procurement management plan, follow these guidelines:

- Identify the project needs that can be fulfilled by acquiring products, services, or results. Determine:
  - What is to be acquired.
  - How to acquire.
  - How much to acquire.
  - When to acquire.
- Study the various input documents required for planning procurements to determine information related to the procurement requirements. The documents include:
  - The project scope baseline.

- The requirements documentation.
- Existing teaming agreements.
- Project risk registers.
- Risk-related contract decisions.
- Activity resource requirements.
- The project schedule.
- Activity cost estimates.
- The cost performance baseline.
- Appropriate enterprise environmental factors.
- Existing organizational process assets.
- Consult technical experts to define specifications for the project needs clearly, concisely, and completely.
- Perform a make-or-buy analysis to determine whether particular work can be accomplished by the project team or must be procured from outside the organization.
- Determine the contract types to be used for specific procurement needs of the project.
- Document the procurement information you identified so far in the procurement management plan.
- After the procurement management plan is created, you will also generate other relevant outputs of the procurement process, including:
  - The procurement statements of work.
  - Make-or-buy decisions.
  - Procurement documents.
  - Source selection criteria.
  - Change requests.

 Note: Some of the information developed in generating these outputs will be used to finalize the procurement management plan.

TOPIC C

Prepare Procurement Documents

After gathering input about procurement resources and developing a procurement management plan, you need to prepare the necessary procurement documents.

The Procurement SOW

The *procurement SOW* is a detailed narrative description of the resources, goods, or services that are being sought from external sources to fulfill a project's requirements. It is distributed to potential sellers, who will use it to evaluate their capability to perform the work or provide the services. In addition, the SOW will serve as a basis for developing the procurement documents during the solicitation process. Information in the project scope baseline is used to create the procurement SOW. The procurement SOW goes through multiple rounds of reviews and fixes until the contract award is signed.

An effective procurement SOW describes the work being procured in sufficient detail so that potential vendors can evaluate their capability to perform this work. The procurement SOW also serves as a basis for developing the procurement documents during the solicitation process.

 Note: Even though a procurement SOW is created for each procurement item, multiple products or services can be grouped and specified in one procurement SOW.

To prepare a procurement SOW, you will need to identify procurement resources with the necessary expertise. If a formal contracting group or department within your organization is not available to support you in your procurement efforts, you will need to obtain those resources and expertise from within your project team. Some of the skills and expertise required for a full-blown procurement effort include:

- Supplier base and supplier qualification
- Contracting expertise
- Negotiating
- Legal services
- Knowledge of company policies and forms

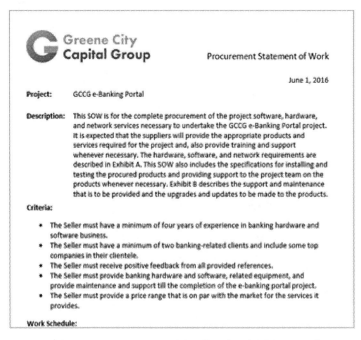

Figure 10-1: A procurement SOW for the GCCG e-Banking Portal project.

Example: Preparing a Procurement SOW to Hold a Public Carnival

The City of Butterfield Visitors' Association decided to hold a public carnival to increase tourism to Butterfield. To create a procurement SOW for this project, the project manager, Rachel, enlisted the help of her organization's chief negotiator and a lawyer. She also hired a consultant to define the specifications of the various carnival rides and attractions that will be utilized.

The organization had no existing preferred SOW format, so the project team researched SOW's used by other companies for similar events. The SOW is laid out in a logical sequence and uses consistent terminology throughout.

The statement also defines acceptable service criteria and includes key elements such as a schedule and acceptance standards. Before sending this SOW to prospective bidders, the project team had the document reviewed and validated by an independent legal firm.

Guidelines for Preparing a Procurement SOW

To prepare an effective procurement SOW, follow these guidelines:

* Review the product description to ensure that you fully understand the scope of the work being procured.
* Consult technical experts to define specifications clearly, concisely, and completely.
* Use a mandated procurement SOW format, if your organization has one. If there is no standard procurement SOW format, modify one from a previous, similar project.
* Present the information in a logical sequence.
* Use consistent terminology and level of detail throughout the procurement SOW.
* Determine whether any collateral services will be required of the vendor as a part of the contract:
    * What are the vendor's performance reporting requirements?
    * Will the vendor be required to provide any post project operational support?
* Determine the acceptable criteria for the product or service.
* Include the following key elements in the procurement SOW:
    * Clear identification of the project name and deliverable name or identification number.
    * A clear description of the deliverable.
    * When, where, and how delivery is required.

- Specifications to which the deliverable must be produced and methods for ensuring that the specifications have been met.
- Acceptance standards for the deliverable.
- Documentation requirements the seller must complete as part of the bidding process (i.e., references, compliance documents, confidentiality agreements, proof of insurance, contractor's license number, and so on).
- Description of any required collateral services that will support the main work activities provided in the contract.
- Any additional instructions the prospective seller will need to bid on the item.
- Have a knowledgeable third-party review the procurement SOW to ensure that it is complete, correct, and understandable.
- Document your make-or-buy decisions.

Procurement Documents

Procurement documents are the documents that are submitted to prospective sellers and service providers to solicit their proposals for the work needed. Many organizations use procurement document terms interchangeably. It is important to be sure that you understand the terms and definitions used by your organization.

All procurement documents must be written to facilitate accurate and complete responses from prospective sellers. The documents should include background information about the organization and the project, the relevant statement of work, a schedule, a description of the desired form of response, evaluation criteria, pricing forms, and any required contractual provisions. They should also be comprehensive enough to ensure consistent, comparable responses, but flexible enough to allow consideration of seller suggestions for improved ways to meet the requirements.

Common documents include:

- Request for Information (RFI)
- Request for Bid (RFB)
- Request for Quote (RFQ)
- Request for Proposal (RFP)
- Invitation for Bid (IFB)

RFI

A *Request for Information (RFI)* is commonly used to develop lists of qualified vendors and gain more input for resource availability.

This document is used to gather relevant information about a vendor's organization and financial history, including:

- Seller organization's history
- Balance sheets
- Business type (family owned, private, publicly listed, etc.)
- Owner's history and background
- Bank statements for the past three years

RFB

A *Request for Bid (RFB)* is commonly used when deliverables are commodities for which there are clear specifications and when price will be the primary determining factor. The RFB is submitted to selected sellers for a formal bidding process. You can anticipate some negotiations.

RFQ

A *Request for Quote (RFQ)* is commonly used when deliverables are commodities for which there are clear specifications and when price will be the primary determining factor. Unlike a Request for Bid (RFB), this solicited price quote is used for comparison purposes and is not a formal bid for work. Negotiation of price is generally not associated with an RFQ.

RFP

A *Request for Proposal (RFP)* is commonly used when deliverables are not well-defined or when other selection criteria will be used in addition to price. Sellers are often encouraged to offer suggestions and alternative approaches to meet the project goals. Preparing the RFP is time-consuming and costly for the seller. Negotiation is expected. Because it is time-consuming and expensive to create a proposal in response to an RFP, it is typical that not all the sellers solicited will respond.

IFB

An *Invitation for Bid (IFB)* is commonly used when deliverables are commodities for which there are clear specifications and when the quantities are large. It is sometimes used interchangeably with an RFQ. Unlike the other documents which are submitted by selected vendors, this invitation is usually widely advertised and any vendor may submit a bid. Negotiation is typically not anticipated.

Guidelines for Preparing Procurement Documents

To create a thorough procurement document, follow these guidelines:

- Examine the procurement need and determine which procurement document to use.
- Use standard procurement forms or templates if available.
- Develop a strong set of source selection criteria based on the real needs of your project.
  - Objective criteria will probably be required when requesting bids for most goods and facilities.
  - However, you may find that using objective criteria alone will be too restrictive when it comes to selecting resources such as a video producer, graphic artist, or central office site.
- Allow room to select from a range of capabilities and experience to get the best possible fit.
- Determine how you want the prospective vendors to respond:
  - Must the response be provided on a specific form?
  - Is there a specific format that must be followed?
  - What is the deadline for proposal submissions?
  - Is there any additional documentation that must be provided?
  - Where and to whom should the proposals be sent?
- Examine the relevant SOW and make any necessary modifications that may have been identified when planning for contracting.
- Verify that the procurement management plan is structured to facilitate consistent, comparable responses from sellers. It should include, at the minimum, the following key elements:
  - Reference to (or inclusion of) the relevant SOW. You may also include other relevant project documents, such as the WBS or network diagram, as appropriate.
  - Clear instructions for how the prospective seller should respond.
  - Any required contractual provisions such as confidentiality agreements and certifications.
  - Criteria by which proposals will be evaluated.
- Identify and consider any regulations that may define the required structure of procurement documents for government contracts.
- When required, include the following information in the procurement management plan:

- Listing of qualified sellers expected to bid (to drive down costs).
- Bidders' conferences.
- Supplier payment plan.
- How change requests will be managed.

ACTIVITY 10-1
Planning Project Procurements Review

Scenario
Answer the following review questions.

1. How can your organization benefit from more effective procurement planning?

2. In the future, what do you plan to use to prepare better SOWs and procurement documents?

Summary

In this lesson, you planned for procuring products or services from external sources. With a procurement SOW and the procurement management plan, you determined how procurement for the project will be handled. This effective planning and documentation of all project procurements up-front ensures the successful outcome of your project.

11 | Planning for Change and Transitions

Lesson Time: 1 hour

Lesson Introduction

You planned for project procurements. As the project advances, you will have to manage the changes that the project will undergo during its execution. Changes are inherent to a project and addressing them in advance can save the project from becoming a failure. A proper approach to changing management activities, diagnosing gaps, and developing corrective actions will increase the chances for project success. In this lesson, you will develop a change control system. You will also develop a plan to transition the completed project to its recipients. This will ensure that it meets their expectations, and will save last-minute rework at the end of the project.

Lesson Objectives

In this lesson, you will:

*   Develop an integrated change control system.

*   Develop a transition plan.

TOPIC A

Develop an Integrated Change Control System

As you continue to plan your project, you understand the important steps you must take toward making sure that your project is conducted with the appropriate internal integrity and oversight. You will further this goal by developing an integrated change control system, which formally governs significant changes to the project work, schedule baseline, and budget. In this topic, you will develop an integrated change control system.

You want to make sure that none of the customers, stakeholders, or members of the project management team are surprised by delays to your schedule or significant cost overruns. By developing an integrated change control system for your project, documenting its parameters, and adhering to its guidelines, you can reduce the risk to your project and maintain its positive forward movement.

Integrated Change Control

Integrated change control is the process of identifying, documenting, approving or rejecting, and controlling any changes to the project baselines. Integrated change control reduces risk to your project by governing the execution of proposed changes that will affect schedule and cost or any other objectives of the project. It allows project managers to record the changes that are requested, make sure that changes are implemented in a standardized and approved manner, minimize their disruptive effect, and monitor their progression from initial request through completion.

Once the change requests are identified, they are documented in a change request form. The form is then sent to the change management team, which can include the sponsors and customers, for review and approval. It is important to define the turnaround time for each change request and initiate a document routing process for a proper communication flow among the reviewers and stakeholders of the project.

Example: Developing an Integrated Change Control System in an Independent Company

A new project manager at a small, independent company, Rad, will be responsible for following the organization's guidelines regarding change control. He will first need to determine if there is a formal change control process in place; if there is not, he will develop one for his project. He will begin by gathering all relevant information and documentation and will identify the changes that require management approval.

He will proceed to identify who the key players are within the management team who need to approve or initiate change requests. This will be very important when it comes to asking for additional funding for the project or deadline extensions. He will identify who will manage changes and give authorization for expenditures. He will also need to document who needs to give consent to change requests and whether the consent of customers is required.

CCB

A *Change Control Board (CCB)* is a formally chartered group responsible for reviewing, evaluating, approving, delaying, or rejecting changes to the project, and for recording and communicating such decisions.

Change Control Systems

A *change control system* is a collection of formal, documented procedures for changing official project documents and project deliverables. An effective change control system includes forms, tracking methods, processes, and approval levels required for authorizing or rejecting requested changes. Change control systems often specify that a CCB will address the issues that affect the scope, cost, time, and product quality.

Example: A Change Control System for an Internal Project

A project manager for an internal project documented the project changes in the change control system. Any changes affecting the original scope, cost, or schedule baselines must be submitted with a standardized change request form, including a description of the change being requested, its relative priority, and the reason behind it. The internal CCB will evaluate each proposed change request for potential risks and benefits and make a decision whether to approve or reject the change.

Types of Project Changes

During a project, some of the types of common project changes include:

- **Timeline**—changes to any activities that can affect the overall schedule.
- **Funding**—changes to activities that can affect the funding allotted to the project; for example, a change that increases the cost of the project.
- **Risk event**—a new risk, or change to an existing risk, than can affect any aspect of the project.
- **Requirements**—changes to the project requirements initiated by a stakeholder.
- **Quality**—changes to the project scope, schedule, or cost that result in a decrease in the quality of project deliverables.
- **Resource**—changes to the project's human or equipment resources.
- **Scope**—changes that require the project scope to be modified.

Causes of Project Changes

Performance variation is an inevitable component of project work and can be caused by several common factors.

Cause	Description
Inaccurate initial estimates	There are many reasons why initial time and cost estimates for completing the project work prove to be inaccurate. These reasons may include lack of experience, lack of information, reliance on inaccurate data, excessive optimism, technological difficulties, and unreliable resources. Getting those original estimates to be as realistic and accurate as possible makes the control process more manageable.
Specification changes	Project work can open up new avenues of development and design that were not considered during the initial planning of the project work and scope. As new options for a product or service become apparent, customers, sponsors, or the project manager may broaden the project's scope to include new specifications and deliverables.
New regulations	As project work is progressing, new governmental or industry-specific regulations may be enacted. This can be especially true for very lengthy projects. Accommodating new regulations or legislation can also mean revisiting the planning process to determine the effect the new regulations will have on resource needs, schedule duration, and quality specifications.

Cause	Description
Missed requirements	Many times the requirements are identified by reviewing the documentation and interviewing the end users and policy makers. However, there are times when complete and comprehensive understanding may not be possible.
	For example, even though the interviewer feels that he or she has understood the point, and the interviewee feels that he or she has expressed everything significant, there still may be no meeting of the minds. Although a Requirements Traceability Matrix (RTM) is prepared, the confusion may still arise in a planning document. Prototyping can help demonstrate the functional and technical requirements of the project, and a missed requirement might surface during development of the prototype.
	Although all these techniques reduce the chances of missing any requirements, they cannot guarantee that every requirement is captured. In many cases, there are some discrepancies that surface at different phases in the project.

Organizational Change Types

The following table describes the organizational changes that would affect a project.

Organizational Change	Description
Mergers/acquisitions	The overall size and number of personnel in your organization is increased to incorporate another organization. This might affect the top-level executives or your project sponsor, and the effects will trickle down to other levels within the project.
De-mergers/splits	Similar to a merger, when organizations separate into two or more smaller organizations, this might affect the top-level executive or sponsor of your project and have trickle-down effects.
Business process change	The organization changes the official processes for getting things done. This might affect how funding and resources are approved.
Internal reorganization	Within the organization. when personnel and functional managers are reassigned, this might affect the project team's members and process.
Relocation	When a project team member leaves the organization or is transferred to another department within the organization, you might have to find a new project team member. If the entire organization relocates, then this might impact the personnel structure throughout the entire organization as well as business processes and preferred vendors.
Outsourcing	When the company decides to procure services from an external resource, this might disrupt the project's workflow processes or the stakeholders involved.

Project Change Categories

Project changes can be classified into three broad categories.

Category	Description
Corrective action	Documented direction on actions that must be carried out to help bring the future project performance requirements back on track and conform with the current project management plan.
Preventive action	Documented direction on actions that must be implemented to diminish the effects of any negative risks.
Defect repair	Formally documented measures that must be undertaken to address the defects in the project components, which are recommended to be either repaired or replaced.

Change Requests

Sometimes, a change in the project scope, work, or process may be necessary to meet the project objectives. *Change requests* are requests for changes that are processed through the change control system for their evaluation and approval. They can also be recommendations for taking corrective or preventive actions. Change requests can be raised by any stakeholder as long as they use the correct procedure. When the change request is approved, you may need to make changes to the related project documents, baselines, and processes. Change requests from vendors must also be carefully documented and approved before implementation.

Configuration Management

Configuration management is a process that is used to manage changes to a product or service being produced. Changes can be of a technical nature and in administrative direction. Configuration management is used to:

- Control product iterations.
- Ensure that product specifications are current.
- Control the steps for reviewing and approving product prototypes, testing standards, and drawings or blueprints.

A *configuration management system* is a set of tools that contains procedures that help provide technical and administrative guidance for identifying and recording the characteristics of a product or service, controlling changes made to the characteristics, documenting the changes and the status of implementation, and verifying the product's conformance to the requirements. One of the subsystems of the configuration management system is the change control system.

Configuration management systems, when combined with integrated change control, provide standardized and effective ways of managing approved changes and baselines within a project. Configuration control involves specifying the deliverables and processes, while change control involves identifying, recording, and supervising changes to project baselines.

 Note: When dealing with government contracts or other large systems, a configuration management system is often required.

Example: Implementing Configuration Management to Control Change Requests

An art director, Reanna, implemented a configuration management system specifically for controlling change requests to the images and animations in customers' advertisements. She created a database to track the project images. When a customer identified a need for an image or animation, the team created a new entry in the database; each entry included the name and size of the image along with a detailed description of the ad. Using this configuration management system, the art director could easily check the database for new entries, assign the change requests to team members, and track them through the approval process.

Guidelines for Developing an Integrated Change Control System

Your goal in developing an integrated change control system should be to ensure that the project management team and the stakeholders are not surprised by schedule delays or cost overruns. By developing a change control process, documenting its parameters, and adhering to its guidelines, you can reduce the risk to your project and maintain its momentum. To develop an integrated change control system, follow these guidelines:

- Use the approved change control system, if it exists. It is your responsibility to implement the approved integrated change control system for your project in accordance with all relevant company procedures and requirements.

- If no integrated change control system is used at your organization, it is your responsibility to develop one for your project. Gather any relevant historical data within the organization that relates to the process of identifying, documenting, approving or rejecting, and controlling changes to the project baselines.

- Identify what will be considered a change that is significant enough to require management approval. For the sake of maintaining forward momentum on project work, project managers will not bring minor changes to schedule and cost estimates to upper management for approval. Make sure that the organizational expectations regarding change control have been clearly defined and documented. How much latitude does the team have in making autonomous decisions about changes? At what point should you bring a change request to the upper management team?

- In conversation with stakeholders and the project management team, identify these responsible parties:

  - The people who are able to initiate change requests. These may include stakeholders, project management team members, and customers, among others.

  - The parties who are authorized to give or withhold business approval to a request for a change. Who will make the decision about whether or not a change is necessary and appropriate?

  - The parties who have the authority to approve additional funding, overtime costs, and purchase orders.

  - The parties who will be responsible for executing the work necessary to satisfy the requested change and evaluate the work for quality assurance.

  - The person(s) who will be responsible for managing changes. In some organizations, this may be the project manager, but in other organizations, it may be one or more functional managers.

  - The parties who are responsible for prioritizing changes and making qualitative decisions about them. Is this change imperative to the success of the project or merely nice to have if time and resources allow?

- Identify how change requests must be approved. Some organizations may require written approval from customers before changes to the scope, schedule baseline, and budget can be implemented.

TOPIC B

Develop a Transition Plan

You developed an integrated change control system and created some of the subsidiary plans of the project management plan. Another plan is the project transition plan, which enables you to manage the project's transition to its recipients—usually a customer or an operations department. In this topic, you will develop a transition plan.

Achievement of expected benefits alone does not mark the completion of a project. You must ensure that the project product obtained is transferred to the appropriate group for sustenance. Transitions are performed in accordance with the transition plan. The project manager is responsible for creating the transition plan.

Product Transition

Product transition is a formal hand-off of a project's outcome to its recipients, which could be a client or the next phase of the project. The project outcome, which includes the products, services, or benefits, is transferred to the next level for *sustainment*. Apart from the product, all required documents, such as training materials, support systems, facilities, and personnel, are also delivered during the transition. The transition process ends only when the receiving entity or organization performs all preparation processes to receive the project's end product and incorporate it. Transitions can be contract-based activities or can occur among functions or projects within an organization.

The Transition Plan

The *transition plan* is a document that describes how the outputs of a project will be transferred either to another organization or to a functional group within the performing organization. Transition plans must be created after detailed discussions with both the sponsors and customers.

Some organizations may add the complete list of tasks specified in the initial list to the transition plan, whereas others may limit the transition plan to tasks that specify the transition of deliverables or resources.

Project transition events need not occur only at the completion of a project. They can happen when necessary, during any phase of the project life cycle. For instance, a project or a non-project work deliverable will be transferred when the specific project activity is complete.

Example: A Transition Plan for an Automotive Company

An automobile manufacturer has taken up the design and launch of a new solar car model. The development of major components, such as the engine, chassis, drive system, solar panels, exterior, and interior, are dealt with as separate projects. The project that deals with the making of solar panels has been outsourced. The vendor responsible for this project created the solar panels and also created a transition plan that specifies the details regarding the transition of the product to the automotive company.

Transition Plan Components

The transition plan is part of the project exit criteria. It includes:

- Creating the scope of the transition and specifying what must be included and what can be excluded in the transition.
- Identifying the stakeholders and their organization or group that must receive the transferred products.

- Ensuring that the project benefits are measured and the benefits sustainment plan exists.
- Ensuring that the products are transferred at the right time.
- Creating a resource release plan that specifies what the resources must do after the benefits are realized and the products transferred.
- Creating a financial closure plan that describes the requirements for the closure of project finances.
- Ensuring that the contract closure requirements are consistent with the terms specified in the contracts.
- Determining the processes to receive deliverable acceptance.
- Communicating the requirements for project closure to the appropriate person with approval from the concerned person.
- Listing the impacts of project closure and describing how the organization or its structure will be affected by it.

Example: Creation of a Transition Management Plan for a New Project at Leaps and Bounds Travel

Linda Perez is the project manager for a new project at Leaps and Bounds Travel. She begins drafting the project management plan and wants to plan project transition. She schedules a meeting with the stakeholders and receiving organization to determine their views and expectations. She also measures the benefits to be obtained and creates the benefits sustainment plan. She is now all set to create the transition management plan that will ensure a smooth transition of the project benefits.

Transition Dates

The transition plan should specify the date when the project product, service, or result will be handed off to its recipients. The transition date has to be specified in the plan so that the products are transferred at the right time. After the product is handed off to the receiving entity or organization, the closure of project finances and contracts will be decided by the managers.

Product Training Events

Product training events are demonstrations provided by the company on a product or service during its transition phase. These training events are undertaken to teach recipients how to use purchased products or services. Modes of training differ from one product to another, and can include instructor-led training, video walkthroughs, handbooks, service manuals, and live demonstrations by experienced personnel.

Example: Product Training for the Anti-Spyware Software

Ristell is one of the companies that supply the latest cellphones to customers worldwide. The anti-spyware software for the cellphones is purchased from another vendor that provides anti-malware solutions. The anti-spyware software has to be integrated into the cellphones along with other software applications. During the product transition phase of the anti-spyware software, the vendor company had to provide a demonstration of the software to the people at Ristell. The vendor company prepared a video walkthrough of the anti-spyware software and how it can be integrated into the cellphones.

Extended Support

Extended support refers to a type of assistance provided by a company to its customers. It is most often a paid service and offers assistance after the expiration of the warranty period of a particular product or service. Extended support may include technical support; customer service; software or product support; troubleshooting; maintenance; and any upgrades, installation, or configuration past the warranty period. These kinds of assistance can be provided over the phone, through email, through technical support personnel, or through a web chat.

 Note: For a detailed discussion of warranties, you can refer to the lesson titled "Monitoring and Controlling Procurements."

Guidelines for Developing a Transition Plan

Planning project transition ensures that the benefits are sustained even after the completion of the project. To create a project transition plan, follow these guidelines:

- Define the scope of project transition.
- Check the project schedule to verify when the product, service, or result is ready for transition.
- Identify the stakeholders in the receiving organizations and their functions, and request their participation for planning project transition. The level of ownership for every involved stakeholder should be mentioned in the transition plan.
- Include any available organizational process assets that are used by the receiving organization if they will affect the project transition plan.
- Create and release the benefits sustainment plan based on the benefits acquired.
- Include any product training events that are planned during the transition process.
- Decide on the period of time when the company can provide support for the product. Also include details on the warranty period and extended support that will be offered.
- Plan the transition of project products, results, or services with the stakeholders and others who are related to the project.

ACTIVITY 11–1
Planning for Change and Transitions Review

Scenario

Answer the following review questions.

1. How will you manage changes in your organization?

2. What has been your experience in developing transition plans? What items did you choose to include?

Summary

In this lesson, you planned for change management and transitions. Building a holistic approach for managing changes and transitions will help you identify the changes that have to be addressed quickly and make an efficient and complete transition of a product or service to the customer or client.

12 | Executing the Project

Lesson Time: 2 hours, 30 minutes

Lesson Introduction

You finished your project planning and integrated the outputs from each of the planning processes into a comprehensive project management plan. Now, your project transitions from planning to executing.

Coordinating the people and resources you need to carry out your project management plan is essential for your project's success. The project team members need a coach to guide them as they undertake the work defined in the scope statement. Executing project work ensures that your team is on the same page and that your project finishes on time, on budget, and with the required quality. In this lesson, you will execute project work.

Lesson Objectives

In this lesson, you will:

- Direct the project execution.

- Execute a quality assurance plan.

- Assemble the project team.

- Develop the project team.

- Manage the project team.

- Distribute project information.

- Manage stakeholders' relationships and expectations.

TOPIC A

Direct the Project Execution

Your project officially advanced from planning to executing. Now, it is finally time to start leveraging the plan. In this topic, you will identify the components and purpose of directing and managing project execution.

Coordinating people and resources to carry out the project plan is like conducting musicians in an orchestra. Effectively directing and managing project execution ensures that the project team starts and finishes the project work according to the project management plan.

Move from Planning to Execution

Throughout the life cycle of a project, various reviews occur. As the project moves from the planning phase (process group) to the executing and controlling phases (process groups), it is important to conduct a review meeting. During the meeting, several items should be verified:

- All roles and skills have been identified, all required resources are available and committed to the project, and high standards for performance are set.
- All project documents have been completed, reviewed, and signed off on, which includes the business, functional, and technical requirements, the project charter, the scope statement, all project plans, and the SOW.
- All issues in regard to planning have been resolved.
- The project is still feasible.
- The expectations of the stakeholders are aligned with the project plan.

PMIS

A *Project Management Information System (PMIS)* is an automated or manual system used by a project team to gather, analyze, communicate, and store project information. The PMIS collects information on the work that has and has not been accomplished in each work package and how that work result compares to the planned schedule, cost, quality, and scope. A PMIS can utilize sophisticated software tools, either those purchased off-the-shelf or custom built by an internal IT group, to manage some of its components.

There is some overlap between a communication plan and a PMIS; a PMIS has a calendar associated with it and includes a lot of communication between the project manager and the team. An example of an off-the-shelf software product that can be deployed as a PMIS is Microsoft® Project.

 Note: A common pitfall associated with using a PMIS is creating a system in which the various pieces of data are incompatible with one another. For example, financial data may be created in one application and reporting in a different application, and there is no way to get these two systems to talk to each other.

Example: Execution of a Project Plan in a Municipal Fire Station

The project team for a municipal fire station completed their project plan, which is well into execution. Using the services of a systems analyst, they designed and implemented a PMIS that includes manual and computerized methods.

The team analyzed the needs of the project and balanced cost and benefits to develop a work authorization system. The system requires an email message to be sent to notify the appropriate people that work can begin on the next component.

Each Monday morning the team has a status review meeting. Before the meeting, the project manager sends out the most recent open task report. During the meeting, the person responsible for a task reports on its progress. If problems or barriers are identified, the administrative assistant logs them in the issues log and the issue is then assigned to an individual.

Common PMIS Problems

Several common PMIS problems arise when directing and managing project execution.

Problem	Description
Reacting to lagging indicators	PMIS reports show problems after-the-fact. Good project management requires proactive problem prevention.
Managing symptoms rather than problems	While the PMIS reports exceptions and overruns, it can't explain the reason for the problem. It is important to focus on finding the cause and solving the problem, rather than making the exception or overrun go away.
Over-reliance on PMIS communication	Project managers need to communicate frequently with team members and other stakeholders. Sending PMIS reports is important, but it should not take the place of other types of communication.
Invalid data in the PMIS	PMIS reports can be wrong, making problems look either greater or smaller than they are. Some very real problems may not show up in the PMIS at all. The project manager must look beyond the PMIS to verify information about the problems, and then concentrate on getting the problems solved.
Too much information	Too much information is counterproductive, forcing people to cope by ignoring some of the messages. It is important to make sure that the right people get the information they need at the right time, but it is equally important not to swamp people with irrelevant or untimely information. Someone has to control the scope of the information in the PMIS, or it will overload the team and the project manager.

Work Performance Information

Work performance information consists of periodically collected information about project activities that are performed to accomplish the project work. This data will reside in your PMIS, if you have one.

This information includes:

- Schedule progress with status information.
- Deliverables that have been completed and have not been completed.
- All schedule activities and their start and finish dates.
- The degree to which quality standards are being accomplished.
- Expenses authorized and incurred.
- Estimates to complete the schedule activities already in progress.
- Percent of completed schedule activities that have been started.
- Lessons learned that are posted to the lessons learned knowledge base.
- Details on resource utilization.
- Status for implementation of change requests.
- Details on corrective and preventive actions and defect repairs.

Work Authorization Systems

A *work authorization system* is a tool that is used to communicate official permission to begin work on an activity or work package. It is a function, or component, of the Project Management Information System (PMIS). Its purpose is to ensure that work is done at the appropriate time, by the appropriate individual or group, within a specific time, and in the proper sequence.

Work authorization systems include the necessary processes, documents, tracking systems, and approval levels required to provide work authorizations. Depending on the project, your work authorization mechanism may be a simple email message or a formal, written notice to begin work. Smaller projects may only require verbal authorization. The work authorization system is integrated with the communications plan.

CONTRACT WORK AUTHORIZATION	
1a. Project Title:	1b. Work Proposal Number:
2. Headquarters Program Point of Contact:	
3. Headquarters Budget Point of Contact:	
4. Responsible Program:	5. Responsible Secretarial Officer:
6. Responsible Field Organization:	
7a. Site and Facility Management Coordinator:	7b. Contractor Point of Contact:
8. Work Authorization Number:	9. Revision Number: *

Figure 12-1: A sample contract work authorization system.

Guidelines for Directing the Project Execution

Throughout the entire execution of a project, the project manager can employ different techniques to coordinate and direct the various technical and organizational aspects of a project. Tools, such as the PMIS and the work authorization system, are powerful work aids that an organization can use to ensure project success. To effectively execute the project plan, follow these guidelines:

 Note: Selecting and implementing a PMIS is outside the scope of this class, but the guidelines presented here are some considerations that you may want to be aware of as you move forward in pursuit of advanced project management skills.

- Comply with any of the organizational policies and procedures that the organization has in place regarding project execution to ensure predictable and consistent results. Make sure that all contractors are familiar with and comply with the procedures.
- Evaluate and select the work authorization system you will use to formally sanction work to begin on an activity or deliverable. The value of the control your system provides should be balanced with the cost (money and time) of designing, implementing, and using the system.
- In line with good project management practice, use the artifacts necessary to get the job done. Use the organization's project management infrastructure. If it is not there already, then invent it.
- If necessary, work with a systems analyst to create a PMIS that is workable for your project. Make sure that the systems analyst understands the following:
  - Who needs to use the information?

- What type of information will be needed by each user?
- When and in what sequence will the information be used?
- Who will generate the initial information to be incorporated in the system?
- Once the system is in place, determine who will be responsible for its day-to-day operation, whether it will be you or someone else. Specifically, you need to determine who will be responsible for:
  - Data entry of initial information. This includes assigning people to enter data and setting up specifications for what data must be entered, how it will be entered, and when it will be entered.
  - Analysis of information. Analysis means summarizing information, drawing conclusions from it, and creating graphical depictions of what the information is saying. Your task here is to assign people to do the analysis and provide specifications of how the data is to be analyzed, how it is to be reported, and what reporting formats will be used.
  - Storage, archiving, and retrieval. This includes assigning individuals to handle day-to-day storage and retrieval and setting specifications for backing up data and archiving it.
  - Systems documentation. Whatever system you choose, it must be documented. Remember that you will be straining the PMIS during project execution. You may need to adjust it, or even repair it, to improve its performance during this phase of the project. Good documentation will allow support staff to make the adjustments and repairs efficiently, without losing data or backing up the project schedule.
- Evaluate the effectiveness of the PMIS for your project.
  - Do not rely too much on the PMIS. Be proactive in managing problems rather than waiting for the PMIS to report a problem before addressing it.
  - Avoid the temptation to manage the PMIS instead of the project.

TOPIC B

Execute a Quality Assurance Plan

Previously in the course, you identified what is involved in creating a quality management plan. Now that you are in the project execution phase, you are ready to move forward with this key element of ensuring that your project meets its stated goals. This is the action phase of your work, in which you will measure, verify, and quantify the progress achieved. In this topic, you will execute quality assurance.

You can set quality goals for your project, but how do you know if they are being met on an ongoing basis? Performing quality assurance ensures that the project will meet the identified quality standards and that stakeholders are confident about the quality of the work being produced.

Quality Audit

A *quality audit* is an independent evaluation, inspection, or review of a project's quality assurance system to improve the quality performance of a project. The audits can take place at scheduled or random intervals. The auditor may be a trained individual from within the performing organization or a qualified representative of a third-party organization. During a quality audit, the quality management plan is analyzed to make sure that it is still reflective of what has been learned in the project and to ensure that the operational definitions are still adequate and valid. The results of a quality audit are important for the current project and for later projects or other parts of the organization.

 Note: You must ensure that quality audits conducted at every interval are logged in an audit log file. Audit logs are referred to as audit trails.

Example: Quality Audits at a Manufacturing Company

An auditor for a manufacturing company performs quality audits regularly. Every six months he walks into the factory and reviews the company's quality management plan, cost of quality, and quality process design to make sure that these processes are up-to-date, being used correctly, and still valid.

Quality Audit Topics

Several topics can be included in a quality audit.

Topic	Description
Quality management policy	May be evaluated to determine how well management uses quality data and how well others in the organization understand how the data is being used. The evaluation may include an analysis of management policies for collection, analysis, and use of data in decision-making or strategic planning.
Collection and use of information	May be evaluated to determine how well the project team is collecting, distributing, and using quality data. Items for analysis in this category may include consistency of data collection processes, speed of information distribution, and use of quality data in decision-making.

Topic	Description
Analytical methods	May be evaluated to determine if the best analytical methods are being used consistently and how well their results are being used. Items for audit may include how analysis topics and analysis methods are selected, what technology is used, and how results are fed back to others in the process.
Cost of quality	May be evaluated to determine the most effective proportion between prevention, inspection, and costs of repair or rework.
Quality process design	May be evaluated to determine how process design, process analysis, and statistical process control should be used to establish and improve the capability of a process.

Process Analysis

Process analysis is the method that is used for identifying organizational and technical improvements to processes. Various techniques are used to conduct the analysis, including flowcharting that shows the relationships between process steps and root cause analysis that helps determine the underlying causes and develop corrective actions. Examples of factors that can be examined when performing the analysis are the process capacity, capacity utilization, throughput rate, flow time, cycle time, process time, idle time, work in progress, set-up time, direct labor time, direct labor utilization, and quality.

Process analysis involves:

- Collecting information about the existing process and documenting a process flow diagram.
- Determining the entry and exit criteria of each step in the process.
- Conducting process analysis interviews with the people to identify the limitations in the process.
- Conducting a *Failure Mode and Effects Analysis (FMEA)* to identify the possible failures in the process.
- Assessing the identified limitations and quantifying their impact.
- Identifying appropriate operating decisions to improve the process.

Quality Assurance Tools and Techniques

The following table describes tools that are used to perform project quality assurance (QA).

Tool	Description
Cause-and-effect diagram	A diagram that illustrates how various factors may be associated with possible problems. Possible causes can be identified by asking "why" and "how" for each problem identified. Cause-and-effect diagrams are also known as Ishikawa or fishbone diagrams.
Control chart	A graphical display of the results or status of a process over time and against established control limits. It helps track the behavior of processes over time and determine if the variances in the process are within acceptable limits.
Flowchart	A process flow diagram that assists the project team's effort to identify potential quality problems, their associated effects on overall project quality targets, improvement areas, and possible improvement measures.
Histogram	A bar chart of variables. Each column symbolizes an element of a problem. The height of each column represents how frequently the element occurs. By using the shape and width of the distribution, causes of problems are identified.

Tool	Description
Pareto	A histogram that shows the causes of problems in the order of their severity.
Run chart	A line graph showing plotted data points in chronological order. It could show trends in a process over time or improvements over time. Trend analysis uses run charts. Trend analysis is a tool you can use to communicate forecasting information based on the project's current performance. It is also used to monitor the project's technical, cost, and schedule performance.
Scatter chart	A diagram showing a relationship between two variables. The diagram plots dependent variables versus independent variables. The more closely the points form a diagonal line, the more closely they are related.

The following table describes techniques that are used to perform project quality assurance (QA).

Technique	Description
Statistical sampling	A sampling technique that is used to measure an entire population based on actual measurement of a representative sample of that population.
Inspection	An official examination of work results to verify that they meet requirements. The inspection may be conducted by an internal or external inspection team.
Approved change requests review	Ensures that all change requests are reviewed and implemented as approved during the perform integrated change control process.
Cost-benefit analysis	Considers the tradeoffs and the benefit of meeting quality requirements of higher productivity and lower costs while increasing stakeholder satisfaction. The business case of each activity is used to compare the cost of each step with its expected benefits.
Cost of Quality (COQ)	Analyzing the costs incurred by preventing non-conformance to requirements, appraising for conformance to requirements, and failing to meet requirements (rework), internal or external.
Benchmarking	Compares the quality of your project's processes and systems to those of other comparable groups, both internally and externally.
Design of Experiments (DOE)	A statistical method of identifying the factors that may influence certain product or process variables. DOE determines the number and type of tests to be used and their influence on the cost of quality.

Example: Execution of a Quality Assurance Plan by a Coffee Brewing Equipment Manufacturer

A leading coffee brewing equipment manufacturer is beginning to produce a new product line, and Kevin Campbell is the project manager for the project. Kevin has been given the task of maintaining a satisfactory level of quality while maintaining the fiscal goals for the project.

A quality audit was commissioned to determine if in-process monitoring produced the expected improvement to cost and quality. Following an examination of the testing procedure outlined in the quality management plan, the audit team analyzed the collected data from the latest series of testing seven days per week.

The analyzed data was compared to the projected quality data based on the in-process monitoring system, and it showed that the projections matched the actual data. Armed with this information, the audit team recommended modifications to the quality management plan requiring testing only twice each week. At a cost of $100 per test, the company is now spending $200 per week on testing instead of $700, therefore saving $500 per week. Through careful review of the quality management plan, analysis of the use and distribution of collected data, and by monitoring the cost of quality, the company achieved marked improvements in quality while realizing an improved bottom-line.

Guidelines for Executing a Quality Assurance Plan

Effective quality assurance provides confidence that the project's product or service will satisfy relevant quality requirements and standards. To execute a quality assurance plan, follow these guidelines:

- Ensure that random and scheduled quality audits are conducted by qualified auditors to evaluate the quality management plan, quality testing procedures, and measurement criteria.
  - Are the quality parameters set forth in the quality assurance plan valid?
  - Are the operational definitions and checklists adequate and appropriate to achieve the desired final results?
  - Are the testing methods being implemented correctly?
  - Is data being interpreted, recorded, and fed back into the system properly?
- Use one or more of the quality assurance tools to determine the causes of quality problems in the project's product, service, systems, or processes.
- Identify and implement the appropriate actions needed to increase the effectiveness and efficiency of the project team's work results and improve the quality in the product or service.

TOPIC C

Assemble the Project Team

Once the project plan has been approved, it is time to execute it. Multitasking of many resources makes negotiation and scheduling components of project management a constant challenge. In this topic, you will look at methods for acquiring and scheduling skilled resources and assemble the project team.

For the project to succeed, you must have the right resources. The most important resource in any project is the intellectual capital that the project team brings to the table. Certain people will have skills that you need. Your job will be much easier if you can negotiate for, effectively assign, and schedule the human and material resources that you need to successfully complete the project. If you lose this battle, all your hard work building that great plan will be for naught. This topic will help you make sure that your project is not in trouble before it even begins.

Project Manager Roles

A project manager has many roles and responsibilities to fulfill on a project.

Role	Description
Leader	The formal authority of project managers is established in the project charter, and the informal authority will be established by their ability to demonstrate leadership skills with the team. Project managers must provide clear direction for where the stakeholders need to go, and credible strategies for how to get there. Project managers must serve as advocates for their project. It is their responsibility to inspire others—stakeholders and non-stakeholders—about the project and enlist their help and support.
Planner and controller	Project managers must facilitate project planning and determine measurement criteria for evaluating the work accomplished. They must also establish systematic processes for measuring the work against the plan.
Communicator	Project managers act as communication central on a project, interfacing with executives, functional managers, customers, vendors, project team members, and other interested parties outside of the project. Project managers must communicate clearly and appropriately to each level, to make sure that the right information is transmitted to the right person at the right time and executive support for the project is maintained.
Negotiator	Project managers need to negotiate for resources—time, money, people, and equipment—in order to complete the project successfully. Depending on the organization, these negotiations may involve an element of "horse-trading" with functional managers. In addition, as the project evolves, project managers may need to negotiate changes in the scope, schedule, or budget with stakeholders. This may involve negotiating trade-offs among the previously established success criteria established for the project.
Problem-solver	Every project is unique, which means that every project has its own unique set of problems to overcome. Project managers must be able to face problems rather than deny them, determine the root causes of problems, and make decisions about the best method for dealing with the problems.

Role	Description
Organizational change agent	Projects exist within organizations. Project managers need to know how to get things done in the organization, how to avoid political issues that may hamper the project's progress, and how to influence the organization to bring about change. They also need to be willing to adapt to project changes that may be imposed upon them by their organization.

Political Capital

Many employees possess a reserve of corporate goodwill that is based on their perceived political position and power in the company. This perception, also known as *political capital*, can come from position, reputation, or both. Often, this goodwill can be used to achieve a desired end.

When a project is threatened, many times the main factor influencing the positive or negative outcome for the project is the political clout of the project manager and the political clout of the sponsor in the senior management realm. If the project manager cannot resolve serious problems, the project manager will need to ask the sponsor to intercede. However, these requests should be done sparingly because there is a limit to the amount of political capital that the sponsor will be willing to use for any given project.

Team Acquisition

Successful completion of a project requires team members with the right skills, knowledge, and ability to deliver project deliverables. Project managers must identify from the resource pool the ideal individuals for the team. *Acquisition* is an approach that is used to obtain resources for the project when there isn't enough staff within the project team or organization to complete the project. Interviewing and recruiting the potential team members and scheduling their availability is one of the core project management responsibilities that contributes to completing the project on time. Organizations hire external resources, if they do not have the required number of appropriate skilled resources on staff.

Example: Acquiring a Project Team for a Fundraising Event

Greg has been assigned the task of organizing a fundraiser for a children's hospital. First, Greg meets with his functional managers, Kim and Rob, to determine what kinds of people should be running each activity, if they need to hire any extra help, and how much resources will cost. They employ about 40 people, and 20 have been preassigned by Kim and Rob to work on activities based on previous experience with the fundraiser. Some activities have already been decided including a hoop-shooting contest, balloon volleyball, and a karaoke contest.

Greg receives a list of everyone who has been assigned to work with him and calls a meeting to develop his team and assign responsibilities. Some team members need to have good organizational skills and some need to have creative skills; however, all need to be good with kids. Based on skills and abilities Greg selects his team, including a high school basketball coach to be in charge of the hoop-shooting contest and an art major to run arts and crafts. Greg finds a local college that agrees to rent its gymnasium to the event for only $100.

The next day, Greg goes over the roles and responsibilities one final time with his team to make sure that all is understood. An organization chart is made and given to the college, Kim, and Rob so that they know exactly how the gym will be used and who will be involved in each activity. Now, organization and setup can begin for the event.

Project Staff Assignments

Project staff assignments are the assignments of people who will work on the project, whether full-time, part-time, or as needed. It usually involves a team directory, memos to or from team members, and project organization charts and schedules.

Pre-Assignment

Pre-assignment is the allocation of project team members to project activities, even before the project has officially kicked-off. These resources could be key resources who have the expertise to perform a particular function in the project or have been promised during a competitive proposal.

Example: Pre-Assigning a Programmer for a Website Development Project

Susan Thomas has been authorized as the project manager for the company's website development project. During the initiation phase, she realized that the services of the company's Java programmer, David Robinson, were required during the month of October in order to complete her project on time. Therefore, she immediately secured the services of the programmer for that time period.

Negotiation

Negotiation is an approach used by individuals or organizations with mutual or opposite interests to come together to reach a final agreement. For example, staff assignments can be negotiated with functional managers, vendors, or external organizations. This ensures that the appropriate staff is assigned within the time frame when there is a need for scarce or specialized resources. Effective negotiation requires knowledge of the economic and strategic worth of the project to effectively bargain for scarce skills resources.

 Note: The book "Getting to Yes: Negotiating Agreement without Giving In" written by Roger Fisher and William Ury provides an interesting approach to problem-solving and negotiating.

Example: Negotiating with Vendors for Supplying Automobile Parts

An automobile manufacturing company decided to employ Greene City Legal Services as vendors to provide consultants for its new project. The project manager negotiated a formal agreement with the supplier on this issue. The negotiation included financial specifications, legal formalities, acceptable quality of items, pricing issues, and so on. Both parties reached a favorable agreement at the end of the negotiation.

Effective Negotiating Skills

Negotiation is indispensable to project management and, when done effectively, will contribute to the success of a project. Some of the skills or behaviors that managers can adapt to negotiate successfully are:

- Analyze the situation.
- Differentiate the needs and wants of both parties.
- Focus on issues and interests rather than on a person's stance or position on the issue.
- Be realistic when making proposals.
- Give concessions and indicate that you are providing something of value.
- Ensure a win-win situation for both parties at the end of the deal.
- Communicate in an appropriate manner.

Virtual Teams

A *virtual team* is a team that is distributed across multiple locations. Some virtual teams have occasional physical meetings, while others may never meet face-to-face. Virtual team building is more difficult, for a number of reasons.

- Bonding and team identity can be hard to create when team members are geographically dispersed because finding ways to provide a sense of team spirit and cooperation may be difficult.
- Communication and information sharing need to rely on various forms of technology because teams cannot meet face-to-face. However, managing electronic collaboration so that everyone on the team can reliably transmit and access information from one another can be challenging.
- Because roles, reporting, and performance can be harder to track on a dispersed team, individual contributions may be overlooked.

Example: Virtual Team for the Apollo 13 Mission

The Apollo 13 spacecraft was launched from the Kennedy Space Center in April, 1970, but an accidental explosion in an oxygen tank aborted its mission to the moon. The virtual team responsible for Apollo 13's launch and its subsequent safe return included the three crew members on board and the staff of mission control in Houston, Texas. Telecommunications included voice and television communication between astronauts and Earth.

Guidelines for Assembling the Project Team

Assembling well-formed project teams will result in meeting the resource needs of the project to fulfill project requirements. To assemble a project team, follow these guidelines:

- Form good relationships with functional managers.
- Know when you need specific resources.
- Negotiate with the appropriate organizations or parties for critical resources timed with project need.
- Ensure that appropriate steps are taken to retain the procured team members.
- Look for synergy and diversity among team members.
- Look outside to competent suppliers where in-house resources are not available.
- Make sure that roles and responsibilities are clearly understood by the team and other stakeholders. If any issues arise among the team members, talk to the team members separately.
- Create and distribute an organization chart to all stakeholders.

TOPIC D

Develop the Project Team

Now that you have acquired your project team, you need to help them achieve peak performance. Team building ensures that you build an atmosphere of trust and open communication. In this topic, you will develop the project team.

Project teams comprise individuals, drawn from different disciplines, who must learn to work together to achieve a common goal in a short period of time. The individuals working on your team, all of whom have their own communication styles, work habits, motivation, and career agendas, have to trust one another and work together rather than compete against one another for resources and time. Team building ensures that you build an atmosphere of trust, collaboration, and open communication.

Interpersonal Skills

Interpersonal skills are abilities that an individual should possess to work harmoniously and efficiently with others. Being in the project management profession, it is important that you develop a balance of conceptual, technical, and interpersonal skills that will enable you to analyze situations and deal with them appropriately. Some of the important interpersonal skills critical to effectively manage a project are:

- Leadership
- Team building
- Motivation
- Communication
- Influencing
- Decision making
- Political and cultural awareness
- Negotiation

Team Development Stages

In his group dynamics research titled "Tuckman's Stages of Group Development," Bruce Tuckman describes the development of a project team in the following five stages.

Stage	Description
1. Forming	Team members are wondering whether the decision to join the team was a wise one. They are making initial judgments about the skills and personal qualities of their teammates, as well as worrying about how they personally will be viewed by the rest of the team. During this stage, conversations tend to be polite and noncommittal because people hesitate to reveal too much about their personal views. In addition, team meetings tend to be confusing, because the team tries to figure out who is in charge.
2. Storming	Team members begin to assert themselves and control issues that emerge. Personality differences begin to arise. Conflicts result because team members differ in the way they want to do the project work or in the way they want to make decisions.

Stage	Description
3. Norming	The team begins to work productively, without worrying about personal acceptance or control issues. There are still conflicts; however, they tend to be focused on process issues rather than personality differences. The team begins to operate on mutual dependence and trust.
4. Performing	The team is working at optimum productivity. It is collaborating easily, communicating freely, and solving its own conflict problems. Team members feel safe in reporting problems, trusting their fellow team members to help them create the best solution for the team as a whole.
5. Adjourning	The team members complete their assigned work and shift to the next project or assigned task. This last stage is sometimes known as "mourning."

The process of forming, storming, norming, performing, and adjourning is not done in a "lock step" fashion by the team. Team members keep coming in and going out of the team. Whenever a new member joins, forming takes place; even if the rest of the team has already crossed the forming stage. So, these stages are not followed one after the other but rather are situational.

Effective Project Teams

The team members should work in a collaborative way to ensure project success. It is the responsibility of the project manager to build an effective project team and foster teamwork. Managers should give opportunities that challenge the team members' abilities, provide support and timely feedback, and recognize and reward good performance. To achieve highest team performance, managers should use effective communication methods, develop trust among team members, manage conflicts, and promote collaborative decision making and problem solving.

Project managers should seek support from management or the appropriate stakeholders to effectively build project teams. This will help improve people skills, advance technical competencies, build good team environment, and increase project performance.

Symptoms of Teamwork Problems

Several symptoms alert the project manager that the team is having trouble working together smoothly.

Problem	Symptom
Frustrated team members	The symptoms may be complaining, negativity, or poor productivity.
Unhealthy conflict or excessive competition	Watch out for factionalism, in which subgroups work to their advantage at the expense of the project as a whole.
Pointless meetings	If meetings are not productive in the sense of solving problems or making team decisions, they can demoralize the team. Check that meetings have a specific and useful purpose and that the purpose is achieved. Also, keep a check on the level of participation of team members.
Lack of confidence in the project manager	The team has to believe that the project manager has a vision, a strategy for making the vision happen, and the ability to translate the strategy into action. If team members begin to second-guess or leave the team manager out of the decision-making loop, something needs to be done.

> **Note:** Remember that all these are problems and symptoms, not causes. To deal with the problem, first identify the root cause and then find the most appropriate solutions.

Barriers to Team Development

The project manager should be aware of barriers that can impair team performance. Some of those barriers include:

- Ambiguous goals or roles.
- Conflicting roles.
- Poor communication.
- Environmental changes.
- Poor support from upper management.
- Conflicting personal and organizational agendas.

Training

Training is an activity in which team members acquire new or enhanced skills, knowledge, or attitude. Training may be provided to teams, small groups, or individuals and can cover management, technical, or administrative topics. It can range from a multi-day, formal workshop in a classroom to a five-minute, informal on-the-job training demonstration at the employee's desk. It may be formulated to provide generic skills or customized to provide a specific skill set that is unique to the project. Training should be made available to team members as soon as the need becomes apparent.

Example: Training on a Software Program

Mark is the programmer assigned to the company website project. Recently, Mark was informed that he will have to create the entire site using a website development software program which he was unfamiliar with because the entire organization was using the program and maintenance will be easier if the tool was standardized.

Because Mark was the only programmer available to work on the project, Carrie, the project manager, arranged for Mark to take a training course to learn the technical program. Not only will Mark's training help the project achieve its objectives and abide by organizational policy, but it will also enhance Mark's skills and help position him to advance within the organization.

Team-Building Activities

Team-building activities or *team-building strategies* are the specific functions or actions taken to influence diverse individuals from many functional areas, each with their own goals, needs, and perspectives, to work as a cohesive team for the good of the project. These activities help the team develop into a mature, productive team. Team-building activities can be formal or informal, brief or extended, and facilitated by the project manager or a group facilitator.

To foster team building within a project team, a project manager may ask each of the veteran employees on the team to partner with a less experienced team member, offering coaching as needed and sharing knowledge, information, and expertise. Working together toward a shared goal is a great way for team members to help each other reach a higher level of performance.

Example: Team-Building Activity

Robin, a new project manager for a line of youth-oriented sportswear, decided that a good way to get to know her team was to plan an outdoor team-building activity. Two of the designers were located on the East Coast and will be working very closely with the manufacturing team at the company's San Diego facility. Robin arranged to fly the two designers to San Diego to participate in the all day, off-site ropes course. Robin also participated in the rope climbing exercise and an experienced team-building coach facilitated the activity.

Ground Rules

Ground rules set clear expectations of the expected code of conduct from team members. This ensures an increase in the productivity and decreases misunderstandings. Ground rules include all actions that are considered acceptable and unacceptable to the project management context.

Example: Ground Rules for a Project

A project manager at a cellular phone manufacturing company has set ground rules for the team members of his new project. The ground rules include:

- The project team members will be consulted about the sensibleness of the plan before the project manager submits the plan for management approval.
- The project team members are responsible for notifying the project manager of any necessary changes to the project plan.
- The project manager is responsible for ensuring that the team members assigned to a team leader are made available for the project at the appropriate time.
- The project team members are responsible for informing the project manager of any potential delay in meeting their scheduled deadlines as soon as it is known to them.
- The project team members are responsible for notifying the project manager or team leader about any anticipated workload conflicts within the project.

Team Logistics

Team logistics is the practice of providing materials and facilities needed by the team to accomplish their tasks. Logistics include:

- Materials needed for the project and project deliverables.
- Facilities for the team, including space, desks, phones, desktops, servers, software, and electrical power.
- Communication equipment for non-co-located team members.
- Software and hardware to create the testbed environment.
- Travel facilities, including transportation, lodging, and other arrangements.

Co-location

Co-location refers to positioning most or all key team members in the same physical location to make communication easier and enhance team performance and team spirit. Although most commonly used on large projects, smaller project teams may also benefit from co-location. There are different degrees of co-location. In some projects, some of the team members may be co-located while others are not.

Example: Co-location for a National Campaign

A political candidate announcing a run for the presidency of the United States will establish a national campaign headquarters office, in which the key members of the campaign's project team will be co-located. The headquarters will serve as a base for national operations and centralize the efforts of the candidate's political machine. The co-location of the project team will only last for the duration of the campaign.

Reward and Recognition Systems

A *reward and recognition system* is a formal system used to reinforce performance or behavior. Reward and recognition systems are generally standardized throughout an organization and approved through corporate channels. The purpose is to motivate the team to perform well.

Rewards can include monetary gifts, additional vacation time or other perks, company plaques or trophies, or small gifts. While it's common for the terms reward and recognition to be used interchangeably, they are different. You can recognize a person without giving them a reward. However, you should never reward a person without recognizing them.

- *Rewards* are tangible, consumable items that are given to a person based on a specific outcome or an achievement. Rewards can also have a defined start and finish, or fixed time, and are usually expected when the specified goal is achieved or attained. For example, receiving a bonus after a successful year is a reward.
- *Recognition* is a more personalized, intangible, and experiential event that focuses on behavior rather than outcome. Recognition is not restricted to a set time, is usually unexpected by the receiver, and is intended to increase an individual's feeling of appreciation. For example, receiving public acknowledgement and appreciation for helping another department that was short staffed is recognition.

 Caution: Rewarding or recognizing a team member for working overtime due to poor planning or in an effort to receive extra pay is not an effective reward and recognition system because it does nothing to motivate the team to perform well or to improve team morale.

Example: Recognizing and Rewarding a Mentor

Tim is an art director assigned to the company website. Often, Tim helps new team members and provides coaching and mentoring. Carrie, the project manager, recognized Tim's extra efforts at the weekly project team meeting by publicly telling the team how Tim has provided new members with beneficial mentoring. She presented Tim with a gift certificate to a new restaurant as a reward and incentive for his outstanding performance.

Individual Performance Rewards

In traditional organizations, rewarding individual performance refers to giving pay increases or promotions to individuals based on merit. In a team environment, it is difficult to tie merit increases to individual performance because of the mutual interdependence of the team members.

 Note: Recognizing and rewarding individual team member performance is considered culturally unacceptable in many countries, particularly China and Japan.

Team Performance Assessments

All project team members have their own areas of expertise that, if identified and used appropriately, can help in completing the project successfully. Project team performance assessment is performed to assess and identify the potential of each team member in order to help improve interaction between team members, solve issues, and deal with conflicts.

A team's technical success is measured on the basis of meeting the project objectives and finishing the project on time and within the decided budget. Continual formal or informal evaluations of the team's performance is an effective way to improve the skills and competencies of project team members and increase team cohesiveness.

You can follow these guidelines to assess team performance.

- Ask key questions of the team members. Questions may include their work experience, likes and dislikes about the projects assigned to them, tasks that they are confident about, and project tasks they will prefer to do.

- Speak to team members frequently through one-to-one meetings and regular project meetings wherein the team may talk about project cost and schedule adherence, milestones, deliverables, change management, risk management, and quality management.
- Provide constructive criticism and acclaim to team members, as necessary. Team successes should be announced while reprimanding should be done in private.
- Evaluate individual performance. Project managers must listen to the team members before responding and must be objective and flexible when necessary.
- In situations where a team member is not performing at the desired level, it may be necessary to remove them from the team and reassign his or her work to another resource. If this is not possible due to the workload and expertise of the other team members, it may be necessary to replace the under-performing resource and to assign his or her work to the new resource.

Example: Developing the Beautification Project Team

A city council passed a proposal for a beautification project, including a new public park. Creation of the new park design fell to a board of citizens and government officials. The Director of Parks and Recreation, Elizabeth Fry, served as the project manager. Elizabeth scheduled a kick-off meeting that included introductions and exchange of information for creating a team directory.

As the project moved through the execution phase, the team performed well for the most part. One team member owned an Internet hosting service and made arrangements for the team to use web-collaboration software, making team communication much easier. To reward team members' efforts, Elizabeth offered small gifts of appreciation, which were donated by local merchants. She also made sure that she recognized the extra effort of her team during city council meetings.

Elizabeth arranged for local landscape architects and gardeners to offer special training seminars to interested team members, which proved to be extremely motivating. When conflicts arose, such as a disagreement over what to use as surfacing materials in the playground, Elizabeth monitored the situations but usually let the team work them out for themselves.

Guidelines for Developing the Project Team

Effective team development results in improved individual and team performance, which increases the team's ability to achieve project objectives. To effectively develop your project team, follow these guidelines:

- Recognize the project team's current stage of development in respect to the Tuckman scale and be proactive in helping the team to be as productive as possible.
  - During the forming stage, conduct activities that will help the team get to know one another and develop a sense of mutual respect. The following is a list of activities for the forming stage:
    - A kick-off meeting that includes time for introductions.
    - Creation of a team handbook documenting the team's goal, the major tasks required to achieve the goal, and any constraints under which the team must operate.
    - Publication of a team directory.
    - Development of a team charter that sets forth guidelines on how team members will behave toward one another, how they will communicate, when they will meet, how they will make decisions, and how they will escalate problems.
    - Selection of a team name or emblem.
    - Initial social events to allow the team members to get to know one another on a personal level.
  - During the storming stage, use conflict management approaches to help the team work through problems.
  - In the norming stage, concentrate on issues of project performance.
    - Focus on the team's productivity toward meeting the project goals.

- If the team is bogged down on certain problems, help create cross-functional teams to work on the problems.
- Eliminate barriers that may be hampering team performance.
- Provide opportunities for recognition for the team's performance from management, customers, or peers.
- In the performing stage, provide recognition for team performance, but stay out of the way when the team manages its own problems. However, if project progress is sluggish, this is a good stage to challenge the team with more stringent performance goals.
- In the adjourning stage, team members complete project work and shift to the next project or assigned task.
  - This phase indicates the transformational phase of achievement through synergy.
  - In this phase, ensure that formal closure and completion of the tasks happen. Also, facilitate the smooth transition of the project team members to the next project.
- Conduct periodic project team and one-to-one meetings to evaluate the team performance and identify the strengths, weaknesses, and requirements of each project team member.
- Provide appropriate feedback to each project team member.
- Develop and implement a formal reward and recognition system.
- Consider co-location to enhance the team's ability to perform as a team and improve communication. When co-location is not feasible, it becomes especially important to encourage and enhance interaction among team members.
- Provide appropriate training and coaching to help team members acquire new or enhanced skills, knowledge, or behavior.

TOPIC E

Manage the Project Team

Virtual teams and matrix organizations make managing project teams more complicated for project managers. However, when team members are accountable to a functional manager and a project manager, this dual reporting relationship becomes a critical component for project success. Effective project managers monitor team member performance and handle conflicts that might arise within the team. In this topic, you will manage your project team.

Causes of Conflict

Conflict arises in most groups and working situations. Causes of conflict include:

- Competition.
- Differences in objectives, values, and perceptions.
- Disagreements about role requirements, work activities, and individual approaches.
- Communication breakdowns.

Examples: Characteristics of Conflicts

Project managers should be aware of certain characteristics of conflict that will help them effectively handle conflicts when they arise. Conflict is a normal aspect of working in a team and forces the need for exploring alternatives. It is a team aspect and openness about the situation or opinions can resolve conflicts. While resolving conflicts, focus should be on the issues and not on individuals; on the present situation and not the past.

Conflict Management

Conflict management is the application of one or more strategies for dealing with disagreements that may be detrimental to team performance. Effective conflict management can lead to improved understanding, performance, and productivity. Conversely, ineffective or nonexistent conflict management can lead to destructive behavior, animosity, poor performance, and reduced productivity—all of which threaten successful completion of the project's deliverables. There are certain conflict resolution methods, and the need to follow a particular method includes the intensity and importance of the conflict, the time given to resolve the conflict, the positions of the conflicting parties, and the motivation to resolve conflicts on a short- or long-term basis.

Example: Conflict Management Between Two Salespeople

Two salespeople accustomed to working independently, on commission, may be asked to partner together on a project to bring in a major new account. If the two become embroiled in conflicts regarding their commission splits and their differing sales styles, and if they cannot agree to work together amicably for the sake of the project, the business will suffer. Conflict management strategies will be used to help them work through their differences.

Conflict Management Approaches

The following table describes six basic approaches for handling conflicts; each is effective in different circumstances.

Approach	Description
Confronting/problem solving	Focuses on identifying the underlying problem and working out alternatives or solutions for it in a way that allows the involved parties to work through their disagreements.
Compromising	Involves working out a middle ground that satisfies all parties to some degree.
Smoothing/accommodating	Focuses on de-emphasizing the differences between points of view and focuses on commonalities.
Forcing	Requires others to yield to the point of view of one side or another. It may increase conflict and end in a win-lose situation.
Collaborating	Incorporates insights and viewpoints from different perspectives, which can lead to commitment between the conflicting parties.
Withdrawing/avoiding	Involves avoiding or retreating from the conflict or potential conflict and allowing the involved parties to work out the conflict on their own.

Note: Different problem-solving business philosophies interpret and categorize compromise and confrontation differently, in terms of their effectiveness and desirability; additionally, different companies may have their own way of interpreting and implementing these approaches. Also, there cannot be one universally effective way to resolve a conflict because conflicts are mostly situational.

Potential Political Barriers

During the executing and controlling processes of a project, political barriers may surface that negatively affect the working relationship between the organization performing the work and the client or business organization. Some of those barriers include:

- The goals and objectives of each organization are different.
- No alignment exists between the different organizations.
- Scheduling issues exist as a result of vested interests.
- Issues exist regarding the resources required for the project.
- User management participation may not exist at the right levels.

A project manager needs to be aware of these barriers to prevent them from occurring or to be prepared to address them when they do occur.

Performance Appraisals

The need for formal or informal *performance appraisals* often relies on project length, project complexity, organizational policy, labor contract requirements, and amount and quality of communication. Evaluation can come from supervisors and people who interact with the team. You can use the performance appraisal to accomplish a number of tasks, including:

- Comparing performance to goals.
- Clarifying roles and responsibilities.
- Delivering positive as well as negative feedback.
- Discovering unknown or unresolved issues.
- Creating and monitoring individual training plans.
- Establishing future goals.

The Issue Log

The *issue log* or *issue register* is a document that is used to list, track, and assign project items that need to be addressed by the project team. It can be used to track the project issue, each issue's unique number, the issue status, and the individuals responsible for resolving certain issues by a specific date. The issue log is useful for regular follow-up with the project team and must be updated regularly. An issue log also serves as an important organizational process asset.

Issue No.	Issue Description	Issue Date	Severity	Originator	Issue Title	Priority Level	Assigned To	Date Resolved	Status

Figure 12–2: An issue log template that is used to register and manage project issues.

Example: Managing the Project Team in an Advertising Company

An advertising company has plans to develop a campaign for a customer over the next four months, and David is acting as the project manager. David wanted to make sure that everything got off to a good start, so he called a kick-off meeting. Before the meeting, he developed a set of metrics to measure team performance and planned to monitor the progress of his team by meeting with them individually once a week.

During the kick-off meeting, David asked the team to submit weekly status reports using email and to use instant messaging software to stay in close contact with one another. He also let the team know how their performance will be monitored and he set up a meeting schedule. However, there was some conflict in the team. Two team members disagreed on the direction for their campaign. One wanted to use a very contemporary, almost edgy approach, while the other wanted to appeal to traditional, more conservative values. After a series of meetings with the customer's product analyst, the team was able to find a middle ground that satisfied both team members and pleased the customer.

From the earliest days of the project, David instituted the practice of using an issues log to track all matters in question or dispute in the project. This became extremely valuable because the project made it to the final stages and was ready for hand-off to the customer. Everyone was clear on exactly what they had committed to, and the customer received the expected deliverables.

Action Items

An *action item* is any piece of work that needs to be performed by a resource. It is not important enough to be included in the issue log, and it does not qualify as an activity in the project schedule. Action items can result from meetings or they can be related to any project objective. The important thing to remember about action items is that they can happen throughout the project, and may or may not be formally documented.

Example: Action Items for a Visiting Client

When an out-of-town client visits, someone might be assigned to pick up the client at the airport and deliver her to her hotel. Another person may be asked to take the client to dinner. And when the client leaves town, another person will need to deliver the client back to the airport.

Guidelines for Managing the Project Team

Successful project team management results in a solid staffing management plan, updated and submitted change requests, resolution of issues, good lessons learned documentation, and productive team members. For effective project team management, here are some guidelines:

- Verify that team members are clear on their roles and responsibilities. Provide any necessary assistance or coaching.
- Communicate the ground rules to each team member.
- Establish good internal and external communication among team members.
  - Be aware of the issues and challenges of virtual teams—especially when team members are in different time zones or different countries.
  - Use proper email etiquette. Typing in all uppercase is synonymous to shouting. Use the phone or a personal visit to discuss contentious issues.
  - Provide cultural-sensitivity training to foster smooth communication for global project teams, especially when English is a second language. Keep communication simple and to the point. Eliminate slang, sports terms, or jokes as they often suffer in translation or can possibly offend others.
- Adjust the communications plan to meet the needs of individual team members, keep information flowing among the team, and provide feedback.
- Ensure that the project team is informed about key milestones and gate reviews when customer or senior manager approval is required.
- Monitor performance of team members on an ongoing basis.
  - Speak individually and directly to each team member. Don't rely on email messages or monthly reports. Personally observe the team's progress and the intangibles (such as morale, engagement, or cynicism) that are at play.
  - Develop a set of metrics to measure team performance for each project. Establish tolerances so that corrective actions can be taken when needed. Use a management-by-exception approach to avoid micromanaging the team.
  - Provide constructive feedback to team members on a frequent basis. Performance reviews can be formal or informal. If disciplinary actions are taken, these must be in writing to avoid any misunderstanding.
  - Consider additional training for those team members who need to improve their performance.
- Consider a quality audit to verify that the team is headed in the right direction to meet the project's quality requirements. An effective quality audit team needs to be independent from the project team.
- Establish how conflicts will be resolved, including escalation procedures.
- Manage conflict using the appropriate approach for the circumstances and individuals involved. Regardless of the approach, apply the following principles:
  - Allow people to have their say—giving both sides a chance to state their case. Demonstrating respect and acknowledging people's different positions are a must to effectively addressing conflicts.
  - Actively listen to what is being said. Paraphrase or ask questions to verify understanding.
  - Find those areas at issue where both sides are in agreement.
  - Encourage both sides to find an agreeable win-win resolution to the problem.
  - Keep the group focused on the goal of finding a resolution to the problem.
  - Set expected ground rules, based on the communications management plan, for the team to operate on.
  - When conflict occurs among team members or between the team and other organizational entities, it may be effective to confront the problem head on—focusing on the problem. It may be advantageous to try to defuse conflicts early to avoid escalation.
- Establish an issues log to track and assign project issues, and enable regular follow-up with the project team. Hold specific team members accountable for resolution of issues.

TOPIC F

Distribute Project Information

During project planning, you developed a communications management plan describing the team's approach to project communication. Now that work results are being accomplished, you need to let project stakeholders know how the project is progressing. In this topic, you will identify the process involved in distributing project information.

In a project, information provides critical links for successfully meeting the project's objectives. Distributing project information efficiently and effectively ensures that meaningful and appropriate information is available to project stakeholders. This in turn assists stakeholders in making appropriate decisions by giving a clear view of the project progress.

Information Distribution Tools

Information distribution tools are distribution methods and presentation tools that are used to provide project information to stakeholders. The tools include:

- Email
- Hard-copy documents
- Presentations
- Video conferencing
- Meetings
- Phone calls

Example: Information Distribution to Stakeholders

As the company website project continues through the executing process, a huge amount of project information is generated and collected. Carrie, the project manager, is diligent in providing the stakeholders with the information they need to make sound decisions. First, she and her team review the communications management plan to make sure that they implement an information retrieval system.

The executive stakeholders present a challenge regarding project communication. On the one hand, they need to make decisions about the project and require enough information to support their decision-making, but they are impatient with lengthy presentations. So Carrie prepares a clear, concise summary of key information and a detailed report with charts and status updates for those who are interested.

Carrie invites the stakeholders to ask questions or provide other feedback. She monitors the communication system to make sure that messages are getting through as planned and that the recipients fully understand the content.

Guidelines for Distributing Project Information

Effective information distribution ensures that project information is appropriately dispensed to project stakeholders. Getting the necessary information in a timely manner enables the stakeholders to make decisions regarding the project in time to make a difference. To distribute project information effectively, follow these guidelines:

- Create and distribute project information, such as project records, reports, and presentations, in accordance with the communications management plan.
- Use effective communication skills to exchange information.
  - Use the communications plan as a guide to ensure that the appropriate level of communication occurs among all project stakeholders.

- Monitor the effectiveness of communications and adjust them accordingly, especially when scope changes occur or risks are realized.
- When communicating new information, include constraints and assumptions, and the impact of that information.
- Verify the immediacy of the need for information and use the appropriate means to communicate it, depending on its urgency.
- Increase communication when stakeholders indicate they need more information or as the project moves into a phase that affects them more directly. Decrease communication when the phase of the project has little to do with a particular stakeholder.
- Modify communication schedules as needed to correct problems that arise.
- Monitor the need to obtain additional information, including feedback, and adjust the plan based on that feedback.
- Verify that new team members are familiar with technologies and tools you are using for communication.
- If schedule changes or risk becomes more likely, ensure that you communicate all changes to the appropriate people and obtain necessary sign-offs.
- Ensure that your reports and other communication are clearly and concisely delivered.
- Ensure that communication delivers a consistent message to all audiences.

- Use an information retrieval system to provide stakeholders' access to project information. Everyone should have access to the information needed. Whether manual, computerized, or a combination of both, make sure that your system complies with the following standards:

  - The system has sufficient storage capacity to hold the necessary project information.
  - The system follows any security protection protocols established in the communications management plan so that sensitive information can be accessed only by appropriate stakeholders.
  - The system provides a method of version control to protect data and to ensure that everyone is working on the same, most recent document.
  - The system is organized to meet the needs of the project and the stakeholders.

- Select the appropriate information distribution method for distributing project information.

  - Sending an email message announcing that a report is posted on the intranet site.
  - Making a telephone call to schedule a one-on-one meeting.
  - Taking notes of phone calls to provide a written record of the communication.
  - Making a presentation to highlight the important points in a report.

- Monitor the communication system for feedback to make sure that messages are getting through as planned. If individuals or organizations are not able to send or receive messages adequately, identify the problem and adjust the communications management plan, information distribution method, or retrieval system accordingly. This might include speaking to individuals directly to get a more straightforward answer.

- Analyze the effects on project execution when unexpected requests for information surface. Take appropriate action to make changes to the plan as necessary. Document such unexpected requests for future use.

TOPIC G

Manage Stakeholder Relationships and Expectations

You informed project stakeholders about how project resources are being used to achieve project objectives. As project issues arise, you need to address and resolve them with the appropriate project stakeholders. In this topic, you will identify the process involved in actively managing stakeholder relationships and working within their expectations.

Managing communication to satisfy the requirements of and resolve issues with project stakeholders can make or break a project. Actively managing relationships with your project's stakeholders and working with their expectations increases the chances that your project will remain on track and that issues are resolved right away to avoid disruptions at a later stage in the project life cycle.

Project Meetings

Project meetings are meetings held among project stakeholders to discuss or convey project-related information. Other meetings, such as team meetings, management meetings, and company meetings, may also include discussions about each project.

Some considerations for conducting effective project meetings include:

- When a meeting is scheduled, an agenda should be written and distributed beforehand so the attendees know what to expect during the meeting.
- The meeting should be led by someone who is familiar with the topics to be discussed, but this person does not necessarily need to be the project manager.
- Discuss any topics outside the agenda at the end of the meeting, if time permits, or defer them to another meeting.
- The meeting should begin and end on time to respect the individual schedules of the attendees.
- And finally, meeting minutes should be prepared, distributed to the appropriate stakeholders, and archived for future reference.

Project kickoff meetings are particularly important, because they set the tone for communications throughout the duration of the project. The agenda for a project team that is meeting for the first time will include:

- Reinforcing project assignment documents.
- Introducing the team members.
- Stating the project goals and expectations.
- Sharing contact information of the team members.
- Establishing timelines and assigning project tasks.
- Discussing potential project issues if any.
- Setting the ground rules.

Expectation-Gathering Techniques

Expectation-gathering techniques help maintain and update the values and expectations of stakeholders. Stakeholder expectations are continuously gathered throughout the project. The progress of the project can be measured against the expectations and stakeholder satisfaction. Conflicts in stakeholder expectations must be resolved and brought to a consensus. Common techniques to gather stakeholder expectations are brainstorming, interviews, and surveys.

Expectation-gathering techniques provide the ability to:

- Compare the project's benefits delivery against the estimated values and expectations.

- Analyze and make recommendations for change when value estimates and expectations are not met.
- Regularly update deliverables with changes, current information, and results.

Example: Managing Stakeholders in an Insurance Company

Alex is a project manager in an insurance company. His team has been developing a new type of insurance plan for car owners. When the project kicked off, Alex created a communications plan and distributed it to the project stakeholders for their review. He met with them and got their feedback, so now a communications plan is in place that seems to be working well.

The communications plan set up a regular status meeting. Before each meeting, Alex prepares a summary of the project status. The stakeholders appreciate this brief summary. Alex also always gives the stakeholders an opportunity to bring up concerns. In the most recent meeting, the stakeholders had an issue with the discount the new insurance plan offers to people with clean driving records. While the stakeholders think this is a good offer, they would like to extend this offer to single car owners with no co-ownership.

Alex agreed that this change is manageable and immediately logged this change in requirements into the database for it to be analyzed and processed through the integrated change control system.

The Stakeholder Expectations Matrix

A *stakeholder expectations matrix* is a document that contains the names of project stakeholders, their expectations from the project, and their influence on the project. This helps the project team understand the commitment levels needed to provide accurate attention on key milestones in the project. The stakeholder expectations matrix may be created through the stakeholder analysis process.

Stakeholder Expectations Matrix Mapping

Stakeholder expectations matrix mapping is the process of mapping goals and expectations of senior managers and sponsors within an organization. Goals and expectations are derived or identified by conducting interviews with key stakeholders along with the business case, project road map, sponsors, and contracts. The matrix is updated continuously with the goals and expectations of new stakeholders as the project planning phase progresses.

The stakeholder expectations may change during the planning and executing stages of a project. Therefore, it is necessary that the matrix is updated regularly and reviewed by everyone related to the project.

Stakeholder Expectations	Validation and Sign-Off	Priority High=5 Low=1	Process to Meet Expectations	Person Responsible for the Process	Measure of Success	Goal	Person Responsible for Reporting Progress
Ensure high quality in the products delivered.	CEO of Greene City Capital Group	4	Effective decision making and proactive resource management.	Project Managers and the PMO	Status against the agreed quality criteria: 96-100%=very satisfied 90-95%=satisfied Below 90%=dissatisfied	Ensure 100% quality in products.	Members of the PMO
Ensure timely delivery of the expected benefits.	The respective PMO	5	Efficient project management.	Project Manager	Each expected benefit to be provided on or before the agreed dates.	Deliver the benefits as scheduled.	Project Manager

Figure 12–3: An example of the stakeholder expectations matrix mapping document.

Expectations Mapping Objectives

The main objectives of the expectations matrix mapping are:

- Cultivating an understanding of the stakeholder groups.
- Identifying and updating stakeholder values and expectations.

- Monitoring and controlling project progress against the expectations and assessing stakeholder satisfaction.
- Defining strategies for resolving conflicts among stakeholder expectations and obtaining consensus.
- Communicating how the project delivers the benefits with the estimated values and expectations.
- Identifying and recommending adjustments in the project if value estimates and expectations are not met.
- Updating deliverables with changes, current information, and results.

Expectations Mapping Matrix Components

The expectations mapping matrix includes several components.

Component	Description
Expectation	Describe the expectation that is to be met by the project.
Validation and sign-off	Validate and sign-off the criteria used to measure the progress when the activity is complete or when the expectation is met. This is usually conducted by the person who defined or provided the expectation.
Priority	Prioritize the level of importance and resources that are assigned to meet the expectation using an appropriate scale of measure.
Process to meet expectation	List the processes and methods used to meet the expectation.
Responsibility for process	List the names and roles of people who are responsible for ensuring that the processes and methods defined to meet expectations are being performed.
Measure of success	List the measurement criteria that are to be used for each expectation.
Goals	List the performance goals of each expectation.
Reporting progress	List the name and role of the person responsible for reporting the progress of meeting the expectation against the standard measures.
Schedule frequency	Determine the frequency of reporting and communicating progress against the measurement criteria.
Current rating	Capture and identify the current progress toward meeting the expectation.

Guidelines for Managing Stakeholder Relationships and Expectations

Actively managing stakeholders ensures that your stakeholders understand the progress your project is making. Managing stakeholder expectations will support your team's project schedule, enhance team performance, and decrease project interruption. To effectively manage stakeholders, follow these guidelines:

- Assess the communications needs of each stakeholder during the planning phase of the project. When managing stakeholders, the project manager needs to follow the plan and periodically obtain stakeholder feedback to make any required adjustments to the plan.
- Hold face-to-face meetings with stakeholders when possible because face-to-face meetings are most effective. Assessing body language provides the project manager with an opportunity to determine whether or not the stakeholder is pleased with the project's progress. For example, if

during a project update the stakeholder is frowning, has arms folded, and is looking at his shoes, it is essential that the project manager determine the stakeholder's concerns. By managing stakeholder expectations, the project will continue to have their buy-in.

- Use a suitable alternative when face-to-face meetings are not practical, such as in global projects. If available to the project team, some useful substitutes might include video/web conferencing, webinars, desktop sharing, net meeting, and video chat.
- Create a stakeholder expectations matrix to help the project team members ensure that all of the stakeholder expectations are implemented in the project. Ensure that the stakeholder expectations are collected frequently.
- Periodically update the stakeholders with the status of the project.
- Be flexible when communicating with the project sponsor or other members of senior management. Be prepared to provide a summary of project status in five minutes or less if the need arises. Flexible communication is the ability to meet the specific communication requirements of each stakeholder. For example, one may prefer extensive numerical data while some others may just prefer a synopsis.
- Use an issue log to assign, track, and resolve open issues that are of interest to stakeholders. Issues that remain unresolved can lead to project delays.
- Change requests need to be processed to update the communications plan reflecting changes in project staffing.
- Take corrective action as needed to bring project performance in line with customer expectations.
- Document lessons learned to reflect the causes of issues and changes made to rectify them.

ACTIVITY 12-1
Executing the Project Review

Scenario
Answer the following review questions.

---

1. What aspects of executing the project plan have you found to be the most challenging? Why?

2. Which tools and techniques will you use to more effectively execute projects in the future?

Summary

In this lesson, you managed project execution. Executing your project according to the project management plan ensures that your project team is on the same page and that your project fulfills the project requirements and delivers necessary deliverables.

13 | Executing the Procurement Plan

Lesson Time: 1 hour

Lesson Introduction

Earlier in the process, you planned project procurement. Now, it is time to execute your procurement plan. As the project manager, it is your responsibility to make sure that your project is completed on time and on budget. Obtaining proposals or bids from vendors gives you confidence that work products will meet project objectives at a fair and reasonable cost. And once you have those documents in hand, you need to be able to follow established techniques for evaluating them accurately and choosing from among them. In this lesson, you will execute project procurement by requesting vendor responses and selecting a vendor.

Lesson Objectives

In this lesson, you will:

- Obtain responses from vendors.

- Determine which vendors to use for the project.

TOPIC A

Obtain Responses from Vendors

During project planning, you prepared a procurement document. Now, you are ready to obtain bids or proposals from prospective vendors to meet project purchasing requirements. In this topic, you will obtain responses from vendors.

Obtaining proposals or bids from vendors gives you confidence that the work products will meet project objectives at a fair and reasonable cost. Mastering the tools and techniques for requesting vendor responses ensures that you obtain relevant, accurate, and appropriate responses from prospective vendors.

Qualified Vendors

Qualified vendors are vendors who are approved to deliver products, services, or results based on the procurement requirements identified for a project. The list of qualified vendors can be obtained from historical information about different vendors who delivered resources required for prior projects executed in your organization.

If the resources you require are new to the organization, you may need to do some research in collaboration with your Purchasing Department to identify qualified vendors for each resource. You can perform an Internet search using specific search criteria to expedite the process. This research will generate a list of possible vendors, and you will need to interview the prospective vendors, visit their work sites, review work samples, interview their references, check with certification boards, or use other approaches to validate whether they qualify as vendors for the procurement requirements. Many vendors publish an Internet knowledge base that contains information about their products and services, where you can search for specifics that will help you determine whether a company should be included in the qualified vendors list.

 Note: In case further information is required about the prospective vendors, you can send an RFI to each of them to gather details about their capabilities.

Example: Qualified Vendors Selection by Mixed Messages Media

Mixed Messages Media invites proposals from vendors for setting up a Wi-Fi network for their new corporate office in New York. The Wi-Fi network needs to meet all specifications of the newly announced governmental regulations. On reviewing the list of their old suppliers, Mixed Messages Media found that none of the suppliers could provide them with a Wi-Fi network that could enable them to meet the governmental regulations.

An advertisement requesting the submission of information about prospective vendors was announced in all the national dailies and business journals. There was an overwhelming response from a large group of vendors. Based on the vendors' information, Mixed Messages Media was able to generate a list of 10 prospective qualified vendors. The qualified vendors were then called in for a conference, where each vendor was asked to demonstrate their capability to deliver the required product. At the end of the presentations, Rudison Technologies and Develetech Industries were selected as the qualified vendors for the Wi-Fi network installation because they met most of the requirements and standards prescribed by Mixed Messages Media. Later, Mixed Messages Media sent the RFP to these two organizations and continued the process of vendor selection.

The Qualified Vendors List

A *qualified vendors list* contains details regarding vendors who meet the organization's requirements and to whom requests can be sent. It is sometimes known as an approved vendor list. The RFI for each vendor is scrutinized and evaluated for qualifying the vendors. The term "qualified vendors" does not mean that the organization is bound to do business with them. It only indicates that when needed, the organization will interact with the vendors and RFPs, IFBs, or RFQs will be sent to the qualified vendors. Generally, vendor identification number or vendor registration number is assigned to the qualified vendors.

Note: In project management, the following terms are frequently used interchangeably: seller, vendor, supplier, and contractor.

Qualified Vendors List

Project Name: Computer Network Upgrade Project

Vendor	Industry/Expertise	Capacity	Staff	Reputation	References
Company 1	Computer networking consultants	100 to 500 machines in local network	60	Able to provide solutions for large businesses on time	*Name 1*: Designation/Contact details *Name 2*: Designation/Contact details
Company 2	Networking hardware router manufacturers	1000	500	Quality equipment providers – rated #1	*Name 1*: Designation/Contact details *Name 2*: Designation/Contact details
Company 3	Networking cable suppliers	Any quantity within 2 weeks	150	Can provide required brands at competitive prices	*Name 1*: Designation/Contact details *Name 2*: Designation/Contact details

Figure 13-1: A qualified vendors list for the Computer Network Upgrade project.

Bidder Conferences

Bidder conferences are meetings conducted by the buyer after issuing an RFP but prior to submissions of a bid or proposal by the vendors. During this meeting, the buyer explains the requirements, proposed terms, and conditions, and the buyer clarifies the vendors' queries. The buyer facilitates the conference to ensure that all prospective vendors have a clear and common understanding of the technical and contractual requirements of the procurement. Bidder conferences can also be called vendor conferences, pre-bid conferences, pre-proposal conferences, or contractor conferences.

Example: Hosting a Bidder Conference for the Wi-Fi Network Project

Mark holds a bidder conference, which is attended by all the prospective vendors. During the bidder conference, a number of clarifications are sought by the vendors regarding the procurement specifications and these are addressed by the project team. The updated procurement documents are now sent along to each prospective vendor. Vendors submit their proposals in response to the RFP which has been previously sent to them.

Guidelines for Obtaining Responses from Vendors

A well-crafted vendor response request, sent to carefully selected vendors, ensures that you obtain relevant, accurate, and appropriate responses from prospective vendors. To obtain responses from vendors, follow these guidelines:

- Gather and review all your procurement documents for accuracy and completeness.
- If necessary, obtain or develop a qualified vendors list.
  - If your organization has a centralized Purchasing Department, there might be available qualified or approved vendor lists, or historical information about different vendors.

- You may also consider talking to the people in your company who will be using the resource being sought, to find out more information about their needs.
- If the resource you require is new to your organization, you may need to collaborate with your Purchasing Department to identify qualified vendors for that resource. You can research using the Internet, telephone and business directories, library services, and trade and professional organizations. After identifying vendors, you will need to take additional qualification steps, such as interviewing the prospective vendors, visiting their work sites, reviewing work samples, interviewing their references, checking with any available certification boards, or other approaches to ensure that they are indeed qualified candidates.
- Determine how and from whom you will request vendor responses.

    - If your list of qualified vendors is sufficient for the work being procured, you may decide to send procurement documents to only those prospective vendors.
    - If your list is insufficient, you might use advertising to expand the list of potential vendors. If your project is a subcontract to a large government project, you may be obliged to advertise the request. Check with your legal consultants or Purchasing Department experts on the wording for the advertisement. Most government projects require that bids or proposals be publicly advertised to ensure that no supplier has unfair advantage over others. Such notification may be in formats that include local newspapers, government publications, professional journals, and other appropriate venues.

- Send the request for vendor responses to the identified prospective vendors. The type of request sent to prospective vendors is dependent on the procurement criteria set for the project. The types of requests sent to obtain responses include RFB, RFP, and RFQ.
- If necessary, hold a bidder conference to allow prospective vendors to ask questions and seek clarification about the deliverables and the requirements for preparing their responses.

    - The questions raised at a bidder conference will be of great interest to the team who prepared the original procurement documents. If there are common misinterpretations of words or if important information is found to be missing, capture this to improve future procurement documents. This might involve modifying the standard documents or templates.
    - If the bidder conference points out serious problems that will cause the vendor's proposals to be in error, you need to amend the original procurement documents and send amended versions to the original vendor list. The amended sections must be clearly identified and the areas of difference annotated.

- Respond to questions asked during the bidder conference. Respond in writing to each recipient of the RFP, so they can include that information in their proposals. This will ensure that all prospective vendors are operating "on the same page."

TOPIC B

Select Project Vendors

As a result of requesting vendor responses, you now have proposals, quotes, or bids from prospective vendors. Now, you can determine which vendor best meets your project's time, cost, and quality commitments. In this topic, you will determine project vendors.

You received proposals from three web designers for your website project. You've worked with two of them in the past. The third person was recommended by a senior level executive in your company. All three proposals are within your price range. Because rolling out your new website is a high-profile project for the business as a whole, you can't afford to make a mistake by selecting the wrong vendor. Using best practices to select the best vendor helps you avoid making critical errors before signing a contract to purchase products or services.

Vendor Proposals

Vendor proposals are responses submitted by potential vendors that are prepared in accordance with the requirements stated in the procurement documents. The proposal should demonstrate an understanding of the procurement need, describe the vendor's ability to provide the service or product, propose methodology for providing the service, and detail the price for delivering the desired goods or services.

Short–Listing (Screening)

Short-listing, or screening, is a technique used to reduce the number of proposals that have been received to a more concise number for further analysis. In this process, the buyer might use an abbreviated scoring system or internal discussions to remove some proposals from further consideration.

Proposal Evaluation Techniques

Proposal evaluation techniques are a set of methods to evaluate, create a short-list, and select a vendor. The fundamental part of any evaluation technique is the set of evaluation criteria. The evaluation techniques may suggest subjective or objective criteria or a combination of both. Though a weighting system is the most commonly used evaluation technique, short-listing (screening) or independent estimating are also used in combination.

Independent Estimates

Procuring organizations may sometimes prepare their own independent cost estimates or have an external professional estimator prepare the project's estimate of costs. If a proposal comes in at an unexpectedly high or low price, you may want to obtain an independent estimate to verify that the proposed price is reasonable. Any significant differences in the cost estimates can indicate that the procurement SOW was ambiguous, deficient, or that the vendors either misunderstood or failed to respond completely to the procurement SOW.

Weighting Systems

A *weighting system* is a method for quantifying qualitative data to minimize the influence of personal bias on source selection. By assigning numerical weights to evaluation criteria, you can objectively prioritize the criteria that best meets the needs of your project. A weighted scorecard is one type of weighting system.

In a *weighted scorecard*, evaluation criteria are grouped in general categories and each category is given a numerical weight. A vendor is rated on a scale of zero to five for each of the technical criteria. These numbers are totaled and then multiplied by the weighting factor to determine the weighted score for that category.

In this example, the company received scores of four, three, and five in the three technical criteria, with a total score of 12 out of a possible 15. When multiplied by the weighting factor, the weighted technical score is 240 out of a possible 300. The weighted score for each of the other categories is calculated in a similar manner. Then all the weighted scores are totaled to obtain a grand total score.

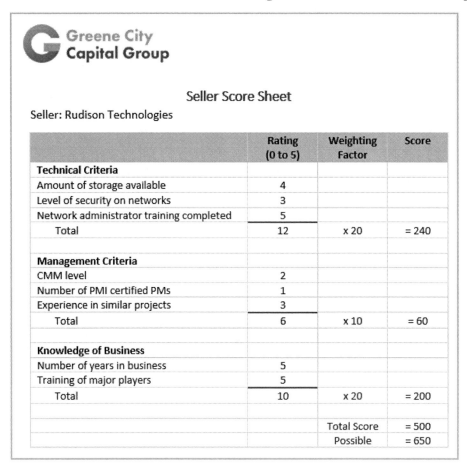

Figure 13–2: A sample weighted scorecard.

Procurement Negotiation Stages

Procurement negotiation is the process of coming to a mutual agreement regarding the terms and conditions of a contract. Before a contract is signed by both parties, a number of procurement negotiation stages are conducted between the concerned parties to arrive at a consensus on the terms and conditions of the contract.

Five different stages for contract negotiation are available.

Stage	Description
1. Introduction	All parties become acquainted and the overall attitude of the negotiation is established; this tone is largely set by the buyer's team leader—normally, the person with authority to sign the contract will lead the contract negotiation team.
2. Probing	Each side attempts to learn more about the other's real position.

Stage	Description
3. Bargaining	Give-and-take discussions take place to arrive at the best possible agreement for all.
4. Closure	The tentative agreement is revised and everyone has an opportunity to tweak the results.
5. Agreement	The team tries to ensure that all parties clearly understand and agree to all terms and conditions of the contract.

Types of Agreements

During procurement, you might encounter some of the following types of agreements. The following agreements will be discussed in more detail in the following pages.

- Memorandum of understanding
- Letter of intent
- Service Level Agreement (SLA)
- Contract
  - Fixed-price
  - Cost-reimbursable
  - Time & Material (T&M)
- Procurement Contract
  - Term contract
  - Completion contract

Memorandum of Understanding

A *Memorandum of Understanding* is an agreement between two or more parties to form a business partnership. It is not legally binding, but is more formal than a "gentlemen's agreement." It is used where the parties do not wish to enter into a formal contract, or when a legally enforceable contract cannot be created.

Similar to a memorandum of understanding, a letter of intent is a non-binding document that outlines the agreement between parties before the official agreement documents are finalized and signed.

SLA

A *Service Level Agreement (SLA)* is a contract between an organization that provides a service, and the user of the service. The contract specifies what the customer will receive and the performance standards the provider is obligated to meet. Performance standards can include, for example, the percentage of time the service will be available; help desk response time; and performance benchmarks that the level of service will be compared to. In many instances, penalties and exclusions are included in the SLA. Information technology companies frequently use SLAs.

Contracts

Contracts are mutually binding agreements that detail the obligations of both parties; in terms of procuring work, they relate to both the buyer and vendor. Although contracts are customized for each agreement, they tend to fall into a number of standard patterns, such as fixed-price, cost-reimbursable, or Time and Material (T&M) contracts.

Example: A Fixed-Price Contract

A project team is procuring the manufacturing unit for its new line of footwear. After seeking the advice of SMEs and reviewing historical records of similar projects, the team estimates the manufacturing cost at $25,000. Including the manufacturer's fee of $10,000, the entire contract will be worth $35,000. This is an example of a fixed-price contract because it establishes a definitive determined total price for a product or service.

Contract Components

In general, any contract must include these elements, at a minimum:

- Description of the project, its deliverables, and scope.
- Delivery date or other schedule information.
- Identification of authority, where appropriate.
- Responsibilities of both parties.
- Management of technical and business aspects.
- Price and payment terms.
- Provisions for termination.
- Applicable guarantees and warranties.
- Limits of liabilities or damages.
- Indemnity or compensation paid for losses incurred.
- Insurance requirements.
- Nondisclosure, patent indemnification, non-compete, or other applicable legal statements.
- Other applicable terms and legal requirements.

Contract Types

Three common types of contracts are used in the procurement of goods and services. Each type of contract has risks associated with it for both the buyer and seller. Some contract types are riskier for the buyer, while others are riskier for the seller.

Contract Type	Description
Fixed-price	Also called a lump sum contract, it establishes a total price for a product or service. The vendor agrees to perform the work at the negotiated contract value. This value is based on anticipated costs and profit, as well as a premium to cover unforeseen problems. The contract may include incentives for meeting requirements such as schedule milestones. Fixed-price contracts provide maximum protection to the buyer but require a long time for preparation and bid evaluation. Because this type of contract is tied to a fixed cost, it is most suited to projects with a high degree of certainty about their parameters. Types of fixed-price contracts include: • *Firm Fixed Price Contracts (FFP)*: This is a commonly used contract type favored by most buying organizations because the price for products or services is set at the outset and not subject to change unless the scope of work changes. • *Fixed Price Incentive Fee Contracts (FPIF)*: This fixed-price contract is flexible in that it allows for deviation from performance. Financial incentives are tied to achieving metrics that are agreed to earlier. • *Fixed Price with Economic Price Adjustment Contracts (FP-EPA)*: This is a fixed-price contract type with special provision to allow predefined final adjustments to the contract price due to changed conditions, such as inflation changes or cost increases or decreases for specific commodities such as fuel, and for currency fluctuations. An FP-EPA contract protects both buyer and vendor from external conditions beyond their control. It is used whenever the vendor's performance period spans a considerable time period. The Economic Price Adjustment (EPA) clause must relate to a reliable financial index, which is used to precisely adjust the final price. • *Purchase Order (PO)*: This can be a type of fixed-price contract, or a separate document that is appended to a contract. It is sent from a buyer to a vendor with a request for an order. When the vendor accepts the purchase order, a legally binding contract is formed. A purchase order is sometimes used for commodity items where the specifications are clear; for example, in a catalog.

Contract Type	Description
Cost-reimbursable	This contract provides vendors with a refund of the expenses incurred while providing a service, plus a fee representing vendor profit. Incurred costs are generally classified as direct costs (those incurred for the project), or indirect costs (costs allocated to the project by the organization as a cost of doing business). These contracts sometimes include incentives for meeting certain objectives, such as costs, schedule, or technical performance targets. This approach is tied to the actual cost to perform the contract, and therefore is most suitable if project parameters are uncertain. The cost-reimbursable contracts include: • *Cost Plus Fixed Fee Contracts (CPFF)*: This contract ensures that the vendor is reimbursed for all allowable costs for performing the contract work. The vendor receives a fixed fee payment calculated based on the initial estimated project costs. This fixed fee does not change due to vendor performance. • *Cost Plus Incentive Fee Contracts (CPIF)*: This contract ensures that the vendor is reimbursed for all allowable costs for performing the contract work. The vendor also receives a predetermined target fee. In addition to this, there is a provision of an incentive fee payable to the vendor, which is based on achieving certain performance objectives as set forth in the contract. In case the final costs are lesser or greater than the original estimated costs, then both the buyer and vendor share the costs from the difference based on the pre-negotiated cost sharing formula; for example, an 80/20 split over or under target costs based on actual performance of the vendor. • *Cost Plus Award Fee Contracts (CPAF)*: This contract ensures that the vendor is reimbursed for all legitimate costs. The majority of the fee is earned based on the satisfaction of certain broad subjective performance criteria defined and incorporated into the contract. The determination of the fee is based on the buyer's subjective determination of vendor performance and is generally not subject to appeals.
Time and Material (T&M)	This type of contract includes aspects of both fixed-price and cost-reimbursable contracts. The buyer pays the vendor a negotiated hourly rate and full reimbursement for materials used to complete the project. This contract is used for staff augmentation, acquisition of experts, and any outside support when a precise SOW cannot be quickly prescribed. Many organizations include not-to-exceed values and time limits in T&M contracts to prevent unlimited cost growth.

Procurement Contract

A *procurement contract* is a mutually binding agreement that details the obligations of the buyer and vendor. The procurement contract, which can be a complex document or in the form of a simple purchase order, is given to each selected vendor. Some of the major components in the contract include: the SOW, the schedule baseline, the period of performance, performance reporting, roles and responsibilities, pricing, payment terms, penalties, acceptance criteria, warranty, liability limitations, change request handling, insurance and performance bonds, termination clauses, and other applicable terms and legal requirements.

Term Contracts vs. Completion Contracts

A *term contract* engages the vendor to deliver a set amount of service—measured in staff-hours or a similar unit—over a set period of time. A *completion contract* stipulates that work will not be considered complete until the vendor delivers the product to the buyer and the buyer accepts the product.

Example: Vendor Contracts for the 2002 Winter Olympics

Salt Lake City, Utah, hosted the 2002 Winter Olympics and needed many contracts for vendors and service providers. Term contracts are appropriate for the independent security firms that were contracted to provide professional security services for the duration of the Olympic events. Completion contracts are appropriate for the construction companies hired to improve interstate roads and build a new light rail system to handle the increased area traffic.

How to Choose Project Vendors

You can use the following procedure to determine which vendor is best for your project.

Choose Project Vendors

To determine a project vendor:

1. Assign a numerical weighting factor to each evaluation criterion or category of criteria based on its relative importance to the success of the project.
2. Develop or obtain a rating scale for scoring the criteria.
3. Score each prospective vendor on each criterion using the rating scale.
4. Multiply the vendor's score by the weighting factor for each criterion or sum of the criteria in a category.
5. Add the final scores.
6. Select the vendor with the highest score.
7. If necessary, negotiate with the vendor on the terms and conditions of the contract.
8. It's a good idea to identify the vendor who will be your second choice in case negotiations fall through with your first choice.

ACTIVITY 13–1
Executing the Procurement Plan Review

Scenario
Answer the following review questions.

1. How will you make sure that you are specifying adequate detail when requesting vendor responses?

2. How do you think assigning numerical weighting factors to the evaluation criteria will help when you are trying to make critical choices about selecting vendors?

Summary

In this lesson, you managed project procurement by requesting vendor responses and selecting a vendor. You identified vendors who can provide the best quality of work for your project, selected vendors after conducting procurement negotiations on the contract, and finally awarded the procurement contract to the selected vendor at a fair and competitive price. By effectively conducting project procurements, you ensured that the procurement requirements of your project were suitably met within the scope of your project's time, cost, and quality commitments.

14 | Monitoring and Controlling Project Performance

Lesson Time: 1 hour, 30 minutes

Lesson Introduction

As the project work accelerates, more effort will be spent on monitoring and controlling project work, which is a key element in your overall goal of controlling the project cost, schedule, and quality.

Monitoring the work results and effectively communicating both good and bad information to project stakeholders is critical to any project. Monitoring project performance allows you to monitor trends that may affect process improvements and it ensures that the project will meet the required expectations. Effectively monitoring the project and reporting its performance is essential for successful project completion. In this lesson, you will monitor the project's performance.

Lesson Objectives

In this lesson, you will:

- Monitor and control project work.

- Manage project changes.

- Report project performance.

TOPIC A

Monitor and Control Project Work

With your project execution well on its way, you need to control changes to the project's performance so that you can best ensure that it meets expectations for schedule, cost, and quality. Change control and several other tasks are part of the monitoring and controlling project work process. In this topic, you will identify the best practices to be followed to monitor and control your project.

As a project manager, it is your responsibility to deliver your project on time, on budget, and to the required specifications. By monitoring and controlling the project work, you will be better positioned to ensure that your project meets stakeholders' expectations for time, cost, and quality performance and maintain an efficient and effective flow of work throughout the project life cycle.

Best Practices of Monitoring and Controlling Project Work

When monitoring and controlling project work, the project manager tracks, reviews, and regulates the project processes to meet the project's performance objectives. Effective monitoring ensures that necessary preventive actions are taken in order to control the project performance.

To effectively monitor and control project work, follow these guidelines:

- Compare and evaluate project performance with the project plan and, if necessary, recommend actions.
- Analyze, track, and monitor risks to make sure they are being recognized and reported, and response plans are being executed.
- Maintain accurate information about the project as it unfolds.
- Maintain the integrity of baselines ensuring that only approved changes are incorporated.
- Provide information to support status reporting, progress reporting, and forecasting.
- Provide forecasts to update recent cost and schedule information.
- Monitor the execution of approved changes when they occur.

 Note: The process of monitoring and controlling project work is not one specific task; it is an overarching process that is ongoing, cyclical, interactive, and interlocking. It involves ongoing work throughout the life cycle of the project.

Example: Monitoring and Controlling Project Work in a Software Development Project

Mike is the project manager for the tax preparation software development project. The project is multiphased and is in its second phase. Mike's programmers have been meeting schedule deadlines and showing good time management skills. However, the documentation department that creates user manuals and help systems works very slowly and is making mistakes. Assessment of reviewer feedback confirmed these observations.

Mike realizes this is a risk for the project. If the deliverables are wrong, he will lose his customer. He decides that the documentation department needs a bit more monitoring. In the company's procedures for documentation, it clearly states that the preliminary software documentation must be created within three days of development of each deliverable from the software department. Mike created a database where the deliverable turnaround time is recorded. After looking through information on past performance, Mike sees that the accuracy of deliverables was 10 percent better than what it is now. Mike believes that with this newly implemented database, the performance and quality will continue to improve.

Technical Performance Measurement

Technical performance measurement is used to identify the overall technical accomplishments made during the project. It compares the project's accomplishments to the planned accomplishments as outlined in the project plan. Objective, quantifiable measures of technical performance are used here. These measures may include the functionality of a deliverable at a milestone, as well as specific measurable criteria such as conformance to specifications. Any differences can help predict if the final project scope will be achieved. The parameters used to measure technical performance include the system, software, and resource performance.

Guidelines for Monitoring and Controlling Project Work

Effective monitoring and controlling of project work ensures that the project achieves the expected organizational objectives. To effectively monitor the project work, follow these guidelines:

* Obtain regular status reports from the project team members.
* Use metrics to report project performance to stakeholders. Care should be taken not to overburden the stakeholders with unnecessary information.
* Conduct effective reviews of the reported project status.

    * Review the current project schedule and cost status and their deviations from the planned values. If variances between the project plan and status are identified, recognize the corrective actions to be taken.
    * Analyze and identify the major concerns of the project.
    * Evaluate and determine the accomplishments since the last review.
    * Review major project risks and challenges.
    * Emphasize the most immediate milestones.
    * Anticipate potential problems and identify possible solutions for the risks.
* If any new changes are introduced by the project team or other stakeholders, document the change in the change control system and track the change until its closure.
* Recognize exceptional performers. Encourage and help lagging performers and provide training or informal mentoring, if necessary.
* Conduct regular project meetings to understand the issues or problems the team members are facing. Use these meetings to convey the overall project performance and status and the accomplishments of the team members.

TOPIC B

Manage Project Changes

Earlier, you developed an integrated change control system to monitor and control project work. While a project is being monitored and controlled, changes that may affect the scope will occur. As a project manager, you need to be able to appropriately handle those changes. In this topic, you will manage project changes.

Because it is the nature of business to get the product for the lowest price, customers will sometimes push the edge of the project scope beyond its limits. If not controlled, this can easily spell disaster for the project. By controlling project changes, you can minimize their impact on the project scope, time, cost, and quality commitments.

The Change Management Process

Change management is the process of managing project changes in a structured and standardized manner. It consists of five main stages.

Stage	Description
1. Change identification	Involves identifying the changes that must be made to a project. The changes may positively or negatively impact the planned project deliverables and performance. The requirement for change can be identified by anyone involved in the project.
2. Change documentation	Involves documenting the changes in the change control form, initiating a formal request for the change.
3. Analyzing the impact of the change	Involves identifying and assessing issues that may arise and adversely impact the various aspects of the project. This will usually be done by the project manager or any other requester.
4. Course of action	Involves coordinating with the appropriate stakeholders, to select the necessary actions to be taken, and implementing the approved changes.
5. Updating related plans	Involves updating the project management plan components that are related to the approved change requests.

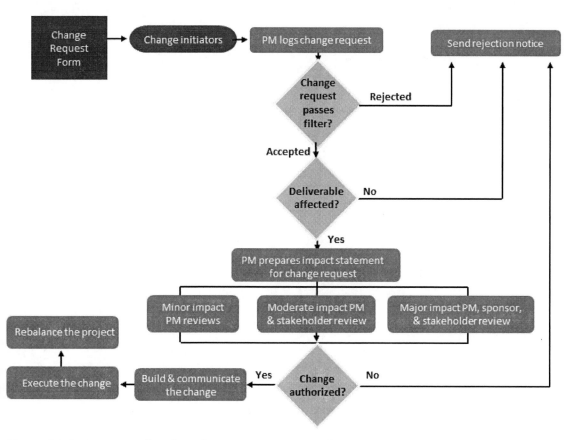

Figure 14-1: A process flowchart for managing project changes.

Example: A Change Control Process for an Elementary School-Age Reading Project

As the project team for an elementary school-age reading program moves through the execution phase, the project manager, Ben, monitors progress by reviewing performance reports and evaluating any variances to the original scope definition and performance baselines. When variances are identified, the project management team members examine the causes and determine the corrective action necessary to bring future performance in line with the project plan. They diligently document the lessons learned for the benefit of future projects.

As change requests are generated, both Ben and the project's CCB review and evaluate their impact on performance baselines as outlined in the change control system. When changes are made that affect performance baselines, Ben updates the project plan to reflect the changes. Using configuration management methods, such as the image tracking database, all changes to the original characteristics of the course are controlled and tracked. The project team's efforts enable them to effectively maintain the original performance baselines and scope definition and keep the project on track.

Change Control Form

A *change control form* is used to request a project change. Change control forms or change management forms are generally referred to as change request forms. A sample change control form template is shown in the following figure.

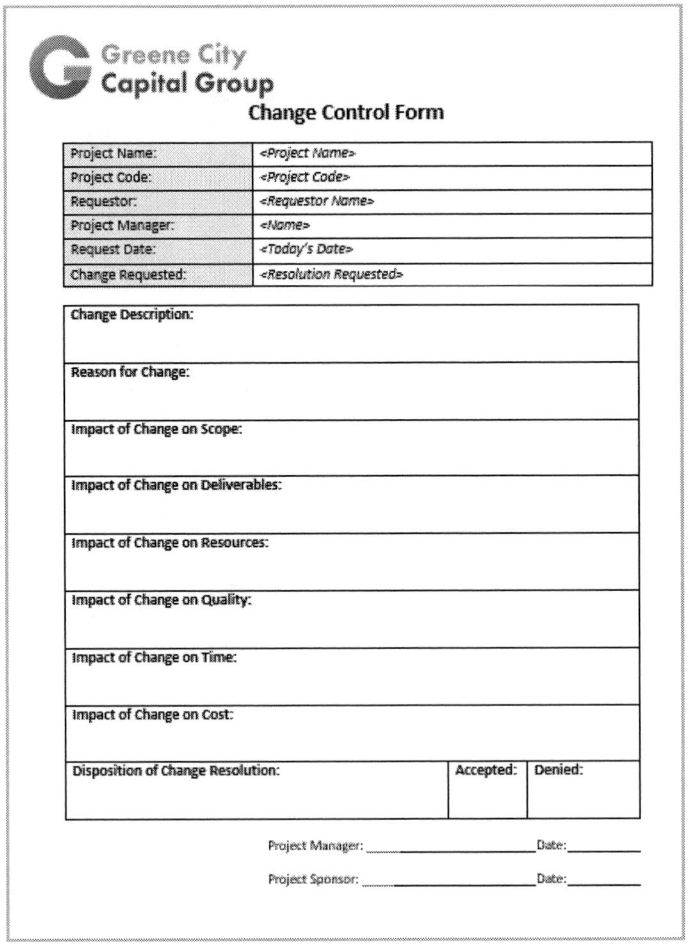

Greene City Capital Group

Change Control Form

Project Name:	<Project Name>
Project Code:	<Project Code>
Requestor:	<Requestor Name>
Project Manager:	<Name>
Request Date:	<Today's Date>
Change Requested:	<Resolution Requested>

Change Description:		
Reason for Change:		
Impact of Change on Scope:		
Impact of Change on Deliverables:		
Impact of Change on Resources:		
Impact of Change on Quality:		
Impact of Change on Time:		
Impact of Change on Cost:		
Disposition of Change Resolution:	Accepted:	Denied:

Project Manager: ____________________ Date: __________

Project Sponsor: ____________________ Date: __________

Figure 14-2: A sample change control form template.

Advantages of Effective Change Management

Effective change management presents several advantages to project managers, including:

- Faster response time.
- Maximum traceability of changes.
- Increased team awareness of change needs.
- Increased engagement of team and stakeholders, internally and externally.
- Better team support for change requirements.
- An organizational framework for moving forward effectively.

The Impact Analysis Process

Impact analysis is the process of evaluating the impact of a change on the project. It involves three major steps.

Step	Description
1. Impact identification	Identifying the impact of a potential change on: • The *triple constraints* (time, cost, scope). • Quality. • Project complexity. • The current and subsequent phases of the project. • The list of project milestones and deliverables. • Project testing needs. • Resources needed for a project.
2. Impact prediction	Forecasting the characteristics, magnitude, and duration of the major impacts.
3. Impact evaluation	Evaluating how the expected impact can be mitigated.

Scope Creep

Scope creep is the extension of the project scope caused by unapproved and uncontrolled changes that impact the cost, quality, or timing of the project. Scope creep contributes significantly to project failure.

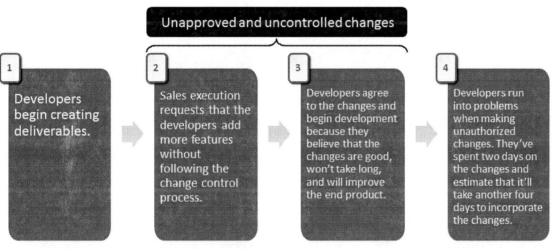

The Project—Creating a PDA for the sales group.

Unapproved and uncontrolled changes

1. Developers begin creating deliverables.

2. Sales execution requests that the developers add more features without following the change control process.

3. Developers agree to the changes and begin development because they believe that the changes are good, won't take long, and will improve the end product.

4. Developers run into problems when making unauthorized changes. They've spent two days on the changes and estimate that it'll take another four days to incorporate the changes.

Impact—Additional cost, time, and resources were used beyond the scope of the project, and now the developers are behind their schedule.

Figure 14–3: An example of scope creep.

Formal Acceptance of Project Work

Formal acceptance of project work is the process for securing approval for completing the remainder of the project work. It requires change requests to be documented and analyzed for their impact on other aspects of project work including time, cost, quality, and risk. It includes a receipt, or documented acknowledgment, that the terms of the contract have been satisfied. It also validates that the acceptance criteria will still be satisfied as a consequence of this change.

Guidelines for Managing Project Changes

Managing project changes ensures that the original project scope and the integrity of performance baselines are maintained. Ensuring that changes are agreed upon and continuously managing changes as they occur minimizes the impact changes may have on project time, cost, and quality concerns. To effectively utilize the change control systems for managing changes in the project, follow these guidelines:

- Make sure that your change control system is cost-effective. It should not cost more money to implement than it saves through controlling.
- Establish or make use of an existing Change Control Board (CCB) composed of project stakeholders to evaluate change requests.
- Make sure that the requested change deals with the project deliverable rather than project structure or controls.
    - Does the requested change address the business, technical, or functional requirements?
    - Does the requested change ask for a deliverable to be added?
    - Does the requested change ask for the modification of a project deliverable? This will need to be negotiated with the customer prior to acceptance.
- Document the effect the changes have on the project. What is the effect of the change on schedule, cost, time, and quality?
- Obtain approval from the appropriate parties for all change requests before implementing the change.
- Use configuration management to document and control changes to original product characteristics.
- Coordinate changes across project attributes as appropriate. For example, does a proposed schedule change affect cost, risk, quality, and staffing?
- Use performance reports to measure project performance and assess whether plan variances require corrective action. Make sure that performance reports are timely and accurate to increase the effectiveness of control decisions.
- Identify corrective action necessary to bring expected performance in line with the project plan.
    - Determine the source and severity of the problem.
    - Review the project plan and objectives.
    - Consider factors inside and outside the project that may influence corrective action decisions.
    - Identify alternative options available.
    - Choose from among the alternatives by evaluating the impact of each alternative on cost, schedule, and quality.
- Update the project plan to reflect changes made that affect performance baselines.
- Document the causes of variances, the steps taken to correct performance problems, and the rationale behind the decision-making process to avoid similar problems on future projects.
- Analyze the impact of the change to verify that no new problems are introduced. If problems arise, be sure to have a regression plan to efficiently reverse any changes that are out of proportion with the benefits or the intended results.

TOPIC C

Report Project Performance

In order to ensure that your project meets stakeholder needs, you need to communicate with your stakeholders about how well your project is performing. This includes monitoring individual and team performance and providing relevant feedback and appraisals. In this topic, you will report project performance.

Implementing control processes into your project work can make a tremendous difference in your ability to communicate project performance to upper management, stakeholders, and customers, and to reassure those with a vested interest in project success that the work is on time and within budget. Performance reports are really the heart of the entire monitoring and controlling process. Effective performance reporting enables you—and your team members, sponsors, stakeholders, and customers—to make reasoned, informed, and timely decisions regarding project status.

Performance Measurement Tools

Project managers have many tools available to them to summarize and analyze data about how well a project is meeting the objectives set forth by the stakeholders. Selecting the right tool and communicating the information the tool provides in an understandable way are important to addressing whether the project is meeting stakeholder expectations. You should be familiar with the most commonly used performance measurement tools, and how to apply them to your project.

Tool	Description
Key Performance Indicators	*Key Performance Indicators (KPIs)* in project management consist of tools that indicate if the project is meeting specific goals. KPIs should be defined early in the project; they should be quantifiable; and they should be measured regularly. Common KPIs relate to how well the project is tracking against the planned schedule and cost baselines and if project milestones are being met. Other indicators can include the status of issues (resolved vs. unresolved); change requests (pending, approved, and disapproved); and effectiveness of risk response strategies. KPIs are often displayed as charts (e.g., line, pie, column, etc.) and indicators (e.g., colored traffic lights).
Dashboards	*Dashboards* are graphical summaries of project measures, often a collection of multiple KPIs. They provide an "at-a-glance" view of important data that managers can base business decisions on. Dashboards can be created from project management software, or purchased from a number of software suppliers. An example of a project dashboard created with Microsoft® Project is shown following this table.
Key Performance Parameters	*Key Performance Parameters (KPPs)* are key system capabilities that must be met for a system to meet its goals. The threshold value of a KPP is the minimum acceptable value (cost, schedule, and technology) below which the system is unacceptable. For more information about KPPs, see **http://www.dtic.mil/cjcs_directives/cdata/unlimit/3170_01a.pdf**.
Balanced Scorecard	The *balanced scorecard* is a tool that integrates project management and portfolio management so that projects are aligned with an organization's strategy. It identifies a small number of financial and non-financial measures and attaches targets to them. When performance deviates from expectations, managers can focus their attention on areas where meaningful improvement in performance is possible.

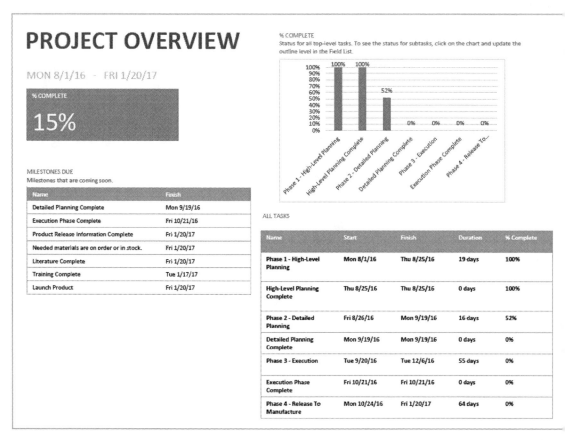

Figure 14–4: An example of a dashboard.

Budget Forecasts

Budget forecast is the estimated budget required to complete the remaining project work. Stakeholders will be given *Estimate to Complete (ETC)* and *Estimate at Completion (EAC)* values for a project.

- The Estimate to Complete value is the estimated cost to finish all the remaining project work.
- The Estimate at Completion value is the estimated total cost of completing all work, expressed as the sum of the actual cost to date and the estimate to complete.

Forecasting Methods

Forecasting methods are classified into various categories.

Category	Description
Time series methods	Estimation of future outcomes is based on historical data. Some of the methods under this category include earned value and moving average.
Causal or econometric methods	Causal forecasting includes the factors that may influence the identified variables, by combining economic theories and statistical information. Some econometric methods under this category include regression analysis and econometrics.

Category	Description
Judgmental methods	Forecasting where there is a complete lack of historical data; for example, when a new product is being launched. Some of the methods under this category include scenario forecasting, Delphi technique, and forecasting by analogy.
	For more information about Judgmental forecasting, see **https:// www.otexts.org/fpp/3**.

Reporting Systems

Reporting systems are tools that help in collecting, storing, and distributing project information to stakeholders. Information can be distributed through various formats such as a presentation and spreadsheet analysis. Project managers use different software applications to collect information from various sources and consolidate them to distribute among stakeholders. Reporting systems are part of the PMIS.

Example: Reporting the Performance of a Construction Project

The project team for a construction project completed the first phase. Before moving on to phase two, the executive board asks the project manager to prepare a mid-project report. The project manager assembles the team and discusses the requirements of the report and explains its value in terms of future development for the remaining work on the current project and for future projects.

The team takes a few days to evaluate the project's accomplishments against expected performance and to discuss and document lessons learned. Because they have regularly monitored and documented project progress and held performance review meetings, they have solid data to evaluate.

Their mid-project report uses the standard format specified in the communications management plan and consists of the following information as required by the plan: a cover page, a narrative description of accomplishments as compared to established goals, interim performance reports and end of project reports, and any appendices or supporting materials. The comparison section also includes a table showing the earned value information for phase one development.

Report Types

The type of report you use will depend on the purpose of the report, the audience, and the message that data is trying to convey. The report format can range from simple to complex depending on the data that is being presented. Some common types of performance reports include:

- **Progress report**: A summary of activities over a period of time, such as a week or month.
- **Status report**: A summary of activities over a cumulative period of time, such as a year-to-date or since the start of a project.
- **Dashboard report**: A simple status report that commonly uses colored indicators, such as red, yellow, and green to provide an at-a-glance identifier for the state of a project component.

Performance Reports

A *performance report* is a document that reports the progress made in the project activities against the specified baseline. Project performance is reported to ensure that the project manager is monitoring the project progress, comparing achievements with the plan, reviewing plans and options against future scenarios, detecting issues during the early phases of the project, initiating corrective action, and authorizing further work.

Performance reports can be classified by either frequency, purpose, or both. The following are common classifications of performance reports:

- **Routine** performance reports aren't necessarily scheduled but might be distributed at intervals that coincide with project phases or milestones. The frequency of performance reports depends on how smoothly the project functions.
- **Exception** performance reports provide project team members with information they need to make a decision on or notify them of a change that affects their work. Exception performance reports are also distributed to stakeholders to inform them that a decision has been made.
- **Special analysis** performance reports contain information about the results of a focused study that might be conducted as part of a project or to determine a solution to a problem encountered during a project. These special reports are not only useful documents for a current project, but are also valuable records of lessons learned for future projects.

Common Problems with Reports

Some frequent problems with performance reports include:

- Too much information or the wrong kind of information.
- Information not distributed in a timely manner.

To avoid these problems when reporting, it is important to:

- Make sure information is current and relevant.
- Create reminders for the due dates of progress reports.

Types of Performance Reports

There are various types of performance reports submitted at different phases of a project.

Performance Report	Description
End stage	Submitted by the project manager to the PMO or senior managers to sign off the stage, having met its required success criteria, and approve transition to the next stage.
Highlight	Submitted by the project manager to the PMO or senior managers at regular intervals as the project progresses. This reports the progress of the stage and project. It also identifies exceptions and issues.
Exception	Submitted by the project manager to the PMO or senior managers when early warnings of any forecast deviations beyond the tolerance levels are identified in the project. Tolerance levels might be ten percent on time and five percent on cost, but of course they will vary from one project to another.
End project	Created and submitted by the project manager to the PMO or the senior manager for the project to be signed off as completed and to consider the necessary follow-up actions.
Post implementation review	Controlled by members external to the project. They are notified whether the expected project benefits have been realized. This review is carried out as soon as the benefits and issues are identified and measured after the project's completion.

Performance Report Components

Performance reports mainly serve the purpose of making the actual versus baseline information with forecasted results available in a consolidated manner. They may be simple or detailed. A simple report may contain information on the project scope, time, cost, and quality, whereas the detailed report may also contain components such as:

- Inferences of the past analysis.

- Current risk status.
- Work completed.
- Work to be completed.
- Summary of approved changes.
- Variance analysis results; for example, Schedule Variance (SV), Cost Variance (CV), Schedule Performance Index (SPI), and Cost Performance Index (CPI).
- Forecasted results; for example, Estimate at Completion (EAC), and Estimate to Complete (ETC).

Benefits of Creating Performance Reports

Some of the overall benefits of creating performance reports include:

- Analysis of the current status of the schedule and budget.
- Feedback to team members and work package owners.
- Communication with upper management and customers.
- Early identification of variance.
- Early implementation of corrective actions.

Guidelines for Reporting Project Performance

Identifying variance to performance as early as possible helps the team pinpoint programmatic and administrative problems that may need to be resolved, and enhances the team's ability to implement corrective actions early enough to make a difference. Final performance reports provide historical information that may improve the likelihood of success for future projects. To effectively report project performance, follow these guidelines:

- Analyze work results against planned performance based on performance elements defined during the planning processes.
  - Involve the team members who are closest to the work in the data analysis. They are the people who understand the work and can probably identify appropriate corrective actions for resolving variances.
  - Use Earned Value Management (EVM) techniques to assess cost and schedule progress against planned performance.
  - Evaluate the results of corrective actions to determine whether they have produced the desired results.
- Hold performance reviews to communicate and assess project status and progress.
  - Keep meetings productive and concise by creating meeting rules that everyone clearly understands and agrees to follow.
  - Define the start and stop times.
  - Prepare and distribute a written agenda.
  - Make sure that the people presenting are ready and understand their role in the meeting.
- Consult your project management plan's subsidiary plans for guidelines and procedures for reporting on the various aspects of project performance.
  - Consult the procurement management plan for guidelines and procedures for analyzing and reporting contractor cost, schedule, and technical performance.
  - Consult the cost management plan for guidelines and procedures for analyzing and reporting project cost performance.
  - Consult the schedule management plan for guidelines and procedures for analyzing and reporting project schedule performance.
  - Consult the quality management plan for guidelines and procedures for analyzing and reporting project quality performance.

- Determine the type of report needed for the information being reported. Make sure that the format of the report adequately provides the type of information and level of detail required by various stakeholders. Refer to the communications management plan for information regarding stakeholder needs.
- Prepare performance reports containing the required information in an appropriate format that enhances understanding of the material. Formal reports should contain:
  - A cover page with the project name, project manager's name, type of report, and date of report.
  - A narrative description of the project's actual accomplishments for the reporting period as compared to the goals established for the period. The description should include qualitative and quantitative terms if possible. In addition, any changes implemented or anticipated should be described.
  - Interim performance reports should include a forecast of how the project is expected to perform in the future.
  - End of project reports should include a brief description of major accomplishments, an evaluation of the project's performance (including in-house staff and contractor performance), an explanation of any variances in the performance and project objectives, and any future plans for the project.
  - Appendices, which may include any supporting material that contributes to an understanding of the project and its progress to date, such as charts, tables, and samples.
  - If available, use standard formats for status, progress, and forecasting reports. These standard formats should be specified in the communications management plan or as part of the PMIS.
- Balance the cost, time, and logistics of preparing performance reports against the benefits gained by the reporting.
- Measure and monitor performance the same way throughout the project life cycle so that meaningful comparisons can be made.

ACTIVITY 14–1
Monitoring and Controlling Project Performance Review

Scenario

Answer the following review questions.

___

1. How can you make the change management processes followed in your organization more effective?

2. In your environment, which elements are the most difficult to control—cost, schedule, or scope?

___

Summary

In this lesson, you determined how to properly manage project performance. By properly monitoring a project, you will be able to meet all project goals, including the cost and schedule. Also, reporting project performance keeps the stakeholders informed of the project progress and helps them make appropriate decisions regarding project status.

15 Monitoring and Controlling Project Constraints

Lesson Time: 2 hours

Lesson Introduction

As a project manager, you identified areas associated with executing a project in your organization. Next, monitoring and controlling a project is essential to ensure that the project is on track with plans. As a project manager, you need to apply monitor and controlling tools, such as performance reviews, and variance analysis to improve your chances of executing the project within the prescribed time, scope, cost, and quality constraints. In this lesson, you will monitor and control project constraints.

Lesson Objectives

In this lesson, you will:

- Control the project scope.

- Control the project schedule.

- Control project costs.

- Manage the project quality.

TOPIC A

Control the Project Scope

You defined your project's scope and developed a Work Breakdown Structure as part of your project planning effort. Now that the project work is moving forward, you need to control changes to project scope using the control scope inputs and tools. In this topic, you will examine how to control the scope of the project.

Because it is the nature of business to get the most for the lowest price, customers will sometimes push the edge of the project scope beyond its limits. Because changes to project scope almost always impact performance baselines, you want to be able to control the project scope. Controlling project scope changes helps you minimize the impact to project time, cost, and quality commitments.

Verified Deliverables

Verified deliverables are project products or results that are completed and verified for their correctness after performing quality control. These deliverables are used as inputs during scope validation of the project to determine if work is complete and satisfies project objectives.

Inspections

An *inspection* is an official examination of work results to verify that requirements are met. It is sometimes referred to as a *review, product review, audit,* or *walkthrough.* An inspection may be conducted by an internal or external inspection team. During scope verification, an inspection typically involves:

- Comparing baseline specifications and any approved changes to the actual project results.
- Determining the likelihood that remaining deliverables will be completed as promised.
- Identifying actions that may be needed to ensure that work results will meet the specifications, scope, or schedule and budget goals.

In some cases, your team will be asked to conduct the inspection. In other cases, stakeholders may decide to ask an outside entity to either conduct the inspection or to participate with you in conducting it.

Example: Inspecting an Educational Toy

An inspector was asked to examine a new children's educational toy to determine whether its design requirements had been met. His inspection revealed that the instruction booklets accompanying the toy had not been adequately translated into all languages; some children and their parents were not able to decipher the instructions. The inspector recommended that the instruction booklets be improved before work requirements could be considered fulfilled.

Inspection Report Components

Inspection reports are necessary and contain several components.

Component	Description
Project-baseline and status comparison	The comparison of baseline specifications, schedules, and budgets to the actual project results for the project phase or deliverable.
Overall project status	A discussion of whether the project as a whole is on track, or whether it is likely to deviate in some way from project plans.

Component	Description
Change recommendations	Based on the inspection result, recommended changes that will be needed in order to meet the specifications, scope, or schedule and budget goals.
Scope and methodology of the inspection	An explanation of what the audit attempted to prove, how it went about proving it, what measurements were used to determine conformance to requirements, and what assumptions or limitations influenced the way that data was collected.

 Note: Some application areas and organizations have specific expectations for scope verification inspections and will probably have documented guidelines and procedures for preparing and conducting them.

Variance

Variance is the quantifiable deviation from the expected results for any component of a product and service being developed, including scope, quality, schedule, and cost. Variance can be extreme or almost undetectable; it may result from many internal and external causes, such as problems with resource availability, or from the skills of personnel assigned to the project. Variance may be obvious the moment a product is produced or may become obvious over time through use and exposure to environmental conditions. To control quality, you must recognize the difference between quality variance within a normal range and variance that indicates a quality error.

Variance Analysis

Variance analysis is the comparison of the difference between the actual or predicted results and the original scope baseline or expected results. Any variances must be analyzed to determine whether they are acceptable or they merit corrective action to keep the performance within specifications. Scope control includes determining the cause and degree of variance relative to the scope baseline and deciding if any corrective or preventive action is necessary.

Work Performance Measurements

Work performance measurements involve calculating the variance between the planned and actual technical performance or other scope performance measurements. The results of performance measurements are documented, generally consolidated in the form of performance reports, and then communicated to project stakeholders. The report may include items such as:

- Features of the product planned versus features of the product being delivered.
- Any addition to or deletion from the features list.
- New changes to the project scope.

Example: Controlling the Project Scope in a Website Designing Project

Two months into the production of a website designed to increase American preschoolers' readiness for kindergarten, the project team received a formal change request submitted through the change control system by one of the team members, an expert in early childhood education. The change request proposed making changes to the site's functionality that were categorized as high priority. Before approving the change request, the CCB asked the team to analyze the change to the schedule, budget, and resources as well as the potential risks and benefits.

The multimedia lead explained that the requested change will require an interface design modification; he estimated that it could be done with current resources and with no significant impact on the schedule. The technical lead agreed that the change could be implemented easily and will not require additional resources because the heavy programming for the course will not start for another month. Both leads felt that the risk to the project was extremely minimal when compared to the potential benefits described in the change request.

Given this information, the CCB approved the change request and documented the decision. The project manager updated the scope statement and the WBS. In addition, the project manager documented the decision and monitored the implementation of the change carefully to ensure that it was properly implemented and that no new risks were introduced.

Guidelines for Controlling the Project Scope

Continually monitoring and controlling changes to the project scope enable you to maintain the original project scope definition and make changes when necessary. In addition, controlling project scope changes ensures that cost, schedule, and quality performance baselines are maintained. To effectively control the project scope, follow these guidelines:

- Develop and implement a scope change control system, possibly integrated with the project's integrated change control system. The system should:
  - Include the paperwork, tracking systems, and approval levels for authorizing scope changes.
  - Comply with relevant contractual provisions when the project is carried out under contract.
  - Comply with the guidelines specified in the scope management plan.
- Evaluate change requests by asking questions:
  - What is the magnitude of the change when compared to the scope statement and WBS?
  - What is the impact of the change on project cost, schedule, and quality objectives?
  - What are the potential risks and benefits of the change?
- Identify and document corrective action to bring expected future project performance in line with planned performance.
- Ensure that formal agreements are reached and new specifications detailed when the project scope is expanded to include either additional work that is clearly outside the original scope, or required as a result of scope boundary clarifications.
- Depending upon the nature of the change, you may need to revise cost, schedule, or quality performance baselines to reflect changes and to form a new baseline to measure future performance against. Notify project stakeholders of any changes made to project baselines.
- Use performance measurement techniques to monitor changes.
  - Are changes being properly implemented?
  - Do changes bring about the desired results?
  - What new risks are introduced as a result of implementing changes? It's prudent practice to conduct a risk review after any scope change.
- Document lessons learned during scope change control for use on future projects. The documentation should include causes of variances, performance baselines affected by the changes, rationale behind the recommended corrective action, and any other lessons learned during scope change control.

TOPIC B

Control the Project Schedule

When you planned your project, you developed a schedule to serve as a baseline during project execution, monitoring, and controlling. Now you need to determine how much variance exists between the actual work completed and the work scheduled. In this topic, you will control the project schedule.

"When was the work scheduled to be completed?" "Can we change the project end date?" "Are we going to finish the project on time?" Answering questions like these is what schedule control is all about. Effective control over the project schedule ensures that you complete your project on time according to the project schedule.

Scheduling Tools

Scheduling tools are tools that use updated schedule data combined with project management software or other methods to perform schedule network analysis and generate an updated project schedule. These tools accelerate the scheduling process by generating start and finish dates of activities based on their inputs, creating network diagrams, and producing resource and activity duration.

EVM

Earned Value Management (EVM) is a method of measuring project progress by comparing the actual schedule and cost performance against planned performance as laid out in the schedule and cost baselines. Assessing the value of work requires first determining what work has actually been performed and, therefore, what value it has contributed to the project.

During planning, project work is broken down into work packages and activities. Each work package is assigned a budget and schedule. Because each increment of work is time-phased, a Schedule Variance (SV) results when work is not completed as scheduled. It is always better to understand the monetary value of work contribution as it relates to the schedule. Therefore, SV is often expressed in terms of the monetary value.

 Note: EVM is often used for government projects but is becoming more popular for private sector projects.

Cost and Schedule Performance

The EVM approach to monitoring cost and schedule performance provides metrics that show variances from baselines. Armed with this information, the project manager can identify appropriate corrective actions. When cost and schedule variance analysis is conducted at appropriate time intervals and levels, it can be effective in controlling against further cost and schedule problems.

PV

Planned Value (PV) is the budgeted portion of the approved cost estimate to be spent during a particular time period to complete the scheduled project work. This amount is specified in the project's cost baseline. In simpler terms, PV indicates the value of work to be done during a particular time period.

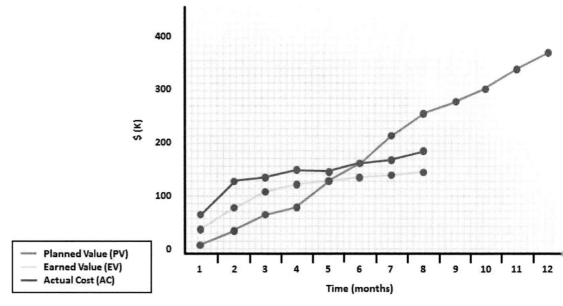

Figure 15-1: An illustration of planned value, earned value, and actual cost.

Example: Evaluating Planned Value

A project to build a shed was proposed. It involved three tasks to be done: flooring, drywalling, and roofing. Flooring was budgeted at $200 and will take two days to complete. The task of drywalling was budgeted at $800 and will take four days to complete. Roofing was budgeted at $600 and will take three days to complete. The total budget for building the shed came to $1,600. The total budget calculated for the first six days of work, involving two days of flooring and four days of drywalling, will be $200 + $800 = $1,000. Therefore, the PV of this project for six days is $1,000.

EV

Earned Value (EV) is a composite measurement of both cost and time performance in relation to scheduled or planned cost and time performance. EV is calculated by multiplying the percentage of work completed by the budgeted cost for the activity as laid out in the cost baseline.

```
Earned Value (EV) = % completed x Planned Value (PV)
```

In order to determine the EV of the project work to date, you will have to look back at the cost baseline to determine how costs were assigned originally. If the PV was determined by the percentage completed to date method, you will apply the same method of assessing the EV. In other words, EV indicates the value of work actually performed during a particular time period.

Example: EV Calculation for Shed Project

The manager of the shed building project receives a project report at the end of day six, which says that the flooring task ($200) is 100% complete and the drywalling task ($800) is 75% complete. To calculate the EV for the completed work, you apply the following formula. Therefore, the calculated EV for the project at the end of day six is $800.

```
EV = (100% x Flooring budget) + (75% x Drywalling budget)
EV = (100% x 200) + (75% x 800)
EV = 200 + 600
EV = $800
```

AC

Actual Cost (AC) refers to the total amount of costs incurred while accomplishing work performed, either during completion of a schedule activity or during the completion of a WBS component. Actual cost is calculated and documented once the work is complete. In other words, AC indicates the actual money that has been spent for work that has been completed.

Example: AC Calculation for Shed Project

The shed building project report also states that the actual money spent on flooring is $180 and on drywalling is $700. So, the actual cost for the project as of day six is $880.

EVM Measures for Schedule Control

The most commonly used EVM measures for schedule control are:

- *Schedule Variance* (SV = EV-PV)
  - A positive SV indicates that the project is ahead of schedule.
  - A zero SV indicates that the project is on schedule.
  - A negative SV indicates that the project is behind schedule.
- *Schedule Performance Index* (SPI = EV/PV)
  - An SPI number greater than 1.0 indicates that the project is ahead of schedule.
  - An SPI of 1.0 means the project is on schedule.
  - An SPI number less than 1.0 indicates that the project is behind schedule.

> **Note:** Content related to schedule and costs has been dealt with as separate topics in this course. For detailed information on Cost Variance (CV) and the Cost Performance Index (CPI), refer to the "Control Project Costs" topic.

Example: Controlling the Project Schedule for an Elementary Reading Course Project

The project team producing an elementary reading course is four months into production. The performance reports indicate schedule performance problems. To get a better picture, the project manager compares the actual work completed to the schedule baseline and calculates the SPI as 0.80. This figure confirms the concern that the project is behind schedule.

The project manager calls a core team meeting to determine the cause of the schedule variance and the magnitude of the variance. According to the multimedia and technical leads, the major rework in the text-to-speech option in the glossary is taking more time to implement than expected. It is taking valuable resources away from other activities on the critical path.

The team members agreed that corrective action is necessary to bring the project back in line with the original schedule baseline. Realizing that they still have to implement the change to the text-to-speech option and that the project's end date cannot be extended, the team brainstorms other corrective action alternatives. The team members decide to recommend adding one graphic artist and one programmer to work on the text-to-speech issues for two months at a total cost of $15,000.

After discussing their recommendation with the project sponsor, the core team submits a change request to the CCB. The CCB approves the change request and the project manager informs project stakeholders of the decision. The project manager carefully monitors the situation and recalculates the SV after one to two months. Trend analysis shows that the corrective action was effective in bringing the schedule back in line with the baseline.

The project manager documents the problem, the causes of the variance, the alternatives considered, the corrective action chosen, and the reason for the decision. In addition, the project manager documents the results of the corrective action and files the documentation in the project archives as lessons learned.

Schedule Control Chart

Another tool you can use to illustrate schedule performance is the *schedule control chart*. This chart can be used to show trends in schedule performance. The following graphic is an example of a schedule control chart plotting the variance in the schedule and shows that the project started behind schedule and that corrective action was probably taken to bring the project back in line with planned schedule estimates.

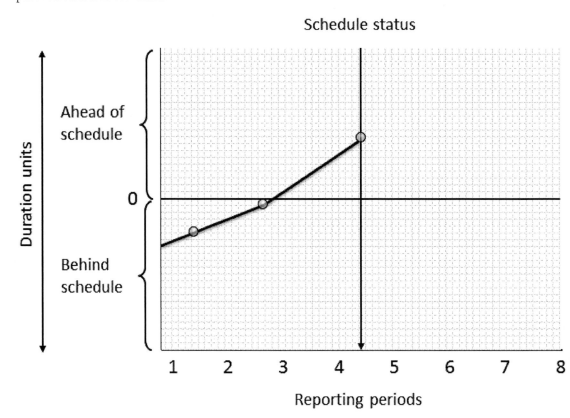

Figure 15-2: Using schedule control chart to track schedule performance.

Gantt Chart

A Gantt chart is an effective tool for providing up-to-date summary information and can be extremely helpful for analyzing the project's overall time performance. The Gantt chart also shows when milestones are scheduled and if those critical dates are still on track. Using the approved schedule baseline as the standard for measuring progress, the project manager can collect reporting information for each activity and use a Gantt chart to summarize data.

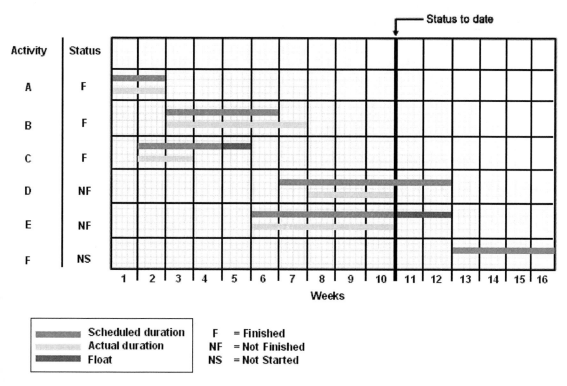

Figure 15-3: A software development Gantt chart.

Example: Gantt Chart for a Software Development Project

Dan is the project manager for a software development project. The estimated duration of the entire project is four months. Dan decides early in the project life cycle that there will be eight reporting periods and that work package owners will supply schedule performance reports every two weeks. On the fifth reporting period, Dan receives schedule reports and plots the results on a Gantt chart, as shown in the figure.

The Gantt chart shows that:

- Activities A, B, and C are finished.
- Activity B finished behind schedule.
- Activity C finished early.
- Activity D started a week late.
- Activity E is behind schedule.
- Activity F has not started yet.

Guidelines for Controlling the Project Schedule

Continually monitoring schedule performance and controlling changes to the approved project schedule enables you to maintain the schedule baseline. To control the project schedule, follow these guidelines:

- Develop and implement a schedule change control system. Make sure that your system:
  - Is integrated with the project's integrated change control system.
  - Includes the paperwork, tracking systems, and approval levels necessary for authorizing schedule changes.
  - Complies with any relevant contractual provisions when the project is done under contract.
  - Complies with the guidelines specified in the schedule management plan.
- Evaluate change requests by asking these questions:

- What is the magnitude of the change when compared to the schedule baseline?
- What is the impact of the change on project cost and quality objectives?
- What are the potential risks and benefits of the change?
- Use performance measurement techniques to compare actual schedule performance to planned performance.
  - Use schedule reports to monitor schedule performance.
  - Calculate SV and SPI to determine whether the project is ahead of or behind schedule.
- Analyze the results of your performance measurements by asking these questions:
  - What is the cause of the variance?
  - What is the magnitude of the variance? Is the activity that is causing the variance on the schedule's critical path? If so, this will indicate that your project finish date will be pushed out.
  - Is it likely that the variance can be made up in the near future without corrective action or is corrective action necessary to bring the schedule performance back in line with the baseline?
- Identify and document corrective action to take to bring expected future project performance in line with planned performance. Depending on the priorities of your project, consider one or more of the following alternatives:
  - Fast-tracking
  - Crashing
  - Outsourcing
  - Resource leveling
  - Reducing the project scope
- Depending upon the nature of the change, you may need to revise the cost, schedule, or quality performance baselines to reflect the changes and to form a new baseline against which to measure future performance. Notify project stakeholders of any changes made to project baselines.
- Use performance measurement techniques, including trend analysis, to monitor the changes.
  - Are the changes being properly implemented?
  - Do the changes bring about the desired results?
  - Are new risks being introduced as a result of implementing the changes?
- Document lessons learned during schedule control for use on future projects. The documentation should include:
  - Causes of variances.
  - Performance baselines affected by the changes.
  - Rationale behind the recommended corrective action.
  - Any other lessons learned during schedule control.

TOPIC C

Control Project Costs

You established a cost baseline for your project. Now that work results are being produced, you need to monitor project costs as your project progresses. In this topic, you will control project costs.

Cost Control

Controlling cost performance is a lot like watching for smoke from a fire tower. The earlier you see the smoke, the easier it will be to put out the fire. Effective cost control will allow you to spot the warning signs early, measure the cost variance, and make the necessary adjustments before cost overruns cause the project to go up in flames.

You also want to monitor the rate at which you are using up your budget, called the *burn rate*, to avoid running out of money before the scope has been completed.

EVM Measures for Cost Control

The most commonly used EVM measures for cost control are:

- *Cost Variance* (CV = EV - AC)
  - A positive CV indicates that the project is performing under budget.
  - A zero CV indicates that the project is on budget.
  - A negative CV indicates that the project is performing over budget.
- *Cost Performance Index* (CPI = EV / AC)
  - A CPI number greater than 1.0 indicates that the project is under budget.
  - A CPI of 1.0 means the project is on budget.
  - A CPI number less than 1.0 indicates that the project is over budget.

Example: Cost Control for a Project

The project team for the preschoolers' educational website implemented the change to the cost baseline required to bring the schedule back in line with the schedule baseline after adding the added functionality. Ben, the project manager, continually monitors the revised cost baseline by calculating the CV and CPI to determine whether the project is performing over or under budget at regular reporting intervals. Using EVM, Ben analyzes any variances to determine their cause and magnitude.

As of the eighth reporting period, only minor variances in cost performance occur. These variances may be corrected by renegotiating contracts and by verifying the estimates of work still to be done, resulting in lower estimates.

Trend analysis conducted at the sixth, seventh, and eighth reporting periods indicates that the corrective actions were effective in maintaining the cost baseline. The project manager documents the cost variances, their causes, corrective action, and the results of the corrective action as lessons learned for future projects.

Cost Control Chart

The *cost control chart* can be used to illustrate trends in cost performance. The following graphic shows the cost variance over time, using data for actual cost and earned value. The actual cost is always greater than the earned value, and we can conclude that the project is progressively more over budget as time goes on.

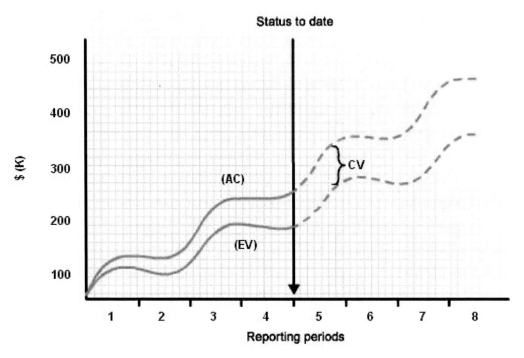

Figure 15–4: Using a cost control chart to track cost performance.

Performance Reporting Techniques

Performance reviews are meetings held to review the schedule activity, work package, or cost account status and progress, usually in concurrence with one or more performance reporting techniques.

Performance Reporting Technique	Description
Variance analysis	Comparing actual project performance to projected performance. For the most part, cost and schedule variances are analyzed. However, variances from the project scope, resource, quality, and risk are taken into consideration.
Trend analysis	Inspecting project performance over a period of time to determine if performance is increasing or decreasing.
Earned value performance	Compares the baseline plan to actual performance.

EVM Performance Measurement Analysis Techniques

The cause and magnitude of variance and corrective action for variance are all important factors in schedule and cost control. Several standard values for a schedule activity, work package, and control account are involved in the earned value technique. The following table provides calculations to determine cost performance efficiency.

 Note: You won't be performing all of these calculations in this course. However, this detailed list is provided for your future reference.

Cost Formula	Description
Estimate to Complete (ETC)	The total budgeted cost of the project at completion. `ETC = BAC - EV or (BAC - EV) / CPI`
Estimate at Completion (EAC) using new estimate	The forecasting technique, based on an updated, mid-project estimate. This method requires making a new ETC for all remaining project work and adding that estimate to the ACs incurred to date. It should be used when original estimating assumptions are flawed and conditions have changed. `EAC = AC + ETC`
Estimate at Completion (EAC) using remaining budget	This forecasting method uses the sum of the ACs and the *Budget at Completion (BAC)* minus the EV. It should be used when current cost variances are atypical of future variances. `EAC = AC + BAC - EV`
Estimate at Completion (EAC) using CPI	This forecasting method involves adding the AC to the difference of the BAC and the EV divided by the CPI. It should be used when current variances are typical of future variances. `EAC = AC + ((BAC - EV) / CPI) or EAC = BAC / CPI`
Variance at Completion (VAC)	The estimated cost overrun or underrun for completing project work. A negative VAC indicates a project overrun; a positive VAC indicates a project underrun. `VAC = BAC - EAC`
To-Complete Performance Index (TCPI) based on BAC	An indicator of the usage of resources for the remainder of the project. `TCPI = (BAC - EV) / (BAC - AC)`
To-Complete Performance Index (TCPI) based on EAC	If management decides that the BAC is not achievable, a new EAC is created by the project manager. `TCPI = (BAC - EV) / (EAC - AC)`

Summary of Earned Value Management Calculations

You can use the information presented in the schedule and cost control topics to evaluate a project from an Earned Value Management perspective. You will compute schedule and cost performance values for each project activity, then use the results to manage those activities that are behind schedule and/or over budget.

The project manager analyzes the information given in the table and graph and determines that the AC to perform the work is more than its EV. This indicates a negative CV and a budget overrun. In addition, the EV is less than the PV, which indicates a negative SV.

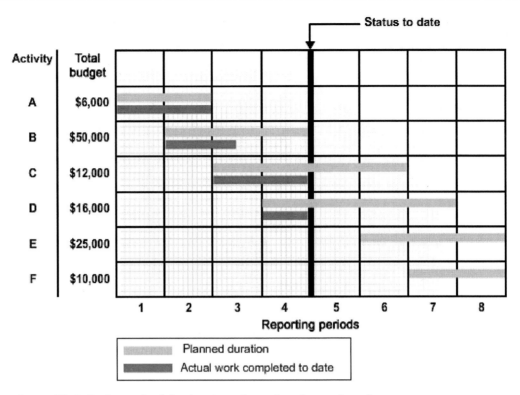

Figure 15-5: Project schedule showing planned and actual work.

Activity	% Complete	PV	AC	EV	SV	CV	SPI	CPI
A	100%	$6,000	$10,000	$6,000	$0.00	-$4,000	1.00	0.60
B	50%	$50,000	$44,000	$25,000	-$25,000	-$19,000	0.50	0.57
C	50%	$12,000	$5,000	$6,000	-$6,000	$1,000	0.50	1.20
D	25%	$16,000	$6,000	$4,000	-$12,000	-$2,000	0.25	0.67
E	0%	0	0	0	0	0	-	
F	0%	0	0	0	0	0	-	
TOTAL		$84,000	$65,000	$41,000	-$43,000	-$24,000	0.49	0.63

Figure 15-6: EVM calculations for project schedule.

The combination of both a negative SV and negative CV indicates that the project is performing over budget and producing less work than scheduled. The project manager uses this information to find out the causes of the variances and determine the appropriate corrective action necessary to bring the cost and schedule performance back in line with the baselines. He repeats the analysis at regular intervals to monitor the results.

 Note: Content related to schedule and costs has been addressed as separate topics. This example is provided to summarize using EVM calculations to monitor and control the project schedule and cost.

Guidelines for Controlling Project Costs

Continually monitoring cost performance and controlling changes to the project's budget enables you to maintain the cost baseline. Controlling project costs also helps avoid budget problems that may jeopardize the successful completion of a project. To control cost performance, follow these guidelines:

- Develop and implement a cost change control system. This can be integrated with the project's integrated change control system. Make sure that your system:
  - Includes the paperwork, tracking systems, and approval levels necessary for authorizing changes to the cost baseline.
  - Complies with any relevant contractual provisions when the project is done under contract.
  - Complies with the guidelines specified in the cost management plan.
- Evaluate change requests by asking these questions:
  - What is the magnitude of the change when compared to the cost baseline?
  - What is the impact of the change on the project schedule and quality objectives?
  - What are the potential risks and benefits of the change?
- Use performance measurement techniques to compare actual cost performance to planned performance.
  - Use performance reports to monitor cost performance.
  - Calculate CV, CPI, and VAC to determine whether the project is performing over or under budget.
  - Use earned value analysis and management to continually measure cost and schedule performance and to assess the value of work performed to date.
- Analyze the results of your performance measurements by asking these questions:
  - What is the cause of the variance?
  - What is the magnitude of the variance? Is the activity causing the variance on the critical path?
  - Is it likely that the variance can be made up in the near future without corrective action, or is corrective action necessary to bring the cost performance back in line with the baseline?
- Identify and document corrective action to take to bring expected future cost performance in line with planned performance. Depending on the priorities of your project, consider one or more of the following alternatives:
  - Recheck cost estimates to determine whether they are still valid. Avoid the temptation to reduce estimates simply to make the cost performance look better.
  - Identify alternate, cheaper sources for materials. For example, consider using a lower grade building material to keep the project costs on target.
  - Brainstorm ways to improve productivity. Consider using an efficiency expert to identify areas where productivity could be bolstered with training or guidance.
  - Change the schedule baseline. When a schedule change is contemplated, make sure that it is done in communication with customers and other key stakeholders to determine the schedule flexibility. If finishing on time is not as important as finishing on budget, cost overruns can be corrected through schedule changes.
  - Reduce the project scope. One way to reduce the scope is to prioritize the remaining work and eliminate work with the lowest priority. Another option is to plan for a Phase 2 project to cover unfinished scope items. Reducing the project scope must be done according to the integrated change control system and with approval of the customer and the sponsoring organization.
- Depending upon the nature of the change, you may need to revise the cost, schedule, or quality performance baselines to reflect the changes and to form a new baseline against which to measure future performance.

- Review the cost management plan as you begin to monitor cost performance. Follow the systematic procedures outlined in the cost management plan as you identify the need for corrective action and baseline adjustments.
  - Notify project stakeholders of any changes made to project baselines.
- Use performance measurement techniques, including trend analysis and EAC, to monitor the changes.
  - Are the changes being properly implemented?
  - Do the changes bring about the desired results?
  - Are new risks being introduced as a result of implementing the changes?
- Document lessons learned during cost control for use on future projects. The documentation should include:
  - Causes of variances.
  - Performance baselines affected by the changes.
  - Rationale behind the recommended corrective action.
  - Any other lessons learned during cost control.

TOPIC D

Manage Project Quality

Your quality management plan describes how your project team will move forward. Now that your project is well underway, you need to monitor the work results to ensure that they meet the quality standards you defined in your quality management plan. In this topic, you will manage project quality.

Companies face fierce competition to minimize development time and bring products to market before competition does. At the same time, organizations are faced with the challenge of staying competitive by keeping customers' costs low. As a result, quality is a component that permeates all aspects of project work. Effective quality control can streamline project work, saving time and money while continuing to maintain customer and stakeholder satisfaction. Controlling quality ensures that your project meets or exceeds your customers' quality requirements.

Quality Control Measurements

Quality control measurements are measurements used to assess a product's adherence to the specified standards. The measurements used may be quantitative or qualitative. Quality control measurements can be used to measure the quality of elements such as products, processes, and performance.

Example: Quality Control Measurements at a Turbine Manufacturing Company

A water turbine manufacturing company made quality specifications for its turbines. The specifications state that the deviation between two blades of a turbine should not exceed 0.20 degrees. The company used a 3D digitizing system to examine the turbines' adherence to the specified quality. If any turbine has blades with inclination more than the specified measurements, the turbine will be rejected.

Causes of Variance

Causes of variance in a process or item are the sources or reasons for deviations from the expected standard. There are two main types of causes of variance: *random* and *special*.

Random, or common, causes are those everyday occurrences that are always present in project work; as such, they may be unavoidable. They may be either insignificant and have little impact on the overall quality performance or they may have a dramatic effect on quality. The corrective actions taken in response to random causes of variance are typically long term and generally involve overall changes to the process.

Special, or assignable, causes are unusual, sporadic occurrences; they are the result of some unexpected circumstance and are typically not caused by a flaw in the overall production process. Like random causes, special causes of variance can also have a dramatic effect on performance. By analyzing instances of the occurrences of special variances, you may be able to isolate the cause and take corrective action to avoid the negative effects on quality performance. The corrective actions taken in response to special causes of variance are typically short term and do not involve overall changes to the process. Special causes do not occur frequently, but it can sometimes be decided not to act upon them because the cost of action may be much more than the benefit.

Example: Causes of Variance in the Metropolitan Bus Schedules

A metropolitan bus company is trying to improve customer satisfaction in one key area: the buses consistently run late. Random causes of the schedule variances include the weather and traffic conditions: these are unavoidable, everyday occurrences that will have an impact on how closely the buses can meet their schedules. A special cause of schedule variance is a minor traffic accident. This is an isolated, unexpected issue that may have a dramatic effect on the bus's schedule that day, but it does not indicate a process flaw.

Significance

Significance of the variance analysis is the weight or importance given to variances to determine whether and what type of corrective action needs to be taken. The project manager must determine the significance of the variance, keeping the balance of the three main constraints in mind.

For example, if the cost variance is $5,000 on a $5 million project, the significance is very low. If the cost variance is $5,000 on a $50,000 project, the significance is much higher.

Example: Schedule Variance

A project manager was responsible for ten projects occurring concurrently and was understaffed. Seven of the projects were performing on schedule. The other three projects had SPIs of 0.98, 0.96, and 0.975. Even though the SV was greater on the second and third projects, they were small and not schedule-driven. The project with the SPI of 0.98 was a mission-critical application that was schedule-driven, so the project manager temporarily diverted team members from some of the other projects to correct the variance on this project.

Root Cause Analysis

Root cause analysis is a technique used to determine the true cause of a problem that when removed, prevents the problem from occurring again.

Example: Root Cause Analysis for a Project

A customized application was in development for the sales force, to enable them to print invoices at the customer location. The program sporadically miscalculated the sales tax due on the invoice. Although initially it appeared that the problem was with the tax calculation portion of the program code, several hours of debugging determined that the root cause was that some of the products in the database had been misclassified, causing the wrong rates to be used.

Tolerances

Tolerances are measurement values that determine if a product or service is acceptable or unacceptable. They are the standards against which data collected will be analyzed. Tolerances are typically expressed in ranges. If the result of the test falls within the range specified by the tolerance, it is acceptable. If not, it is considered unacceptable. Tolerances are specified in the quality management plan.

Example: Tolerance Level for a Product's Weight

The tolerance for a product's weight may be 5.8 grams $\pm$ 0.2 grams. If a product weighs more than 6.0 grams or less than 5.6 grams, it is considered unacceptable because it exceeds the tolerance and does not meet the specification.

Variability Indications

Measurements that exceed the upper and lower control limits in a control chart are considered to be an indication of instability. The variability expressed is atypical for the process and may be an indication of a special source of variance.

It is important to remember that, although control charts can effectively show variability, they can neither indicate the source of the variability nor show performance in relation to expected performance. The control chart shows only the capability of the process to produce similar products. It does not show the conformity of that process to a customer's specifications.

Standard Deviation and Variability

Project managers use control charts to check for instability because processes always have some fluctuation and variability. In measuring deviations, if one has six standard deviations between the process mean and the nearest control limit defined in the control chart, practically no items will fail to meet specifications. This is termed the *Six Sigma limit*. In terms of controlling processes, the Six Sigma limit is significant because it provides a guideline for monitoring quality and adjusting it as necessary for processes where extremely high-quality results are required.

Data in a statistically normal distribution will exhibit deviation as follows:

- About 68.26% of the values lie within ±1 standard deviation of the mean.
- About 95.46% of the values lie within ±2 standard deviations of the mean.
- About 99.73% of the values lie within ±3 standard deviations of the mean.

The Six Sigma Process

Six Sigma has also evolved into a business management strategy that seeks to improve the quality of process outputs by identifying and removing the causes of defects and variability in processes. To achieve process Six Sigma, a process must not produce more than 3.4 defects per million opportunities.

Histograms

Histograms are quality control tools that organize individual measured values in a data set according to the frequency of occurrences. Frequency can be either the number or percentage of occurrences. Histograms can be used to track many items, such as the frequency of failures. Histograms show the shape of the distribution of values as a bar chart. In addition, they make it easy to show the range, mean, and variation of data. You can use histograms to:

- Show the distribution of data.
- Evaluate both attribute (pass/fail) and variable (measurement) data.
- Determine how variable the process is.
- Analyze whether the variation is random.

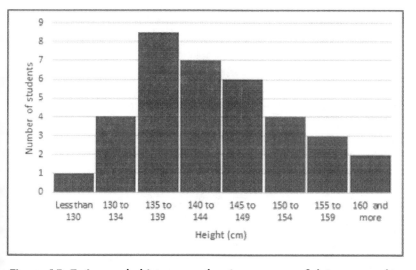

Figure 15-7: A sample histogram showing a range of data grouped together into intervals.

Pareto Charts

A *Pareto chart* is a histogram that is used to rank causes of problems in a hierarchical format. The goal is to narrow down the primary causes of variance on a project and focus the energy and efforts on tackling the most significant sources of variance. The variables in the chart are ordered by the frequency of occurrences.

A typical Pareto chart is used to represent data, which is first organized in descending order of occurrences and then plotting the cumulative curve. The bars represent the number of failures for each of the causes (A through E). In this example, approximately 72 percent of the total number of failures are due to causes A and B (320 out of 440). The project team can easily see that they should focus most of their corrective action efforts on those two causes.

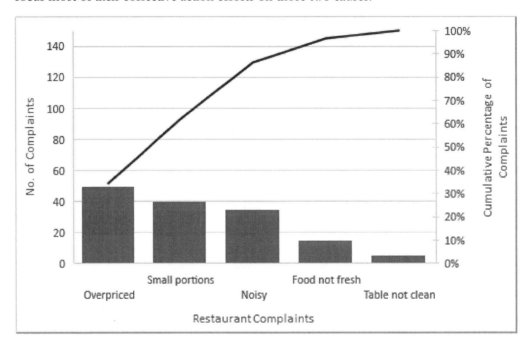

Figure 15-8: A Pareto chart.

Pareto Analysis

The analysis used to develop Pareto charts is referred to as a Pareto analysis, after Vilfredo Pareto, an Italian economist of the late 19th and early 20th century. In his analysis, Vilfredo Pareto found that 80 percent of the land in late 19th century Italy was controlled by 20% of the population.

During a Pareto analysis, data is collected in various forms, such as reports, inspections, and surveys. This data is then analyzed to isolate the major causes of project variance and is assigned a frequency or percentage value. The resulting chart is a histogram that identifies specific sources of variance and ranks them according to their effect on the quality performance. Pareto charts can be very useful tools throughout the entire project for prioritizing and focusing on corrective actions. Comparative analysis of Pareto charts at different points in the project can be an effective tool for determining and communicating the effect corrective actions have had on curtailing or eliminating variability.

The 80/20 Rule

Pareto charts are based on Pareto's law, also known as the *80/20 rule*. The 80/20 rule is a general guideline with many applications; in terms of controlling processes, it contends that a relatively large number of problems or defects, typically 80 percent, are commonly due to a relatively small number of causes, typically 20 percent.

Run Charts

A *run chart* is a line graph showing plotted data points in chronological order. It could show trends in a process or improvements over time. Trend analysis is a tool that uses run charts to communicate forecast information based on the project's current performance. It is also used to monitor technical, cost, and schedule performance.

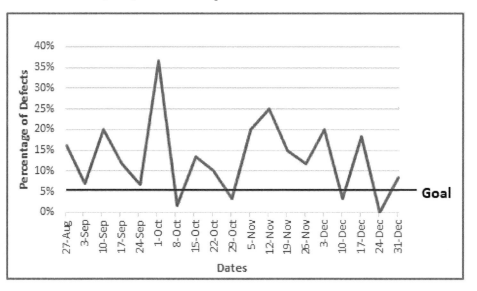

Figure 15-9: A sample run chart displaying plotted data points in chronological order.

Example: Managing Quality for the Arithmetic on a Stick Project

As the project team for the Arithmetic on a Stick project continues through production, the team continually monitors work results by conducting online reviews of the completed lessons and documenting any problems in the project's database. During one of the core team's meetings, the project manager does a quick trend analysis and notices that there is an unusually high number of problems in the database for the fifth lesson when compared to the previous four lessons.

The project manager asks the quality control engineer to evaluate the problems to determine which are generating more problems. The quality control engineer does a Pareto analysis and plots the results on a Pareto diagram. Because curriculum changes and technical problems are generating most of the problems, the team decides to focus on those two issues. Further analysis of the problems caused by technical reasons reveals that one technical problem was the cause of all trouble. The technical lead was able to isolate the problem and resolve the issues.

The curriculum changes were not so easily resolved. A new curriculum developer had been hired recently. The new curriculum developer was having difficulty understanding the project team's development process and consistently changed lessons after they had already been produced and programmed. This resulted in change requests for the art director and for the programmers. Intensive training sessions were suggested and implemented.

Trend analyses conducted on the sixth, seventh, and eighth lessons indicated that the corrective actions were effective in reducing the number of problems due to curriculum changes and technical problems. Now, the highest number of problems was due to curriculum and programming errors, so the team focused their attention on those issues. As they moved through the remaining lessons, the overall number of problems in the database significantly declined, indicating an overall increase in project quality.

Scatter Charts

A *scatter chart* (or diagram) is a diagram that displays the relationship between two variables. The diagram plots dependent and independent variables. The independent variable is usually marked on the X-axis and the dependent variable on the Y-axis. The more closely the points form a diagonal line, the more closely they are related.

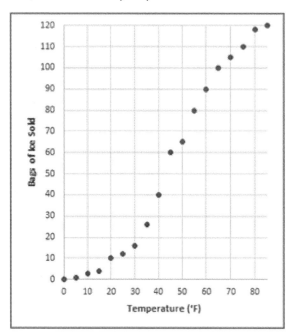

Figure 15-10: A sample scatter chart.

Statistical Sampling

Statistical sampling is a technique that is used to determine the characteristics of an entire population based on actual measurement of a representative sample of that population. Sampling is a way to determine if large batches of a product should be accepted or rejected without having to test every single item produced. Its goal is to produce a process that does not require inspection of every item. The size of samples and the frequency and cost of sampling must be determined when planning for project quality.

A common example of statistical sampling is polling. Polling organizations ask questions to a small, random sample of participants. The answers given by the sample group are used to suggest how an entire group may feel regarding an issue.

Sample size can affect the accuracy of results. Generally speaking, the larger the sample size, the higher the likelihood the sample will truly represent the variability of the population. In quality terms, the larger the sample size, the more confidence you can have that your measurements reflect the quality level of the entire product population.

 Note: It is important that members of a team whose focus is on quality control have a strong understanding of statistics. Other members need only have a basic understanding of statistical concepts.

Example: Statistical Sampling Through Polling

A common example of statistical sampling is polling. Polling organizations ask questions of a small, random sample of participants. The answers given by the sample group are used to suggest how an entire group may feel regarding an issue.

The Statistical Sampling Process

The *statistical sampling process* involves dividing sampling data into two categories—attribute and variable—each of which is gathered according to sampling plans. Because corrective actions are taken in response to analysis of statistical sampling and other quality control activities and because trend analysis is performed, defects and process variability should be reduced. The use of statistical sampling during quality control can reduce the overall quality cost by helping to forecast and prevent errors before they occur.

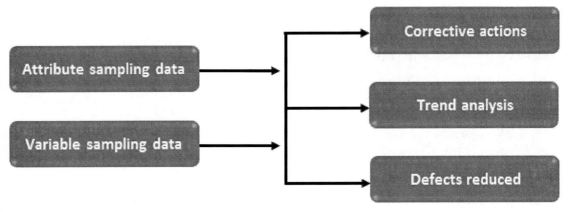

Figure 15-11: The statistical sampling process.

Attribute Sampling Data

Attribute sampling data is data from the sample that is counted, such as the number of employees participating in profit sharing, the number of customer complaint calls, and the number of returned items.

Attribute sampling uses no scale. It simply tells you whether or not a standard has been met. Implementing an attribute sampling plan is fairly simple. Team members may be required to count the number of items that do not conform to a quality specification or that show evidence of a quality defect. If the number exceeds a certain limit, the sample fails to meet quality specifications.

Example: Attribute Sampling for a Random Sample of Widgets

A project team is given a sampling plan that involves taking a random sample of 500 widgets and counting the number of widgets that do not meet the relevant operational definition. The plan states that there must be fewer than 10 defective widgets in order for the sample to pass the inspection. The team inspects each of the widgets, compares them to the standard specified by the operational definition, and determines that 30 of the widgets do not meet the standard. The sample did not pass the inspection because the number of defective widgets exceeded the minimum acceptance level of 10.

This is an example of attribute sampling because no scale is used. The test was a pass-or-fail inspection to determine whether the sample exceeded a certain acceptance level.

Variable Sampling Data

Variable sampling data is data from a sample that is measured on a continuous scale, such as:

- Time
- Temperature
- Weight

For variable data, the compliance to specifications is rated on a continuous scale. Measurements can fall between an upper and a lower range. To implement a variable sampling plan, you will collect a sample of the product and take some specific measurement to determine if the sample meets quality specifications. Variable samples typically provide the same level of accuracy as attribute samples with much smaller sample sizes.

Example: Variable Sampling by an Ice Cream Manufacturing Company

A company manufacturing premium ice cream will use variable sampling data to ensure quality control. Not every batch of ice cream produced will be tested for quality measurements, but testers will take measurements of random batches and test for flavor, consistency, color, texture, visual appeal, and other internal markers for quality.

Guidelines for Managing Project Quality

Managing project quality ensures that the quality complies with relevant quality standards. Meeting quality standards enhances the team's ability to deliver an overall project performance that meets project objectives. To effectively manage project quality, follow these guidelines:

- Conduct inspections to detect quality errors as project work is ongoing.
    - Consult the quality management plan for the procedures and guidelines to use during quality control.
    - Check work results against relevant operational definitions and checklists. Document the results.
    - Use statistical sampling to determine whether large batches of a product should be accepted or rejected based on the quality of the sample(s). Ensure that samples are chosen randomly and that the sample size is large enough to demonstrate the variability of the entire group.
- Analyze quality variance to determine the root cause of the problem.
    - If the same problem keeps recurring, you have treated the symptoms rather than solving the root cause of the problem. Before you can take corrective action, you must determine the root cause of the problem.
- Use Pareto diagrams to focus corrective actions on the problems having the greatest effect on overall quality performance and to measure and monitor the effect of corrective actions over time.
- Use control charts to analyze and communicate the variability of a process or project activity over time. As you analyze performance with control charts, you must not only look for variability outside the control limits, but you should also analyze patterns of data within control limits.
- Identify ways to eliminate causes of unsatisfactory results in order to minimize rework and bring nonconforming items into compliance. Use flowcharts to identify redundancies, missed steps, or the source of quality performance problems.
- Initiate process adjustments by implementing corrective or preventive actions necessary to bring the quality of work results to an acceptable level. Major adjustments must be made according to the project's change control system.
- Continue to monitor, measure, and adjust quality throughout the project life cycle.

ACTIVITY 15-1
Monitoring and Controlling Project Constraints Review

Scenario
Answer the following review questions.

---

1. Of the three components, schedule, cost, and scope, which according to you has the most impact on the program outcome?

2. What performance measurement techniques will you use in the future to measure schedule performance?

Summary

In this lesson, you monitored and controlled project constraints. Without controlling project constraints, your project may exceed its promised deadline and go over budget. Monitoring and controlling the project schedule, scope, cost, and quality helps your organization maintain its competitive advantage in the marketplace.

16 | Monitoring and Controlling Project Risks

Lesson Time: 45 minutes

Lesson Introduction

During project planning, you developed a risk management plan that describes how the project team will respond to identified risks. Now that your project is in full swing, you need to continue to monitor project work for new and changing risks.

Monitoring and controlling project risks may involve choosing alternative strategies, executing a contingency plan, or taking corrective actions to keep the project on track. If an assessed risk changes during the project's life cycle, it is important to analyze it quickly to determine if a threat or opportunity may result. As the project manager, your command of the tools and techniques to monitor and control project risks will enhance your ability to successfully complete your project. In this lesson, you will continue to monitor and control the project, focusing on project risk.

Lesson Objectives

In this lesson, you will:

- Monitor and control project risks.

TOPIC A

Monitor and Control Project Risks

In the planning process group, you developed a risk management plan and a risk response plan. During project execution, you need to implement those plans. In this topic, you will monitor and control project risks.

You identified the project risks, quantified and ranked them, and planned an appropriate response to each risk. That's just the beginning. It is up to you, as project manager, to implement these risk response plans appropriately. Effective project risk monitoring and control ensures that you respond in a reasoned manner.

Project Status Meetings

Project status meetings are regularly scheduled meetings that are conducted to discuss the current status of the project with the project team members and other stakeholders. Risk identification and management is one of the agenda items in the project status meeting. The time taken to address the identified risks depends on what risks have been identified, their priority, and complexity of response.

Example: Handling Project Risks During Organizational Restructuring

As the project work for a driver's safety video nears completion, the parent organization announces a restructuring of the department. As part of the restructuring effort, two of the project's resources, one graphic designer and one video producer, are transferred. The transfer of those resources will significantly impact the project and may cause some turbulence in the team.

In addition to their regular risk review meetings, the project manager calls an emergency core team meeting to develop a strategy for dealing with this new risk. The risk officer and the project sponsor attend the emergency meeting in which the group brainstorms alternative strategies in response to the risk.

Because two other projects have been canceled as part of the organization's restructuring plan, other graphic designers are now available. Those resources will be distributed among the various other projects that had lost resources. The new team members will need to be trained.

With the deadline looming, the project manager allocates a portion of the contingency reserves to cover the additional expenses that will be incurred to complete the video production, which had to be outsourced. This is a serious setback because four videos still need to be written and produced.

The multimedia lead takes ownership of this new risk. He hires a seller to edit the videos using the in-house editing equipment. He also collaborates on rewriting the scripts to make use of stock footage rather than having to shoot new footage to produce the four remaining videos. A risk response audit shows that the team's response plan for dealing with this unforeseen risk was effective in reducing its impact on the project objectives. The team updates the project's risk database to reflect the actions taken and the results of those actions.

Risk Reassessment

Risk reassessment is the process of reexamining and reevaluating the risks in a project risk register. It involves identifying new risks, reassessing current risks for their probability and impact, and closing the outdated risks. Risks can be reassessed during project status meetings. The extent of risk assessment at the status meetings depends on how the project is flowing compared to its objectives. For example, if an unanticipated risk develops, it may be necessary to have additional response planning.

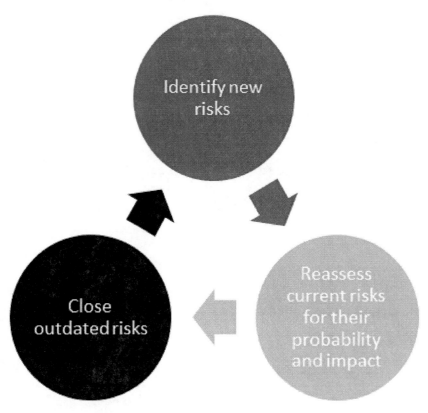

Figure 16-1: The process of risk reassessment.

The Project Risk Response Audit

The *project risk response audit* is the process of examining the team's ability to identify risks, the effectiveness of risk response plans, and the performance of risk owners. The audit may be conducted by a third party, the project's risk officer, or other qualified personnel.

The auditor reviews the risk register and data concerning project work results to determine whether the risk management activities are producing the desired results. In addition, the auditor evaluates the performance of the risk owner in implementing the response plan. The auditor documents the results of the audit and makes recommendations for improvement in the project's risk management efforts.

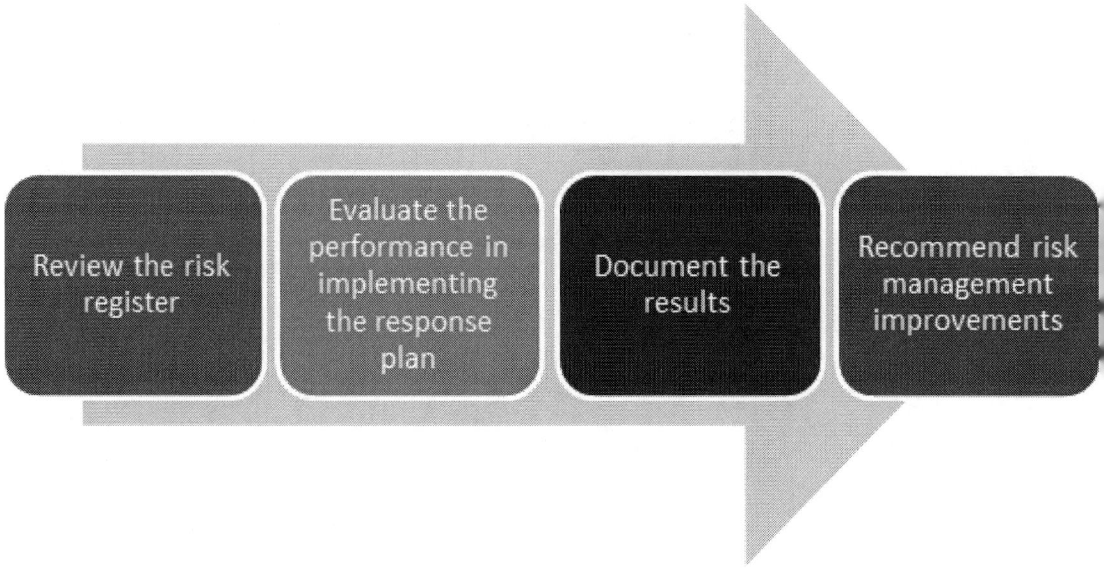

Figure 16–2: Risk response audit for a project.

Trend Analysis

Trend analysis is the process of examining project results over time to determine if performance is improving or deteriorating. A risk or a risk category is tracked over a period of time to determine whether its exposure to the project is increasing or decreasing. Trend analysis helps determine the categories of risks that are increasing or decreasing in their exposure to the project. It involves reviewing the various trends in project performance on a regular basis and can be used to predict future performance. Project trends should be reviewed using data collected on performance. Results from trend analysis may forecast a difference of cost and schedule from their initial targets. Earned value analysis and various other techniques can be used to monitor project performance.

Guidelines for Controlling Project Risks

Controlling project risks ensures that appropriate responses to risk events are implemented. To effectively control project risks, follow these guidelines:

- When an event affects the project objectives, consult the risk response plan to execute actions as mentioned in the risk response plan.
- Monitor the environment for any new risks that may arise due to:
    - Changes in the project objectives. Any change to the overall cost, schedule, or quality or performance level of your project will change your overall risk picture.
    - Changes to the scope. Whether the scope of the project increases or decreases, the risk picture changes. For example, increasing the scope of the project without assessing the impact on time or cost can spell disaster. Changes in the scope require iterating the risk management process.
    - Changes within the organization, such as restructuring within functional departments, that may mean some of the resources you were counting on will no longer be available for assignment to the project.
    - Changes outside of the organization such as technological changes, changes in industry standards, economic or market changes, or legal or regulatory changes.
- Monitor the effectiveness of the risk response, contingency, and fallback plans laid out in the risk response plan. Make sure that your monitoring is done in accordance with the policies and procedures defined in the risk management plan.

- Conduct project risk response audits to examine and document the effectiveness of the risk response plan and the performance of the risk owner.
- Perform earned value analysis to monitor overall project performance against the baselines. If the project is deviating significantly from the baseline, reiterate the risk identification and analysis processes.
- Conduct periodic project risk reviews that are part of the project schedule to communicate risk response effectiveness and to identify new risks or triggers that may require additional response planning.
- Measure technical performance to determine whether variances are significant enough to warrant additional risk response planning.
- If the response plans are not effective in reducing or eliminating risk, consider implementing the fallback plan.
- Deal with unforeseen risks by systematically planning a reasoned response.
  - Develop workarounds for risks with low risk values.
  - Perform additional response planning for risks with significant impact on project objectives.
- Update project documentation as changes to risks are indicated.
  - Keep the risk response plan up-to-date when risks occur and response plans are changed or added.
  - Issue change requests in accordance with the integrated change control system.
  - Update performance baselines if the changes are significant.
  - Update risk identification checklists to help manage risk in future projects.
  - Update the risk register with the status of each risk. Add any new risks that have been identified.
- Identify the variances and trends in project performance and manage the contingency reserve so that the additional time, money, and resources are utilized as planned.
- Periodically check the project performance and compare the project's technical performance to the planned performance as outlined in the project plan.

ACTIVITY 16–1
Monitoring and Controlling Project Risks Review

Scenario

Answer the following review questions.

1. How have changes to the business environment affected your project's risk control efforts?

2. What is your biggest challenge when it comes to monitoring and controlling risks?

Summary

As the project manager, you are responsible for monitoring the risks facing your project and controlling them appropriately to ensure the successful completion of your project.

17 | Monitoring and Controlling Procurements

Lesson Time: 45 minutes

Lesson Introduction

You selected a vendor to fulfill your project's procurement requirements. Now, you need to ensure that the vendor's performance meets the contract requirements. In this lesson, you will administer project procurements.

Lesson Objectives

In this lesson, you will:

- Monitor and control vendors and procurements.

- Handle legal issues associated with procurements.

TOPIC A

Monitor and Control Vendors and Procurements

Keeping the project on time and within budget focuses on monitoring and controlling the vendors, procurement documentation, contract change control system, and other systems that relate to the payment, records, and budget-related issues for the project.

Vendor Management

Vendor management is a management technique that is used to obtain and oversee contracted resources, including people, facilities, equipment, and materials. Managing project vendors is important for obtaining procured project elements without any delays. Contracts must be established to stipulate the quality and services of vendors. In a large project involving many vendors, web-based applications, such as Vendor Management Systems (VMS), can be used. In addition, performance must be closely monitored to ensure that services meet the quality objectives of the project. Change requests from vendors must be carefully documented and approved before implementing them.

The WBS must be thoroughly reviewed before determining which tasks and deliverables should be provided internally and which should be purchased from vendors. Factors to consider when selecting vendor services include:

- Impact on other projects.
- Initial and ongoing maintenance costs internally versus externally.
- Intellectual capital considerations. For example, will the organization lose the opportunity to gain a critical competence if the work is done externally?
- Performance capabilities.
- Compatibility with existing support structure.
- The organization's capability to manage a vendor relationship.

Example: Vendor Management for a Construction Project

The project manager for an industrial construction project, Christopher Young, is planning the procurement of the necessary raw materials for the construction. Christopher contracted two external vendors for the supply of construction materials. One of his site managers complained of repeated delays in the delivery of construction materials by one of the contracted vendors. The schedule is so far unaffected by using the contingency reserve. Christopher examines the vendors' contract and revisits the clause stipulating that any delay in the delivery of materials, excluding adverse climatic changes, will result in levying a 10 percent delay fee to cover additional costs of the schedule delay. Christopher directs the site manager to remind the vendor that any further delays in material supply will invoke the additional costs clause without notice. After a week, the site manager reported improvement in supply according to the schedule.

Procurement Documentation

Procurement documentation contains information about vendor performances on the cost, scope, quality, contract change notes, approved and rejected changes, payment notifications, and claims. It can also include technical documentation, deliverables, seller performance reports, warranties, financial documents, and results of contract inspections. Procurement documentation is acknowledged and validated for contract closure. The documentation is created when administering project procurements.

The Procurements Administrator's Duties

On a small project, the project manager may play the role of a procurements administrator. On a larger project, the project manager may delegate this task to one or more team members and monitor them.

In either case, the procurements administrator has the following duties:

- Act as a contract compliance officer.
- Interpret contract specifications and ensure that their terms are met.
- Monitor vendor performance.
- Integrate subcontracted elements.
- Manage change requests.
- Resolve disputes and manage payments.
- Deal with contract breach, early termination, and so forth.

Procurement Performance Reviews

A *procurement performance review* is the evaluation of the vendor's work. It verifies that the work performed is in accordance with the scope, schedule, quality, and cost as defined by the contract. It can include a review of documentation submitted by the vendor, inspections, or quality audits. The purpose of this review is to identify strengths and weaknesses with project performance and to monitor the progress of schedules and tasks.

Example: Contract Performance Review of Construction Materials

A company contracted four suppliers to supply construction materials for an industrial complex construction project. Because the quality standards for the project are stringent, the project manager wants the quality of the materials reviewed periodically. He appoints a team member to regularly monitor the material quality and send a weekly report on it.

The Contract Change Control System

The *contract change control system* might be a component of the integrated change control system or it might be a separate system, but it is dedicated specifically to control contract changes. It specifies the process by which project contract changes can be made. It includes the documentation, dispute-resolution processes, and approval levels to authorize the changes to contract specifications.

Example: Documenting Changes in the Contract Change Control System

A global service providing company contracted a website designing company to develop an online portal for one of its services. After the initial designing phase, the website design was sent to the customer for review. The customer, after reviewing the design, asked for additional features to be added to the website. The web designers analyzed the changes and identified that the implementation of these changes will extend the project schedule by one week. Upon approval by the customer, the change in the project deadline and the reasons for changes were documented in the contract change control system.

Vendor Inspection and Audit

Inspections and audits are conducted by the buyer to verify compliance in the vendor's work processes or deliverables. This is always outlined in the contract. Some contracts allow buyer procurement personnel as part of their inspection and audit teams. The goal of the audit is to establish a record that may be used to shape procurement practices in other contracts for this project or for other projects. The lessons learned from an audit can be valuable information for future contracts.

A *vendor audit* seeks to answer several questions about the procurement process.

- Were the contract specifications completed as specified and were all terms and conditions met?
- Were the quality, timelines, and cost acceptable?
- Were the vendor's project management, contract management, financial management, and communications management practices acceptable?
- Was the vendor able to accommodate requested changes?
- Were the members of the vendor's staff acceptable? Did any individuals merit special recognition?
- Was there anyone you will not recommend for future assignments?
- Were there areas for improvement?
- What were the lessons learned from this contract?

Example: Procurement Audit of Marketing Materials

A project manager, Dave, asked each of his core team members to evaluate the vendors they used during the course of the project for new marketing material. Dave gave the team leads a checklist and asked them to answer each of the questions that were relevant to the type of contract used. Randy, the multimedia lead, used over 50 freelance illustrators, video producers, audio producers, photographers, and animators throughout the project. Randy developed a template to use for each vendor.

This is an example of an effective procurement audit because it provides valuable information regarding the vendor's performance that will be helpful in future projects. It also provides lessons learned information that will increase the freelance illustrator database.

Contract Evaluation

Project Name: **Marketing Illustrations**

Contractor Name: **Jonathan Smith**

Job Role: **Illustrator**

Description of Scope of Work:
Create 20 illustrations for the new marketing print material.

Performance Assessment:
(Rating scale: 0=Poor, 1=Fair, 2=Good, 3=Above Average, 4=Excellent)

Skill	Rating
Quality	4
Timeliness	4
Price	2
Communication	4
Interpersonal skills	3

Recommend for future work? **Yes**

Terms or conditions of contract met? **Yes**

Lessons learned:
We met Jonathan through an artist's representative. Although his prices were considerably higher than that of other illustrators and graphic designers we have used, the results were worth the extra costs. We should continue to work with artists' representatives because of the time saved in finding a contractor. This will increase our pool of available talent.

Figure 17-1: A sample vendor audit document.

Payment Systems

Payment systems are used to make payments to vendors that are made contingent on the acceptance of the delivered goods or services and on the receipt of a valid invoice. Typically, invoices are sent to the organization's Accounts Payable department, which in turn checks with the project organization to verify that the goods or services were delivered and accepted and then authorizes payment.

Claims Administration

Disputes that arise when buyers and vendors cannot agree on changes are referred to as *claims* or *appeals*. Claims are handled in accordance with contract terms and are managed throughout the term of the contract. If the buyer and vendor do not resolve the claim, it will be handled according to the dispute resolution procedures in the contract. Contract clauses may include arbitration or litigation and may be brought up after contract closure.

The Records Management System

The *records management system* is a software application that is used to generate, track, and retrieve documents and for correspondence purposes. It is also used to manage the project vendors, procurements, and contract documentations. It contains the processes, control functions, and automation tools. The records management system is a subsystem of the PMIS.

Guidelines for Monitoring and Controlling Procurements

Regardless of the size of the project, the project manager is responsible for administering procurements for the project. Experienced project managers always rely heavily on the contract administration expertise of their organizations' Procurement, Purchasing, and Legal departments. Effective procurement administration ensures that the vendor's performance meets contractual requirements and objectives.

To administer procurements, follow these guidelines:

- Index and store all contract correspondence for ease of retrieval.
- Develop and implement an effective contract change control system. The system might be integrated with the project's overall change control system. It should include these elements:
  - Forms and paperwork required to request a contract change.
  - Contract performance-tracking mechanisms.
  - Procedures for submitting and approving change requests, including approval levels based on cost or impact of change.
  - Procedures for reviewing and resolving contract disputes.
- Evaluate the risk of each contract change request.
- Document all contract changes and incorporate any effect of the changes into the project plan.
- Develop and implement an effective performance reporting system for the vendor. The performance reporting system should include these elements:
  - Project performance baselines such as baseline time, cost, and quality specifications.
  - Actual time, cost, and quality specifications.
  - Performance of contractual reports including status reporting, on-site visits, and product inspection.
- Spell out in the contract any performance reporting specifications to be imposed on the vendor.
- Set performance milestones to monitor project progress.
  - Depending on your project, you may use partial deliveries, completion of selected portions of the product, or preliminary versions of the finished product as milestones.
  - Make sure that the milestones are arranged and agreed upon with the vendor ahead of time.

- Negotiate a deadline for each milestone and quality and completeness specifications for the milestone.
- If work is performed at another site, conduct site visits to determine how the vendor's work is progressing.
    - Be sensitive to the cost of site visits in terms of time and impact on vendor relationships.
    - Schedule the visits up-front, set an agenda for each visit, and use only the time required.
- Verify that the objectives of the project are being met.
- Approve the submitted invoices for payment in accordance with the contract and the project's payment system.

TOPIC B

Handling Legal Issues

When working with procurement matters, you will need to understand and deal with legally binding documents, such as contracts. When you experience changes to any procurement relationships, you might need to change the terms of a contract or other legal document.

Whether or not you were involved in procurement negotiations, you must understand your rights and responsibilities under the contract so that problems can be worked out with a minimum impact on project goals. Meanwhile, you need to be careful not to take actions that could undermine your organization's legal position, should litigation be necessary later on.

Changes to Contract Terms

Either party can propose *contract change requests* for any of the contract terms, including the scope, cost, delivery date, or quality of goods or services.

Contract Change	Description
Administrative changes	These are non-substantive changes to the way the contract is administered. This is the most common type of contract change. Administrative changes should be documented and written notification sent to the vendor with a clear expectation that the vendor will approve and return the change document. Administrative changes require no adjustment in payment.
Contract modification	This is a substantive change to the contract requirements such as a new deadline or a change to the product requirements. Contract modifications should be documented and a formal change order should be sent to the vendor. Contract modifications may result in claims for payment adjustment.
Supplemental agreement	This is an additional agreement related to the contract but negotiated separately. A supplemental agreement requires the signatures of both buyer and vendor. A separate payment schedule is attached for the work in a supplemental agreement.
Constructive changes	These are changes that the buyer may have caused through action or inaction. As a result of constructive changes, a vendor is required to change the way the contract is fulfilled. The vendor may claim a payment adjustment as a result of constructive changes.
Termination of contract	A contract may be terminated due to seller default or for customer convenience. Defaults are typically due to nonperformance, such as late deliveries and poor quality, or nonperformance of some or all project requirements. Termination due to customer convenience may result due to major changes in the contract plans, through no fault of the seller.

Example: Administering a Contract for a Website Project

With his change request approved, Peter, a project manager, becomes responsible for monitoring the graphic artist's contract for his company's website project. Peter fills out a conversation log for each conversation he has with the artist about the project and files the conversation logs in the seller's file.

Peter schedules meetings with the artist to monitor progress and to clarify expectations if necessary. As partial deliverables are made according to predetermined milestones, he reviews them for quality before signing and submitting the artist's invoices to the Accounts Payable department for payment. Peter places a copy of each invoice in the seller's file.

As the project team gets closer to completing the project, it decides to add another section to the website. This change to the project goes through the appropriate change control system set up for the project. After being analyzed for its impact on project cost, schedule, and quality, the change request is approved.

The additional section requires a modification to the contract for the design and production of the graphics for the new section. Peter negotiates the terms of the change with the artist and submits a change request for the contract modification using the change request form specified in the contract change control system.

This change request is also evaluated for its impact on the project cost, schedule, and quality before being approved and signed. Peter submits the request for the contract modification to the Legal Department, which incorporates the change and sends the modified contract to the artist to sign and return. Peter then files the signed modification in the seller's file.

The vendor's work goes smoothly with no legal issues. Eventually, the final deliverable is made and accepted, and the seller submits the final invoice for payment. Peter signs and submits the invoice for payment and thanks the artist for a job well done.

Legal Concepts

Project managers should be familiar with some of the common legal issues related to procurement administration.

Legal Issue	Description
Warranty	A promise, explicit or implied, that goods or services will meet a predetermined standard. The standard may cover features such as reliability, fitness for use, and safety. Some warranty agreements may promise repair or replacement of products or services for certain months, years, or for life.
Waiver	The giving up of a contract right, even inadvertently.
Breach of contract	Failure to meet some or all of the obligations of a contract. It may result in damages paid to the injured party, litigation, or other ramifications.
Non-disclosure agreement (NDA)	A legal contract that outlines confidential material, information, or knowledge that two parties wish to share only with each other. It is used to protect confidential and proprietary information, often including trade secrets, from being shared with other parties.
Cease-and-desist letter	A document sent to an individual or a business to stop (cease) allegedly illegal activities and to not undertake them again (desist). Such a letter can be used as a warning of impending legal action if it is ignored.
Letter of intent	A document that outlines an agreement between two parties before the agreement is finalized. It is sometimes used to highlight fundamental terms of an agreement before potentially expensive legal negotiations are begun, or to indicate that the parties have begun negotiations.

Legal Issue	Description
Force majeure clause	A common clause that refers to a superior force added to contracts that addresses the actions from both the parties when an extraordinary circumstance beyond the control of either party occurs. The extraordinary circumstances include war, strike, riot, crime, or a natural disaster (a so-called "Act of God" that includes floods, earthquakes, and storms) that prevent one or both parties from fulfilling their obligations under the contract. The force majeure clause is not intended to excuse negligence or other misconduct by the parties, and nonperformance is caused by usual and natural consequences.

Example: Warranty Agreement for a Solar Panel

The manufacturer of a new solar car model outsourced the project that deals with the making of solar panels. The vendor responsible for this project created the solar panels and delivered them within the allotted time and budget. The company signed a warranty agreement with the vendor that extends for a year. The agreement listed all the services the vendor may provide in case of any serious defects found in the solar panels. They even agreed to a replacement of panels if the defect is found within a month of its manufacturing date.

Types of Warranties

As a project manager, you may encounter several types of warranties.

Warranty Type	Description
Express warranty	If the predetermined standard for quality or performance is specified, either in a formal warranty or in the manufacturer's description of the product, it is considered an express warranty.
Implied warranty	If the predetermined standard for quality or performance exists but is not specified, it is considered an implied warranty. This type of warranty takes effect if the buyer depends on the seller's expertise when making a purchasing decision. If you purchase items that are widely available on the market, it is assumed that you are relying on the seller's expertise in determining that the goods are merchantable and fit for a particular purpose.
	On the other hand, if you are a technical expert, and you require an unusual modification to the product or you intend to use the standard product in an unusual way, you will not be able to claim implied warranties.
	Similarly, if you provide detailed product specifications and the seller meets them, you will not be able to claim that the seller breached an express warranty if the goods do not meet your needs.
Warranties of merchantability	A type of implied warranty that requires goods to be fit for ordinary usage. Any sale of an item is subject to warranties of merchantability. The sale of an item for use in a particular project will mean that the item was also subject to warranty of fitness if it can be proven that the seller knew how it will be used.
Warranties of fitness for purpose	A type of implied warranty that requires goods to be fit for the usage that was intended by the buyer.

Types of Waivers

It is possible for a party on a contract to explicitly waive a contract right. However, project managers should be particularly aware of the ways in which they can inadvertently waive their contract rights. These include:

- Accepting a product that fails to meet standards for quality or performance.
- Accepting late deliveries.
- Overlooking some other aspect of non-conformance to contractual obligations.

To protect against losses incurred by an inadvertent waiver of contract rights, some contracts are written to specifically exclude the possibility of waiving a specified right.

Types of Breaches of Contract

Project managers may encounter different types of breaches of contracts.

Type of Breach	Description
Anticipatory	An unavoidable indication that the other party will not be able to produce the performance necessary to fulfill the contract.
Fundamental	A breach so serious that it negates the very foundation of the contract.
Material	A serious breach that prevents the injured party from benefiting from the contract. In a material breach, the injured party can claim damages, but is no longer obligated to fulfill any contract commitments.
Immaterial	The contract is breached in such a way that there is no resulting damage to the injured party; because there are no damages, the injured party is not entitled to receive compensation. This is also called a minor breach.

Guidelines for Handling Legal Issues

Project managers should have a general understanding of contracts and breaches of contracts, but they are not expected to be legal experts. The best way to protect yourself, your project, and your organization is to make sure that your legal department reviews and approves all contracts before you sign them. As a general guideline, you should never sign a contract unless you are sure that you understand all its terms. Other guidelines for handling legal issues include:

- Have a good understanding of the differences between important legal terms that can, if ignored, have a significant impact on the project—warranty, waiver, and breach of contract.
- Be sure to consult with somebody in your company's legal department or seek advice from an outside legal expert so you thoroughly understand any contracts that affect your project.
- If your contract isn't written specifically to exclude inadvertent waivers, avoid doing any of the following that would waive your contract rights:
  - Accept a product that fails to meet standards for quality or performance.
  - Accept late deliveries.
  - Overlook an aspect of non-conformance to contractual obligations.

ACTIVITY 17–1

Monitoring and Controlling Procurements Review

Scenario

Answer the following review questions.

1. How will developing and implementing an effective performance reporting system help you administer contracts on future projects?

2. What are the most common legal issues you've encountered when monitoring and controlling vendors?

Summary

In this lesson, you monitored project procurements, and examined the importance of executing the project contracts effectively so that you can successfully bring your project to its conclusion.

18 | Closing the Project

Lesson Time: 1 hour, 30 minutes

Lesson Introduction

You successfully completed the last project deliverable and approved the last invoice for payment. You are almost done! But first, you must properly close out the project.

Unfinished business, contracts not correctly closed out, and poor documentation can turn into months of additional work and expenditure. The last thing you do on a project will be the first thing people remember about your efforts overall. Mastering the techniques of effective project closure helps ensure that there are no loose ends that could unravel the good work of your team and the success of your project. In this lesson, you will perform project closure.

Lesson Objectives

In this lesson, you will perform project closure.

- Deliver the final product.
- Close project procurements.
- Close a project.

TOPIC A

Deliver the Final Product

You monitored and controlled the project and the project's product is ready to be handed off to the customer. In this topic, you will complete various tasks associated with delivering the final product.

There are many tasks involved in handing off the final product to the customer. Although those tasks are not difficult or time consuming, it is important to ensure that you covered all the bases and obtained final sign-off from the customer. Then, you will know that you successfully completed the project according to the customer's expectations, and it can go a long way toward building your credibility with sponsors of future projects.

Accepted Deliverables

Accepted deliverables are all deliverables that are completed, accepted, and formally signed-off. The deliverables that have been formally signed-off or acknowledged by the sponsors or customers are moved toward project closure.

The Final Product, Service, or Result Transition

The final product, service, or result transition is the process of transferring the final product that the project was authorized to produce. The final product is usually reviewed for completeness and accuracy before it can be transitioned to its recipients.

Example: Release of the Final Product

The financial module of an ERP package was ready to be released to production. The project team members completed the customization of the package, managed data migration, and performed unit and functional testing, including a final pre-release test in a duplicated production environment testing facility. They documented the known issues, errors, and customizations done to the software They compiled technical documentation for support personnel and provided early release information for training so that end user training could be prepared.

The training department first conducted change management training, because a number of accountants had serious concerns about changing how they were currently doing things. They then conducted special technical training sessions for the help desk personnel. A series of web-based training sessions were set up to train the accountants on the new software, prior to its release. One month prior to release, the company posted product highlights, release information, and a FAQ to the company intranet. The installation of the software was scheduled at the beginning of the month so that it wouldn't conflict with month-end closeouts. A representative from the team was scheduled to provide floor support during the first week after release and was on hold for the second week if needed. To put a positive spin on the release, email notices were sent daily to stakeholders during the two weeks prior to release, with a countdown to the big day. The project manager coordinated a kickoff celebration with the VP of finance.

Guidelines for Delivering the Final Product

Accurate delivery of a final product ensures that all deliverables are transferred in a quality-controlled format with a smooth transition and according to the stakeholders' expectations. To deliver the final product, follow these guidelines:

- Perform the final user acceptance or operational test. Test systems performance to ensure that stated quality standards and performance targets are being met.

- Verify that known issues and errors have been identified and that information has been transferred to support personnel.
- Provide operational support personnel with the documentation created.
- Verify that the transfer date has been communicated and that stakeholders are prepared to accept the deliverables:
  - Determine who is responsible for future support to provide operational continuity.
  - Determine who has ownership rights to the intellectual capital represented by the deliverables.
- Double-check to make sure that all the stakeholders' hand-off requirements have been met.
- Ensure that the training plan has been executed and that the team performed those responsibilities as specified in the transfer plan.
- Ensure that the project team is prepared to provide floor support for the specified time during the initial launch. This support is critical for a smooth transition, but it's easy to lose team members to other projects when the current project winds down.
- Conduct any other activities that were specified in the hand-off deliverables checklist.
- Manage customer perceptions:
  - Many times the hand-off is a non event—technical or installation experts install the product or process and then leave.
  - Consider creating a formal transfer event to provide a sense of closure, such as a formal demonstration event, a walkthrough, or a ribbon-cutting ceremony.
  - Highlight the benefits of the new system.
- Secure the appropriate approvals and sign-offs.

TOPIC B

Close Project Procurements

You and your project team successfully carried out your project plan, produced work results, and controlled the project's performance baselines. You also need to close any contracts with service providers and vendors who were contracted for part of the project. In this topic, you will close project procurements.

Incomplete or inaccurate project records indicate poor organizational skills. Although you may never have to go back into your procurement files, other project managers in your organization may want to use them as historical information for their projects. Proper closure of a contract ensures that contract records will serve as valuable information for future contracts and that work completed under the contract was accomplished completely and correctly.

Procurement Audits

A *procurement audit* is a formal evaluation of the effectiveness of the procurement process itself. The goal of the audit is to establish a record that may be used to shape procurement practices in other contracts for this project or for other projects. This audit considers the following elements of the procurement process:

- Make or Buy Analysis.
- Preparation of the procurement SOW and procurement documents.
- Selection of selected vendors.
- Adequacy of the procurement contract.
- Contract administration.

Procurement Audit Lessons Learned

The lessons learned from a procurement audit can be invaluable information for future contracts. For example, the contract structure or payment terms that seemed appropriate at the start of the contract may have acted as disincentives to performance during the contract itself. By including as much anecdotal detail in the lessons learned as possible, you help others in the organization apply the learning to their situations.

Negotiated Settlements

Negotiated settlements are undertaken to arrive at a final equitable settlement for all outstanding issues, claims, and disputes by negotiation. The parties may resort to Alternative Dispute Resolution (ADR), which includes mediation and arbitration, if settlement cannot be achieved through direct negotiations held between the parties.

Closed Procurements

Closed procurements are usually a formal written document between the buyer and the seller stating that no considerations are pending from either party. This can be done whenever a procurement contract is satisfied and can happen on a rolling basis throughout the project. The buyer receives what was expected and is satisfied; the seller receives the payment and other aspects as prescribed in the contract. The contract spells out the terms and conditions for contract acceptance and closure. These terms and conditions are usually included in the procurement management plan.

Special Issues in Contract Closeout

The following table describes special issues that may impact contract closeout.

Issue	Description
Incomplete contract closeout	• Contracts may be terminated early due to vendor nonperformance or through no fault of the vendor whatsoever. • If a project is shut down prematurely due to issues within the customer or project organization, how does that impact contract closeout? In this situation, the contract itself will probably provide guidance as to how to deal with early termination. • For example, the contract may have a clause that specifies that either side may withdraw from the contract with a 30-day written notice to the other side. During the 30-day notice period, the vendor may continue working on the project, tying up loose ends, taking receipt of material ordered for the project, and so forth. Once the project has been terminated, the project manager should take whatever steps are necessary to provide the appropriate written notice as soon as possible, in order to start the termination clock. • In addition, an explanatory call to the vendor in advance of the written notice is an expected courtesy. If the contract ties payment to specific deliverables, the procurement audit should verify that the deliverables were received as specified and that the invoices reflect only those deliverables that were received. Issues of time, cost, and quality are still relevant. • Be sure to evaluate these issues based on the version of the deliverable you are paying for, rather than for the final deliverable. For example, say the vendor was contracted to supply a beta version of the product in January and a final version in March. But the project was canceled in February. • The product quality audit should be based on whether it met the specifications for a beta product, not for a final product.
Vendor staff evaluations	• In some cases, vendors will request that you participate in evaluating their staff members who are participating in your project. • In other cases, you may wish to send letters of commendation to a vendor, in order to recognize the performance of some of their staff members. • Your organization may have a policy that limits your participation in evaluating the ongoing performance of vendor staff. You should consult this policy before providing any sort of written performance evaluation. • Most organizations allow letters of commendation that recognize the contribution of particular vendor staff members. This practice is highly motivating to the vendor staff. • Usually, a copy is sent both to the staff member individually and to the vendor organization.

Guidelines for Closing Project Procurements

Use can use the following guidelines to properly close the project procurements:

• Ensure that all required products or services were provided by the vendor.
• Make sure that any buyer-furnished property or information was returned to the buyer.

- Settle any outstanding contracting issues. Are there any claims or investigations pending on this contract?
- Conduct a procurement audit to identify successes and failures of the procurement process.
- Conduct a vendor inspection and audit to evaluate the performance of the vendor.
- Address any outstanding invoices and payments.
- Archive the complete contract file with the project archives.
- Provide the vendor with formal written notice that the contract has been completed.

TOPIC C

Close a Project

You and your project team successfully carried out your project plan, produced work results, and controlled the project's performance baselines. It is time to tie up all the loose ends and close your project or phase. In this topic, you will perform the administrative portion of project or phase closure.

Ending a project or phase requires the same care and attention as starting the project or phase. As a project manager, the way in which you end your project or phase says a great deal about you to your stakeholders. Obtaining formal acceptance of your project's or phase's final product, service, or result ensures that the project or phase is properly closed.

Knowledge Management

Closing a project involves more than simply completing the project's scope and getting sign-off from the customer and other key stakeholders. You will need to prepare several closure documents and make them available to future projects, so they can benefit from what you learned during your project and hopefully avoid some of the rough spots that you were faced with. You will also organize the data you collected during your work—status reports, performance measurement information, and all of the change requests—so other people can learn from your experiences.

These reports and data can be archived on a company intranet site, rather than stored in boxes in a warehouse. People with the appropriate permissions can then find them long after your project has ended and the team has moved on to other work. If your organization uses one of the popular collaboration tools, you will not need to "start from scratch" to develop your archiving system.

 Note: Microsoft® SharePoint® is a widely used collaboration tool, and an Internet search will provide many other options.

Administrative Closure

Administrative closure involves verifying and documenting project results to formalize project or phase completion on all aspects. During the administrative closure process, the project team gathers and updates project documentation and relevant records and reports. Project results are compared with customer and stakeholder expectations and requirements. A properly completed administrative closure process ensures that:

- The project or phase requirements were met and formal acceptance was granted.
- The project objectives were completely met.

After the administrative closure is complete, you should conduct a project evaluation whereby you will review the original proposed financial and operational benefits and determine whether or not they have been achieved over time. If they have not been achieved, you should evaluate and determine if further action is required.

Project Records to Archive

During administrative closure, it may be beneficial to archive selected project records such as:

- The project management plan with its subsidiary plans and supporting detail.
- Project performance records, audit reports, and financial records.
- Contract documentation as completed in closed procurements.
- Copies of all relevant communication, status reports, meeting minutes, and change requests.

- Relevant project databases.
- Staff evaluations.
- Lessons learned reports and the final project report.
- Formal acceptance documentation.

It may be helpful to construct a list of outstanding items that must be resolved, addressed, or completed before the customer will accept the final work results. Include the actions taken to resolve any outstanding issues and any time frames associated with completion.

Lessons Learned Reports

Lessons learned reports are documents that capture salient and helpful information about the work done in a project; they identify both the project team's strengths and areas for improvement. They can be formal or informal, depending on the organizational norms or requirements. The lessons learned reports can be built by contributions from the project team throughout the project, and edited into a clean document during closing. This minimizes the need for contributors to recall details at the end of the project.

Lessons learned reports will be beneficial to future project teams. Having this knowledge base enables project teams to capitalize on work that has already been done, avoid repeating mistakes, and benefit from ongoing organizational learning.

Example: Lessons Learned When Launching a New Product Line

After a particularly challenging project involving the launch of a new product line, the project manager finalized the lessons learned report based on inputs provided by the project team. Also, in a meeting with key team members and stakeholders, the participants were asked about what went well in the project and what they will do differently next time. The project manager documented their responses into a report for future reference; it captured the challenges that had been overcome, suggestions that were generated, and other lessons that had been learned.

Considerations of Lessons Learned

During administrative closure, project managers should take into account the following considerations of lessons learned.

Consideration	Description
Scheduling lessons learned	These include any relevant scheduling problems or issues. They also document the management strategies that were implemented to deal with schedule or resource constraints. Capture beneficial approaches to implement as new best practices.
Conflict management lessons learned	These include any issues that arose within the team or between the team and customers. They include documentation of the nature and source of the conflict and the impact that the conflict had on the project. The documentation should also specify how management intervened in response to the conflict.
Vendor lessons learned	New seller experience and performance should be documented and provided to the procurement department.
Customer lessons learned	If a customer is excessively litigious or unreasonable to work with, that information should be conveyed to the sales and legal departments and documented in the lessons learned repository. If the customer experience is positive, then capture the potential for future sales or working together.

Consideration	Description
Strategic lessons learned	Strategic lessons learned are those that typically impact some aspect of the organization's project management methodology or significantly improve a template, form, or process. These address the questions: Can we reuse this project's artifact to get more done with the same resources and deliver work sooner?
Tactical lessons learned	Tactical lessons learned are those that answer the question: If we were to do this type of project again, what should we stop, start, and continue so that we can execute the project flawlessly? They focus on developing recommendations, reviewing recommendations with other managers in other departments, developing implementation plans, and implementing those plans.
Other aspects of lessons learned	Project managers should take into account scope, schedule, cost, quality, and customer satisfaction and any corrective action taken in response to issues, as well as any new practices to adopt.

Closure Meetings

Closure meetings, or closeout meetings, are sessions held at the end of a project or phase; they involve discussing the work and reviewing lessons learned. Closure meetings include stakeholders, team members, project resources, and customers. They typically follow a formal agenda and may require official minutes to be recorded. Conducting closeout meetings is essential, and not all organizations or projects require closeout meetings in a formal manner. Some organizations require the minutes from closure meetings to be completed in full, approved by management, and preserved in a specific manner.

Some organizations require official closure meetings so that they can obtain the customers' formal project acceptance, while others use them as an opportunity to discuss the project with the customers as a prelude to soliciting additional business. Other organizations use closeout meetings for internal purposes, for the edification of the staff and improvement of internal processes. From an organizational standpoint, good endings lead to good beginnings on subsequent projects.

Example: Fire Safety Closure Meetings

A project manager responsible for fire safety equipment and inspections will hold a closure meeting at the conclusion of the inspection process. He will invite the stakeholders, project team members, and representatives from the fire marshal's office. They will review inspection documentation records; complete and sign inspection certificates; review, approve, and sign the plans for evacuation procedures; and document the inspections and testing of fire safety equipment. Those signed, official documents will be filed both with the fire marshal and at the company in accordance with fire safety procedures.

Auditing vs. Debriefing

Auditing is an examination of a project's goals and achievements, including adequacy, accuracy, efficiency, effectiveness, and the project's compliance with applicable methodologies and regulations. It tends to be a formal, one-sided process that can be extremely demoralizing to team members.

Debriefing is a less formal, more cooperative means of discussing the positives and the negatives of the project, what worked, and what will be done differently next time. This discussion includes technology issues, people issues, vendor relationships, and organizational culture.

Example: Obtain Candid Feedback with a Debriefing Meeting

At the conclusion of an 18-month, $2 million project that came in on time, but $200,000 over budget, the project manager knew she would be subjected to an organizational audit to verify the project's use of resources to accomplish the goal of the project. She chose, however, to use facilitated debriefing in the final project review, knowing that she would be able to keep the meeting positive and get better feedback from her team. Also the intermediate closeout meetings conducted at the end of every phase of the project helped keep the final closeout meeting short and effective. The meeting was then followed by a team celebration.

Historical Information

Historical information is an aggregate of lessons learned and other useful information collected from preceding projects. This information can be used as best practices in similar projects. *Artifacts*, such as plans, standards and procedures, estimations, metrics, and risks, are some of the historical information that can be referred to when managing pertinent projects. Historical information that describes successes, failures, and lessons learned is particularly important during planning and managing projects. The project manager is responsible for maintaining these artifacts that often prove useful when a significant amount of work is done by virtual teams or when it involves multicultural communication.

Example: Project Closure for Renovation of a Manufacturing Plant

The renovation of a manufacturing plant project is in its last stages. The project manager developed documents, technical and managerial, such as plant layouts, minutes of meetings that took place at different points, and so on. The specifications for renovated plants were compared with the actual work. The key stakeholders who were involved in finalizing the specifications were invited for validating the deliverables. A detailed presentation containing photographs, images, key issues faced, best times, and worst times on the project was developed. The team members were invited for the final ceremony of project conclusion. They were awarded based on their contributions to the project. The team had a project postmortem meeting and at the end they came up with ideas for improvements in the next project. The project stakeholders were happy and the managing director commended the team on the systematic approach taken toward the project.

Guidelines for Creating a Project Closure Report

When you accurately create a project closure report, you clearly and concisely document the project life cycle, its effectiveness, value, issues, and cultural impact so that this information is easily communicated and can be used for future reference on projects of a similar nature. When you create a project closure report, be sure to do the following:

- Define the organization of the project.
- Document project strengths and weaknesses and the techniques used to get results:
  - Project effectiveness: Use the project charter and scope statement to validate whether the project achieved the strategic objectives.
  - Project efficiency: Define whether or not the project was on time, on specification, and on budget.
- Document project team recommendations.
- Define the project's cultural impact—the impact of the project upon the organizational structure and culture.
- Explain the value—define the capability or capabilities added to the organization and explain how they will support the strategic objectives.
- Lay out recommendations for maintenance—get stakeholders involved and identify ongoing responsibilities of the operational management for supporting and leveraging the new capability to ensure operational continuity.

- Consider using a corporate intranet site, groupware repository, such as a SharePoint team site, or other shared location as you collect, document, and share information with people who need to know it.

Guidelines for Closing a Project

Each phase of the project must be properly closed to ensure that valuable information is safeguarded for future projects. To properly close a project, follow these guidelines:

- Some organizations and application areas have a project termination checklist that may be useful when closing out a project or phase. You may find it useful to prepare one if there is not one available. This helps to ensure that you are thorough in your administrative closeout.
- Gather and organize performance measurement documentation, product documentation, and other relevant project records for ease of review by stakeholders.
- Release project resources. Recognize and reward team members who have performed well in the project.
- Update records to ensure that they reflect final specifications. Be sure to update the resource pool database to reflect new skills and increased levels of proficiency.
- Analyze project success and effectiveness and document lessons learned.
- Finalize lessons learned reports and a final project report.
- Obtain project approval and formal project acceptance. Demonstrate to the customer or sponsor that the deliverables meet the defined acceptance criteria to obtain formal acceptance of the phase or project. This may involve preparing an end-of-project report or giving a presentation.
- Archive a complete set of indexed project records.
- Celebrate the success of the project with the team and other stakeholders.

ACTIVITY 18-1
Closing the Project Review

Scenario
Answer the following review questions.

---

1. What steps do you plan to take to improve the project closure process in the future?

2. How will compiling a formal lessons learned report help you manage future projects effectively? Explain your ideas.

Summary

In this lesson, you learned how to effectively close a project. Your efforts to create a smooth and orderly closure will help shape stakeholders' perceptions of the overall project. In addition, effectively closing the project provides valuable lessons learned and input for your organization's future projects.

A | Taking the Exams

When you think you have learned and practiced the material sufficiently, you can book a time to take the test.

Preparing for the Exam

We've tried to balance this course to reflect the percentages in the exam so that you have learned the appropriate level of detail about each topic to comfortably answer the exam questions. Read the following notes to find out what you need to do to register for the exam and get some tips on what to expect during the exam and how to prepare for it.

Questions in the exam are weighted by domain area as follows:

CompTIA Project+ PK0–004 Certification Domain Areas	Weighting
1.0 Project Basics	36%
2.0 Project Constraints	17%
3.0 Communication and Change Management	26%
4.0 Network Security	21%

Registering for and Taking the Exam

CompTIA Certification exams are delivered exclusively by Pearson VUE.

- Log on to **Pearson VUE** and register your details to create an account.
- To book a test, log in using your account credentials then click the link to schedule an appointment.
- The testing program is CompTIA and the exam code is **PK0-004**.
- Use the search tool to locate the test center nearest you, then book an appointment.
- If you have purchased a voucher or been supplied with one already, enter the voucher number to pay for the exam. Otherwise, you can pay with a credit card.
- When you have confirmed payment, an email will be sent to the account used to register, confirming the appointment and directions to the venue. Print a copy and bring it with you when you go to take your test.

When You Arrive at the Exam

On the day of the exam, note the following:

- Arrive at the test center at least **15 minutes before the test** is scheduled.
- You must have **two forms of ID**; one with picture, one preferably with your private address, and both with signature. View CompTIA's candidate ID policy for more information on acceptable forms of ID.

 Note: See the candidate ID policy at **https://certification.comptia.org/testing/test-policies/candidate-id-policy**.

- Books, calculators, laptops, cellphones, smartphones, tablets, or other reference materials are not allowed in the exam room.
- You will be given note taking materials, but you must not attempt to write down questions or remove anything from the exam room.
- It is CompTIA's policy to make reasonable accommodations for individuals with disabilities.
- The test center administrator will demonstrate how to use the computer-based test system and wish you good luck. Check that your name is displayed, read the introductory note, and then click the button to start the exam.

Taking the Exam

CompTIA has prepared a **Candidate Experience video**. Watch this to help to familiarize yourself with the exam format and types of questions.

 Note: The Candidate Experience video is available at **https://www.youtube.com/embed/kyTdN2GZiZ8**.

- There are up to 90 multiple-choice questions and **performance-based items**, which must be answered in 165 minutes. The exam is pass/fail only with no scaled score.
- Read each question and its option answers carefully. Don't rush through the exam as you'll probably have more time at the end than you expect.
- At the other end of the scale, don't get "stuck" on a question and start to panic. You can mark questions for review and come back to them.
- As the exam tests your ability to recall facts and to apply them sensibly in a troubleshooting scenario, there will be questions where you cannot recall the correct answer from memory. Adopt the following strategy for dealing with these questions:
  - Narrow your choices down by eliminating obviously wrong answers.
  - Don't guess too soon! You must select not only a correct answer, but the best answer. It is therefore important that you read all of the options and not stop when you find an option that is correct. It may be impractical compared to another answer.
  - Utilize information and insights that you've acquired in working through the entire test to go back and answer earlier items that you weren't sure of.
  - Think your answer is wrong - should you change it? Studies indicate that when students change their answers they usually change them to the wrong answer. If you were fairly certain you were correct the first time, leave the answer as it is.
- As well as multiple-choice questions, there will be a number of performance-based items. Performance-based items require you to complete a task or solve a problem in simulated IT environments. Make sure you read the item scenario carefully and check your submission.
- The performance items are usually positioned at the start of the exam, but it is not required that you complete them first. You may consider completing the multiple-choice items first and returning to the performance items.
- Don't leave any questions unanswered! If you really don't know the answer, just guess.
- The exam may contain "unscored" questions, which may even be outside the exam objectives. These questions do not count toward your score. Do not allow them to distract or worry you.
- The exam questions come from a regularly updated pool to deter cheating. Do not be surprised if the questions you get are quite different to someone else's experience.

 Caution: Do not discuss the contents of the exam or attempt to reveal specific exam questions to anyone else. By taking the exam, you are bound by CompTIA's confidentiality agreement.

After the Exam

Note the following after taking the exam:

- A score report will be generated immediately, and a copy will be printed for you by the test administrator.

- The score report will show whether you have passed or failed and your score in each section. Make sure you retain the report!
- If you passed your CompTIA exam, your score report will provide you with instructions on creating an account with the Certmetrics candidate database for viewing records, ordering duplicate certificates, or downloading certification logos in various file formats. You will also be sent an email containing this information. If you failed your CompTIA exam, you'll be provided with instructions for retaking the exam.
- Newly-certified individuals will receive a physical certificate by mail. If six weeks have passed after taking your exam and you haven't received a copy of your certificate, contact CompTIA support.

Retaking the Exam and Additional Study

If you fail the first attempt of your certification, you can retake it at your convenience. However, before your third attempt or any subsequent attempt to pass such examination, you are required to wait a certain amount of time since your last attempt. Review your score report to understand how long before you can attempt again. Note that you will have to pay the exam price each time you attempt.

Mapping Course Content to CompTIA® Project+® Exam PK0-004

Obtaining CompTIA® Project+® certification requires candidates to pass exam PK0-004. This table describes where the objectives for exam PK0-004 are covered in this course.

Exam Objective	Lesson and Topic Reference
Domain 1.0 — Project Basics	
1.1 Summarize the properties of a project.	
• Temporary	Lesson 1, Topic A
• Start and finish	Lesson 1, Topic A
• Unique	Lesson 1, Topic A
• Reason/purpose	Lesson 1, Topic A
• Project as part of a program	Lesson 1, Topic A
• Project as part of a portfolio	Lesson 1, Topic A
1.2 Classify project roles and responsibilities.	
• Sponsor/champion	Lesson 1, Topic A
• Approval authority	Lesson 1, Topic A
• Funding	Lesson 1, Topic A
• Project charter	Lesson 1, Topic A
• Baseline	Lesson 1, Topic A
• High-level requirements	Lesson 1, Topic A
• Control	Lesson 1, Topic A
• Marketing	Lesson 1, Topic A
• Roadblocks	Lesson 1, Topic A
• Business case/justification	Lesson 1, Topic A
• Project Manager	Lesson 1, Topic A; Lesson 12, Topic C
• Manage team, communication, scope, risk, budget, and time	Lesson 12, Topic C

Exam Objective	Lesson and Topic Reference
• Manage quality assurance	Lesson 12, Topic B
• Responsible for artifacts	Lesson 18, Topic C
• Project coordinator	Lesson 1, Topic A
• Support project manager	Lesson 1, Topic A
• Cross-functional coordination	Lesson 1, Topic A
• Documentation/administrative support	Lesson 1, Topic A
• Time/resource scheduling	Lesson 1, Topic A
• Check for quality	Lesson 1, Topic A
• Stakeholder	Lesson 1, Topic A
• Vested interest	Lesson 1, Topic A
• Provide input and requirements	Lesson 3, Topic B
• Project steering	Lesson 2, Topic D
• Expertise	Lesson 1, Topic A
• Scheduler	Lesson 1, Topic A
• Develop and maintain project schedule	Lesson 1, Topic A
• Communicate timeline and changes	Lesson 1, Topic A
• Reporting schedule performance	Lesson 1, Topic A
• Solicit task status from resources	Lesson 1, Topic A
• Project team	Lesson 1, Topic A
• Contribute expertise to the project	Lesson 1, Topic A
• Contribute deliverables according to schedule	Lesson 1, Topic A
• Estimation of task duration	Lesson 1, Topic A
• Estimation of costs and dependencies	Lesson 1, Topic A
• Project Management Office (PMO)	Lesson 1, Topic A
• Sets standards and practices for organization	Lesson 1, Topic A
• Sets deliverables	Lesson 1, Topic A
• Provides governance	Lesson 1, Topic A
• Key performance indicators and parameters	Lesson 1, Topic A
• Provides tools	Lesson 1, Topic A
• Outlines consequences of non-performance	Lesson 1, Topic A
• Standard documentation/templates	Lesson 1, Topic A
• Coordinate resources between projects	Lesson 1, Topic A
1.3 Compare and contrast standard project phases.	
• Initiation	Lesson 1, Topic B; Lesson 2, Topic A

Exam Objective	Lesson and Topic Reference
• Project charter	Lesson 2, Topic C
• Business case	Lesson 2, Topic C
• High-level scope definition	Lesson 2, Topic B
• High-level risks	Lesson 2, Topic B
• Planning	Lesson 1, Topic B; Lesson 3, Topic A
• Schedule	Lesson 4, Topic A; Lesson 5, Topic A
• Work Breakdown Structure	Lesson 4, Topic A
• Resources	Lesson 4, Topic D
• Detailed risks	Lesson 3, Topic A; Lesson 9, Topic A
• Requirements	Lesson 3, Topics A and B
• Communication plan	Lesson 8, Topic B
• Procurement plan	Lesson 3, Topic A; Lesson 10, Topic B
• Change management plan	Lesson 11, Topic A
• Budget	Lesson 6, Topics A and C
• Execution	Lesson 1, Topic B; Lesson 12, Topics A-G; Lesson 13 throughout
• Deliverables	Lesson 12, Topics A, B-E, G; Lesson 13 throughout
• Monitor and Control	Lesson 1, Topic B; Lesson 14, Topics A-B; Lesson 15, Topics A and C; Lesson 16, Topic A; Lesson 17, Topic A
• Risks/issues log	Lesson 12, Topic E; Lesson 16, Topic A
• Performance measuring and reporting	Lesson 14, Topic C; Lesson 15, Topic A
• Quality assurance/governance	Lesson 15, Topic D
• Change control	Lesson 11, Topic A; Lesson 14, Topic B; Lesson 15, Topic B; Lesson 17, Topic A
• Budget	Lesson 15, Topic C
• Closing	Lesson 1, Topic B; Lesson 18 throughout
• Transition/integration plan	Lesson 11, Topic B
• Training	Lesson 11, Topic B
• Project sign off	Lesson 18, Topics A and C
• Archive project documents	Lesson 18, Topic C
• Lessons learned	Lesson 18, Topic C
• Release resources	Lesson 18, Topic C

Exam Objective	Lesson and Topic Reference
• Close contracts	Lesson 18, Topic B
1.4 Identify the basics of project cost control.	
• Total project cost	Lesson 4, Topic E; Lesson 5, Topic C; Lesson 6 throughout; Lesson 15, Topic C
• Expenditure tracking	Lesson 6, Topic C
• Expenditure reporting	Lesson 6, Topic C
• Burn rate	Lesson 15, Topic C
• Cost baseline/budget	Lesson 6, Topic B; Lesson 15, Topic C
• Plan vs. actual	Lesson 15, Topic C
1.5 Identify common project team organizational structures.	
• Functional	Lesson 1, Topic C
• Resources reporting to Functional Manager	Lesson 1, Topic C
• Project Manager has limited or no authority	Lesson 1, Topic C
• Matrix	Lesson 1, Topic C
• Authority is shared between Functional Managers and Project Managers	Lesson 1, Topic C
• Resources assigned from Functional area to project	Lesson 1, Topic C
• Project Manager authority ranges from weak to strong	Lesson 1, Topic C
• Projectized	Lesson 1, Topic C
• Project Manager has full authority	Lesson 1, Topic C
• Resources report to Project Manager	Lesson 1, Topic C
• Ad hoc resources	Lesson 1, Topic C
1.6 Given a scenario, execute and develop project schedules.	
• Work Breakdown Structure	Lesson 4, Topic A
• Scheduling activities	Lesson 5, Topic B
• Determine tasks	Lesson 4, Topic B; Lesson 5, Topic B
• Determine task start/finish dates	Lesson 5, Topic B
• Determine task durations	Lesson 5, Topic B
• Determine milestones	Lesson 4, Topic B
• Set predecessors	Lesson 4, Topic C
• Set dependencies	Lesson 4, Topic C
• Sequence tasks	Lesson 4, Topic C
• Prioritize tasks	Lesson 4, Topic C

Exam Objective	Lesson and Topic Reference
• Determine critical path	Lesson 5, Topics A and B
• Allocate resources	Lesson 4, Topic D
• Set baseline	Lesson 5, Topic D
• Set quality gates	Lesson 1, Topic B
• Set governance gates	Lesson 1, Topic B
• Client sign off	Lesson 1, Topic B
• Management approval	Lesson 1, Topic B
• Legislative approval	Lesson 1, Topic B

1.7 Identify the basic aspects of the Agile methodology.

• Readily adapt to new/changing requirements	Lesson 1, Topic D
• Iterative approach	Lesson 1, Topic D
• Continuous requirements gathering	Lesson 1, Topic D
• Establish a backlog	Lesson 1, Topic D
• Burndown charts	Lesson 1, Topic D
• Continuous feedback	Lesson 1, Topic D
• Sprint planning	Lesson 1, Topic D
• Daily standup meetings/SCRUM meetings	Lesson 1, Topic D
• SCRUM retrospective	Lesson 1, Topic D
• Self-organized and self-directed teams	Lesson 1, Topic D

1.8 Explain the importance of human resource, physical resource, and personnel management.

• Resource management concepts	Lesson 4, Topic D
• Shared resources	Lesson 4, Topic D
• Dedicated resources	Lesson 4, Topic D
• Resource allocation	Lesson 4, Topic D
• Resource shortage	Lesson 4, Topic D
• Resource overallocation	Lesson 4, Topic D
• Low-quality resources	Lesson 4, Topic D
• Benched resources	Lesson 4, Topic D
• Interproject dependencies	Lesson 4, Topic D
• Interproject resource contention	Lesson 4, Topic D
• Personnel management	Lesson 12, Topics C-E
• Team building	Lesson 12, Topic D
• Trust building	Lesson 12, Topic D
• Team selection	Lesson 12, Topic C

Exam Objective	Lesson and Topic Reference
• Skill sets	Lesson 12, Topic D
• Remote vs. in-house	Lesson 12, Topics C and D
• Personnel removal/replacement	Lesson 12, Topic D
• Communication issues	Lesson 8, Topic B; Lesson 12, Topic E
• Conflict resolution	Lesson 12, Topic E
• Smoothing	Lesson 12, Topic E
• Forcing	Lesson 12, Topic E
• Compromising	Lesson 12, Topic E
• Confronting	Lesson 12, Topic E
• Avoiding	Lesson 12, Topic E
• Negotiating	Lesson 12, Topic C

Domain 2.0 — Project Constraints

2.1 Given a scenario, predict the impact of various constraint variables and influences through the project.

• Common constraints	Lesson 15, Topics A-D
• Cost	Lesson 15, Topic C
• Scope	Lesson 15, Topic A
• Time	Lesson 15, Topic B
• Deliverables	Lesson 15, Topic A
• Quality	Lesson 15, Topic D
• Environment	Lesson 15, Topic D
• Resources	Lesson 15, Topic D
• Requirements	Lesson 15, Topics A-D
• Scheduling	Lesson 15, Topic B
• Influences	Lesson 12, Topic G; Lesson 14, Topics A and B; Lesson 15, Topic A
• Change request	Lesson 14, Topic B; Lesson 15, Topic A
• Scope creep	Lesson 14, Topic B
• Constraint re-prioritization	Lesson 3, Topic C
• Interaction between constraints	Lesson 3, Topic C
• Stakeholders/sponsors/management	Lesson 3, Topic C
• Other projects	Lesson 3, Topic C

2.2 Explain the importance of risk strategies and activities.

• Strategies	Lesson 9, Topic E

Exam Objective	Lesson and Topic Reference
• Accept	Lesson 9, Topic E
• Mitigate	Lesson 9, Topic E
• Transfer	Lesson 9, Topic E
• Avoid	Lesson 9, Topic E
• Exploit	Lesson 9, Topic E
• Risk activities	Lesson 9, Topics A, B, and D
• Identification	Lesson 9, Topic B
• Quantification	Lesson 9, Topic D
• Planning	Lesson 9, Topic A
• Review	Lesson 16, Topic A
• Response	Lesson 9, Topic E
• Register	Lesson 9, Topics B and C
• Prioritization	Lesson 9, Topic D
• Communication	Lesson 9, Topic A; Lesson 16, Topic A

Domain 3.0 — Communication and Change Management

3.1 Given a scenario, use the appropriate communication method.

• Meetings	Lesson 8, Topic A; Lesson 12, Topics F and G; Lesson 18, Topic C
• Kick-off meetings	Lesson 12, Topic D and G
• Virtual vs. in-person meetings	Lesson 8, Topic A
• Scheduled vs. impromptu meetings	Lesson 8, Topic A
• Closure meetings	Lesson 18, Topic C
• Email	Lesson 8, Topic A
• Fax	Lesson 8, Topic A
• Instant messaging	Lesson 8, Topic A
• Video conferencing	Lesson 8, Topic A
• Voice conferencing	Lesson 8, Topic A
• Face-to-face	Lesson 8, Topic A
• Text message	Lesson 8, Topic A
• Distribution of printed media	Lesson 8, Topic A
• Social media	Lesson 8, Topic A

3.2 Compare and contrast factors influencing communication methods.

• Language barriers	Lesson 8, Topic A
• Time zones/geographical factors	Lesson 8, Topic A

Exam Objective	Lesson and Topic Reference
• Technological factors	Lesson 8, Topic A
• Cultural differences	Lesson 8, Topic A
• Inter-organizational differences	Lesson 8, Topic A
• Intra-organizational differences	Lesson 8, Topic A
• Personal preferences	Lesson 8, Topic A
• Rapport building/relationship building	Lesson 8, Topic A
• Tailor method based on content of message	Lesson 8, Topic A
• Criticality factors	Lesson 8, Topic A
• Specific stakeholder communication requirements	Lesson 8, Topic B
• Frequency	Lesson 8, Topic B
• Level of report detail	Lesson 8, Topic B
• Types of communication	Lesson 8, Topic B
• Confidentiality constraints	Lesson 8, Topic B
• Tailor communication style	Lesson 8, Topic B

3.3 Explain common communication triggers and determine the target audience and rationale.

• Audits	Lesson 8, Topic B
• Project planning	Lesson 8, Topic B
• Project change	Lesson 8, Topic B
• Risk register updates	Lesson 8, Topic B
• Milestones	Lesson 8, Topic B
• Schedule changes	Lesson 8, Topic B
• Task initiation/completion	Lesson 8, Topic B
• Stakeholder changes	Lesson 8, Topic B
• Gate reviews	Lesson 8, Topic B
• Business continuity response	Lesson 8, Topic B
• Incident response	Lesson 8, Topic B
• Resource changes	Lesson 8, Topic B

3.4 Given a scenario, use the following change control process within the context of a project.

• Change control process	Lesson 11, Topic A; Lesson 14, Topic B
• Identify and document	Lesson 14, Topic B
• Evaluate impact and justification	Lesson 14, Topic B
• Regression plan (Reverse changes)	Lesson 14, Topic B
• Identify approval authority	Lesson 14, Topic B

Exam Objective	Lesson and Topic Reference
• Obtain approval	Lesson 14, Topic B
• Implement change	Lesson 14, Topic B
• Validate change/quality check	Lesson 14, Topic B
• Update documents/audit documents/ version control	Lesson 14, Topic B
• Communicate throughout as needed	Lesson 14, Topic B
• Types of common project changes	Lesson 11, Topic A
• Timeline change	Lesson 11, Topic A
• Funding change	Lesson 11, Topic A
• Risk event	Lesson 11, Topic A
• Requirements change	Lesson 11, Topic A
• Quality change	Lesson 11, Topic A
• Resource change	Lesson 11, Topic A
• Scope change	Lesson 11, Topic A

3.5 Recognize types of organizational change.

• Business merger/acquisition	Lesson 11, Topic A
• Business demerger/split	Lesson 11, Topic A
• Business process change	Lesson 11, Topic A
• Internal reorganization	Lesson 11, Topic A
• Relocation	Lesson 11, Topic A
• Outsourcing	Lesson 11, Topic A

Domain 4.0 — Project Tools and Documentation

4.1 Compare and contrast various project management tools.

• Project scheduling software	Lesson 4, Topics C and D; Lesson 5, Topic A
• Charts	Lesson 4, Topic C; Lesson 7, Topic B; Lesson 15, Topics B and D
• Process diagram	Lesson 7, Topic B
• Histogram	Lesson 12, Topic B; Lesson 15, Topic D
• Fishbone	Lesson 12, Topic B; Lesson 7, Topic B
• Pareto chart	Lesson 12, Topic B; Lesson 15, Topic D
• Run chart	Lesson 12, Topic B; Lesson 15, Topic B
• Scatter chart	Lesson 12, Topic B; Lesson 15, Topic D

Exam Objective	Lesson and Topic Reference
• Gantt chart	Lesson 5, Topic A; Lesson 15, Topic B
• Dashboard/status report	Lesson 14, Topic C
• Knowledge management tools	Lesson 1, Topics A and D; Lesson 5, Topic A; Lesson 13, Topic A; Lesson 18, Topic C
• Intranet sites	Lesson 1, Topic C
• Internet sites	Lesson 5, Topic A; Lesson 13, Topic A
• Wiki pages	Lesson 1, Topic A
• Vendor knowledge bases	Lesson 13, Topic A
• Collaboration tools	Lesson 1, Topic C; Lesson 12, Topic D; Lesson 18, Topic C
• Performance measurement tools	Lesson 14, Topic C
• Key performance indicators	Lesson 3, Topic C; Lesson 14, Topic C
• Key performance parameters	Lesson 14, Topic C
• Balanced score card	Lesson 14, Topic C
• SWOT analysis	Lesson 9, Topic B
• Responsible, Accountable, Consulted, Informed (RACI) Matrix	Lesson 7, Topic A

4.2 Given a scenario, analyze project-centric documentation.

• Project charter	Lesson 2, Topic C
• Project management plan	Lesson 3, Topic A
• Issues log	Lesson 12, Topic E
• Organizational chart	Lesson 1, Topic C
• Scope statement	Lesson 3, Topic C
• Communication plan	Lesson 8, Topic B
• Project schedule	Lesson 5, Topic A
• Status report	Lesson 14, Topic C
• Dashboard information	Lesson 14, Topic C
• Action items	Lesson 12, Topic E
• Meeting agenda/meeting minutes	Lesson 8, Topic A; Lesson 12, Topic G; Lesson 18, Topic C

4.3 Identify common partner or vendor-centric documents and their purpose.

• Request for Information	Lesson 10, Topic C
• Request for Proposal	Lesson 10, Topic C

Exam Objective	Lesson and Topic Reference
• Request for Quote	Lesson 10, Topic C
• Mutually binding documents	Lesson 13, Topic B; Lesson 17, Topic B
• Agreements/contracts	Lesson 13, Topic B; Lesson 17, Topic B
• Non-disclosure agreement	Lesson 17, Topic B
• Cease and Desist letter	Lesson 17, Topic B
• Letters of Intent	Lesson 17, Topic B
• Statement of Work	Lesson 2, Topic B; Lesson 10, Topic C
• Memorandum of Understanding	Lesson 13, Topic B
• Service Level Agreement	Lesson 13, Topic B
• Purchase Order	Lesson 13, Topic B
• Warranty	Lesson 17, Topic B

Solutions

ACTIVITY 1-1: Defining Project Management Fundamentals Review

---

1. **What types of project management experiences have you had?**

   A: Answers will vary, but may range from very informal, short-term projects to a full blown, long-term project that involves a large number of people in your organization.

2. **How does the ability to tailor each of the project management process groups to each project or phase improve your chances of project success?**

   A: Answers will vary, but might include: the five project management process groups are a recognized worldwide standard that was created over time by experienced project management professionals. The process groups have been tried and tested and have found immense success in project management. No two projects are the same, and therefore the activities and processes in the process groups will not be applicable for all the projects. Therefore, project managers should tailor these processes to meet the specific requirements or needs of a project or phase. Also, tailoring helps achieve more predictable outcomes.

ACTIVITY 2-1: Initiating the Project Review

---

1. **How is the project initiation phase (process group) important while managing a project in your organization?**

   A: Answers will vary, but may include: because project initiation involves defining and agreeing upon the project purpose, the project's relationship with the organization's strategic plans, the scope of work to be done, the project deliverables, and the acceptable criteria for the product, project initiation can be called the cornerstone of the project.

2. **How do you think creating the Project SOWs in your organization helps you manage your projects?**

   A: Answers will vary, but may include: a Project SOW gives the project management team a clear perspective of the project and its components. It can include the name of the project, description of high-level deliverables, key milestones, business need, description of the project's product or services, priority of the project, high-level risks, and key resources. The SOW helps the project manager manage the expectations of the project and project changes. Because the Project SOW lists the key project stakeholders, the project manager can easily keep them informed about the project's status and issues.

ACTIVITY 3-1: Planning the Project Review

---

1. **Which factors are important to your organization while defining the project scope?**

   A: Answers will vary, but may include: the accurate definition of the project objectives, clear definition of boundaries, stable definition of requirements, deliverables, acceptance criteria, constraints, and assumptions. During the project scope definition, you could also include descriptions of the product, service, or result of the project and involvement of the key stakeholders. Alternative identification on product or project outcome processes also provides a clear understanding of the project scope.

2. **In your experience, what are the most critical inputs for developing a project scope statement?**

   A: Answers will vary, but may include: the project deliverables, the project timeline, the project charter, client requirements, resource availability information, and the available budget.

ACTIVITY 4-1: Preparing to Develop the Project Schedule Review

---

1. **How do you think creating an activity list for projects will help ensure that your project activities are tied to the project scope?**

   A: Answers will vary, but may include: the activity list is developed by the decomposition of the WBS of the project. The project WBS is a project scope description. Because the activities are derived from the validated WBS, it ensures that activities are tied up to the project.

2. **Reflect on the advantages of creating a project schedule network diagram. How do you think this will help you organize your project more effectively?**

   A: Answers will vary, but may include: the project schedule network diagram depicts the flow of project execution. With such a diagram, you can identify flaws in the flow of project activities and immediately rectify the flaws.

ACTIVITY 5-1: Developing the Project Schedule Review

1. **In your experience, which schedule format do you find to be the most beneficial and why?**

   A: Answers will vary. Each of the schedule formats (bar chart, milestone chart, programming diagram, or Gantt chart) has its advantages and disadvantages.

2. **When developing a project schedule, which element or component of the schedule do you find to be the most crucial?**

   A: Answers will vary. Some might say that identifying the critical path is the most important element of the schedule, whereas others might say that establishing the schedule baseline is crucial for getting management approval of the project.

ACTIVITY 6-1: Planning Project Costs Review

1. **How do you think the ability to effectively estimate costs will improve your performance on the job?**

   A: Answers will vary, but may include: the ability to estimate costs effectively will help you make sound financial decisions on the project, avoid cost overruns by implementing cost saving methods, identify cost alternatives, and determine the cost baseline, which helps in planning project performance. These factors will definitely improve your performance on the job and ensure project success.

2. **How do you think incorporating good funding reconciliation practices will help in completing a project within the allocated budget?**

   A: Answers will vary, but may include: incorporating good funding reconciliation practices helps in judicious usage of funds allocated by the sponsor for the project.

ACTIVITY 7-1: Planning Human Resources and Quality Management Review

1. **Which components will you include while creating a staffing management plan in your organization?**

   A: Answers will vary, but may include: components such as staff acquisition, staff release plan, training needs, recognition and rewards, compliance, and safety. Smaller organizations might not be as formal when creating staffing management plans. The plans will be tailored to their particular project needs.

2. **What is the purpose of a quality management plan in your organization?**

   A: Answers will vary, but may include: a quality management plan describes how the project structures its quality system; areas of application; the quality policies and procedures; and roles, responsibilities, and authorities. The quality management plan will help projects produce deliverables of high quality with few or no errors. It also enables the project team to identify errors at the early stages of a project and avoid rework.

ACTIVITY 8-1: Communicating During the Project Review

1. **In your experience, which communication methods did you find to be the most effective? Which methods were the least effective?**

   A: Answers will vary, but might include one-on-one status updates being an effective method of communicating the necessary information with the right person at the right time. Another effective method might be posting project status updates on a shared team site so everyone has the information at their fingertips when they need it and don't have to waste time searching for what they need. The least effective methods would probably involve lengthy, large group meetings where attendees feel as if their presence is unnecessary or wasted.

2. **Share a situation when you were required to communicate a difficult message about the project to its sponsor or a top-level executive. What approach and communication method did you take?**

   A: Answers will vary, but will probably include the need to be as clear and concise as possible. In addition to communicating the difficult or bad news, it's beneficial to provide the steps or process that will be used to correct the situation so the sponsor knows you're working on solving the root cause of the problem and not just patching the symptoms.

ACTIVITY 9-1: Planning for Risk Review

1. **How could your organization benefit from comprehensive risk planning?**

   A: Answers will vary, but may include: a disciplined approach on risk planning is absolutely necessary for any organization. Early identification of project risks through various tools and techniques and implementing immediate corrective actions will increase the probability of project success and reduce possibilities of failure. It is the responsibility of the project manager to proactively identify potential risks before they occur and implement appropriate risk response measures.

2. **Which tools and techniques will you use to effectively perform qualitative risk analysis for future projects you manage?**

   A: Answers will vary, but may include: risk probability and impact assessment, probability and impact matrix, risk data quality assessment, risk categorization, risk urgency assessment, and expert judgment.

ACTIVITY 10-1: Planning Project Procurements Review

1. **How can your organization benefit from more effective procurement planning?**

   A: Answers will vary, but may include: effective procurement planning ensures better sourcing and selection of sellers by your organization using the detailed product and service specifications, seller analysis and identification, and guidelines for carrying out project procurement.

2. In the future, what do you plan to use to prepare better SOWs and procurement documents?

A: Answers will vary, but may include: product analysis, alternative identification, required quality standards, risk-related suggestions, and the WBS dictionary. Having the right information helps in preparing thorough procurement documents. You will be continually looking for small improvements.

ACTIVITY 11-1: Planning for Change and Transitions Review

1. How will you manage changes in your organization?

A: Answers will vary, but may include: it is important to have a well-developed change control system in place in order to manage changes in a project. The general process includes: 1. Identifying the changes that have occurred or need to occur. 2. Identifying the impact of the changes to the project scope, time, and cost. 3. Documenting the changes in a change request form. 4. Sending the change request form to the change management team (sponsors and customers) for review and approval. 5. Developing change management plans. 6. Taking actions to implement the changes. 7. Verifying the changes made.

2. What has been your experience in developing transition plans? What items did you choose to include?

A: Answers will vary based on students' real-world experiences. The transition plan components that are included might be the project schedule, project scope, and stakeholder expectations.

ACTIVITY 12-1: Executing the Project Review

1. What aspects of executing the project plan have you found to be the most challenging? Why?

A: Answers will vary, but may include: among the various processes involved in project execution, developing the project team is one of the most challenging processes. Because projects depend on collective performance of the project team, acquiring and improving skills required for the project, communicating project information to all team members, and motivating them to improve performance becomes one of the most important tasks. These tasks may become challenging when the project team members are inexperienced and require a learning curve and when the project team is spread across different countries or organizations, which makes communication among the team members difficult.

2. Which tools and techniques will you use to more effectively execute projects in the future?

A: Answers will vary, but may include: the PMIS, quality auditing, negotiation, training, team-building activities, observation and conversation, conflict management, project performance appraisals, process analysis, interpersonal skills, and lessons learned.

ACTIVITY 13-1: Executing the Procurement Plan Review

1. **How will you make sure that you are specifying adequate detail when requesting vendor responses?**

   A: Answers will vary, but may include: verify your procurement documents to ensure that you included measurable technical specifications as mentioned in the SOW and proposed terms and conditions of the contract, the regulatory and statutory requirements, the necessary documentation required, and details for the proposal submission process when requesting vendor responses.

2. **How do you think assigning numerical weighting factors to the evaluation criteria will help when you are trying to make critical choices about selecting vendors?**

   A: Answers will vary, but may include: using a weighting system enables quantifying qualitative data to minimize the influence of personal bias in selecting vendors. It also enables you to focus on what is important.

ACTIVITY 14-1: Monitoring and Controlling Project Performance Review

1. **How can you make the change management processes followed in your organization more effective?**

   A: Answers will vary, but may include: change management processes can be made effective by implementing an integrated change control system for the projects in accordance with all the relevant company procedures and requirements; by clearly identifying the roles responsible for initiating, authorizing, and approving change requests; and by effectively managing the approved changes.

2. **In your environment, which elements are the most difficult to control—cost, schedule, or scope?**

   A: Answers will vary, but may include: almost all project managers will find controlling project costs, schedule, and quality challenging in project management. Paying more attention to project quality may increase the project cost and duration. Maintaining quality while keeping the project cost and duration under check can be one of the most difficult tasks for a project manager.

ACTIVITY 15-1: Monitoring and Controlling Project Constraints Review

1. **Of the three components, schedule, cost, and scope, which according to you has the most impact on the program outcome?**

   A: Answers will vary, but may include: any of the three components, cost, time, and scope. Cost change may affect the need for the increase in money that needs to be spent, change in schedule may affect the time that may be required to perform an individual activity, and scope change may affect the efforts that need to be put in to complete a project successfully. Answers will depend on the objectives of the project and what its alignment will be to the three components.

2. **What performance measurement techniques will you use in the future to measure schedule performance?**

   A: Answers will vary, but may include: Schedule Variance (SV), Schedule Performance Index (SPI), trend analysis, variance analysis, schedule reports, and Estimate at Completion for time (EAC - time).

ACTIVITY 16-1: Monitoring and Controlling Project Risks Review

1. **How have changes to the business environment affected your project's risk control efforts?**

   A: Answers will vary, but may include: changes, such as a change in leadership or regulatory changes might introduce new risks that may affect the performance of the project. These changes need to be analyzed during the risk assessment conducted in periodic project status meetings to understand the impact on the project.

2. **What is your biggest challenge when it comes to monitoring and controlling risks?**

   A: Answers will vary, but might include developing a plan for responding to all risks, especially those that are unforeseen or unexpected. Also, identifying new risks in an ongoing project.

ACTIVITY 17-1: Monitoring and Controlling Procurements Review

1. **How will developing and implementing an effective performance reporting system help you administer contracts on future projects?**

   A: Answers will vary, but may include: developing and implementing an effective performance reporting system helps maintain a historical record of vendor performance with regard to contractual obligations and provides future projects with information on risks that affect the project schedule, cost, or quality.

2. **What are the most common legal issues you've encountered when monitoring and controlling vendors?**

   A: Answers will vary, but might include breaches of contract caused by various resource problems or scheduling issues.

ACTIVITY 18-1: Closing the Project Review

1. **What steps do you plan to take to improve the project closure process in the future?**

   A: Answers will vary, but may include: defining the closure procedures for closing project or phases and procurements, documentation, final results transition, and final verification of the products received from vendors or delivered to buyers.

2. **How will compiling a formal lessons learned report help you manage future projects effectively? Explain your ideas.**

   A: Answers will vary, but may include: compiling lessons learned implies indexing it for easy storage and access. The formal lessons learned report captures salient and helpful information about the work done in the project or phase and will serve as historical information for future projects. If lessons learned are stored in a systematic manner and are accessible for future projects, mistakes are less likely to be repeated. Also, by making best practices easily accessible, you can avoid spending time on issues that have already been identified. It also helps improve the performance of the projects based on the knowledge of the strengths, weaknesses, opportunities, and threats that affect projects in an organization.

Glossary

8/80 rule
A general guideline regarding work packages; they require more than 8 and fewer than 80 hours of effort to be completed.

80/20 rule
A general guideline with many applications; in terms of controlling processes, it contends that a relatively large number of problems or defects, typically 80 percent, are commonly due to a relatively small number of the causes, typically 20 percent.

AC
(Actual Cost) The total amount of costs incurred while accomplishing work performed, either during completion of a schedule activity or during the completion of a WBS component.

acquisition
An approach that is used to acquire resources when enough staff is not available within the project team or organization to complete the project.

action item
Any piece of work that needs to be performed by a resource at any time during the project.

activity
A discrete, scheduled component of work performed during the course of a project; it has estimated duration, cost, and resource requirements.

activity dependency
A logical relationship that exists between two project activities.

activity list
A definitive list of activities that must be completed to produce the desired project deliverables.

activity resource requirements
A description of resources and quantities necessary to complete project activities.

administrative closure
The project management process of verifying and documenting project results to formalize project or phase completion.

Agile project management
An iterative and incremental project management approach that focuses on customer value and team empowerment.

alternatives analysis
The process of analyzing the different methods of accomplishing activities and determining a globally preferred method.

alternatives identification
The act of generating different plans for achieving project goals.

analogous estimating
A top-down estimating technique using duration of previous similar activities to estimate future duration.

anticipatory breach
An unavoidable indication that the other party will not be able to produce the performance necessary to fulfill an agreed-upon contract.

appeals
See "claims."

appraisal costs
Costs associated with evaluating whether the programs or processes meet requirements.

artifact
Items such as plans, standards and procedures, estimations, metrics, risks, and other historical information that provide evidence for lessons learned.

assumptions
The statements that must be taken to be true in order to begin project planning.

assumptions analysis
The process of exploring and validating the assumptions made during project planning.

attribute sampling data
Data that is counted, such as the number of product defects or customer complaints.

audit
See "inspection."

auditing
An examination of a project's goals and achievements, including adequacy, accuracy, efficiency, effectiveness, and the project's compliance with applicable methodologies and regulations.

average
The number that typifies the data in a set. It is calculated by adding the values of a group of numbers and dividing that total by the number of objects included.

BAC
(Budget at Completion) The total budgeted cost of the project at completion.

balanced scorecard
A tool that integrates project management and portfolio management so that projects are aligned with an organization's strategy.

baseline
An approved time phased plan for a project, a WBS component, a work package, or an activity, plus the approved scope, cost, schedule, and technical changes.

benchmarking
A method of addressing the evaluation of a group's business or project practices in comparison to those of other groups. It is used to identify best practices in order to meet or exceed them.

benefit measurement models
A project selection decision model that analyzes the predicted value of the completed projects in different ways. They may present the value in terms of forecasted revenue, ROI, predicted consumer demand in the marketplace, or the Internal Rate of Return (IRR).

bidder conferences
Meetings conducted by the buyer prior to submissions of a bid or proposal by the vendors.

bottom-up estimating
A method of estimating the cost for each work package in the WBS. The estimates are then rolled up or aggregated for progressively higher levels within the WBS.

breach of contract
Failure to meet some or all of the obligations of a contract. It may result in damages paid to the injured party, litigation, or other ramifications.

budget forecast
The estimated budget required to complete the remaining project work.

burn rate
The rate at which you are using up your budget.

burndown chart

A tool that is used to track the progress of the project by plotting the number of days of Sprint against the number of hours of work remaining.

business case

A brief document that justifies the investments made for a project and describes how a particular investment is in accordance with the organization's policy.

business partner

Individuals and organizations who are external to the company and provide specialized support to tasks such as installation, customization, training, or support.

business requirements

The pressing organizational needs that drive decision makers to sponsor projects and prioritize competing projects.

business risk

The inherent risk in any business endeavor that carries the potential for either profit or loss. Types of business risks are competitive, legislative, monetary, and operational.

capital budgeting

A decision-making process that is used to evaluate fixed asset purchases.

cause-and-effect diagram

It provides a structured method to identify and analyze potential causes of problems in a process or system.

causes of variance

The sources or reasons for deviations from the expected standard in a process or item.

CCB

(Change Control Board) A formally chartered group responsible for reviewing, evaluating, approving, delaying, or rejecting changes to the project, and for recording and communicating such decisions.

cease-and-desist letter

A document sent to an individual or a business to stop (cease) allegedly illegal activities and to not undertake them again (desist). Such a letter can be used as a warning of impending legal action if it is ignored.

change control form

A document that is used to request a project change. They can also be recommendations for taking corrective or preventive actions. See also "change request."

change control system

A collection of formal, documented procedures for changing official project documents and how project deliverables will be controlled, changed, and approved.

change management

The process of managing project changes in a structured and standardized manner.

change request

Request for change that is sent to the upper management or the Change Control Board (CCB) for its evaluation and approval. See also "change control form."

checklist

A job aid that prompts employees to perform activities according to a consistent quality standard.

checklist analysis

The process of systematically evaluating the pre-created checklists and developing a checklist based on relevant historical information.

claims

Disputes that arise when buyers and vendors cannot agree on changes.

closed procurement

A formal written notification from the buyer and the vendor stating that no considerations are pending from either.

closure meetings

Sessions held at the end of a project or phase in which you discuss and document areas for improvement and capture lessons learned for use in future projects.

co-location

The placing of most or all key team members in the same physical location to make communication easier and enhance team performance and team spirit.

code of accounts

Any system that is used for numbering the elements in a WBS.

communication requirements

The project stakeholders' documented communication needs.

communication requirements analysis

An investigation that leads to a clear articulation of the stakeholders' communication needs.

communication technology

Any type of technology that is used for communicating information, including websites, email, instant messaging, phones, and video conferencing. Some technologies are instantaneous, whereas others take time; some are interactive, whereas others are one-way only.

communications management plan

A document that describes the project team's approach to communicating project information.

completion contract

A type of contract that is completed when the vendor delivers the product to the buyer and the buyer accepts the product.

composite organizational structure

An organizational structure with a combination of functional, project-based, and matrix organization structure types.

conditional branch

Activities that will be implemented only under specific conditions.

conditional diagramming method

A network diagramming method that allows for non-sequential activities such as loops or conditional branches.

configuration management

A controlling tool for applying technical and administrative direction and surveillance to manage changes that affect the function or characteristics of the product or service being produced.

configuration management system

A set of tools that provide technical and administrative guidance for identifying and recording the characteristics of a product or service, controlling changes made to the characteristics, documenting the changes and the status of implementation, and verifying the product's conformance to the requirements.

conflict management

The application of one or more strategies for dealing with disagreements, struggles, and compatibility issues that may be detrimental to team performance.

conformance costs

The amount spent to avoid failures, such as prevention and appraisal costs, that factor into the total cost of quality.

constraints

The factors that limit the way that the project can be approached.

contingency allowances

Additional funds that are sometimes built into cost estimates to allow for unanticipated events, or known unknowns.

contingency plan

See "contingent response strategy."

contingency reserve

A predetermined amount of additional time, money, or resources set aside in advance to be used to further the project's objectives in the event that unknown risks or accepted known risks become reality.

contingent response strategy

A risk response strategy developed in advance; it is meant to be used in the event that identified risks become reality.

contract

A mutually binding agreement that details the obligations of the buyer and vendor.

contract change control system

An offshoot of the overall change control system, but dedicated specifically to controlling contract changes.

contract change requests

Any requested change to contract terms.

control chart

A graph that is used to analyze and communicate the variability of a process or project activity over time.

cost aggregation

A technique that is used to calculate the cost of a whole component by finding the aggregate of the cost of the constituent parts of the whole component.

cost baseline

A time-phased budget that will monitor and measure cost performance throughout the project life cycle.

cost control chart

Used to illustrate trends in cost performance.

cost management plan

A document that outlines the criteria for planning, estimating, budgeting, and controlling project costs.

cost of quality

The total cost of effort to achieve an acceptable level of quality in the project's product or service.

cost–benefit analysis

A comparison of the predicted costs versus the predicted benefits of a project.

cost–reimbursable contract

A contract type that provides vendors a refund of the expenses incurred while providing a service, plus a fee representing vendor profit.

CPAF contract

(Cost Plus Award Fee contract) A cost-reimbursable contract which ensures that the vendor is reimbursed for all legitimate costs. The majority of the fee is earned based on the satisfaction of certain broad subjective performance criteria defined and incorporated into the contract.

CPFF contract

(Cost Plus Fixed Fee contract) A cost-reimbursable contract which ensures that the vendor is reimbursed for all allowable costs for performing the contract work. The vendor receives a fixed fee payment based on the initial estimated project costs.

CPI

(Cost Performance Index) A measurement of cost performance that is used to determine whether the project is over or under budget. The formula for calculating CPI is $CPI = EV/AC$.

CPIF contract

(Cost Plus Incentive Fee contract) A cost-reimbursable contract which ensures that the vendor is reimbursed for all allowable costs for performing the contract work. The vendor also receives a predetermined target fee with provision of an incentive fee.

CPM

(Critical Path Method) An analysis method that uses a sequential Finish-to-Start network logic and calculates one early and late start and finish date for each activity using a single-duration estimate.

crash cost plotting methods

Techniques for analyzing the crash costs by creating a graph or visual representation.

crashing

A schedule compression method that analyzes cost and schedule trade-offs to determine how to obtain the greatest schedule compression for the least incremental cost.

criteria profiling

A decision model that is used to evaluate and score alternatives on each criterion.

critical activities

The activities that are on the critical path.

critical chain method

An analysis method that allows you to consider resource limitations and adjust the schedule as appropriate to work within those limitations.

critical path

The network path that has the longest duration in a project or work package.

cultural feasibility

An organizational characteristic that measures the extent an organization's shared values support the project's goals.

customer

Individuals or companies with varying requirements and specifications. Can also be referred to as users.

customer requirement

A requirement that documents the customers' needs and expectations to meet the project objectives.

CV

(Cost Variance) The difference between the EV and the AC incurred to complete that work. The formula for calculating CV is CV = EV - AC.

daily standup meeting

A meeting in which the complete team gets together for a quick status update. These meetings are short, 15-minute meetings that are conducted by standing in a circle.

dashboard

Graphical summaries of project measures, often a collection of multiple KPIs, that provide an "at-a-glance" view of important data that managers can use when making project-related decisions.

data gathering

The process of collecting project-related data using techniques such as interviewing, questionnaires, expert brainstorming, and Delphi techniques.

DCF

(Discounted Cash Flow) A method that is used to evaluate the opportunity of an investment.

de facto regulations

Regulations that are widely accepted and adopted through use.

de jure regulations

Regulations that are mandated by law or have been approved by a recognized body of experts.

debriefing

A less formal, more cooperative means of discussing the positives and the negatives of the project, what worked, and what will be done differently next time.

decision tree

A type of screening system decision model that uses a branch diagram to choose among two different alternatives. This model incorporates probabilities of occurrence and the costs or rewards of each decision.

decision tree analysis

An assessment of the data obtained using the decision tree method to evaluate various possible outcomes.

decomposition

A technique for creating the WBS by subdividing project deliverables to the work package level.

delaying

A project scheduling process where activities are postponed to accommodate the availability of resources.

deliverable

The end result of work; it can be a product, service, or outcome that responds to a business need or fits the sponsor's requirements.

Delphi technique

A group technique that extracts and summarizes anonymous group input to choose among various alternatives. This technique is often used to arrive at an estimate or forecast.

dependency determination

The identification of the dependencies of one activity over the other. It involves establishing the precedence relationships among activities and creating logical sequences.

discretionary dependency

Defined by the project and the project management team at their discretion. It is defined based on the best practices followed in a specific application area or on specific requirements. If there is no mandatory or external dependency between two activities, the team has some flexibility in activity sequencing. Also known as "soft logic," "preferential logic," and "preferred logic."

documentation reviews

The structured reviews of project plans and related documents that are conducted to improve the quality of the documents.

DOE

(Design of Experiments) A technique that is used to systematically identify varying levels of independent variables.

duration

The amount of time expressed in days, weeks, months, or years taken to complete a particular task or work package from start to finish.

EAC

(Estimate at Completion) A forecast of total costs needed to complete the project; it is used to predict and control cost problems.

effect-based risk classification

A way of analyzing the major risks that are inherent to a project that could have an impact on its success. These major risks include time, cost, quality, and scope.

effort

The measure of labor expressed in time over unit format that is applied to the completion of a particular task or work package.

effort-driven

A term that is used to describe a task that can be completed faster through the application of additional energy or labor resources.

elapsed time

The actual calendar time required from start to finish of an activity. May or may not be the same as duration.

EMV analysis

(Expected Monetary Value analysis) A method of calculating the average outcome when the future is uncertain.

end-users

The people who will be affected by the product or service generated by the project. This might be the individuals or organization in the customer role, but can also be someone else.

enterprise environmental factors

Internal or external factors that can have a positive or negative influence on the project outcome.

entry/exit criteria

Conditions or circumstances defined by the project manager that are required to enter into or exit from a particular milestone.

ETC

(Estimate to Complete) A forecasting technique based on a new estimate that is more accurate and comprehensive; it is independent for all outstanding work.

EV

(Earned Value) A composite measurement of both cost and time performance in relation to scheduled or planned cost and time performance. EV is calculated by multiplying the percentage of work completed by the budgeted cost for the activity as laid out in the cost baseline.

EVM

(Earned Value Management) A methodology that measures project progress by comparing actual schedule and cost performance against planned performance as laid out in the schedule and cost baselines.

expert judgment

Advice sought from individuals having expertise in a particular knowledge area, an application area, an industry, or discipline.

express warranty

A warranty in which the predetermined standard for quality or performance is specified, either in a formal warranty or in the manufacturer's description of the product.

external dependency
Contingent on inputs from outside the project activities.

external failure costs
Costs due to rejection of the product or service by the customer.

facilitated workshops
Group sessions that bring together key stakeholders to define the project or product requirements for the project.

fallback plan
Included in the contingent response strategy, this plan is implemented if the initial response strategy is ineffective in responding to the risk event.

fast tracking
The process of compressing the project duration by performing some activities concurrently that were originally scheduled sequentially.

feasibility analysis
An analysis that provides technical and operational data to management to help determine if a project will work for the organization or if an alternative should be pursued.

FF
(Finish-to-Finish) The precedence relationship between two activities where the predecessor activity must finish before the successor activity can finish. It can be expressed as, "Activity A must finish before Activity B can finish."

FFP contract
(Firm Fixed Price contract) A commonly used contract type favored by most buying organizations because the price for products or services is set at the outset and not subject to change unless the scope of work changes.

first-time/first-use penalty
Any disadvantage or obstacle created by the fact that a project will generate an outcome

that has never been created before, and consequently nobody within the organization has any experience with the operation of the new capability.

fixed duration
A term that is used to describe a task or work package that requires a set amount of time to complete.

fixed-price contract
Also called a lump sum contract, it establishes a total price for a product or service. The vendor agrees to perform the work at the negotiated contract value.

float
The amount of time an activity can be delayed from its ES without delaying the project finish date or the consecutive activities. Also called slack.

flowchart
A diagram that shows the relationships of various elements in a system or process.

FMEA
(Failure Mode and Effects Analysis) A system that consists of reviewing components, assemblies, and subsystems to identify how they might fail, and the causes and effects of a failure. It is often the first step in a system reliability study, and it is sometimes used in risk mitigation.

focus group
Trained moderator-guided interactive discussions that include stakeholders and Subject Matter Experts.

force majeure clause
Translated from French as "superior force," this common clause is added to contracts that addresses the actions of both parties when an extraordinary circumstance beyond the control of either party occurs, such as war, strike, or natural disasters usually deemed as acts of God.

form study
This prototyping model enables you to check the primary size and appearance of a product without simulating its exact function or design.

formal acceptance of project work

The process for securing approval for completing the remainder of the project work; it requires change requests to be documented and analyzed for their impact on other aspects of project work including time, cost, quality, and risk.

FP–EPA contract

(Fixed Price with Economic Price Adjustment contract) A fixed-price contract type with special provision to allow predefined final adjustments to the contract price due to changed conditions.

FPIF contract

(Fixed Price Incentive Fee contract) A fixed-price contract that is flexible in that it allows for deviation from performance.

free float

The amount of time an activity can be delayed without delaying the ES of any activity that immediately follows it.

FS

(Finish-to-Start) The precedence relationship between two activities where the predecessor activity must finish before the successor activity can start. It can be expressed as, "Activity A must finish before Activity B can begin."

functional

This prototyping model enables you to check the appearance, materials, and functionality of the expected design.

functional managers

Individuals who are part of management in the administrative or functional side, such as human resources, finances, accounting, or even procurement of the business in the organization. They sometimes act as subject matter experts or may provide services needed for the project.

functional organizational structure

An organizational structure where reporting is hierarchical, with each individual reporting to a single manager.

functional requirements

Project requirements that detail the desired functionality, capacity, or capability expected from the project.

fundamental breach

A breach of contract so serious that it negates the very foundation of the contract.

funding limit reconciliation

A method of adjusting, spending, scheduling, and resource allocation in order to bring expenditures into alignment with budgetary constraints.

Gantt chart

The visual representation of a project schedule in bar chart form. Activities are listed down the left side and dates across the top or bottom with bars to indicate start and finish dates. Time is represented with horizontal bars that correspond to the activities. Gantt charts may also show the dependencies of the project activities, as well as the percentage of the activity completed to date and the actual progress in relation to planned progress.

GERT

(Graphical Evaluation Review Technique) An analysis method that provides a graphical display of the conditional and probabilistic treatment of logical relationships; it illustrates that not all the activities may ultimately be performed.

ground rules

Rules that set clear expectations of the expected code of conduct from team members so as to increase productivity and decrease misunderstandings.

group decision-making techniques

Assessment processes that assess multiple alternatives to arrive at an expected outcome.

hammock activity

See "summary activity."

histograms

They are quality control tools that organize individual measured values in a data set according to the frequency (number or percentage) of occurrence.

human resource plan

A document that provides guidance on how the human resources required for a project should be defined, staffed, managed, controlled, and eventually released after the end of the project.

IFB

(Invitation for Bid) Used interchangeably with RFP, an IFB is commonly used when deliverables are commodities for which there are clear specifications and when the quantities are very large.

immaterial breach

A breach of contract in which there is no resulting damage to the injured party; because there are no damages, the injured party is not entitled to receive compensation.

impact analysis

The process of evaluating the impact of a change on the project.

impact scale

The assignment of a value that reflects the magnitude of the impact of a risk event on project objectives.

implied warranty

A warranty in which the predetermined standard for quality or performance exists but is not specified; it takes effect if the buyer depends on the vendor's expertise when making a purchasing decision.

influence diagram

A visual representation of a decision situation that helps make appropriate decisions when planning for project risks.

information–gathering technique

Any method or approach used to collect data that will assist the project team in identifying risks to the project.

inspection

An official examination of work results to verify that requirements are met; it involves measuring, examining, and verifying results to be sure work and deliverables meet requirements and acceptance criteria. It may

also be referred to as reviews, product reviews, or walkthroughs.

insurable risk

A risk that has only the potential for loss and no potential for profit or gain. An insurable risk is one for which insurance may be purchased to reduce or offset the possible loss. Types of insurable risks are direct property, indirect property, liability, and personnel-related.

integrated change control

The process of identifying, documenting, approving or rejecting, and controlling changes to the project baselines, which include the cost baselines and schedule baselines.

internal dependency

Contingent on inputs from within the organization.

internal failure costs

Costs associated with making the product or service acceptable to the customer after it fails internal testing and before it is delivered to the customer.

interpersonal skills

Abilities that an individual should possess to work harmoniously and efficiently with others.

IRR

(Internal Rate of Return) The discount rate that makes the Net Present Value (NPV) of the future cash return equal to the initial capital investment.

ISO 9000 series

A quality system standard that is applicable to any product, service, or process in the world.

issue log

A document that is used to list, track, and assign project items that need to be addressed by the project team.

issue register

See "issue log."

job shadowing

Another term for observation, which is a direct way of viewing individuals in their work environment or while using the product to identify the project or product requirements.

KPI

(Key Performance Indicator) In general, these metrics are used to evaluate factors crucial to the success of a project or organization. In project management, a KPI consists of tools that indicate if the project is meeting specific goals. The best practice is to define KPIs early in the project; and they should be quantifiable and measured regularly. Common KPIs relate to how well the project is tracking against the planned schedule and cost baselines and if project milestones are being met.

KPP

(Key Performance Parameters) The key system capabilities that must be met for a system to meet its goals. The threshold value of a KPP is the minimum acceptable value (cost, schedule, and technology) below which the system is unacceptable.

lag

A delay in the start of a successor activity.

LCL

(Lower Control Limit) The bottom limit in quality control for data points below the control or average line in a control chart.

lead

A change in a logical relationship that allows the successor activity to start before the predecessor activity ends in an FS relationship.

lease, rent, or buy decision

Business analysis that determines the most cost-effective way to procure the necessary equipment for a project.

lessons learned reports

Formal documents that capture salient and helpful information about the work done in a project or a project phase; they include information about what worked well on the project and areas for improvement.

letter of intent

A document that outlines an agreement between two parties before the agreement is finalized. It is sometimes used to highlight fundamental terms of an agreement before potentially expensive legal negotiations are begun, or to indicate that the parties have begun negotiations.

levels of uncertainty

A way of analyzing the risks of a project based on how much is known about them.

loop

Activity sequences that must be revisited or repeated.

make-or-buy analysis

A technique that is used to determine whether it will be better to produce a product or service in-house or to procure it from an outside vendor.

management horizon

The time frame within which the management team calculates potential risk and rewards. Many organizations use a three-year horizon, but this will vary from organization to organization.

management reserves

Buffers added to the project tasks for unplanned changes to the project scope and cost.

mandatory dependency

Inherent to the work itself. It is usually affected by physical constraints. Activities must be performed in a specific sequence for the work to be successful. Also known as "hard logic."

material breach

A serious breach of contract that prevents the injured party from benefiting from the contract; the injured party can claim damages, but is no longer obligated to fulfill any contract commitments.

mathematical models

A project selection decision model that uses different types of mathematical formulas and algorithms to determine the optimal course of action. Variables such as business constraints, the highest possible profit that could be made on a project, and the laws and safety regulations that govern business operations may be considered.

matrix organizational structure
An organizational structure with a blend of functional and project-based structures in which individuals still report upward in the functional hierarchy, but they also report horizontally to one or more project managers.

mean
The sum of the events divided by the number of occurrences.

median
The number that separates the higher half of a probability distribution from the lower half. It is not the same as the average, although the two terms are often confused.

memorandum of understanding
An agreement between two or more parties to form a business partnership. It is not legally binding, but is more formal than a "gentlemen's agreement."

milestone
A control point event in a project with zero duration that triggers a reporting requirement or requires sponsor or customer approval before proceeding with the project.

milestone list
A document that contains the project milestones and indicates if achieving the milestones are mandatory or optional.

Monte Carlo analysis
A technique that is used by project managers to make predictions about the optimistic, most likely, and pessimistic estimates for variables in the model, and simulates various outcomes of the project schedule to provide a statistical distribution of the calculated results.

NDA
(Non-Disclosure Agreement) A legal contract that outlines confidential material, information, or knowledge that two parties wish to share only with each other. It is used to protect confidential and proprietary information, often including trade secrets, from being shared with other parties.

negative risk strategies
Methods that specify how to deal with risk scenarios that have a possible negative impact on the project.

negative risks
Risks that have a negative impact on the project.

negotiated settlements
Are undertaken to arrive at a final equitable settlement of all outstanding issues, claims, and disputes by negotiation.

negotiation
An approach used by individuals or organizations with mutual or opposite interests to come together to reach a final agreement.

networking
A technique that is used during human resource planning to gather resources.

non-conformance costs
The amount spent to rectify errors, such as internal failure and external failure costs, that factor into the total cost of quality.

normal distribution PDF
A visual depiction of a PDF in which the data is distributed symmetrically in the shape of a bell with a single peak.

NPV
(Net Present Value) The present value of an investment minus the initial investment.

objective probability
Probability that is deduced mathematically.

ongoing risk assessment
An iterative process of identifying, analyzing, and documenting the risks facing your project; it is conducted throughout the project life cycle.

operational relevance
A project responsibility that requires that the desired future state described in the project concept definition is aligned with, coordinated with, or in support of the operational priorities authorized by tactical management for the stated management horizon.

operations

Ongoing, repetitive tasks that produce the same outcome every time they are performed.

operations manager

An individual who manages a core business area such as the design, manufacturing, provisioning, testing, research and development, or maintenance side of the organization.

opportunities

See "positive risks."

organization chart

A visual representation of the project's organizational structure.

organizational process assets

Any assets that can be used to influence the success of a project.

organizational structure

The compositional makeup of an organization that dictates how the various groups and individuals within the organization interrelate.

outsourcing

Moving beyond the organization to secure services and expertise from an outside source on a contract or short-term basis.

ownership

Refers to a condition where everyone in the project claims to understand the roles and responsibilities assigned to them.

parametric estimating

A technique that is used to predict total project costs by using the project's characteristics and historical information in a mathematical model.

Pareto chart

A bar chart or histogram that illustrates the causes of problems and their relative severity. Used for prioritizing efforts to solve problems.

payback period

The time taken to reclaim the original investment that was made.

payment systems

Systems that are used to make payments to the vendors that are made contingent on the acceptance of the delivered goods or services and on the receipt of a valid invoice for the goods or services.

PDF

(Probability Density Function) A visual depiction of probability distribution in which the vertical axis refers to the probability of the risk event and the horizontal axis refers to the impact that the risk event will have on the project objects.

PDM

(Precedence Diagramming Method) A project schedule network diagramming method that produces a type of project schedule network diagram that uses rectangular or circular nodes to represent activities and arrows to represent precedence relationships between activities.

performance appraisal

Project team reviews that are conducted to clarify the roles and responsibilities of project team members, provide constructive feedback, identify unknown or unresolved issues, develop individual training plans, and establish future goals.

performance report

A document that reports the progress made in the project activities against the scheduled performance.

performance reviews

Meetings that are used to measure, analyze, and compare schedule performance. This includes comparing the actual start and finish dates, percent complete, and the time needed to complete the work in progress.

phase-gate review

A checkpoint review of project deliverables and performance at the end of each phase or subphase of a project at which point a management review or sign-off may be required. This is also known as a governance-gate review.

PMBOK

(Project Management Body of Knowledge) A process-based approach to manage most projects. PMBOK is a process framework and not a methodology like Agile. The PMBOK recognizes processes that fall into five process groups: Initiate, Plan, Execute, Monitor and Control, and Close. These five process groups have knowledge areas.

PMIS

(Project Management Information System) An automated or manual system used by a project team to gather, analyze, communicate, and store project information.

PMO

(Project Management Office) A centralized, ongoing administrative unit or department that serves to improve project-management performance within an organization by providing oversight, support, tools, and helpful methodologies to project managers.

PO

(Purchase Order) This can be a type of fixed-price contract, or a separate document that is appended to a contract. It is sent from a buyer to a vendor with a request for an order. When the vendor accepts the purchase order, a legally binding contract is formed.

political capital

A reserve of corporate goodwill that is based on a person's perceived political position and power in the company. This capital can come from a person's position, reputation, or both. It is often spent by project managers and project sponsors when a project is threatened.

portfolio

A collection of projects, programs, and operational work to achieve the strategic business objectives of an organization.

portfolio managers

Individuals, often executives, in the portfolio review board who are part of the project selection committee and belong to the high-level project governance side of the organization.

positive risk strategies

Methods that specify how to deal with risk scenarios that have a possible positive impact on the project.

positive risks

Risks that when taken, produce a positive project outcome.

pre-assignment

The allocation of project team members to project activities, even before the project has officially kicked-off.

precedence relationship

The logical relationship between two activities that describes the sequence in which the activities should be carried out.

predecessor activity

When sequencing two activities, the activity that must take place prior to the other.

prevention costs

Upfront costs of programs or processes needed to meet customer requirements or design in quality.

probability and impact risk rating matrix

The assignment of risk rating to risks or conditions.

probability distribution

The scattering of values assigned to a likelihood in a sample population.

probability scale

A graph showing the assignment of value to the likelihood of a risk occurring.

process

A sequence of activities designed to bring about a specific result in response to a business need.

process analysis

The method that is used for identifying organizational and technical improvements to processes.

process control structure
The formal organization of the modifications made to deliverables that are controlled by configuration management.

process flowchart
It shows the sequence of events and the flow of inputs and outputs between elements in a process or system.

process improvement plan
A subsidiary plan of the project management plan that describes the steps to analyze and identify areas of improvements in project process.

process improvement planning
The process of analyzing and identifying areas of improvement in project processes and enumerating an action plan based on the project goals and identified issues.

procurement audit
A formal evaluation of both the vendor's performance of the contract and the effectiveness of the procurement process itself.

procurement contract
A mutually binding agreement that details the obligations of the buyer and vendor. This agreement can be a simple purchase order or a complex contract.

procurement documents
Documents submitted to prospective vendors or service providers to solicit their proposals for the work needed.

procurement management
The management of processes involved in acquiring the necessary products and services from outside the project team.

procurement management plan
A document that outlines the specifications for procuring work from outside sources. It specifies the types of contracts that will be used, describes the process for obtaining and evaluating bids, mandates the standardized procurement documents that must be used, and describes how multiple providers will be managed.

procurement negotiation
The process of bargaining to come to a mutual agreement regarding the terms and conditions of a contract.

procurement performance review
The evaluation of the vendor's work that verifies that the work performed is in accordance with the scope, quality, and cost as defined by the contract.

Procurement SOW
The procurement SOW (Statement of Work) is a narrative description of the resources, goods, or services that are being sought from external sources to fulfill a project's requirements; it is distributed to potential vendors, who will use it to evaluate their capability to perform this work or provide the services.

product analysis
An evaluation of the project's end product and what it will take to create this product.

product backlog
A prioritized list of customer requirements. It is the first step of Scrum.

product review
See "inspection."

product training events
Demonstrations provided by the company on a product or service during its transition phase.

product transition
A formal hand-off of a project's outcome to its recipients.

program
A group of related projects that have a common objective.

program manager
An individual who works in coordination with the project managers, and oversee related projects in a program to obtain maximum benefits. They also provide guidance and support to every individual project.

progressive elaboration
A process of development in which additional layers of detail are defined over the course of a project.

project
A temporary work endeavor that creates a unique product, service, or result.

project charter
A document for project sign-off that varies from company to company and indicates the customer's authorization of a project.

project coordinator
The individual who supports the project manager and provides cross-functional coordination between the functional managers. The project coordinator might also provide administrative support and documentation assistance, time and resource scheduling, and quality checking.

project deliverables
Any tangible, measurable result or outcome required to complete a project or portion of a project.

project governance
A comprehensive methodology to control a project and ensure its success.

project interfaces
The various reporting relationships that occur within a project.

project life cycle
A process that defines the five phases that a project goes through from the beginning to the end.

project management
The planned effort for executing and monitoring a project in order to accomplish its defined goals and objectives.

project management plan
A document that details how a project will be executed to achieve the specified objectives.

project management processes
Activities that underlie the effective practice of project management; they include all the phases of initiating/pre-project setup, planning, executing, monitoring/controlling, and closing a project.

project management software
A software application that generates and organizes resource information, such as cost estimates and Work Breakdown Structures, which helps optimize resource utilizations.

project management team
Members of the project team who perform management activities, such as acting as the procurement manager for projects that involve multiple contracts and vendors, being responsible for inputting data into the PMIS and confirming the accuracy of that data, and assuming the role of Project Manager in his or her absence.

project manager
The individual who is responsible for managing all aspects of the project.

project meetings
Meetings held among the project stakeholders to discuss or convey project-related information.

project objectives
The criteria used to measure whether a project is successful or not.

project phase
A group of related project activities that results in the completion of a major deliverable.

project prototyping
The process of creating a mock-up of a product or an information system.

project requirement
A statement that defines why a project is being undertaken, the functionality that a project is designed to accommodate, or how the functionality will be achieved and satisfied by the solution.

project resource
Any useful material object or person necessary to complete project work.

project risk ranking
The overall risk ranking for producing the final deliverable of the product or service of the project.

project risk response audit
The process of examining the effectiveness of risk response plans and the performance of the risk owner.

project schedule
The project team's plan for starting and finishing activities on specific dates and in a certain sequence. The schedule also specifies planned dates for meeting project milestones.

project schedule network diagram
A graphical representation of the sequence of project activities and the dependencies among them.

project scope statement
Defines the project and what it does and does not need to accomplish.

project selection
The act of choosing a project from among competing proposals.

project selection criteria
The standards and measurements that the organization uses to select and prioritize projects.

project selection decision model
A framework for comparing competing project proposals by helping decision makers compare the benefits of one project with another.

project selection method
Any systematic approach that is used to analyze the value of a proposed project in order to choose among competing proposals.

project stage
A group of related project activities that results in the completion of a major deliverable.

project stakeholder
A person who has a business interest in the outcome of a project or who is actively involved in its work.

project status meetings
Short project meetings conducted to discuss the current status of the project among the team members and other stakeholders.

project team
Consists of the project manager, the project management team, and other individual team members. The project team contains people from different groups who possess knowledge on specific subjects or have unique skill sets to carry out project work.

projectized organizational structure
An organizational structure where the project manager and a core project team operate as a completely separate organizational unit within the parent organization.

proof-of-principle
This prototyping model enables you to check some aspects of the product design without considering the visual appearance, the materials to be used, or the manufacturing process.

proposal evaluation techniques
A set of methods to evaluate, short-list, and select the vendor.

prototype
A simulated version of a new system, essential for clarifying information elements.

published estimating data
The commercial publications about production rates, resource cost, and labor requirements, for different countries and regions.

PV
(Planned Value) The budgeted portion of the approved cost estimate to be spent during a particular time period to complete the scheduled project work; previously known as the budgeted cost of work scheduled (BCWS).

Q-sorting
A decision model that uses groups of people to rate the relative priority of a number of alternatives.

qualified vendors
The vendors who are approved to deliver the products, services, or results based on the

procurement requirements identified for a project.

qualified vendors list
Contains details regarding vendors who are qualified by the organization and to whom requests can be sent. It is sometimes known as an approved vendor list.

qualitative risk analysis
The process of determining the probability of occurrence and the impact of identified risks by using logical reasoning when numeric data is not readily available.

quality
The totality of features and characteristics of a product or service that bear on its ability to satisfy stated or implied needs.

quality audit
An independent evaluation, inspection, or review of a project's quality assurance system.

quality control measurements
Measurements used to assess a product's adherence to the specified standards.

quality gates
Used in software development projects, this special type of phase gate is a formal way of specifying and recording the transition between stages in the project life cycle.

quality management plan
A document that describes a team's approach to implementing the quality policy; it outlines how quality control and quality assurance will be performed.

quality metrics
An actual value that describes the measurements for the quality control process.

quantitative analysis methods
Risk analysis methods that allow project managers to consistently determine the probability and impact of each risk.

quantitative risk analysis
A numerical method that is used to assess the probability and impact of risk and measure the impact.

RACI chart
(Responsible, Accountable, Consulted, and Informed) This chart is a type of Responsibility Assignment Matrix (RAM) that helps detect the level of responsibility for each project team member.

RAM
(Responsibility Assignment Matrix) A chart that links key project stakeholders to specific project deliverables or activities by assigning responsibilities to each stakeholder for each element of work.

random causes of variance
Those everyday occurrences that are always present in project work; as such, they may be unavoidable. They may be either insignificant and have little impact on the overall quality performance, or they may have a dramatic effect on quality.

RBS
(Risk Breakdown Structure) A hierarchical arrangement of identified risks that helps project managers organize potential sources of risk to the project.

recognition
A personal, intangible, and experiential event that focuses on behavior rather than outcome. Recognition is not restricted to a set time, is usually unexpected by the receiver, and is intended to increase an individual's feeling of appreciation.

records management system
A software application that is used to manage the project vendors, procurements, and contract documentations.

regulations
Compliance-mandatory characteristics for specific products, services, or processes.

relative authority
The project manager's authority relative to the functional manager's authority over the project and the project team.

reporting systems
Tools used to collect, store, and distribute project information to stakeholders.

requirements documentation

A process of describing how individual requirements meet the business requirements for the project.

requirements management plan

A document that describes how project requirements will be analyzed, documented, and managed throughout the project life cycle.

reserve analysis

The process of identifying and adding extra time that will serve as contingency or management reserves to the duration estimates.

resource breakdown structure

A hierarchy of identified resources, organized by category and type.

resource calendar

A calendar that lists the time during which project resources can participate in the project tasks.

resource leveling

One of the four common methods for achieving schedule network analysis; a technique that is used to analyze the schedule model. Resource leveling allows you to readjust the work as appropriate.

review

See "inspection."

reward

A tangible, consumable item that is given to a person based on a specific outcome or an achievement. A reward can have a defined start and finish, or fixed time, and is usually expected when the specified goal is achieved.

reward and recognition system

A formal system used to reinforce behaviors or performance. The purpose is to motivate the team to perform well and achieve and maintain the desired level of individual and team morale.

RFB

(Request for Bid) Commonly used when deliverables are commodities for which there are clear specifications and when price will be the primary determining factor.

RFI

(Request for Information) Commonly used to develop lists of qualified vendors and gain more input for resource availability.

RFP

(Request for Proposal) Commonly used when deliverables are not well-defined or when other selection criteria will be used in addition to price.

RFQ

(Request for Quote) Commonly used when deliverables are commodities for which there are clear specifications and when price will be the primary determining factor. Unlike an RFB, this solicited price quote is used for comparison purposes and is not a formal bid for work.

risk

An uncertain event that has either a positive or negative effect on the project. Its primary components are a measure of probability that a risk will occur and the impact of the risk on a project.

risk analysis

The evaluation of the probability and impact of the occurrence of a risk.

risk categorization

A risk ranking technique that categorizes risks to identify the areas of the project most exposed to the effects of uncertainty.

risk data quality assessment

The evaluation of the usefulness of the available data concerning the risk.

risk impact

The likely effect on project objectives if the risk event occurs. In risk analysis, each risk is assigned a value representing the likely consequences of the risk event occurring.

risk management plan

A document that describes the team's approach to manage risks.

risk probability

The likelihood that a risk event will occur or prove true. In risk analysis, each risk is assigned a value to represent its probability or degree of uncertainty.

risk probability and impact assessment

A risk assessment technique that is used to evaluate the likelihood of occurrence and potential impact of the identified project risks.

risk reassessment

The process of reexamining and reevaluating the risks in a project risk register.

risk register

A document that identifies and categorizes risks, potential risk responses, and their triggers, or warning signs.

risk tolerance

The level of risk a project manager or key stakeholder is willing to take when the investment is compared to the potential payoff.

risk urgency assessment

The evaluation of project risks and prioritizing them based on their urgency.

risk–related contract decisions

Risk response approaches agreed upon by both the parties when procuring materials from a third party.

rolling wave planning

A technique that is used to address the progressive elaboration characteristic of the project. It is nothing but the progressive detailing of project plans.

root cause analysis

A technique used to determine the true cause of the problem that, when removed, prevents the problem from occurring again.

RTM

(Requirements Traceability Matrix) A document that is created by associating the project's deliverables with the requirements for creating each deliverable.

run chart

A line graph showing plotted data points in chronological order. It could show trends in a process over time or improvements over time.

scatter chart

Diagram that displays the relationship between two variables.

scenarios

A method for developing potential or likely eventualities for different situations.

schedule baseline

The management-approved version of the project schedule; it is drawn from schedule network analysis and includes baseline start and finish dates.

schedule compression

The act of shortening the project schedule without affecting the project scope.

schedule control chart

Used to illustrate trends in schedule performance.

schedule management plan

An approach to develop, maintain, and manage the project schedule.

schedule network analysis

Any technique that is used to calculate the theoretical early and late start and finish dates for all project activities.

schedule performance measurement

Any technique that is used to determine how the project is performing in terms of time as compared to its planned performance.

scheduler

The individual who is responsible for developing and maintaining the project schedule, communicating the timeline and any changes to it, reporting schedule performance, and soliciting task status from resources.

scope baseline

A component of the project management plan that describes the need, justification, requirements, and boundaries for the project. Components of the scope baseline include the detailed project scope statement, the WBS, and the WBS dictionary.

scope creep

The extension of the project scope caused by unapproved and uncontrolled changes that impacts the cost, quality, or timing of the project.

scope management plan

A planning tool that describes how a project team will define, verify, manage, and control the project scope.

scope statement

See "project scope statement."

Scrum

An Agile methodology that has been developed over the last decade and can be applied to a variety of projects. It focuses on iterative and incremental delivery of products. Scrum owes its popularity to a simple approach, high productivity, and its scope for applicability to multiple areas.

sensitivity analysis

A method of assessing the relative impact of changing a variable in the project to gain insight into possible outcomes of one or more potential courses of action.

seven-run rule

When the variability of a process is more than seven consecutive points above or below the mean, indicating situations that are out-of-statistical control and, therefore, there should be a shift in the mean.

SF

(Start-to-Finish) The precedence relationship between two activities where the predecessor activity must start before the successor activity can finish. It can be expressed as, "Activity A must start before Activity B can finish."

short-listing

A technique used to reduce the number of proposals that have been received to a more concise number for further analysis. In this process, the buyer might use an abbreviated scoring system or internal discussions to remove some proposals from further consideration.

significance

It is the weight or importance given to variances to determine what type of corrective action needs to be taken by the project manager.

silos

Compartmentalized functional units, such as sales, engineering, production, and so on.

simulation

A technique that uses computer models and estimates of risk to translate uncertainties at a detailed level into their potential impact on project objectives at the total project level.

Six Sigma limit

In terms of controlling processes, the Six Sigma limit is significant because it provides a generally accepted guideline for monitoring quality and adjusting it as necessary

SLA

(Service Level Agreement) A contract between an organization that provides a service, and the user of the service. The contract specifies what the customer will receive and the performance standards the provider is obligated to meet.

slack

See "float."

SME

(Subject Matter Expert) A person with technical expertise in a particular subject area.

source selection criteria

The standards used to rate or score proposals, quotes, or bids and form a part of the procurement solicitation documents.

source-based risk classification

A method of analyzing risk in terms of its origins.

SOW

(Statement of Work) A document that describes the products or services that the project will supply, defines the business need that it is designed to meet, and specifies the work that will be done during the project.

special causes of variance

Unusual, sporadic occurrences; they are the result of some unexpected circumstance and are typically not caused by a flaw in the overall production process.

specifications

Descriptions of the work to be done or the service or product to be provided; they define the requirements that must be met in exacting detail.

SPI

(Schedule Performance Index) The ratio of work performed to work scheduled. The formula for SPI is SPI = EV/PV.

sponsor

Individuals or groups that provide financial assistance to the project. If the sponsor is outside of the company, such as a customer, their duties may be the responsibility of the project manager.

Sprint

See "Sprint cycle."

Sprint backlog

A list of user stories selected from the Product Backlog that the Scrum Team chooses and commits to complete in that Sprint cycle.

Sprint cycle

In Agile project management, this represents a complete process from planning to delivery and demo of a part of the product. The Sprint cycle begins when the Product Owner defines and prioritizes the Product Backlog. (This can also be known as *Sprint*.)

SS

(Start-to-Start) The precedence relationship between two activities where the predecessor activity must start before the successor activity can start. It can be expressed as, "Activity A must start before Activity B can start."

staffing management plan

A subsidiary plan of the human resources plan that forecasts the staff who will work on a project, where they will be needed, how they will be recruited, and when they will be released from the project.

stakeholder analysis

The formal process of identifying all the stakeholders by gathering and analyzing quantitative and qualitative information and building coalitions at the onset of a project by identifying their needs, objectives, goals, and issues.

stakeholder analysis matrix

A document that describes the strategies to manage the stakeholders of a project.

stakeholder expectations matrix

A document that outlines the deliverables or results that each stakeholder hopes to receive from the project.

stakeholder management strategy

A management strategy that is created to ensure increase in support and minimize the negative impacts of stakeholders throughout the entire project life cycle.

stakeholder register

A document that identifies stakeholders of a project with information that includes their identification, assessment, and stakeholder classification.

standard deviation

This is the measure of the spread of the data, or the statistical dispersion of the values in your data set.

standards

Non-mandatory guidelines or characteristics that have been approved by a recognized bod of experts such as the ISO.

statistical sampling

A technique that is used to determine characteristics of an entire population based o actual measurement of a representative sampl of that population.

statistical sampling process

Dividing sampling data into two categories—attribute and variable—each of which is gathered according to sampling plans.

strategic relevance

Determines whether the project should be done and requires that the desired future state established in the project concept definition is aligned with, coordinated with, or in support of the organizational strategic objectives set by senior leadership.

subjective probability

Probability based on people's opinions, which may be shaped by information, experience, and attitude.

subproject

An independently manageable component of an existing project.

successor activity

When sequencing two activities, the activity that must take place after to the other and is driven by the relationship.

summary activity

A group of related activities that are reported as an aggregate activity.

sustainment

(of a product) It ensures that a project's end product is maintained so that the product is in operable condition irrespective of whether or not the product is used by the end user.

SV

(Schedule Variance) The measured difference between the actual completion of an activity and the planned or scheduled completion of an activity. The formula for calculating SV is EV − PV = SV.

SWOT analysis

The process of examining the project from the perspective of strengths, weaknesses, opportunities, and threats.

system flowchart

See "process flowchart."

T&M contract

(Time and Material contract) A type of contract that includes aspects of both fixed-price and cost-reimbursable contracts. The buyer pays the vendor a negotiated hourly rate and full reimbursement for materials used to complete the project.

tailoring

The act of determining which processes are appropriate for any given project.

TCPI

(To-Complete Performance Index) An estimate that is derived by dividing the budgeted cost of remaining work by the remaining project budget.

team logistics

The practice of providing materials and facilities needed by the team to accomplish their tasks.

team-building activities

Specific functions or actions taken to help the team to develop into a mature, productive team.

team-building strategies

See "team-building activities."

teaming agreements

A legal contractual agreement between two or more parties to form a partnership, joint venture, or other arrangement as defined by the parties to meet the requirements of a business opportunity.

technical feasibility

A feasibility study to analyze the hardware, software, facilities, and databases needed for a proposed project.

technical performance measurements

Measurements used to identify the overall technical progress of a project by comparing the actual versus planned parameters related to the overall technical progress of the project.

technical requirements

The technical needs that are crucial for a project.

term contract

A type of contract that engages the vendor to deliver a set amount of service—measured in staff-hours or a similar unit—over a set period of time.

threats

See "negative risks."

three-point estimating

A method of activity duration estimating in which three types of estimates are incorporated into a singular duration estimate scenario: most likely, optimistic, and pessimistic.

tolerances

The measurement values that determine if a product or service is acceptable or unacceptable.

top-down estimating

See "analogous estimating."

total float

The total amount of time that an activity can be delayed without delaying the project finish date. It is obtained by subtracting an activity's EF from its LF or its ES from its LS.

TQM

(Total Quality Management) An approach to improve business results through an emphasis on customer satisfaction, employee development, and processes rather than on functions.

training

An activity in which team members acquire new or enhanced skills, knowledge, or attitudes.

transition plan

A document that describes how the outputs of a project will be transferred either to another organization or to a functional group within the performing organization.

trend analysis

The process of examining project results over time to determine if performance is improving or deteriorating.

triangular distribution PDF

A visual depiction of a PDF in which the data is skewed to one side, indicating that an activity or element presents relatively little risk to project objectives.

triggers

Warning signs or indications that a risk is about to occur in a project.

triple constraints

They are limitations that concern scope, time, and cost.

UCL

(Upper Control Limit) The top limit in quality control for data points above the control or average line in a control chart.

uniform distribution PDF

A visual depiction of a PDF in which all outcomes are equally likely to occur so that the data is shown in a straight line.

urgent risks

Risks that require immediate attention.

use case analysis

A method for designing information systems by breaking down requirements into user functions. Each use case is an event or sequence of actions performed by the user.

user stories

In Agile methodology, these are the customer requirements or features. Each user story emphasizes the functionality of the feature and how it adds to the final product.

VAC

(Variance at Completion) It is the difference between the BAC and the EAC. The formula to calculate VAC is BAC - EAC.

variable sampling data

Data that is measured on a continuous scale, such as time, temperature, or weight.

variance

The quantifiable deviance or amount of departure from the expected results for any component of product and service being developed, including quality, schedule, and cost.

variance analysis

The analysis of variance from the original scope baseline or the quantification of departure from expected results.

vendor audit

Conducted by the buyer to verify compliance in the vendor's work processes or deliverables.

The goal of the audit is to establish a record that may be used to shape procurement practices for current and future projects.

vendor bid analysis

A cost estimation technique based on the bids obtained from vendors.

vendor management

The management technique that is used to obtain resources, such as people, facilities, equipment, and materials, for the project through an external organization, while developing, maintaining, and improving relationships with the vendors.

vendor proposals

Responses submitted by potential vendors that are prepared in accordance with the requirements stated in the procurement documents.

vendors

External parties who enter into a contractual agreement with the organization and provide components or services needed for the project. Seller, contractor, and supplier are also used when referring to vendors.

verified deliverables

Project products or results that are completed and verified for their correctness while performing quality control.

virtual team

A team that is distributed across multiple locations. Some virtual teams have occasional physical meetings, while others may never meet face-to-face.

visual

This prototyping model enables you to check the design and imitate the appearance, color, and surface textures of the product, but will not contain the functions of the final product.

waiver

The giving up of a contract right, even inadvertently.

walkthrough

See "inspection."

warranty

A promise, explicit or implied, that goods or services will meet a predetermined standard. The standard may cover reliability, fitness for use, safety, and so on.

warranty of fitness for purpose

Implied warranties that require goods to be fit for the usage that was intended by the buyer.

warranty of merchantability

Implied warranties that require goods to be fit for ordinary usage.

WBS

(Work Breakdown Structure) A logical grouping of project deliverables arranged in a hierarchical structure that defines the total scope of work required to complete the project.

WBS dictionary

An auxiliary document containing details about each element in the WBS.

weighted factor

A decision model that applies a multiplier based on importance to each criterion, which is factored into the scoring.

weighted scorecard

One type of weighting system that groups evaluation criteria into general categories and assigns a numerical weight to each category. A vendor is rated on a scale of zero to five for each of the technical criteria. These numbers are totaled and then multiplied by the weighting factor to determine the weighted score for that category.

weighting system

A method for quantifying qualitative data to minimize the influence of personal bias on source selection.

what–if scenario analysis

An analysis method that allows you to plan for unexpected issues or problems that will interfere with the schedule.

work authorization system

A tool for communicating official permission to begin work on an activity or work package.

work flow analysis

A technique that formally documents the manner in which work gets done and displays that work in a flowchart.

work package

The smallest, most granular deliverable that is displayed in the lowest-level component of the WBS.

work performance information

Periodically collected information about project activities being performed to accomplish the project work.

Index

ISBN-13 978-1-64274-115-5
ISBN-10 1-64274-115-9